THE PEOPLE'S REPUBLIC OF KAMPUCHEA
1979–1989

THE PEOPLE'S REPUBLIC OF KAMPUCHEA, 1979–1989

THE REVOLUTION AFTER POL POT

MARGARET SLOCOMB

Silkworm Books

ISBN 978-974-9575-34-5

First published in 2003 by

Silkworm Books
430/58 M. 7, T. Mae Hia, Chiang Mai 50100, Thailand
info@silkwormbooks.com
http: www.silkwormbooks.com

Typeset by Silk Type in Janson 10 pt.
Cover illustration: From the 1979 edition of Kampuchea, the official newspaper of the Kampuchea United Front for National Salvation.

CONTENTS

ACKNOWLEDGMENTS

The People's Republic of Kampuchea (PRK), as its name implies, was a revolutionary regime. This book attempts to study the nature of the Cambodian revolution itself and the reasons why it did not persist. The continuities with the previous regime, Democratic Kampuchea (DK), cannot be denied despite the fact that the remnants of Democratic Kampuchea were the mortal enemy of the PRK throughout its decade of rule. The history of revolution in Cambodia is complex and the consequences of its failure during the initial period 1975 to 1978 were painful and destructive. The focus of this book is on the PRK and its failed attempts to revive the revolution despite its very real achievements in rebuilding and defending the state and the nation.

Controversy still surrounds the history of Democratic Kampuchea and in this monograph I offer no more than a synopsis of what other historians have already revealed and discussed. Some of those historians have altered their original interpretations of events surrounding the revolution and its aftermath. For the most part, however, I have recorded the arguments they gave at the time when Cambodia was barely recovering from the catastrophe of the DK years. For the PRK period, I have relied heavily on the official documents of the Council of Ministers and the Council of State, partly in an attempt to avoid the rhetoric and controversy that dogged the regime established with the support of the Socialist Republic of Vietnam, but largely by choice as the internal documents provided a narrative structure and official evidence with which a history could be recorded. I am indebted to the director and staff of the State Archives of Cambodia for making the documents available and for their generous assistance throughout the research period, and also to Peter Arfanis for telling me that the documents existed. My doctoral thesis supervisor, Dr. Martin Stuart-Fox of the University of Queensland, and Dr. Michael Vickery, who guided me through several revisions, provided sound advice and support. Long-term expatriate friends in Cambodia, particularly Onesta Carpene, and long-term friends of Cambodia including Raoul Jennar, Serge Thion, and Nayan Chanda were generous with their time, memories and reflections. Above all, many Cambodian friends and colleagues tirelessly answered questions for several years about their direct experience of the period. Finally, I would like to thank the former and current government leaders and officials for their courtesy, time, and personal interest in the documenting of this history of the People's Republic of Kampuchea. I take total responsibility for errors and omissions.

INTRODUCTION

During the final quarter of the twentieth century, Cambodia experienced radical political revolution. Power was effectively and forcibly transferred from the monarchy and the traditional elite which derived its power from the patronage of the king and links to the royal court to a social stratum which identified with and drew its popular support almost exclusively from the rural agricultural laboring class. The power of the king to govern in his former style as semi-divine monarch was irretrievably abrogated. At the same time, the goal of social revolution, genuine transformation in the way that social relations are constructed and social power is articulated, was not achieved. Despite the massive upheavals which Cambodia experienced, particularly during the first stage of revolution from 1975 to 1979, Cambodian political society functions today in much the same way as it always has despite the trappings of multi-party democracy which have largely been imposed on it by the processes of the peace settlement, globalization and the need for external assistance to fund its development agenda. The Cambodian revolution ultimately succumbed to what its leaders called "objective reality" and from there to the necessity for maintaining power. Cambodian society was not transformed by the era of revolution and by the time the People's Revolutionary Party of Kampuchea officially disclaimed its socialist goals and then abandoned its socialist ideology in October 1991, the traditional patterns and inequalities of Cambodian society had largely reasserted themselves.

From the 1930s until 1975, the Indochina Peninsula was engulfed by war and revolutionary movements. Patriotic groups of resistance fighters of Vietnam, Cambodia and Laos, organized by the Indochina Communist Party, cooperated first in the struggle for national independence from French colonization and then fought to rebuild their nations according to the principles and models of international socialism. In Cambodia's case, however, the revolution that was achieved in April 1975 was a disaster. During the first phase of the revolution which lasted from 1975 to 1979, the vanguard party led by Pol Pot and Ieng Sary adopted extreme Maoist theories and practices. As a consequence of misguided policies, poor management and ineffectual party leadership, more than one million people died prematurely, many of them horribly, the economy was destroyed, and the populace left dispirited and scattered. To save both the nation and the revolution, a group of dissidents led by Heng Samrin turned to Vietnam for assistance to overthrow the Pol Pot–led regime of Democratic Kampuchea (DK). In this way, even Cambodia's hard-fought national independence had to be bartered for ten years of military protection and tutelage provided by Vietnam during the ensuing civil war between the rival factions of the Cambodian communist movement. This debilitating civil war was played out both as an endgame in the ideological Cold War with players from all sides supporting and directing it, and as a continuation of ancient regional rivalries. During those ten years, the Cambodian revolution struggled to survive by returning to more orthodox Marxist-Leninist principles of social transformation which had to be modified to accommodate the realities of a nation stripped of its educated and skilled human resources and most especially of its trained and trusted party and military cadres. In effect, this meant tacit acceptance of a free market economy and dependence on a petty bourgeoisie which rehabilitated itself with alacrity and later proved intractable to efforts to control.

The scale of the problems faced by the new regime, the People's Republic of Kampuchea (PRK), was huge. Other social revolutions in the region were also confronted by massive problems of post-war reconstruction, as well as those produced by excesses of revolutionary zeal and misguided policies which affected both popular support and economic development. In Cambodia's case, the damage caused to the revolution by the Pol Pot era was probably irreparable and it may have been beyond the capacity of any socialist government to deal with those problems in any but pragmatic ways. The PRK administration was always conscious of the people's outrage with the excesses of the Pol Pot years, and yet what it aimed to achieve was essentially the same goal. Therefore, the PRK had to win the people's trust and convince them that "genuine" socialism was in their own best interests.

In order to do this, the new leadership had to rebuild a viable state from an extremely low base, both the structure and the superstructure, in such a way that the people themselves would assume mastery over the forces of production and, in effect, over their own destiny, while at the same time proving to the people that their faith in the party was justified. In other words, winning ideological hegemony was equally as important as economic and social reconstruction. Without the people's trust, the simultaneous efforts of national defense against the regrouped forces of the DK and its allies would have failed, with disastrous consequences.

The PRK did not achieve its political goals for many reasons, and, in fact, these goals may have been inherently unrealizable. On the other hand, it did rebuild the state and it did defend its people so that by the time the regime came to an end in 1989, the people's lives had resumed a level and rhythms not vastly dissimilar from what they had been prior to the outbreak of the war in 1970 which preceded the revolution.

Most importantly, the reconstruction and defense of Cambodia was achieved with the minimum recourse to state coercion. This is not meant to deny that the people did indeed experience some abuse at the hands of state officials. Old habits die hard. Patronage and clientelism, nepotism, official corruption, and other forms of misuse of power were not eradicated by the PRK. Moreover, as the security situation worsened, military conscription eventually become inevitable and the labor of thousands of civilians was levied for the war effort, particularly during the notorious K5 Plan to protect the Cambodian-Thai border from incursions by the rebel forces.

Foreign scholars have so far examined and analyzed some

particular stages of the Cambodian revolution. To date, however, the second stage of the revolution, the PRK, has received only scant attention. Most of the emphasis on Cambodia's revolutionary history has concentrated on the Pol Pot period mainly for the purpose of estimating the scale of the atrocities committed during that time and attributing blame to the perpetrators. The PRK regime which ousted the Pol Pot clique was, by contrast, anti-climactic. For the most part, it was assumed, with good reason, that the PRK was a satellite, a client state of the Socialist Republic of Vietnam and therefore lacking genuine Cambodian credentials. Most of the attention paid to the PRK by foreign commentators at the time related not to internal events but to the war fought by the resistance coalition from their bases on the Cambodia-Thailand border and to the diplomatic struggle which finally resolved what was generally called the "Cambodia problem."

The purpose of this book is to focus on the PRK, on the agenda it set for itself and the strategies it adopted for restoring the Cambodian society. Inherent in those strategies are some of the reasons for its failure to complete the revolution. More importantly, the history of the PRK suggests a model for reconstruction of other societies, at similar levels of development, which are torn apart by war to the point of near annihilation. Cambodia was rebuilt by the PRK, not as is often assumed by the international peace-making effort led by the United Nations in the early 1990s. By the time of the Paris Peace Agreement in 1991, Cambodia already had a functioning economy, with a vibrant if relatively small free market which was prepared for expansion. There was a sound administrative structure which reached from the center to the smallest hamlet. Despite acute levels of rural poverty, children attended school, and literacy programs and evening classes or "complementary schools" were available for those who were deprived of the opportunity to receive or complete their formal education during the chaotic decade which preceded the PRK. A social security system of sorts was provided by the state and more usefully by the semi-structured traditional system of *provas day kinear*, or mutual support built around the *krom samaki*, the solidarity production teams.

Poverty was the single defining feature of the PRK. The struggle to rebuild the country was carried out in a storm of international outrage over the so-called "occupation" of Cambodia by the armed forces of the Socialist Republic of Vietnam. The international embargo on credit and trade which was imposed on Vietnam in 1979 naturally fell on Cambodia also. Given the extent of the damage to the economy and its infrastructure by the massive aerial bombardment of Cambodia during the final years of the Second Indochina War by US B-52 bombers and then by the virtual neglect of the economy during the years of the DK, Cambodia's need for external assistance was total. A great deal of assistance was provided, largely by Vietnam and the USSR and also by other members of the Soviet bloc. Cambodia received both technical and financial assistance and while it may be argued that the assistance provided was inadequate for the country's needs, it was offered on a scale and at a level which could be absorbed and applied to ease the worst of the country's ills without creating excesses which in turn produce their own problems.

The poverty of the PRK was both caused and exacerbated by the on-going war and by the failure of the new regime to win international recognition of its legitimate right to govern Cambodia. Although the forces of Democratic Kampuchea were routed by the combined forces of the Salvation Front and the People's Army of Vietnam, they soon regrouped and dug in, establishing bases that ranged along the northwestern border of the country. In 1982, the Khmer Rouge forces were strengthened and their counter-insurgency efforts were legitimized by the formation of the Coalition Government of Democratic Kampuchea, that unlikely mélange of communist, republican, and royalist factions which was backed financially, technically, and materially by the US, the People's Republic of China, and the ASEAN member states. During the 1984–1985 dry season offensive, those forces were driven off Cambodian territory into Thailand. From there, they used corridors to infiltrate Cambodia and launch their guerrilla raids against the villagers and particularly against the offices of the local administration. The cost of the war effort, and the cost to the regime in terms of its loss of popular support by having to conscript civilians to defend Cambodia's sovereignty ultimately proved too much for the young regime to bear. Shifts in the international power balance and regional pressure to end the destabilizing war finally brought all four factions to the negotiating table. In October 1991, the Paris Peace Agreement paved the way for a settlement of the Cambodia problem. By then, the PRK had already transformed itself into the State of Cambodia which laid no claims at all to socialist credentials, and the last of the Vietnamese troops and advisers had left for home.

NOTE ON SOURCES

During the ten years of the PRK, foreign journalists and academics made regular visits and their views and observations made valuable contributions to understanding the nature of the regime. There were also foreign aid workers resident in Cambodia from as early as 1980 who cooperated in the rebuilding of the society. It must be noted, however, that the period 1979–1989 represented the final years of the Cold War and that ideological tension sometimes provoked extreme reactions, particularly to the so-called occupation of Cambodia by Vietnam. In view of this, the main sources for this text have been the internal documents of the regime, particularly the official documents of the Council of Ministers and the Council of State which are now housed in the State Archives in Phnom Penh. These circulars, laws, minutes of meetings, reports, memos, and *prakas* or regulatory laws offer insights into the working of the regime almost on a daily basis. As internal documents, they are largely free of the rhetoric and posturing which can plague public statements or broadcasts. The aim of this text is to allow the documents their own voice to recount the history of the People's Republic of Kampuchea. Transliteration of proper nouns and key terms are, as far as possible, those regularly used by other scholars; otherwise they are transliterated into their closest approximation in English.

ABBREVIATIONS

ANS	National Sihanoukist Army
ARVN	Army of the Republic of Vietnam
ASEAN	Association of Southeast Asian Nations
CGDK	Coalition Government of Democratic Kampuchea
COM	Council of Ministers
COMECON	Economic Community of the Communist bloc
COSVN	Central Office South Vietnam
CPK	Communist Party of Kampuchea
DK	Democratic Kampuchea
DRV	Democratic Republic of Vietnam
FEER	*Far Eastern Economic Review*
FULRO	Front Uni de Liberation des Races Opprimées
FUNCINPEC	United National Front for an Independent, Neutral, Peaceful, and Cooperative Cambodia
FUNK	National United Front of Kampuchea
FUNSK/KUFNS/KNUFS	Kampuchean United Front for National Salvation
GRUNK	Royal Government of National Union of Kampuchea
ICP	Indochina Communist Party
ICRC	International Committee of the Red Cross
JIM	Jakarta Informal Meetings
KPNLF	Khmer People's National Liberation Front
KPRAF/PRKAF	People's Revolutionary Armed Forces of Kampuchea
KPRP	Khmer People's Revolutionary Party
KR	Khmer Rouge

KUFCDM	Kampuchean United Front for Construction and Defense of the Motherland
NADK	National Army of Democratic Kampuchea
NLF	National Liberation Front
NVA	North Vietnam Army
PAVN	People's Army of Vietnam
PLA	People's Liberation Army
PRC/PRCK/KPRC	People's Revolutionary Council of Kampuchea
PRG	Provisional Revolutionary Government
PRK	People's Republic of Kampuchea
PRPK	People's Revolutionary Party of Kampuchea
SNC	Supreme National Council
SOC	State of Cambodia
SPK	*Sar Pordemien Kampuchea* (Kampuchea Press)
SRV	Socialist Republic of Vietnam
UIF	United Issarak Front
UNHCR	United Nations High Commission for Refugees
UNICEF	United Nations Children's Fund
UNTAC	United Nations Transitional Authority in Cambodia
USAID	United States Agency for International Development
USSR	Union of Soviet Socialist Republics
VCP	Vietnamese Communist Party
VVAK	Vietnam Volunteer Army in Kampuchea
VWP	Vietnam Workers' Party

MAP OF THE PEOPLE'S REPUBLIC OF KAMPUCHEA

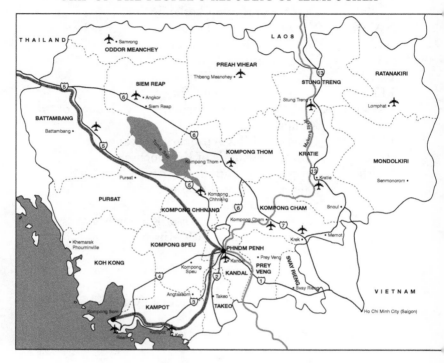

After Antonin Kubes, *Kampuchea* (Prague: Orbis Press Agency, 1982), p. 28

Chapter 1

THE CAMBODIAN COMMUNIST
MOVEMENT, 1951–1975

IN THE 1960s, despite or because of King (then Prince) Sihanouk's frantic efforts to remain neutral in the Second Indochina War, the fire that he allowed to singe the fringes of his country ultimately engulfed it. The old regime could not cope with the crisis that the war created and which was fanned by the internal leftist insurgency. The indigenous communist movement of Cambodia developed as it did in other countries in the region out of the struggle for independence from colonialism that was born during the respite granted by the absence of European overlords during World War II. Cambodia's incipient movement was given some impetus by the communist parties of both Thailand and Vietnam, particularly the latter. Nevertheless, this support was small. Cambodia was not considered to be ready for revolution. Despite some small-scale industrial development in the city, Phnom Penh, there was nothing even resembling a working-class which might have been termed a "proletariat." The rubber plantations, established by the French and which might have produced an organized base for the mobilization of support, were worked largely by Vietnamese immigrant laborers. Cambodia's economy was overwhelmingly agrarian and under-developed to the point of self-sufficiency in many areas. Poor soils, the vagaries of a marginal monsoon climate and a significant lack of natural resources, apart from timber and fish, made Cambodia a poor candidate for independent economic development. The majority of the population was rural and uneducated. From an orthodox Marxist perspective, therefore, Cambodia most definitely was not ripe for revolution. When the revolution succeeded in 1975, it did so almost by default.

I

THE ORIGINS OF THE COMMUNIST MOVEMENT

The Indochina Communist Party (ICP) was founded in 1930, *de facto* a communist party of Vietnam with an original membership throughout the three countries of French-controlled Indochina dominated by ethnic Vietnamese and Chinese organizers. The Cambodian movement, in contrast with its Lao counterpart, received only scant attention and little impetus for development prior to World War II. According to the research of Engelbert and Goscha, "the extensive work of [Vietnamese] northerners in western Laos and upper northeastern Thailand in the late 1920s and early 1930s is in striking contrast to the virtual inattention paid to Cambodia by their southern counterparts."[1] They note that "there were few—if any—bases along the western Cambodian and lower northeastern Siamese frontier" prior to the war. The arrival of Japanese troops in Cambodia in World War II initiated popular nationalist uprisings against colonial domination as it did elsewhere in East and Southeast Asia. The first Cambodian anti-French Issarak (independence) organizations were set up in Battambang province in 1944. The Cambodian northwestern provinces of Battambang and Siem Reap/Oddar Meanchey had been occupied by Thailand, with Japanese approval, in 1941 and these organizations were "apparently the work of (a Bangkok-based) Issarak Committee and of the ICP and the Communist Party of Thailand."[2] By 1946, a Viet Minh unit of two hundred men was located in Battambang and at the end of that year, revolutionary committees were established in Cambodian provinces adjacent to southern Vietnam.

Early in 1948, the Khmer People's Liberation Committee headed by Dap Chhuon, "a traditional warlord rather than a leftwing nationalist" according to Kiernan, was formed by the Issarak movement and by the end of that year it had divided the country into four military zones: the Southeast, the Northeast, the Southwest and the Northwest headed respectively by Keo Moni, Son Sichan, Son Ngoc Minh and Dap Chhuon. Except for Dap Chhuon, who would surrender to Sihanouk's Royal Government the following year, they were all members of the ICP. Son Ngoc Minh (aka Achar Mean), an ethnic

Khmer from Kampuchea Krom and a former professor of Pali at Wat Unnalom in Phnom Penh, would become the chairman of Cambodia's first communist party.[3] In those early years, he worked closely and successfully with the Vietnamese but the anti-French resistance consisted of many different strands and, as Kiernan notes, "they were able to win the loyalty of many Khmer nationalists but could not capture unchallenged leadership of the independence movement the way the Viet Minh had done in their own country."[4] The support that they held was almost exclusively rural; the revolutionary movement in Phnom Penh was almost negligible before independence. Nevertheless, their numbers were sufficiently large to worry the colonial government (about 10,600 rebels by early 1949, less than a thousand of whom were Vietnamese, according to police estimates), despite the fact that they were "poorly-armed, vulnerable concentrations of forces rather than entrenched guerrilla units."[5] In April 1950 some 200 delegates of whom 105 were Buddhist monks, according to Kiernan, held the "First National Congress of the Khmer Resistance" in the Southwest Zone. The congress was preceded by a meeting between Le Duc Tho, other Viet Minh leaders, Son Ngoc Minh and other Khmer communists which voted to establish the United Issarak Front (UIF) and a proto-government called the Provisional People's Liberation Central Committee headed by Son Ngoc Minh with three deputies, including Tou Samouth (aka Achar Sok).

Acting on the orders of the Comintern, the second congress of the ICP held in early February 1951 dissolved the party into three national communist parties. The party in Cambodia was to be the Khmer People's Revolutionary Party (KPRP) and its founding congress on 28 June that year "approved a program of activities and party statutes, and appointed a leadership commission of the party among whom were comrades Son Ngoc Minh and Tou Samouth."[6] The party statutes were adopted in 1952. Kiernan observes that they were similar to those of the Vietnam Workers' Party (VWP), with two exceptions: "There was no mention of Marxism-Leninism or its founders, only a vague statement that 'the doctrine of the Party is the doctrine of People's Democracy.'"[7] The KPRP's goal at that stage was independence from France, not revolution. Kiernan suggests that both the Cambodians and the Vietnamese recognized that the proletarian movement in Cambodia was still small and undeveloped and both parties recognized the need for Cambodia's modernization.

INDEPENDENCE FROM FRANCE AND CONSEQUENCES FOR THE PARTY

In June 1951, Le Duc Tho gave the directive for the VVAK, the Vietnamese Volunteer Army in Kampuchea, to fight with the Khmer Issarak armed forces under a unified command. This radicalization of the independence movement provoked concern and outrage in the court and King Sihanouk's coining of the term "Khmer Viet Minh":

> We can affirm that this situation of insecurity is provoked by the infiltration of the Viet Minh, with communist loyalties. These disruptive foreign elements, by pressure or lying propaganda, have managed to win to their cause a great number of our compatriots. Most of the Issarak bands which call themselves nationalists to deceive us, are nothing else but Khmer Viet Minh . . . We must scorn them and collaborate with the forces of order.[8]

The king was to take the credit for winning the struggle for independence. In June 1952, Sihanouk dismissed the new, popular government of the Democratic Party, declared himself prime minister, and ruled by decree until appointing a new government at the end of January 1953 with Penn Nouth as prime minister. He launched his own "Royal Crusade for Cambodian Independence" and with a familiar ploy, put himself into exile, threatening not to return to Phnom Penh until independence was achieved. On 9 November 1953, Sihanouk won limited independence for Cambodia from France.[9] By mid-1954, the combined forces of the UIF and VVAK, under Vietnamese military control, had laid claim to more than one third of the Cambodian countryside.[10] In spite of this, the UIF

4

representatives, Keo Moni and Mey Pho, were not admitted when the Geneva Conference convened in May 1954 to settle the Korean and Indochinese conflicts. In response to the DRV Deputy Premier and Foreign Minister Pham Van Dong's request for discussion of a proposal to invite representatives of the resistance governments of the Pathet Lao and the Khmer Issaraks to the conference, Sam Sary, head of the Cambodian delegation, denied that the Khmer Issaraks constituted a government and argued that they were "foreigners who are being manipulated by a foreign bloc."[11] According to the terms of the Indochina settlement, all Viet Minh forces would withdraw from Cambodia and from Laos. The UIF were not granted regroupment zones as were their equivalent partners in Vietnam and Laos and they were ordered to disarm and prepare to take part in national elections to be held in 1955. This was a bitter blow for the incipient revolutionary force of just over two thousand members. Wilfred Burchett reported:

> When historians put their fingers on the major impediment to the Cambodian revolution, they must point to the consequences of the 1954 Geneva Conference on Indochina . . . The Khmer resistance fighters who had participated in that struggle were robbed at Geneva of their share of the fruits of the common victory by the three peoples of Indochina over French colonialism.[12]

On the other hand, one must wonder about the easy acquiescence of the Khmer Issarak leaders to the arrangements made on their behalf by the Viet Minh delegation. Randle hypothesizes:

> Even with the guarantees of their civil rights in Article 6, the insurgents may have been displeased with the DRVN's arrogation of the right to speak on their behalf . . . [On the other hand], in view of the fact that Son Ngoc Minh, president of the Khmer resistance "government," appealed for the observance of the settlement in late July, it is not impossible that the Khmer Issaraks freely consented to Viet Minh representation in June and to the terms of the ceasefire agreement relat-

ing to demobilization. Also, Khmer Issarak leaders never challenged the obligatory force of the agreement, and their conduct after July evinced an intent to adhere to its terms.[13]

The Geneva Conference and its outcomes highlights the extent of Vietnamese authority over the Cambodian revolutionary movement at this stage. For the young firebrand revolutionaries like Saloth Sar (aka Pol Pot), who returned from studies in France in the year prior to the conference, this easy adherence by the Khmer Issarak leaders to the terms of the agreement and subservience to Vietnamese leadership whose strategic thinking subjugated the role of Cambodia and Laos to the defense of Vietnam, must have been a cause of deep frustration and resentment.

The withdrawal of Viet Minh forces was to be completed within ninety days of the entry into force of the Geneva Agreement, that is, no later than ninety days after 23 July. Demobilization of the Khmer Issarak forces was carried out so quickly that it was almost completed before the International Supervisory Commission (ISC), composed of representatives of India, Canada, and Poland, began to function. Evacuation of the Viet Minh units began on 12 October and by 18 October, the ISC had verified the withdrawal of 2,384 Viet Minh troops. Despite Cambodian government claims to the contrary, the ISC concluded that "no substantial number of former Viet Minh soldiers or irregulars remained in Cambodia."[14]

Just over one thousand Cambodians joined the departing Viet Minh troops on the ships carrying them north to Hanoi.[15] No doubt these Khmer Viet Minh feared government reprisals, despite the assurances of Article 6 of the Agreement on the Cessation of Hostilities. Those who went represented "the best and the brightest . . . ranking military and party leaders who had acquired valuable experience in working with the Vietnamese for years."[16] They included Nuon Chea, So Phim, Keo Moni, Son Ngoc Minh, and Sieu Heng.[17] Some of those who went to study and work in Vietnam and other communist states at that time were still only adolescents.[18] After 1970, they returned to fight for the revolution and all except fifty-seven of them who would become the leaders of the early PRK regime, including Pen Sovann, Chan Si, Keo Chenda, Ros Samay, Say Phouthang, Bou Thong, and Chea Soth, would number among the dead in Pol Pot's killing fields.

ISOLATION AND SELF-RELIANCE

Approximately half of those committed to revolution remained in Cambodia, some forming a legitimate political party, the Pracheachon (People's) Party and others going underground to escape the savage sweeps of the Khmer Royal Forces throughout the former KPRP zones. By Carney's definition, the period from 1954 to 1967 was the "era of political struggle, a time of open and clandestine educational efforts to rouse and develop public awareness of national and class problems."[19] Most importantly, these efforts were conducted without the supervision and for the most part without even the knowledge of Vietnam. According to Engelbert and Goscha, "[W]hile the Vietnamese left behind 'a number of their comrades' after 1954 and while they undoubtedly had their own ways of gathering intelligence, by the end of the 1950s their large-scale withdrawal saw them fall out of touch with the events confronting what remained of the KPRP in Cambodia, with one Vietnamese internal study conceding that Vietnam had only one (un-named) person located within the KPRP."[20]

For the VWP, from 1955 on, support for Prince Sihanouk's policy of neutrality in foreign affairs was an essential part of their strategy for achieving national reunification. According to Dmitry Mosyakov:

> The North Vietnamese leaders who were preparing for a re-newal of armed struggle in the South, found in Sihanouk, with his anti-imperialist and anti-American rhetoric, a far more im-portant ally than the KPRP. Moreover, Sihanouk had real power.[21]

The benefits of this support were borne out in fact: in August 1963, Sihanouk broke diplomatic relations with South Vietnam; in November, he terminated all US assistance programs in Cambodia, and in May 1965, he broke diplomatic relations with the US; from 1965 on, the Chinese, Soviets, and Czechs were allowed use of the port of Sihanoukville to supply Vietnamese communist troops in South Vietnam, and the North Vietnamese and the Viet Cong were allowed use of eastern Cambodian provinces as a sanctuary in their fight against the US. For the Khmer communists who remained in Cambodia and who suffered at the hands of Sihanouk's secret police and armed forces, "the story gained currency that Hanoi had simply betrayed them, used them as hostages for the sake of reaching agreement with the then leader of Cambodia, Norodom Sihanouk."[22] Mosyakov continues that their evaluation of Vietnamese policy was "an unrighteous betrayal of the Cambodian revolution."

There was yet another struggle for those Cambodian communists left behind after 1954, that for control of the party itself. Young Khmer students studying in France in the late 1940s and early 1950s came heavily under the influence of socialist idealism. Kiernan writes that ten of them had become members of the French Communist Party by 1951, including Saloth Sar (Pol Pot) and Ieng Sary, and that another twenty or so including Khieu Samphan, Hou Yuon, and Vorn Veth, had joined by 1953. On their return to Cambodia they gradually took control of a party which had been fractured by the events of 1954 and further crushed by the process and outcome of the 1955 national election. The failure of the as yet clandestine KPRP seemed complete with the 1959 defection to the government of Sieu Heng, the in-country leader of the party.

From 30 September to 2 October 1960, the second party congress was held secretly at the Phnom Penh railway station with twenty delegates attending. The propaganda document which was prepared for the fifth, and final, party congress states:

> At the end of the 1950s, the Sihanouk authorities savagely oppressed the mass struggle movement. Many members were arrested and killed. Some wavering members left their duty. The party base was destroyed in many places. Of the highest leadership institutions of the party only Tou Samouth was left.

8

The situation made it necessary to strengthen the administrative organization and to have measures to care closely for the movement. The party cadre conference called a secret meeting in Phnom Penh on 30 September 1960. This conference was considered to be the second congress of the party. The congress approved a program of struggle within the new situation, approved the essence of changes to the statutes and appointed a central committee including eight full rights members and two candidates, with comrade Tou Samouth as secretary-general. Pol Pot and Ieng Sary took advantage of this opportunity to infiltrate the central committee and Pol Pot joined the politburo.[23]

The politburo then consisted of Tou Samouth, with Nuon Chea as his deputy, and Saloth Sar (Pol Pot) as member. The Cambodian revolution was about to take a course radically different from that foreseen and planned by Son Ngoc Minh and his Vietnamese mentors. Kiernan believes that the main difference between this group of French-educated revolutionaries and the party veterans was in conflicting perceptions of the nature of the Sihanouk regime and the nature of relations with Vietnam:

> The Pol Pot group tended to be implacably opposed to [the Sihanouk regime], as a backward, dictatorial monarchy . . . The veterans, on the other hand, were much more inclined to see Sihanouk's neutrality and his increasingly anti-imperialist stance as positive factors in an Indo-China-wide struggle for socialism.[24]

In mid-1962, KPRP Secretary-General Tou Samouth disappeared. The next generation of revolutionaries claimed that he was betrayed to Sihanouk's secret police, under the command of Lon Nol, by Pol Pot himself although Pol Pot vehemently denied this in an interview with journalist Nate Thayer not long before his death.[25] "At that time I was his aide," Pol Pot said. "If Tou Samouth had talked, I would have been arrested. He was killed at Stung Meanchey pagoda. We loved each other." Ney Pena argues that following Tou Samouth's death,

Saloth Sar deliberately set out to destroy Nuon Chea's reputation by claiming that he had a close relationship with the defector, Sieu Heng, "and had money to buy a house in Phnom Penh as well."[26] The ruse appeared to work and, Ney Pena claims, Nuon Chea asked permission to resign from his politburo position. In this way, Saloth Sar controlled the party alone until he called an extraordinary party congress in January 1963 in order to elect a new central committee. Saloth Sar was then elected secretary-general of the party with Nuon Chea and Ieng Sary as his deputies; So Phim and Vorn Veth completed the politburo.

A few months later, both Pol Pot and Ieng Sary fled Phnom Penh for the maquis where they established their headquarters on the border of Kompong Cham and Vietnam.[27] This was the main area of Vietnam's secret bases.[28] The Central Office of South Vietnam/COSVN headquarters (of the VWP branch for South Vietnam), for instance, was located within the Memot Plantation which straddled the border.[29] During that period, in June 1965, Pol Pot made a visit to Hanoi and held talks for the first time with ranking Vietnamese politburo members. Engelbert and Goscha note that top Vietnamese officials in Hanoi were aware of the rise of this younger group of Cambodian communists.[30] However, because they had allowed the relationship with the Cambodian party to become estranged after 1954, "there were people in the highest posts of the Khmer Communist Party little-known to the Vietnamese and inevitably suspect because they were educated in France, instead of in Hanoi. Besides, the majority of them had not participated in the anti-colonial war and were not checked for allegiance 'to the elder brother.'"[31] The KPRP's political platform which had been prepared for the party's second congress in 1960 stating the importance of self-reliance and armed action against Sihanouk was coolly rebuffed by Secretary-General Le Duan who reportedly told Pol Pot that "for the moment its emphasis on 'protracted, difficult, and self-reliant struggle' was inappropriate."[32] The document was reworked, "written in Vietnamese and proof-read by Duan himself."[33] Pol Pot is said to have left the meeting "without saying anything at all. He did not say one word."[34] Apart from the deep insult to Cambodian pride, the Vietnamese response to the Khmer party's plan for armed action reconfirmed the suspicion that Hanoi placed its own strategic interests and objectives above its obligations to a fraternal party. Pol Pot then proceeded to Beijing where he met with high-ranking CCP officials, including Liu Shaoqi and Deng Xiaoping, and was reassured by their praise for his political platform and their urgings to rely on the peasantry and oppose American imperialism.[35]

Towards the end of 1966, because of US bombing raids, the headquarters of the renamed Communist Party of Kampuchea were relocated to Ratanakiri province. It was, Sara Colm notes, "a logical place for Pol Pot to build the party's first base of popular support" with a generally supportive population bitter over brutal Khmerization policies, land confiscation, excessive taxation, and other abuses inflicted on the indigenous highland people by state authorities; ample natural resources; and secure hiding places for military training camps.[36] A Brou leader who attended a month-long training session given by Pol Pot recalled that the message of the meeting was ". . . that there should be solidarity between Vietnam, Laos and Cambodia; we should not abandon each other. We needed to prepare arms in order to have enough military force for the struggle. Finally, we needed to take over lowland Cambodia from the mountains. Once we got to the lowlands, we must then take the cities."[37] He recalled that the people loved Pol Pot at that time: "He would live and die with the people . . . Pol Pot really liked the ethnic minorities—he said we were the best."[38]

REACTIONS IN THE ROYAL COURT

While Pol Pot was building his popular base in the countryside, Sihanouk's policy of neutrality was beginning to falter. In the 1962 general election, all seventy-seven of his Sangkum candidates were returned unopposed and he incorporated a number of members of the Sangkum's left-wing faction, including Hou Yuon, Hu Nim, and Khieu Samphan, into his post-election cabinet.[39] However, pressure from the right and subversion by the left were leaving him with little room to maneuver. In late 1963, alleging that Washington was supporting right-wing rebel movements against his government, he renounced US economic and military aid and severed relations with South Vietnam. His new economic measures to account for this, including nationalization of all banking and import-export business, inevitably cost him valuable support from the traditional elite. To increase export earnings, especially rice export earnings, the official price at which rice was purchased from the peasants was reduced by 20 percent between 1963 and 1964. Stephen Heder notes that this reduction not only tended to lower peasant incomes but also contributed to stagnation in rice production which brought about a general economic crisis in the countryside after 1963:

> The rural economic and political situation drew the CPK deeper into involvement with peasant grievances against the Sihanouk regime and improved its prospects for organizing peasants around the theme of land reform, which became a party slogan in 1964.[40]

In the city, the Chinese and Sino-Khmer traders readily found ways to circumvent government control over the import-export trade and to evade the payment of duties. Nevertheless, according to Milton Osborne, "Although they continued to live at a level of luxury that astounded many foreign visitors, the Cambodian elite, by 1966, had a strong sense that their personal economic position was endangered, and that Sihanouk was to blame."[41] Sihanouk could have weathered the discontent of the Phnom Penh elite but by cutting off US assistance to the military, the prince was courting disaster. In 1962, the US had provided over 30 percent of the armed forces' budget.[42] The US contribution represented the funds that financed the salaries of the officers and the troops, provided equipment and training within the country, and sent officers to training schools in America. As Osborne notes, "By 1966 many, including Sihanouk, were aware that there was deep dissatisfaction within the army."[43] However, in a rare but vital misjudgment, in the lead-up to the September 1966 general elections, Sihanouk concluded that his main threat came from the left. He abandoned his usual policy of nominating Sangkum candidates, thereby ensuring that the candidates who were rich enough to buy their support would win. The result was an overwhelming victory for the rightwing of the Sangkum. As testament to the esteem in which they were held by the urban electorate for their integrity and intelligence, Khieu Samphan, Hou Yuon, and Hu Nim on the left were returned as deputies to the National Assembly despite the best efforts of Sihanouk's officials to undermine their campaigns. General Lon Nol was asked to form the new and fractious Cambodian government.

By 1967 rice exports had collapsed. Given such low official rice prices, the farmers preferred to sell their paddy illegally to Chinese middlemen who profited by sales to the Vietnamese troops. The government reacted with a program of forced rice collection with the support of the military. Opposition to this practice, combined with pent-up grievances, precipitated a major peasant rebellion in the Samlaut region of Battambang province in April 1967. Sihanouk accused the communists of fomenting violence in the countryside and on 22 April he charged Khieu Samphan and Hou Yuon with primary responsibility for Samlaut. Two days later, both fled Phnom Penh for the maquis.

ARMED STRUGGLE

By the middle of August 1967, the Samlaut rebellion had been crushed. Heder believes that it was at this point that the party "decided that it was time to abandon all forms of cooperation with the Sihanouk regime and to make preparations to form, as soon as possible, a revolutionary army with which to wage all-out armed struggle against it."[44] The decision was an autonomous one and possibly even unknown to the Vietnamese for whom bases in eastern Cambodia, supplied with arms shipped from China and Hanoi through Sihanoukville, were crucial staging areas for their planned Tet offensive of 1968.

Any action on the part of the CPK to jeopardize this vital supply route would have been roundly condemned by the VWP leaders. In view of the fact that the CPK needed Vietnam's cooperation in order to maintain its own supply of arms from China down the Ho Chi Minh Trail, most of its attacks took place in the northwest, far from the Vietnamese sanctuaries. Mosyakov suggests that Pol Pot reached a "compromise" with Hanoi "to reserve to himself authority in the party leadership, to provide the material and military aid for fighting groups, which he called the Revolutionary Army."[45] He adds that Pol Pot "even showed readiness for close union and 'special solidarity' with the DRV." The period of armed struggle from 1968 to victory in April 1975 was hard and bitter. It was, in Heder's words, "a period of isolated defiance, self-confidence and, as evidenced by the growth of the CPK's forces, success."[46] From January 1968, the KR launched a widespread guerrilla campaign throughout the northeast and western provinces and David Chandler estimates that the number of guerrillas under arms in Cambodia doubled to "some four thousand" between 1968 and 1970.[47] Militarily, however, these poorly armed actions were unsuccessful and were swiftly put down by the military forces led by General Lon Nol. According to Mosyakov, ". . . this army conducted unsuccessful operations against the forces of the ruling regime, sustaining heavy losses, and did not have the slightest hope of coming to power."[48]

The secret bombing of Cambodia by US aircraft began in March 1969 in an attempt to flush out and destroy the key Viet Cong bases along the Cambodian-Vietnamese border. It continued for over a year with more than three thousand raids against Cambodian targets.[49] As Chandler adds, "Sihanouk's neutralist policy was in tatters. The game he had played since 1955 was lost."[50] On 19 March 1970, during his absence from Cambodia, Sihanouk was voted out of office by the National Assembly in a bloodless *coup d'état*.

VICTORY

Hun Sen, prime minister of Cambodia from 1985 and a member of the struggle from 1967 or 1968,[51] has often stated that if it had not been for the 1970 coup, the ensuing civil war which Serge Thion calls "the most savage onslaught ever launched against a peasantry"[52] and the terror caused by intensive US bombing,[53] there would not have been a Kampuchean revolution. There is evidence for his claims. On 23 March, from Beijing, Sihanouk declared war on the coup plotters and proposed a National Union Government (GRUNK) with Penn Nouth as president and Khieu Samphan as deputy, a National Liberation Army and a National United Front of Kampuchea (FUNK).[54] In his broadcast he called on his "children . . . to engage in guerrilla warfare in the jungle against our enemies."[55] Thousands responded to the call. Thanks to Beijing's diplomacy, the Khmer Rouge were now part of a Vietnamese-Sihanouk alliance. They not only gained recruits under the aegis of Sihanouk's patronage; they also gained arms and training from Vietnam. Much of this political and military training of new recruits was conducted by those same young communists, the Khmer Viet Minh, who had gone to North Vietnam in 1954. According to Carney, the North Vietnamese told Sihanouk that eight thousand Khmer had gone south to support his return to power.[56] As this number is far greater than that of the original 1954 group, Carney suggests that it may "reflect additional men who continually filtered north during Sihanouk's rule."[57]

The Democratic Republic of Vietnam's response, a denunciation of the Lon Nol coup as the work of the US and a pledge of its support to Prince Sihanouk, was fast but not immediate. According to Engelbert and Goscha, the Vietnamese were unsure if the US had supported the coup, "[a]nd before committing Vietnam to taking up armed action in Cambodia, Le Duan's diplomats made a last minute effort to gain Lon Nol's continued acquiescence to Vietnamese sanctuaries in eastern Cambodia."[58] Assured of the new Khmer Republic's stand, between April and May 1970, "significant" North Vietnamese forces entered Cambodia in response to a request made by

Nuon Chea, Pol Pot's deputy, to Hanoi.[59] By the end of 1970, there were four North Vietnamese combat divisions in Cambodia.[60] One can well imagine the uneasiness of Pol Pot and the CPK in the face of this veritable invasion of Vietnamese troops and Khmer Viet Minh advisers. The size of their own forces paled in comparison. There was a very real possibility that power over the Cambodian communist movement could slip out of their control and that Vietnam would place the Khmer Viet Minh returnees in positions of power and control. In fact, however, the returnees never attained leadership positions above that of village or *damban* (district or sector) level. Despite this effort on the part of Vietnam to maintain a working relationship, it became increasingly obvious after mid-1971 that the Khmer Viet Minh had a role only as long as the Vietnamese troops were in place. In the second half of that year, a CPK "congress" made the decision to break with Vietnam, naming it the long-term "acute" enemy of the Cambodian revolution.[61] By late 1971, there were frequent clashes between the Cambodian and Vietnamese communist forces. The VWP leaders were aware of these incidents, although it is less likely that they considered the conflict as a product of deliberate policy. Their response was to urge conciliation "in order to concentrate all our forces in the liberation of the south."[62]

The withdrawal of Vietnamese troops from Cambodia in October 1972 in accordance with the preconditions for the Paris Peace Accords in many ways represented a re-enactment of what had happened after the 1954 Geneva Conference. "Hanoi has dropped us," is how Sihanouk described the state of Cambodian-Vietnamese relations following his tour to the liberated zones in March–April 1973.[63] At the same time, the withdrawal provided the opportunity for the "domestic" Cambodian communists to assume real power. Chandler records:

> Freed at last from Vietnamese supervision and control, CPK forces in some areas organized demonstrations against the Vietnamese, dismantled guerrilla forces supporting Sihanouk's return to power, and purged returnees from North Vietnam.[64]

Some of the returnees managed to escape back to Vietnam. In early August 1986, two representatives of the Central Commission for Foreign Relations of the Communist Party of Vietnam reported to a special meeting of the powerful Central Administration Commission of the People's Revolutionary Party of Kampuchea in Phnom Penh. The minutes of that meeting record that 1,015 Khmer Viet Minh had gone to North Vietnam in 1954. Fifty-two of them died before 1970 but all 963 of the remainder returned to Cambodia between 1970 and 1974. In 1979, there were only 57 of the original 1,015 alive so "we can conclude that the number that died in the Pol Pot time was 906 comrades."[65] The Cambodian revolution never recovered from the loss of these highly trained, experienced, and committed cadres. It destroyed a whole generation of its own core leaders and replaced them with young zealots. David Chandler observes:

> Even before victory, Cambodians thirteen and fourteen years old were often taken from their homes in liberated areas and subjected to short indoctrination courses from which they emerged, according to a US embassy study in early 1975, "fierce in their condemnation of the 'old ways,' contemptuous of traditional customs, and ardently opposed to religion and parental authority." Freed from family obligations, they displayed a loyalty to the Organization that was often absolute . . . These boys and girls became the revolution's cutting edge.[66]

Despite warnings from Vietnam of severe reprisals, Pol Pot rejected US Secretary of State Henry Kissinger's demands for negotiations between the Khmer revolutionary movement and the Lon Nol government of the Khmer Republic. Almost immediately after the 27 January 1973 signing of the Paris Peace Accords ending the war in Vietnam, intensive US aerial bombardment of Cambodia began. For two hundred days and nights, B-52 bombers rained more than a quarter of a million tons of bombs on the Cambodian countryside. In the wake of the chaos and terror that the bombing caused, tens of thousands of rural Cambodians crowded into Phnom Penh, while in the liberated zones the KR supervised the creation of cooperatives and the collectivization of private property. By 1974 the KR had liberated virtually the whole country; only the capital and some provincial centers remained in government hands. The people in the towns were fed by airdrops of USAID rice while just a few kilometers away their relatives were "growing rice for the KR." On 17 April 1975, the KR entered and took Phnom Penh. The first stage of the revolution had been secured.

Chapter 2

THE REVOLUTION AND ITS AFTERMATH, 1975–1978

FRANCOIS PONCHAUD, A Catholic priest who had spent ten years in Cambodia prior to 1975, published one of the first detailed accounts of the revolution in October 1976.[1] He used the title "Year Zero" to help to define the scale of the transformation of Cambodian society wrought by the political revolution of April 1975. Cambodia was returned to its origins, stripped of all forms of foreign influence, and pared down to a lifestyle which relied only on food for survival and the labor required to produce it. Those who did not acknowledge the new rules perished, either at the hands of the enforcers of the changed order or because the conditions created by that order permitted only the fittest to survive. It is generally accepted that approximately 1.7 million people died during the regime of Democratic Kampuchea, what has become popularly known as the Pol Pot Regime, which lasted for a few months short of four years.[2] The whole society was profoundly affected and very few families were untouched by the death of at least one immediate family member. At a deep psychological level, therefore, April 1975 is Year Zero for many older Cambodians. For them, there is time "before Pol Pot" and time "after Pol Pot." The year is the benchmark for everything that Cambodians believe they have lost and it justifies their profound nostalgia for the past which was for them in every way perfect. By corollary, it is a convenient and much-used excuse for current problems in Cambodia and also a way to explain them. The "Pol Pot time" is both reference point and watershed. Like other defining eras in world history, or in the history of societies whose lives were dramatically changed by political events or natural disasters beyond their control and comprehension, the first stage of the Cambodian revolution, April 1975 to January 1979, has gradually shaped a collective memory of experience. At the same time, it has also developed something like collective amnesia. Nobody, it seems, can understand why the Khmer Rouge, the leaders of Democratic Kampuchea and their followers, were driven to such rage that they were able to defy the religious precepts, kill with impunity, and deny those deeper instincts produced by age-old traditions. In truth, however, violence and confrontation were no more absent from Khmer culture than from any other. Within the living memory of the victims was the brutal civil war when neither side took prisoners. Even the better-off citizens of Phnom Penh who were shielded from the worst of the terror created by the war were made to pay witness at that time to public acts of violence committed against the transgressors of state power. Nevertheless, for those who survived the catastrophe of 1975 to 1979, no amount of explanation or historical evidence, it seems, can ever make sense of the wild irrationality of those years.

IDEOLOGY IN THE REGIME OF DEMOCRATIC KAMPUCHEA

Foreign scholars who have researched and analyzed the history of Democratic Kampuchea (DK) question the use of "social revolution" to explain the nature of that regime. Michael Vickery, for instance, argues that it was in the nature of a peasant rebellion, inspired more by millenarianism than adherence to communist theory and practice.[3] Those who made this revolution, however, seem to have believed that what they were doing was indeed creating a new society committed to communist goals. A captured document dated Phnom Penh, 1975 entitled *A Short Guide for Application of Party Statutes* begins:

I. Party Name
Our party is called "The Communist Party of Kampuchea" in accordance with the recommendations passed by the central committee in September 1966.

II. Goal of the Party

1. The immediate goal of the party is to lead the people to succeed in the national democratic revolution, to exterminate the imperialists, feudalists, and capitalists, and to form a national revolutionary state in Cambodia.

2. The long range goal of the party is to lead the people in creating a socialist revolution and a communist society in Cambodia.[4]

The two-stage revolution and its general analysis that the root causes for revolution were exploitation and oppression committed against the people by foreign imperialists and the landlord class thus put the Cambodian revolution squarely in the mold of other regional Marxist-Leninist revolutionary movements from the Philippines to North Korea at that time.

In an early 1977 Party document entitled *Abbreviated Lesson on the History of the Kampuchean Revolutionary Movement led by the Communist Party of Kampuchea*, the author declares:

> We say that we made the National-Democratic Revolution because analysis showed that the feudal landlords were in antagonistic contradiction within our country, and outside [it] there were the imperialists. In our party some friends said that this was not so. In the [international] world there were also some friends who said this was not so.[5]

In practice, it hardly mattered whether their class analysis was valid or not, or whether the real problem of rural poverty and backwardness was landlordism, ethnic Chinese usury, or the fault of "imperialist" external forces, because for the DK regime, theory bore little relevance to practice and making revolution was really all that mattered. "We did not act with the guidance of definite theories," Ieng Sary is reported to have told a Palestine Liberation Organization visitor in 1976, "but followed our feelings and carried out the struggle in a practical way . . . What is important is the determination and faith of the principal revolutionaries. We did not study in ideological schools, but practiced a struggle in the light of the concrete situation."[6]

THEORY IN PRACTICE

The Pol Pot years are remembered almost exclusively for their brutality, although this view must be tempered by the evidence that the regime was not always and everywhere the same, that rule in some parts of the country, in areas of Kratie and some parts of Kompong Thom provinces, for instance, was almost benign, and that some local Khmer Rouge cadres did what they could within the restrictions imposed on them to lessen the suffering of the people, and even gave warning of impending executions in order to save lives. The evacuation of the cities, particularly Phnom Penh, the systematic torture and liquidation of party dissidents in S-21 (Tuol Sleng), and the mountains of skulls excavated from mass graves all over the country have become the emblems of the excesses of DK power.

The brutality towards the returning Khmer Viet Minh in 1970 has already been noted. For the ordinary rural people, however, before "liberation," the good behavior and correct attitude of the Khmer Rouge cadres attracted many to their cause. Ith Sarin was a former primary school inspector who spent nine months with the revolutionaries in the maquis from April 1972. His short book, *Sronoh Proloeung Khmer* [Regrets for the Khmer Soul], which was published in Phnom Penh in July the following year, provides interesting and, for the most part, positive commentary on the communist movement's level of organization, self-reliance, and "serving the people":

> The Khmer Rouge *Angkar* strongly forbids disturbing the produce or goods of the people . . . Another effective point in Khmer Rouge "Psychological Activity" toward peasants is help during troubles . . . This being "together with the people" in order to "serve the people," closely associating with the people, is the implementation of one of the Khmer Rouge theories in educating Khmer Rouge cadre. These kinds of psychological activities were really successful and deeply affected the people more than the instruction in theory did. The farming people of the base areas who knew nothing of socialist revolution quickly began to love and support the *Angkar* because of its sentiments of openness and friendliness.[7]

After winning power, however, "loving the people" was not sufficient for effective government. David Ashley argues that the DK leadership was "strikingly unrealistic and incompetent."[8] One failed policy was replaced with another failure. Ashley quotes a former DK intellectual:

> Of the leaders, only Pol Pot was good at thinking and analyzing. When speaking about an issue, Pol Pot was very good at explaining it in a very lucid, clear way which convinced you that he had found a complete solution to the problem. But when it came to implementation, his solution would fail. Then he would put forward another idea which would again seem very convincing and yet the same thing would happen again.[9]

When all else failed, Pol Pot did what other failed demagogues had done before him and resorted to ultranationalism, rule by fear and casting blame on a traditional enemy.

The compilation of eight documents entitled *Pol Pot Plans the Future*, translated and edited by David Chandler, Ben Kiernan, and Chanthou Boua, offers interesting insights into the workings of the regime. The earliest of these, *Decisions of the Central Committee on a Variety of Questions*, is dated 30 March 1976. By then, the first revolutionary stage, the national democratic revolution, was seen to have been completed with the eradication of the feudal, capitalist regime and the evacuation of its remnants to the countryside where they were termed the "new" people to distinguish them from the "old" or "base" people, that is, the peasants who had remained on the base and in the liberated zones before 1975. The revolution had already entered the stage of building socialism, so the document begins: "Let there be a framework of procedures for implementing our revolutionary authority." On this matter, "the aim of our revolutionary struggle is to establish state power within the grasp of the worker-peasants, and to abolish all oppressive state power." To this end, as the document notes, the constitution had been written, and elections had been held in preparation for forming the assembly, the state presidium and the government. As for the GRUNK, that Royal Government of National Union of Kampuchea created by the coalition of left-wing and monarchist exiled forces in 1970, the document merely advises that "there is no problem with Penn Nouth" and as for Sihanouk, "we have decided to retire him, according to the wishes of others."

The constitution was drafted by a constitution commission headed by Khieu Samphan and in late August 1975 an early draft was presented to Sihanouk and Penn Nouth, who were still in China. The constitution was approved on 14 December 1975 at the National Congress that was convened in Phnom Penh with 1,115 delegates attending. Stephen Heder notes:

> On 5 January 1976, five days after his return to the country, Sihanouk presided as chief-of-state over a meeting of the GRUNK cabinet, at which the text of the constitution was presented as a *fait accompli* for promulgation. On that date Cambodia thus formally became "Democratic Kampuchea."[10]

The preamble to the constitution justified the regime in terms of the highest ideals:

> . . . Whereas the entire Kampuchean people and the entire Kampuchea Revolutionary Army desire an independent, unified, peaceful, neutral, nonaligned, sovereign Kampuchea enjoying territorial integrity, a national society informed by genuine happiness, equality, justice, and democracy without rich or poor and without exploiters or exploited, a society in which all live harmoniously in great national solidarity and join forces to do manual labor together and increase production for the construction and defense of the country.[11]

Laura Summers interprets the preamble as "tap[ping] profound moral roots in Khmer political tradition even as it breaks with part of that tradition."[12] The radical political and social changes wrought by the revolution were, paradoxically, justified as reviving the cosmic order and reestablishing the harmony between man and nature that had been shattered by the civil war. However, Summers continues, "If the constitution clarifies some of the goals of the revolution, it reveals very little about the current use of revolutionary power."[13]

Polling for the 515 candidates standing for the 250 seats in the Kampuchean People's Representative Assembly as specified by Article 5, Chapter 5 of the constitution was held on 20 March 1976. As explained in the 30 March document, the assembly president was to be Nuon Chea, the state presidium would consist of Khieu Samphan, Penn Nouth, and Ros Nhim and the government would be headed by Pol Pot as prime minister with three deputies: Ieng Sary in charge of foreign affairs, Vorn Veth in charge of the economy and finance, and Son Sen in charge of national defense. According to Heder, the assembly met just once and for only two hours on the afternoon of 12 April and "having thus served its purpose of formally ending the united front, the assembly never met again."[14]

The former administrative system based on provinces was replaced by one based on zones or regions. Each zone (*phumipheak*) was divided into sectors (*damban*), then districts (*srok*), communes (*khum*), and finally the village (*phum*). Each administrative level was the charge of a committee but "in the *khum* where the chairman did not understand about the revolution, they designated a party political commissar to assist the committee."[15] The core of the organization of the country, however, was the cooperative and it was here that power and control were most effectively exercised. In 1972, the Front (FUNK) had started organizing solidarity production teams (*krom samaki bongkor bonkaun phol*) of ten to fifteen farming families as the basic unit of agricultural work, and these *krom* later formed the basis of the cooperative.[16] The population of these cooperatives, of which about half contained between seven hundred and one thousand families by 1977, was formed into permanent labor teams as well as mobile labor brigades.[17]

The war mentality permeated every structure and activity of the regime. "Grasping hold of the cooperatives" is the theme of the second document, *Excerpted Report on the Leading Views of the Comrade Representing the Party Organization at a Zone Assembly*, which was reported in *Tung Padevat* (The Flag of the Revolution) of June, 1976.[18] How was this to be done?

By grasping politics tightly, to make people understand the very important political line of the party. Grasp hold of their

25

consciousness, make things clear to them. The party's every task and plan must be explained to them until they understand and things become clear. Dikes, canals, three tons—(all of this) is to build and defend the country. If they understand clearly, they are happy, they do their own fighting, they have their children join the army or the work brigades to raise dikes and dig canals.

This, in turn, would be achieved by the whole zone administration going down to the cooperatives "in order to broadcast the party line" because "unless we pursue this experiment, we cannot maximize the strength of this socialist revolutionary movement."

The author feared that "socialist consciousness" had not gone deeply among the people. As the party had decided that agriculture would be transformed into a modern system within ten to fifteen years, the key question was how to organize the "action line." The answer was as in war:

> We raised the principle of attacking wherever we (could) win, wherever the enemy was weak. And the same goes for the economy. We attack wherever the opportunities are greatest . . . We must prepare offensives for the whole country.

The document is filled with war analogies and as in guerrilla warfare, speed was of the essence because "if we are not strong and do not leap forward quickly, outside enemies are just waiting to crush us . . . for that reason we must strive to move fast." It was the party's role "to consider, to lead, to administer" and it had the strength to do so because "our forces now, compared to 1970, are a thousand times, ten thousand times stronger. From this position we want to build socialism quickly, we want our country to change quickly, we want our people to be glorious quickly. But especially, to prevent the enemy from making us suffer." The revolution depended on agriculture, and everything else—health services, social action, "scientific culture"—would come later, "but now we must produce rice." "When we have the food, we will expand simultaneously into the learning of reading, writing, and arithmetic."

In its haste and hubris, the DK declared they were not "preparing ourselves as a step towards socialism" because, in their own estimation, they had achieved their goal in just one great bound. In the introduction to *The Party's Four-Year Plan to Build Socialism in all Fields* of July–August 1976,[19] the party center document claims that the Cambodian situation was completely different from that of other socialist countries, especially China, Korea, and North Vietnam:

> We are faster than they are . . . We have new relations of production; nothing is confused, as it is with them . . . We didn't go through a period of land reform or social change. Instead, we leaped from a people's democratic revolution into socialism. Our line is correct, both in terms of strategy and tactics . . . We don't follow any book. We act according actual situation in our country.

There was always the concern over "shortcomings" in party leadership, however, and niggling reminders that while their own propaganda convinced them that they, in fact, loved the people, that love was not really reciprocated.

In all of these documents, the problem was identified as inadequate consciousness on the part of the masses, not the fact of the matter which was, according to David Ashley, that "the masses were never allowed to know the party's true line and leadership."[20] The following quotation from the undated document entitled *Summary of the Results of the 1976 Study Session from the Party Center*[21] suggests that the recalcitrance of the masses may also have had something to do with hunger:

> Always nurture the people in politics and consciousness. Take care to gather forces, strengthen and propagate the allied worker-peasant forces to make them ever more powerful. Do whatever is necessary to make the people warm to our system. Therefore, do not be restrictive. Implement the target of 13 *thang* (per person per annum) absolutely, to make it general,

so that the people can eat their fill and keep enough seed for next year.

If there had been a hint of compassion within the leadership of the DK prior to 1977, the events of that year and the one that followed proved that only paranoia and brutality remained. On 27 September 1976, Pol Pot temporarily resigned because there had been a coup attempt against him. In the interview of October 1997 referred to previously, Pol Pot acknowledged that he had ordered the arrest and murder of his political rivals, including Vorn Veth, Hu Nim, and Hou Yuon:[22]

> Those people were in the central leadership of Democratic Kampuchea, but they were not the people of Democratic Kampuchea. In 1976 . . . that group of people . . . , they set up a *coup d'état* committee, especially against me. In that committee there were Vietnamese agents in the majority.

He named comrade Ya (aka Men San), commander of the northeast region, as chief conspirator.

The sixth document, *Report of Activities of the Party Center According to the General Political Tasks of 1976*,[23] most probably written by Pol Pot, was dated after that coup attempt, 20 December 1976. It refers to a "sickness inside the party, born in the time when we waged a people's and a democratic revolution" but because the fever of those revolutions was insufficient "at the level of people's struggle and at the level of class struggle," the illness had not yet emerged and "we search for the microbes within the party without success." Contradictions threatened to rot the party, the society, and the army. Despite the fact that political consciousness had been of considerable importance in 1976, "in comparative terms, political consciousness lags behind the other aspects. It has not yet transformed the collectivity, even in economic terms . . . the crucial problems are the problem of the party and the problem of cadre":

The tasks of nourishing our cadre's politics isn't complete. We need to build up our cadre as a strategy, covering ten, twenty, thirty. . . a hundred years . . . This problem is of great importance . . . Proletarian patriotic consciousness and proletarian internationalism can transform people's nature into something new. As for the problem of nurturing a Marxist-Leninist viewpoint, we should allow this to seep in according to our chosen method.

He admitted that they could only expand the party slightly but did not consider this to be very important because "the party has been strengthened and has become purer; that's more important." He then immediately went on to say that in 1977, the plan was to expand party membership in the collectives by 100 percent, thereby allowing every collective to have a party branch. The road to progress was by boldly encouraging democracy and encouraging gatherings because "if we use this method the masses will innovate; they won't merely perform their assigned tasks as if they were machines. Their potential won't be buried." Should some "crazy faction" take advantage of such liberties and "raise one difficult problem and then another, asking for this, asking for that," then "we will be fearless. Our line is correct; so is our rationale." In time, and in accordance with the theory of the natural evolution of an organic cadre "class," Pol Pot says:

As time goes on, the masses will draw closer and closer to the party, becoming bolder in expressing their opinions and at building cadres for us. As time goes on, our cadres will emerge increasingly from the masses. Thus, we're not only forming cadres on the collectives, we're forming the masses as a whole.

He then loses his own argument by declaring, "To increase and expand state power, state power on the cooperatives must be party power . . . The party must, in fact, seize power at every level so as to be rooted in terms of consciousness, politics, and tasks."

OUTCOMES OF THE REVOLUTION

Transformation is a mild term for the changes that were imposed on Cambodian social and cultural institutions by this regime. The old structures were "rooted out," one of Pol Pot's favorite metaphors. The Buddhist religion was forbidden by the end of 1975, markets were closed, and currency was abandoned; the forced relocations and the separation of children from their parents in some regions undermined the family unit, as did communal eating. Youths were given special status and powers over their elders, sometimes even the power of life and death, according to published accounts of survivors' experiences. The creation of associations, the mass organizations for mobilizing popular support, such as the Youth League, the Women's Association, the Farmers' League, and the Trade Union Federation, was very new for Cambodian rural society. Another new phenomenon, May Ebihara notes, was the meeting, a blunt instrument for indoctrination when the regime "attempted to instill revolutionary and socialist consciousness through self-and mutual-criticism sessions, speeches, songs, and the like. Associations, political study schools, radio broadcasts, magazines, newspapers, and theatrical performances with song and mime were further vehicles for instruction."[24]

What the DK regime tried to do in Cambodia was not essentially different from what other revolutionary regimes were doing elsewhere in the region or attempting to do. Theoretically, socialist revolution was waged to transform the society, its people, and its values into one with a higher consciousness, better values, imbued with social justice. As means to that end, the new state first had to achieve and establish its control, but the period of rule for the DK, as Ebihara continues, was too short for those "reformulations" to take hold:

> There is, in any event, a question as to how wholeheartedly
> much of the population had adopted DK doctrine. Cadre
> terrorism in various places engendered distrust and hatred
> of the Pol Pot regime. DK leaders had largely ignored (except
> for select purposes) or underestimated the shared and deep-

seated commitment to various institutions and norms that constitutes a people's culture; they evidently assumed further that a society could be remolded by fiat and force.[25]

Was their failure in part at least due to the short time they had to establish ideological hegemony over the society? Given the emphasis on haste and speed and great leaps which is so obvious in the documents referred to above, the DK did not prefer a gradualist approach whether they had the time or not. This was a vital error. The party destroyed its own vanguard elite in 1972–1973 and in savage purges after 1976 decimated its own ranks. "Indeed, only six of the original twenty-two members of the Democratic Kampuchea party central committee survived their years in power unscathed . . . "[26] Newly recruited and hastily trained cadres, illiterate and unsophisticated young men and women from among the base people, hardly had the skills to understand let alone to pass on the basic doctrines of socialist theory to the masses. Nor could they have had the self-confidence to adapt and adjust policy as it came down to them from the center. Fearful of meeting the same fate as their unlucky comrades, they forced the people to meet production and work quotas. Opposition, even hesitation, could not be tolerated because this represented a challenge to the very thin patina of real authority among them, in the sense of their ability to understand and cope with a situation. This was as true at the top level of leadership as it was at the base. The reactions were predictably coercion, violence, panic, and scapegoating, attitudes which were diametrically opposed to the forces required to establish genuine ideological hegemony.

"I do not reject responsibility," Pol Pot said, "our movement made mistakes, like every other movement in the world. But there was another aspect that was outside our control—the enemy's activities against us. I want to tell you, I'm quite satisfied on one thing: If we had not carried out our struggle, Cambodia would have become another Kampuchea Krom in 1975."[27]

WAR WITH VIETNAM

The fear of being swallowed by larger neighbors is the nationalist rallying-point in Cambodia. It was certainly a fear that Pol Pot played on in those final years of panic. Clashes over territorial claims between the forces of Cambodia and Vietnam occurred regularly between 1975 and 1977 and tensions had increased to flash point by 1978. Following the withdrawal of Vietnamese troops from Cambodia after October 1972, the massacre of the Khmer Viet Minh returnees, armed attacks on Vietnamese soldiers and liaison officers, and the intolerable B-52 bombing waged as reprisal by the US against the defiant Cambodian communist rebels, the relationship between the VWP and the CPK reached its nadir.[28] In a conversation with the Soviet ambassador in April 1973, Le Duan is reported to have said that "the initiative in Cambodian affairs is not in our hands."[29] He continued, "the Cambodian People's Revolutionary Party has contentions both with Sihanouk and with its own members. Their organization is situated in Beijing. Even the Chinese embassy in Hanoi has more contacts with them than we have. However, Khmer comrades are very careful. Our help to them is substantial. There is a possibility to get closer to them gradually."[30] That "possibility" was through control over access to the Ho Chi Minh Trail, the route by which Chinese military supplies could reach Cambodia. From 1974, Mosyakov notes a marked improvement in the VWP-CPK relationship, "up to the level of close cooperation" and, in preparation for the takeover of Phnom Penh, "in 1974, Vietnam granted military aid with no strings attached."[31] This was self-interest on the part of North Vietnam which needed the civil war in Cambodia to continue at least until it could fulfill its own plans for a complete takeover of South Vietnam, a point that would not have been lost on Pol Pot. It also shows that Vietnam was not prepared to accept a total breakdown of relations with the CPK.

In June 1975, after the victories of the Indochinese communist parties, Pol Pot made a protocol visit to Hanoi during which he politely refused "special relations" with Vietnam. Border clashes and "misunderstandings" occurred regularly between the two states throughout the DK period, which were patched over by seemingly fraternal, diplomatic expressions of solidarity. Escalation of savage cross-border attacks on Vietnamese villages in mid-1977, the worsening rift in Sino-Vietnamese relations, and "the appearance of Chinese military personnel backing the Khmer Rouge training and arming their troops, building roads and military bases," however, all represented a renewed threat to Vietnamese security.[32]

Plans to recruit an army and a political front from among the Cambodian refugees in southern Vietnam commenced in October 1977. Two months later, on 25 December, a PAVN force of twenty thousand troops launched a brief but massive retaliatory attack on Cambodia. One prong of the attack reached close to the provincial capital of Kompong Cham and another reached the outskirts of Svay Rieng town. Nayan Chanda observes, "The regional units, even the Fourth Division belonging to the center—under Heng Samrin's command—had dispersed before the advancing Vietnamese columns."[33] On 31 December 1977, "the government of Democratic Kampuchea decided to temporarily sever diplomatic relations with the SRV."[34]

Historians can only speculate on the motives of So Phim, Eastern Zone party secretary, to lead a rebellion against the DK Center in May 1978. His revolutionary credentials were sound: peasant origins, ICP/Issarak member, Khmer Viet Minh who went to Hanoi in 1954 and returned soon after to help reorganize the party, politburo member from 1963, and deputy chief of staff of the Khmer Rouge army throughout the war against Lon Nol.[35] In a conversation with the Soviet ambassador in early September 1978, Le Duan is supposed to have said that Vietnam was at that time trying to establish contacts with So Phim. According to Morris, "The Vietnamese leader stated that 'he is our man,' and that Hanoi wanted So Phim to 'take over the leadership of the movement inside Kampuchea.'[36] By then, as Morris points out, So Phim had been dead for three months. There is no corroborative evidence that So Phim was ever, or was even likely to be, an agent of the Vietnamese. What is reasonable to accept, however, is that the Eastern Zone leaders who had had the

33

most frequent contact with Vietnam from the earliest days of the Cambodian communist movement were those most at odds with Pol Pot's radical approach to social transformation, and while not necessarily being actively pro-Vietnamese, they probably supported a more classical line. Stephen Heder is perhaps correct when he speculates:

> I think the eastern region, which had suffered most extensively from the clashes with Vietnam, was arguing that some kind of diplomatic time had to be bought with this country in order to prepare more adequately for dealing with the Vietnamese. This was also considered treasonous . . . [37]

The suicide or death in battle of So Phim, following the punitive expedition of forces sent by the Center from the Southwestern Zone, produced an insurrection of Eastern Zone forces in May 1978. By July, the rebellion had been crushed and then the vengeance killings began. Rebel leader Heng Samrin sent emissaries to Vietnam for assistance. In early September, Vietnam again invaded Cambodian territory, this time to contact Heng Samrin and to escort him and his followers back to Vietnam. "With the arrival of Heng Samrin, Chea Sim, and other Khmer Rouge survivors, the future government of a pro-Vietnamese Cambodia was assembled."[38]

Vietnam invaded Cambodia in huge military force on 25 December 1978 and after a brave initial stand, the KR forces made a tactical withdrawal to the northwest and established their bases along the Cambodian-Thai border where they resumed guerrilla warfare against the newly installed government.

The question of why Vietnam invaded as it did, at great cost in terms of world opinion and the severe consequences of the international embargo which was placed on credit and trade with Vietnam, not to mention China's ire, has never been satisfactorily answered and speculation is dangerous. Essentially, however, Vietnam needed a reliable ruling power in Cambodia that would not jeopardize its own efforts to consolidate the Vietnamese revolution and achieve national reunification. Between 1955 and 1968, Prince Sihanouk, with his policy of neutrality in international affairs, fulfilled this role. Even after the March 1970 coup, the Vietnamese first tested the waters of the Lon Nol government to see if they would be permitted to maintain bases on Cambodian territory before they gave their full support to the FUNK. In view of its commitment to international socialism, Vietnam's expediency in relation to the Cambodian revolution during this stage is both understandable and reprehensible. Without access to Cambodian territory in order to establish staging bases and sanctuaries, the war for national unification would have been seriously protracted. Moreover, in fact, Democratic Kampuchea did not behave as a reliable revolutionary partner. DK's close ties with China at a time when Vietnam's own relationship with the People's Republic of China was deteriorating created a most serious contradiction; the border clashes were highly provocative; its domestic politics were in turmoil. At the same time, in terms of its professed principles of international socialism, Hanoi had been negligent. Such expediency was a severe blow to Cambodian pride and it placed Vietnam's own reliability in question. Furthermore, as the quotes from VCP leaders, especially Le Duan, suggest, there were serious gaps in what Hanoi knew or understood about the situation of the communist movement in Cambodia right throughout the period to 1979. Vietnam's support for the Cambodian revolution had been erratic, due as much to Vietnam's preoccupation with its own internal affairs as to the intransigence of the DK. This was a lesson well learned by Vietnam but at great cost.

The Pol Pot–Ieng Sary faction of the Cambodian communist movement was rigidly, fanatically opposed to any form of solidarity with the Vietnamese revolution. It would be wrong, however, to presume that the dissident faction who would form the leadership of the PRK along with the Khmer Viet Minh survivors were unconcerned about Vietnam's intentions with regard to the Cambodian revolution. The fundamental contradiction between the two revolutionary states over the independence of the Cambodian revolution continued to haunt the relationship between Cambodia and Vietnam throughout the years of the People's Republic of Kampuchea.

Chapter 3

REBELLION AND SALVATION, 1978–1979

THE KHMER ROUGE had controlled the people by terror. The accounts of the eyewitnesses who survived and the reports of refugees who managed to escape across the country's borders recreated a pervasive atmosphere of unrelenting surveillance, silence and intense personal isolation where even intimate family members avoided speaking with each other for fear of being overheard by those with the power of life and death over them. Other very real forms of control included the strict rationing of food, which meant that even if groups did form and plan escape, they could not stockpile supplies needed for the journey, as well as the almost total absence of information and control over the very few details about the organization, *Angkar*, which dictated their lives.

The terror of the people and their social atomization was both a reflection and consequence of the fear and paranoia of their leaders. Fears that their power was not total and therefore not secure were probably well-founded. From its beginnings during the war of liberation against the French, the Cambodian communist movement had lacked unity and trust. In 1963, Saloth Sar had effectively usurped leadership of the party. His move towards China and away from Vietnam's orthodox approach to social revolution widened the cracks inherent in the Cambodian Communist Party. During the evacuation of Phnom Penh, some people witnessed at least one street battle which broke out between Khmer Rouge soldiers who arrived in the city from different zones, noting that those from the Eastern Zone wore gray or khaki uniforms as distinct from the more usual black. A 1979 secret report of Chinese

politburo member Geng Biao suggests that there were at least
three factions at the time of the 1975 victory:

> If these three factions were properly handled when the Kam-
> puchean army began to consolidate its ranks in 1976, the
> situation could have been better. But the Kampuchean Com-
> munist Party did not follow the correct approach in handling
> them, thus leading to an expansion of mutual contradictions.[1]

The first of these factions, in Geng Biao's analysis, were
the "old soldiers", the Sihanouk supporters of the post-1970
FUNK who resented the way the victors had treated the king
and who were punished for their "recalcitrance" and "even
treated . . . as reactionary troops and reactionary families, who
were subject to either persecution, or the fate of disbandment
or disarmament." This way of doing things, he added, "inad-
vertently forced a part of the forces previously in support of
the Communist Party to revolt and turn around to merge with
those remnant units of Lon Nol who had become bandits in
the hills and change into counter-revolutionary armed guerrillas." The second faction was pro-Vietnam and here "the
commanding officers also failed to make a distinction between
the question of stand and the question of ideology, grabbing
all at once more than four thousand of them, who were either
put to death or imprisoned; thus everybody felt threatened and
ultimately ended up in open revolt." The third faction, the
victors, were pro-China but it was far from a homogeneous
group. The "Great Proletarian Cultural Revolution" engulfed
China in wave after wave of ideological "rectification" from
1966 until the arrest of the Gang of Four in October 1978.
There was one officially sanctioned "stand" at any one time
but that position changed suddenly, radically, and erratically
to sweep away perceived reactionary elements. The Cambodian Communist Party's decade of armed struggle and then
fortuitous victory and power coincided with China's decade of
Cultural Revolution. At that time, what did it mean to be
pro-China? Factionalism was almost synonymous with having
a pro-China stand. Ben Kiernan also believed that there were
three major factions making up the Cambodian communist

movement during the 1960s and 1970s: a chauvinist group led by Pol Pot whose nationalist perspective was a traditionalist and revivalist one not unlike that of Lon Nol; a group closely associated with Hu Nim which was attracted by "mass democracy" ideology of China's Cultural Revolution; and a third group including people like Keo Moni, So Phim, and Non Suon who were attracted to the Vietnamese socialist model.[2] After 1970, Kiernan argues, these groups seem to have crystallized into regions based on their politics, with the Pol Pot group in the north and northeast, the pro-Vietnamese group in the east, and the "Cultural Revolution" group in the southwest.[3] Thus there was a web of fault lines not far below the surface of Pol Pot's apparent total power which tore the regime apart when external factors applied critical pressure. Ultimately, it was Pol Pot's suicidal foreign policy which sealed the regime's fate.

REBELLION

Anti–Pol Pot resistance occurred sporadically throughout the DK years. In the southwest, for instance, in the area around Koh Kong province bordering Thailand and the Gulf of Siam, Say Phouthang, an ethnic Thai and a former Issarak leader who would become head of the powerful Administration Commission within the new party structure after 1979, had been part of the "Free Khmer Rouge" rebel group since 1974. The first uprising against the regime is believed to have taken place in Siem Reap in September 1975 but it was ruthlessly put down as were other attempts in Battambang, Kandal, Siem Reap, and Koh Kong the following year.[4] These acts of rebellion were unconnected and some were even inexplicable but they all served to fuel the regime's sense of insecurity and then to provide the rationale for the bloody waves of purges as the party began to consume itself.

The Siem Reap incident, which occurred on 25 February 1976, was blamed by the regime on the United States of America. On that day, Siem Reap town was "rocked by two waves of five-hundred-pound bombs, six hours apart."[5] Democratic Kampuchea announced that fifteen people had been killed and a further thirty injured by US F-111 bombers which it said had flown off towards Thailand. Other Cambodian watchers at the time suspected Thai Air Force jets, Vietnamese MiGs, or even Chinese-built MiGs from Phnom Penh.[6] As late as December 1978, however, just two weeks before Vietnam military forces overthrew the regime, DK officials in Siem Reap told Malcolm Caldwell, one of three Westerners invited to witness the revolution in order to dispel refugee stories of widespread atrocities occurring within Cambodia, "We have evidence that it was not Vietnam but was done by the CIA, by agents in Thailand."[7] On 2 April 1976, the day scheduled for the resignation of Prince Sihanouk as head of state, grenades exploded near the Royal Palace in Phnom Penh and shots were fired at the nearby National Museum close to the compound occupied by the top leaders of the regime. No one seems to have been killed or injured in the attack, nor was there any material damage. Ten days later, suspects were arrested and interrogated at the notorious S-21, headquarters of the regime's internal security police or *santebal*. As a result of their "confessions," Chan Chakrey, a political commissar of Division 170 and deputy secretary of the newly formed national army's general staff, was arrested and charged with plotting a coup.[8] After some months of interrogating Chakrey, the *santebal* chief, Deuch, reported to Pol Pot that he had uncovered a larger "espionage" organization, which he called "the rubber plantation network," a reference to cadres from the Eastern Zone whose secretary was So Phim.

There are few recorded accounts of popular uprising against the regime, and brief explosions of the people's anger such as that which occurred in Chikreng district, southeast of Siem Reap town in March 1977 and which spread as far south as Staung district in Kompong Thom province, are likely to have been incited and manipulated by those at the center of the regime for their own political motives.[9] Hunger, fear, and rigidly enforced isolation guaranteed the victims' powerlessness. There were individual acts of defiance and some survivors have memories of prisoners shouting their outrage from the back of ox-carts as they were taken to the killing fields, but these acts seem to have been born out of a sense of hopelessness rather than sacrifice. When organized resistance did finally succeed, it was in the east and the northeast, the regions that Lon Nol could never dominate and the regions where the Viet Cong had trained the Khmer revolutionaries in politics and military strategy throughout the Second Indochina War. By November 1977 the mutiny of the 155th Regiment led by Nom Samouth in Prey Veng had spread to eight provinces and by the following May the insurgents had created liberated zones.[10] Keo Chenda, the first minister for information and culture in the PRK regime, told a visiting journalist in February 1979 that he had been based in a liberated area of the northeast for many months before liberation and that life there had been quite stable since the end of 1977, while in other liberated areas schools and hospitals had been rebuilt and were operating normally.[11] Pockets of lasting resistance such as those described by Keo Chenda may have remained, but for the most part, like the other attempted uprisings, that of the Eastern Zone was savagely crushed by the center which was supported by troops from the Southwest. The zone's cadre force was purged and tens of thousands of people were forcibly evacuated to the northwest in one of the bloodiest episodes of the regime's brief history. The consequences of this uprising, however, were quite different because several hundred of its survivors either fled to Vietnam or, as in the case of future PRK president, Heng Samrin, were eventually escorted to safety by Vietnamese troops in October 1978. Four months later, these dissidents and asylum seekers would return with a massive PAVN military force to overthrow the Pol Pot regime.

VIETNAM'S ROLE

As David Chandler suggests, the S-21 confessions act as a barometer of changes in DK domestic and foreign policy. At the time of Chan Chakrey's incarceration, for instance, in mid-1976, his interrogators were looking for "links with the United States rather than with the Vietnamese Communists or for plots inside the higher echelons of the party."[12] On 8 September 1976, Mao Zedong died and within one month of his death, the Cultural Revolution was over. Chandler says that following Mao's death, a factional fight broke out inside the CPK that resulted in the execution of several veteran Communists.[13] That month, Radio Phnom Penh announced that Pol Pot had resigned "for reasons of health" and that Nuon Chea had temporarily replaced him. Ieng Sary had also resigned. Both of them were back in office in October. As Nuon Chea was never purged or even demoted, Chandler suggests that Pol Pot's resignation was tactical rather than imposed, "He may indeed have been genuinely ill."[14] The Vietnamese were also unsure about the changing situation within Cambodia. In early November, Prime Minister Pham Van Dong suggested to the Soviet ambassador that Pol Pot was actually sick.[15] Le Duan is reported to have welcomed the pair's removal because they constituted a "pro-Chinese sect conducting a crude and severe policy," adding that "these are bad people."[16] On the other hand, Hanoi does not appear to have taken real measures to support Pol Pot's opponents or may have been powerless to act. "In any case," as Mosyakov points out, "the attempt at Pol Pot's removal from power ended extremely pitiably for Hanoi: thousands of 'brother number one's' opponents were imprisoned and executed, and the winner having regained his power, could now openly conduct his anti-Vietnamese policy."[17]

Suspicions about those with Vietnamese or Soviet connections seemed to have coalesced after September 1976, beginning with the arrest and torture of party veteran Keo Meas and later other veterans and intellectuals who were connected with the Vietnamese-backed Khmer People's Revolutionary Party which originated in 1951. In December, a foreign ministry official confessed under torture in S-21 that "the USSR and Vietnam were plotting to overthrow DK in order to place a pro-Vietnamese regime in power in Phnom Penh."[18] Two Vietnamese diplomats in Phnom Penh were supposed to have been orchestrating the conspiracy. To outward appearances, however, close fraternal ties continued to exist between Cambodia and Vietnam. While Keo Meas was being tortured, the air service between Hanoi and Phnom Penh started operations, a Cambodian women's delegation visited Vietnam, and the

CPK was congratulating the Vietnam Workers' Party on the occasion of its Fourth Congress.[19] In fact, relations between Vietnam and Cambodia worsened steadily from the beginning of 1977 and full-scale conflict, "almost certainly instigated by DK," according to Chandler, broke out in the middle of 1977.[20] The fighting continued, at varying levels of intensity until the final Vietnamese offensive of December 1978 led to the overthrow of the regime. War with Vietnam was an act of supreme folly but, as Elizabeth Becker said, "The party leaders were so caught up within the sudden turns in the regime's policies they could not see how this new stage would lead to their own demise."[21] Even Ieng Sary did not believe that a border dispute with Vietnam would lead to war. Becker adds,

> Though he accepted on blind faith that there were Vietnamese agents planted in the uppermost levels of the party, he said he did not see how this would lead to war between the two countries. "We had let the Vietnamese come [to set up their embassy] before the Chinese. We let the Vietnamese travel where they requested. They traveled by car from Saigon to Phnom Penh and made some trips inside Kampuchea . . . I never wished for war between Vietnam and Kampuchea . . . The fear for me was a coup on the inside, not the threat of an invasion from the outside . . . I said the main problem was internal, because of Vietnamese agents on the inside."[22]

From October 1977, the Vietnamese started recruiting a united front to rid Cambodia of Pol Pot from among the remaining members of the Khmer Viet Minh, including Pen Sovann, Chan Si, and Chea Soth, as well as Bou Thong, who led the resistance among Cambodia's northeastern ethnic minorities, and also among those who had taken refuge in camps in parts of southern Vietnam.[23] Defectors from the DK army would form a vital component of this new front but given the state of relations between the two countries and their armies, their sincerity was naturally suspect. Hun Sen, a former regimental commander in charge of the border region from Kratie to Kompong Cham, was one of these. He had received orders in early 1977 to ready his units for attacks inside Tay Ninh province. Instead, on 20 June he and four others crossed the border and eventually joined efforts to organize the new front.[24] The brutal attack on Tay Ninh which finally took place on 24 September 1977, leaving hundreds of civilians dead, not only shook the Vietnamese government into considering long-term options for a settlement of the border problem with Cambodia, it also provided sufficient evidence that the defectors such as Hun Sen's group were reliable.

On 31 December 1977, Radio Phnom Penh broadcast the news that Democratic Kampuchea had severed diplomatic relations with Vietnam. In mid-February the following year, the Vietnamese politburo met in Ho Chi Minh City to devise a plan for setting up a Cambodian communist party and a resistance organization and shortly after that meeting, Le Duc Tho and Le Duan, long-term allies of the development of the communist movement within Cambodia, met with some of the remnants of the Khmer Viet Minh and with those who had escaped the purges of the Eastern Zone.[25] The Khmer Viet Minh survivors included Pen Sovann, Chan Si, and Khang Sarin, who had been made majors in the Vietnamese army since their evacuation to Hanoi after the signing of the Geneva Accords in 1954; Taing Sarim, who had been working as a labor supervisor in a coal mine; Keo Chenda, who was a broadcaster for Radio Hanoi; and Chea Soth, a news editor from the Vietnam News Agency. Political cadres who had escaped from the purges included Hun Sen, Hem Samin, Yos Por, and Bou Thong.[26] All of them would be founding members of the People's Republic of Kampuchea. Nayan Chanda observed:

> Dragged out of their nondescript offices and refugee barracks, they were suddenly presented to the top Vietnamese leaders whom they had previously known only in pictures. By a turn of fortune they too were to be leaders in a new Cambodia still in the womb of the future. Le Duc Tho told them that the time had come to restore the ties of cooperation that had existed between Vietnamese and Cambodian Communists.[27]

In October 1978, Chea Sim, party secretary of Ponhea Krek district near the border, crossed into Vietnam with three hundred Eastern Zone people who were fleeing the terrible purges following the death of So Phim, and soon after his arrival, the Vietnamese army launched a special attack inside Cambodia in order to reach Heng Samrin, commander of the Fourth Division based in the Eastern Zone, and his troops and take them back to Vietnam. Two hundred potential cadres, among them the surviving veterans of the 1954 group, defectors from the DK army, as well as members of the educated classes of former regimes who could be persuaded to join the Kampuchean United Front for National Salvation (FUNSK) received training in the former police training school in Thu Duc, Ho Chi Minh City.

THE SALVATION FRONT

On the morning of 2 December 1978 several thousand Cambodians assembled in a clearing in a rubber plantation within a liberated zone near Snoul, Kratie province under the banner of the red flag with a yellow, five-towered Angkor Wat which had been the flag of the Issaraks in the days of anti-French resistance. The Front's president, Heng Samrin, read the official declaration of the FUNSK and its eleven-point program on behalf of the Front's fourteen-member central committee.[28] He claimed that "a dictatorial and militarist regime of unequalled ferocity has been installed in Kampuchea. The reactionary Pol Pot–Ieng Sary clique and their families have totally usurped power, betrayed the country and harmed the people . . . The Chinese authorities have encouraged and backed to the hilt these traitors and tyrants."[29] The DK regime, he argued, was "neo-slavery" and had nothing to do with socialism. The immediate revolutionary task of the Kampuchean people following the overthrow of this regime was "to establish a people's democratic regime, to develop the Angkor traditions, to make Kampuchea into a truly peaceful, independent, democratic, neutral, and non-aligned country advancing to socialism, thus contributing actively to the common struggle for peace and stability in Southeast Asia."[30]

The eleven-point program set the agenda for the new

regime. The policy was one of "great national union" and to this end there would be general elections to a national assembly, a new constitution, and the reorganization of "people's democratic power at all levels." Mass organizations (of youth, women, trade unions, peasants, and intellectuals) would be built "with a view to toppling the reactionary and nepotist Pol Pot–Ieng Sary clique and bringing to all strata of our people the right to be the real masters of the country."[31] The army would be formed and developed. The people would be granted rights to genuine freedom and democracy, of residence, movement, and franchise. The economy would be both planned and market, meeting the needs of social progress while advancing towards socialism; there would be mutual-aid and cooperative organizations on the basis of "the full consent of the peasants" and an eight-hour day with pay according to labor for the workers; banks, currency, and trade would be restored. There was concern for restoring "the happy life of every family" by encouraging free choice in marriage and equality between men and women, care for the infirm, the aged, the victims of war, and orphans. A new culture would eliminate illiteracy, develop education at all levels, and preserve and restore historical relics and structures. "Reactionary chieftains who persist in opposing the people" would be punished, but leniency would be shown to those captured members of the DK administration and army and help given for them to become "honest people, useful to society."[32] The foreign policy would be one of peace, friendship and nonalignment, disputes with neighboring countries would be settled through peaceful negotiations, and there would be strong solidarity with all revolutionary and progressive forces throughout the world.

Following the Snoul meeting, armed propaganda units of the Front went into the villages along the border explaining the eleven-point program and building support. Leaflets calling for an uprising were dropped by Vietnamese aircraft over Cambodian territory near the border, and the radio station, Voice of the Cambodian People, in Ho Chi Minh City relayed the same message.[33]

LIBERATION

The PAVN military onslaught against Democratic Kampuchea commenced at midnight, 24 December 1978. Tank-led columns spearheading some 150,000 troops moved quickly along the major routes towards Phnom Penh. By 4 January, they had control of all Cambodian territory east of the Mekong. On 6 January, they crossed the river and by the morning of the following day they were on the outskirts of Phnom Penh. According to Carney, the Front's forces were "enough to form a plating on the PAVN spearhead, but little more."[34] Hun Sen later explained that prior to the formation of the FUNSK, the combined dissident forces amounted to perhaps thirty battalions (*kong vore sena touch*) compared with Pol Pot's twenty-three divisions.[35] He argued that " although the victory of 7 January 1979 involved the combined national forces with the support of the volunteer forces of Vietnam, and the PAVN had an important function in dispersing the Pol Potists, the forces of the Kampuchean revolution had the decisive function because for a revolution [to succeed] in any country, it must be the people of that country who are the ones to act and no other country can come and replace [that]."[36] The support given by Vietnam was "in answer to the request of the Kampuchean people."[37] In this argument there are echoes of Truong Chinh, then President of the National Assembly of the SRV who claimed:

It is clear that the revolution of a country cannot be imported. The revolutionary war of the Kampuchean people was born and grew in the soil of the Angkorian civilization. It has internal causes and is due to antagonistic contradictions within a monstrous society which the Pol Pot–Ieng Sary reactionaries, under the orders of Beijing, put at the feet of Kampuchea . . . The Kampuchean people were undertaking a revolutionary war with the nature of a war of liberation . . . It is a sacred right of self-determination of a people and no one has the right to interfere. The armed forces and the people of Vietnam were helping the Kampuchean brothers to fight against the genocidal clique in the pay of Beijing to take back independence and freedom.[38]

The victory came so quickly that its announcement inter-rupted the third party congress which had been convened in Memot from 5–8 January. According to Hun Sen, this "Con-gress to Re-Build the Party" as it came to be known was held with the participation of sixty-two party members, represent-ing more than two hundred members who were working in different places.[39] This congress was intended to erase the January 1963 "third congress" where

> Pol Pot lied about many historical matters, lied about tradi-tional relations between the Kampuchean party and the Viet-namese party and changed the name of the party to the Com-munist Party of Kampuchea, expanded the composition of the party, and where his group joined the party center with Pol Pot as secretary-general.[40]

This Memot Congress, the document noted, was a struggle for the right of highest leadership within the party and for the right to practice a regime of state authority separate from that of Pol Pot. The congress decided to "develop the revolution-ary tradition of the party which originated in the Indochina Communist Party and it took the name of the People's Revo-lutionary Party of Kampuchea; it discussed all measures towards rebuilding the party as a pure Marxist-Leninist one, approved the political program of the party and appointed a commission for building the party throughout the country" which later became the party central committee.[41] Hun Sen claims that "by the end of the congress, the motherland of Kampuchea had been liberated completely from the bloody claws of the Pol Potists."[42] Although this claim would prove to be premature by twenty years, the military victory had been sufficiently decisive to allow for the establishment of a new government in Phnom Penh.[43] The eight-member Kampu-chean People's Revolutionary Council (PRCK) was instituted on 8 January 1979.[44] The PRCK, which remained the provi-sional government of Cambodia until the 1981 constitution provided for a regular distribution of legislative and executive authority, issued a declaration on the founding of the People's Republic of Kampuchea on 12 January 1979.

In his speech at the victory celebration ceremony in January 1979, Heng Samrin, president of the FUNSK and chairman of the PRCK declared the stand of the new regime:

> Under the watchword of "cooking the animal's meat in a pot of its leather," [the Pol Pot–Ieng Sary reactionaries] compelled our revolutionaries to commit crimes against the people. They poisoned the young people and gave them the taste for blood . . . Such was the genocidal policy put into practice by the reactionary Pol Pot–Ieng Sary clique on the orders of their masters in Peking . . . [Their genocidal policy] had been conceived according to the plans and on the orders of the reactionary elements within the Peking ruling circles. It aimed at undermining national independence and peace in Southeast Asia and in the world, and at annexing the whole of Kampuchea. Once this goal was attained, they would annex the whole of Southeast Asia and seek to establish their hegemony over the world . . . Millions of our compatriots have fallen bravely. Their bones have piled up into mountains, and their blood has turned our rivers red. Their examples inspired our people to join the revolutionary bases and adopt the objectives of the patriots. It was in this spirit that the FUNSK was born and made public its 11-point Political Program on 2 December 1978 . . .[45]

The eight-member council reflected the diverse origins of the new regime. Heng Samrin, the new president, and Chea Sim and Hun Sen, holding the portfolios of the interior and foreign affairs, were former Khmer Rouge military cadres of the Eastern Zone who had defected in 1977 and 1978.[46] Pen Sovann, the vice president with extra responsibility for defense, and Keo Chenda, Mok Sakun, and Nou Beng who were respectively in charge of information, economy, and health, were veterans of the Issarak movement who had gone to Vietnam in 1954 and remained there until 1979 apart from a couple of years spent inside Cambodia after 1970 when most of their peers were massacred.[47] Chan Ven, the new minister for education, was a former teacher and college director who had fled across the border in 1978. He had no revolutionary background and represented the small band of intellectuals, monks, administrators, professionals, and technically skilled people who were prepared to serve the new regime. Much of the analysis of this early period of the PRK by foreign historians such as Vickery, Heder, and Kiernan concentrates on the real or potential divisions within the new administration along these fault lines of revolutionary experience. In the first six years in particular, rifts would occur which could be interpreted in this way and ultimately the former KR group would hold sway. Nevertheless, among the eventual power-holders, some members of the group that had returned from Vietnam remained very influential, notably Chea Soth and Bou Thong, who were deputies to two successive prime ministers of the PRK, and Say Phouthang, who was without doubt the most powerful member of the party throughout the PRK regime. Differences were partly determined by shared and unshared experience but there were also personality differences that were difficult to resolve. In the end, however, party discipline held up remarkably well and factionalism, which had torn apart so many governments of the late Sihanouk years and the Khmer Republic and which had destroyed the regime of Democratic Kampuchea, was kept carefully in check.

They were, generally speaking, a very young group. Foreign Minister Hun Sen, for instance, was only twenty-six years old when the PRK was founded. In view of their youth, the challenges ahead of them were huge and probably exciting rather than daunting. The 1954 veterans, most of whom returned to Phnom Penh with Vietnamese wives, had waited twenty-five years in exile to apply their revolutionary training. As they had been schooled in the Vietnamese model of state-making, it was inevitable that the key administrative positions would be given to them. Ironically, although perhaps not entirely unexpectedly, they were the ones who resisted Vietnamese authority over the Cambodian revolution most vehemently. These were the idealists who believed that a Marxist-Leninist revolution with Cambodian characteristics was both possible and desirable, and while they were prepared to compromise some socialist principles in the face of the concrete reality of post-DK Cambodia, they held other, nationalist, principles which were unbreachable. The pragmatists bided their time and eventually won power, only to lose the revolution.

The situation which confronted the new leaders required turning socialist theory on its head. As Michael Vickery aptly notes, "the PRK inherited a truly classless society, yet in order to move toward socialism they had to recreate social classes."[48] At the beginning of 1979 there was no Cambodian state, no economy, no industry. The farmers could somehow have picked up the shattered remains of their village life and returned with relief to subsistence agriculture until the routed Pol Pot forces managed to regroup and return with a vengeance. Therefore, there were no options and little time. Vickery adds:

> The problem faced by the PRK was thus to recreate from scratch a non-productive administrative and service sector, reactivate and restore a small essential industrial sector, and persuade the majority food producing sector to support administration and industry with minimal return for the immediate future.[49]

This had to be done with little external assistance, in a storm of foreign censure against the prolonged Vietnamese military occupation of Cambodia and in the face of mounting security threats which amounted, in fact, to civil war.

The one constant factor in the early life of the PRK was the grinding poverty of the people. There were no precedents for restoring revolution in such conditions. The Chinese revolution had taken a severe battering from those disastrous experiments of the Great Leap Forward and the Great Proletarian Cultural Revolution but there was at least the decade before all that on which the people could look back with pride in their achievements. The DK regime had dragged the revolution headlong into an abyss from which, perhaps, there could be no recovery. The PRK and its Vietnamese advisers thus attempted a daring socialist experiment; socialist reconstruction based, as Vickery says, on the middle peasant and industrious urban trader and artisan:

If the Cambodian revolution indeed represents a class victory for the petty bourgeoisie, both in small-scale family production as the dominant form of production and in the free markets and artisanal production which have dominated the urban economy, how will such a social formation—unforeseen in any theory of revolution—develop? A petty-bourgeois formation based on small peasantry and without exceptionally valuable raw materials for export or specialized high-technology manufacture has little available surplus for development beyond basic self-sufficiency.[50]

The Pol Pot experiment had alienated the people of all social strata from both socialist theory and practice. If the revolution was to survive, the state had to secure the consent and full cooperation of the masses. This was fundamentally a motivational task. Having once achieved ideological hegemony, these young revolutionaries believed they could then gradually reverse their laissez-faire policies and introduce taxation and compulsory deliveries to the state, extend their control over the market and persuade the farmers to accept collectivization and central planning. Many factors intervened to defeat a task which may or may not have been inherently unachievable, but it was a bold endeavor. To quote Vickery:

> What in normal times had held (Cambodians) all together in an organic whole was an ideological superstructure culminating in monarch and church and which legitimized the nonproductive sectors and their claims on a living supplied by the peasantry. That superstructure had been damaged by the Khmer Republic, totally destroyed by DK, and the PRK intended, not to restore it, but [to] replace it by a different one. There was no state for them to take over. They had to create it anew.[51]

The immediate tasks of the new administration, therefore, were to build the administrative and economic structure of the new state while at the same time creating both the public and private superstructures where their hegemony would be established.

Chapter 4

INSTITUTION-BUILDING: THE ADMINISTRATIVE STRUCTURE OF THE NEW STATE

ALTHOUGH PHNOM PENH was liberated on 7 January 1979, the new government of Cambodia cannot really be said to have had even nominal control over the territory of Cambodia until July or August that year when the Khmer Rouge forces were finally driven out of the northwest provinces of Battambang and Siem Reap/Oddar Meanchey. Even then, the hold over the northwest part of the country remained tenuous for a further five years. Most of the country, however, appears to have succumbed quickly to the advancing PAVN/FUNSK forces. Apart from a daring stand by Pol Pot's forces along the border with Vietnam in that region between the Fish Hook and the Parrot's Beak, "after we had advanced about twenty kilometers, it seemed as if there was no more resistance" because the Khmer Rouge simply melted away before them in a well-planned strategic retreat.[1] The PAVN/FUNSK forces easily took the provincial centers because they had been virtually empty for three years. Wherever possible, the KR rounded up the population they controlled in the countryside and drove them towards the border with Thailand, setting fire to granaries and the rest of the yet unharvested rice crop and destroying roads and bridges behind them. Stories from people in different parts of the northwest at that time tell of the final atrocities committed before the final withdrawal. At public meetings, the remaining family groups were told to select the strongest among them to send on a foraging mission to gather food for a long journey they would take together and on this pretext, they were led to the pits already filled with the rotting bodies of previous victims for their own execution. Another acquaintance, then a child, spoke of huddling in a corner of his shack and hearing grown men scream for their mothers as their throats were slit the night before the Vietnamese soldiers arrived.[2] Like roads, bridges and a ripe harvest, human assets had to be destroyed to spite the conquerors. However, within a month of the liberation of Phnom Penh, Richard Nations was reporting that "there are clear signs that the damage was not great. The Khmer Rouge army has remained largely intact . . . [has] restored its command and control structure with two new military headquarters communicating with tactical units and [is] capable of operating on a nationwide scale."[3] His military source estimated that "four-fifths of the army—or about 60,000 men—remained intact and have re-formed . . ."[4] This figure was probably exaggerated and it is more likely that the KR forces were then 30,000–35,000; they remained at roughly that size for the next ten to fifteen years.[5] Perched in their northern border sanctuaries and later settled in refugee camps inside Thailand, the KR loomed like a dark shadow over the new regime in Phnom Penh, and forced it to depend on the promise of continued Vietnamese military and logistical support. The security factor, the virtual annihilation of the economic infrastructure, the dearth of loyal, trained personnel, and a rural population broken in health and spirit, all determined the shape that the structure of the new regime, its administration and its economy, would take.

FORMING THE NEW ADMINISTRATION AT THE CENTER

Until May, as eyewitness Bui Tin reported, "hundreds of thousands of gaunt and diseased people, dazed as if they were returning from hell, wandered shoeless along dusty roads . . . reduced to a state where they did not speak or smile any more," moving across the Cambodian landscape and returning to their former homes or searching for their relatives.[6] A ring of temporary settlements was set up around Phnom Penh for those wishing to return to the city. These settlements, each housing between six thousand and sixty thousand people, acted as screening centers for a government effort to select and rebuild an administration. Foreign journalists reported that those who could establish their skills and former residency in Phnom Penh were assigned jobs which they took up following completion of a two to three-week "reeducation" course in Phnom Penh.[7] This basic political training was in general orientation on the goals of socialism and the aims of the Front's eleven-point program. Within the ring, the new regime was installing itself and deciding on a system for governing the country. The system evolved from its predecessor, the regime of Democratic Kampuchea, and borrowed essential elements from the system of the Socialist Republic of Vietnam but it also adapted itself to the concrete situation of Cambodia at that time.

The early documents suggest that 1979 was a year of general confusion. Slowly, however, order was pulled out of chaos and by the end of that year a system of government had emerged that revolved around the power of the Communist Party of Kampuchea, specifically its central committee, which had at its core the permanent commission (*kenna achentrey*), that is, the politburo.[8] The authority of the party was exercised and upheld by the People's Revolutionary Council of Kampuchea (PRCK), which provisionally conducted the executive and legislative duties of government until a constitution could be written and general elections held for a national assembly, and by the FUNSK, which was responsible for mass organizations, mass mobilization and party recruitment. Details concerning the new administration were set out in a lengthy decision issued by the central committee in 1979.[9]

In theory at least, the party was the embodiment of collective democracy while "each individual must be master of his/ her own contribution to the collective leadership. When that happens, then we can ensure that the leadership of the party is precise and relevant; then it can expand well its function of management of the PRCK and its function as the one that raises the spirit of organization and education for the masses of the Front and all mass organizations."[10] Actual party leadership was provided by the eight-member central committee. By February 1979, the central committee consisted of:

- Pen Sovann, party general secretary, vice chairman of the PRCK, minister for national defense;

- Heng Samrin, chairman of the PRCK, president of the Front;
- Chea Sim, politburo member, member of the PRCK, vice-president of the Front;
- Say Phouthang, politburo member, chairman of the Central Administration Commission;
- Van Sorn, party secretary of the Phnom Penh Committee;
- Bou Thong, chairman of the Propaganda and Education Commission;
- Hun Sen, member of the PRCK, minister of foreign affairs, member of the Front;
- Chan Kiri, chairman of the Monitoring Commission.[11]

The four permanent members, Pen Sovann, Heng Samrin, Chea Sim, and Say Phouthang, who made up the politburo, prepared the issues to be discussed at meetings of the central committee and guided the ministries and departments in preparing written accounts for discussion at those meetings. All government circulars and directives had to have politburo approval.

The affairs of the central committee were coordinated by three commissions and a general department. The most powerful of these was the Central Administration Commission (*kenna chat tang*). Under the leadership of Say Phouthang, its role was to oversee the work of all the administrative organizations of the party/state. "Managing cadres' dossiers, managing party members, their distribution and preparation for work" was the duty of this commission.[12] Because of the power he had over the assignments of party members, not to mention the power of information he held about them, Say Phouthang was unarguably the most influential leader of the PRK. Pen Sovann, party secretary general and prime minister until his dismissal at the end of 1981, said that Say Phouthang had as much power as the prime minister.[13] The fact that Say Phouthang was able to remove Pen Sovann at the end of 1981 suggests that this was an under-estimate. The second most powerful commission was the Propaganda and Education Commission led by Bou Thong. This commission's task was to develop the correct "attitude" within the party and to carry out propaganda work among the masses and on the international stage. It held in-country political training courses for cadres and party members and helped the government ministries to upgrade their cadres' political skills. The Monitoring Commission was supposed to ensure that the party statutes were upheld. However, this commission does not appear to have functioned at all before the fifth party congress in 1985 when Say Phouthang was appointed to lead it.[14] The Department of the Central Committee had the important bureaucratic function of preparing the circulars and decisions, guaranteeing the work of management and government of the center and its various committees and so on.

The People's Revolutionary Council executed the policies determined by the central committee. The document cited above termed it the *"kbal machine,"* the engine of implementation in all sections of the work: "economy, livelihood, culture, social action" after the center had made a decision concerning major principles and policies.[15] This executive body also consisted of eight members: the chairman (Heng Samrin), the vice chairman who was minister for defense (Pen Sovann), and six members who were ministers for foreign affairs (Hun Sen), the interior (Chea Sim), economy and livelihood (Mok Sakun until his death in April 1979 and then Ros Samay), health and social action (Nou Beng), propaganda, information and culture (Keo Chenda), and education (Chan Ven). The council had a secretariat (*kenna pracham*) with functions similar to those of the party's politburo, comprising three members, one of whom was minister for national defense. The responsibility of members was to present "their own personal opinions on the general work of the council, approve matters of the council and, in line with this, act as chief directors of ministries for which they are responsible. They have the duty to prepare and take care of various matters of their own section of work in order to present them to the council for approval."[16] The council met once a month and the *kenna pracham* met weekly. The PRCK guided the work of all the people's revolutionary committees of the administrative sub-divisions of the country.

The FUNSK gathered the ideas, opinions and wishes of the

masses "in order for the center to grasp [them]."[17] The central meeting of the Front was held every three months and the members of the Front met with the masses once a month in each center in order to "give propaganda about mass movements, implement all the principles and policies of the party and the state and recognize the ideas and wishes of the masses."[18]

The major problem at the beginning was finding people with sufficient education, let alone experience or party affiliation, to staff the ministries and departments set up by the new administration. In April 1979, Nayan Chanda wrote:

> East European sources admit that the central leadership in Kampuchea now consists only of 25 people and an initial search for those with secondary school education who could be considered "intellectual" and given administrative responsibility has produced only 106 others.
>
> In the early 1970s the number of people with such attainments was reportedly 20,000 . . . [and] whatever administration the provinces now have is provided by freshly-recruited former Lon Nol soldiers and by Vietnamese advisers.[19]

Towards the end of 1979, the PRCK circulated a decision which described the general chaos within the civil service.[20] It noted that "the people who have work to do are few while those who have nothing to do are numerous" and "those who have technical skills are few while the civil service is very large."[21] Worryingly, "some staff are the enemy and they take advantage of our negligence . . . in order to creep into the ministries and enterprises to carry out their destructive activities."[22] Therefore, the PRCK decided that ministries and enterprises had to stop selecting people by themselves, and they had to distinguish clearly between workers and their dependants. They had to monitor their workers according to the assigned task and required skills and explain to the relevant section of the ministry why a certain staff size was necessary. Those surplus to requirements or not meeting the criteria had to be dismissed and bad elements had to be handed over "to the region where that individual lives for management and further education."[23] In the future, every ministry and section had to negotiate with the Central Administration Commission and the Ministry of Finance concerning the employment of staff. The decision ordered that the complicated situation of cadres, workers and staff had to be resolved by the end of January 1980.

In 1979, hundreds of Cambodians were sent to Vietnam to train as cadres for the new administration. Their place in Cambodia was taken by a veritable army of Vietnamese experts. Resulting tension within the ministries and work places between the proud Khmers and the sometimes condescending Vietnamese experts was inevitable. As Bui Tin, himself an expert with the Cambodian Press Agency, SPK, recalled:

> True, there were some who were well-informed, dedicated and helpful. As such they were valued and respected, but unfortunately there were very few, too few of them. There were far too many experts who were false or venal or had been appointed as 'privileged experts.'[24]

A decision of the central committee suggested six points to calm the situation in order to make for good working relations.[25] Both sides were asked "to act properly and in conditions of loving and wholeheartedly respecting each other and helping each other, with mutual respect and awareness of the pure solidarity of the international proletariat and learning from each other."[26] All affairs were to be discussed first with the experts, and their opinions heeded, but "whatever the experts do must have the approval of our leadership organizations and, most importantly, be enacted according to our decision."[27] Information had to be shared in good time and joint reports were prepared each week; programs and plans of activities for each week and each month were worked out together. In this difficult marriage of convenience, "solidarity and consensus, modesty, learning from each other on various issues" were recommended.[28] "If there is some affair that we cannot yet do, we should ask the experts to help our cadres to do it or help to do it while starting the conditions for our cadres to work by themselves. Anything which our cadres can do, then our cadres will do. Asking the experts to help will let our cadres become increasingly better but we must not rely on our friends for everything."[29] By the end of 1980, the number of Vietnamese experts had been scaled down. Ben Kiernan, who spent several months in Cambodia in 1980, gave the following examples:

> A year ago, Takeo had forty, now Khmer officials there say there are none; two officials in Kompong Cham told me in separate private conversations that the advisers to their province had been reduced in number from twenty to eight . . . in Phnom Penh's Ministry of Foreign Affairs, there were twelve in 1979, two in 1980. All Vietnamese advisers have apparently gone from the Ministry of Education. Vietnam's ambassador in Phnom Penh, Ngo Dien . . . told me that the number of Vietnamese advisers in Kampuchea had been reduced by fifty percent, although this number was increased again by thirty percent with the arrival of technical and 'more qualified' personnel.[30]

Staffing the provincial administration with reliable, skilled people loyal to the regime was a major problem and the new government relied heavily on Vietnamese assistance. Communication between the center and the base was not exact. An early party decision referred to "the phenomenon of [the provinces] working according to impulse without reports or without requesting the opinion of the central committee."[31] There was, it said, a need for "clarity, democracy, unity and collective leadership."[32] The administration at the provincial/municipal level had to reflect that of the center: the party committee acting as the hub while the people's revolutionary committee conducted the work of government and the mass organizations of the Front were responsible for mass mobilization, maintaining popular support and finding new party recruits. The party committees had to establish their *chivepheap* (the routine system for meetings, criticism and self-criticism sessions, work plans, etc.) quickly and securely, and develop and promote production, especially agriculture. At the same time, they had "to continue to sweep clean the groups of soldiers of the routed enemy army as well as take care to defend the security system at the base."[33] Other concrete duties of the provincial party committees set down in this decision were "to lead and expand the sectors of health, education, training and culture, to mobilize the masses to build and strengthen the state authority, and to proceed with the work of building the party. . . ."[34]

AT THE BASE

The party committee at the provincial/municipal level had from three to five members. The provincial party secretary could (and usually did) also act as chief of the people's revolutionary committee with overall responsibility and direct responsibility for the economy and livelihood. There was a member for "organizing and monitoring," and another for "propaganda, education, culture and social action." The chief of the regional and provincial battalion, or the political commissar of the battalion, was part of the people's revolutionary committee, with duties on the military and security side. In a committee of just four members, the member responsible for "organizing and monitoring" was also responsible for the mass organizations.

Apart from the municipality of Phnom Penh, the party committee and the people's revolutionary committee tended to be one and the same thing. Most provinces were desperately short of party members. Kiernan noted that "most of the peasantry have no relations with the party whatsoever . . . in 1981 in fact several of the country's eighteen provinces still had only one party member."[35] Therefore, this decision granted the party committee the right to "choose some cadres with quality and potential for the committee in the various sections of work such as organization, propaganda and education, and monitoring the departments."[36] It was stressed that "the work must be as a collectivity and genuinely democratic, bringing together and assigning duties to individuals to accept responsibility."[37]

The people's revolutionary committee at each level of the national administration acted on and guided the implementation of all party and government circulars and decisions in its own base in the important areas of politics, economy, culture, social action and the military. The committee had, if possible, from five to seven members, three of whom formed the permanent commission to resolve the day-to-day work of administration and management. Below the level of province (*khet*), and the municipalities (*krong*), of Phnom Penh and Kompong Som, were the district (*srok*), commune (*khum*), and village (*phum*). A party decision of July 1979 claimed, "We have liberated more than four million people so basically our people throughout the country have been liberated."[38] The figures given to illustrate the extent of the revolutionary state authority, however, were little more than wild guesses: 3,400–3,500 villages in 1,100–1,900 communes in 80–120 districts.[39] The author of the document noted: "The state authority in the provinces and at the center is strengthening and expanding its orderliness."[40] On the other hand, it was admitted, "we are not yet strong, we are still weak in quality, still lacking importantly in quantity in the districts and the local state authority [there] still doesn't have enough strength to manage all the sectors of the lives of the people."[41] According to this document, the district and commune people's revolutionary committees consisted of five people: the chief with responsibility for economy and livelihood and members responsible for military, security, information/culture/society, and education/health. The writer admitted:

> The organization of our state authority is still weak and we haven't strengthened the important parts at the level of commune and district where it is very weak. The enemy are taking advantage of the gaps that we have by burrowing into our ranks in order to organize a state authority with two faces.[42]

At that stage, the central committee proposed elections to "select and appoint the state authority at all levels: village, commune, district, province."[43] The commune (and municipal counterpart, *sangkat*) elections were deferred until 1981, when the National Assembly general elections were also held. Provincial and district committees remained appointed rather than popularly elected, while the village chief assumed his position by various means that were decided locally.

The village, as Heder correctly observed in 1980, remained "fairly autonomous."[44] Even at the commune level, he claimed, there were party people, "local 'domestic' communists who survived the purges" and while not all communes had Vietnamese experts, most of them were garrisoned by "at least a platoon and sometimes a company of Vietnamese troops who often engage in non-military activities such as control of rice and supply depots and 'civil action' projects."[45] However, there were no Vietnamese experts exercising administrative responsibilities in the village and although most villages were regularly visited by Vietnamese patrols, "no more than 10–20 percent of the villages have a permanent Vietnamese troop presence."[46] Even when there was a presence, he continued, the troops had no responsibility for village administration whose members consisted "almost exclusively of locally recruited or even locally elected people . . . who before January 1979 had nothing to do with the Vietnamese or the FUNSK."[47] The central committee decision concerning arrangements for the country's administration referred to previously made little mention of the village, saying only, "in any village where there still isn't a state authority, we must monitor and grasp the state of affairs within the village and then make a plan to organize to raise the masses to select and appoint people with a good attitude and qualities to join the state authority."[48] Heder confirms this:

> The general line on the composition of the village committees was a political line and not a class one . . . local 'clean' people having no associations with any past regime were . . . supposed to be favored . . . Thus the class and ideological tendencies within village committees were often mixed and sometimes more than a little contradictory and the dominant tendencies differed widely from village to village.[49]

Heder contends that it was the Vietnamese and Pen Sovann who decided how the villages would be organized: each village had a three-member village committee and a militia (*svay tran/chhlop*) of between ten and fifty men who may or may not have had arms, and the village was divided into a number of groups or teams (*krom*)—"the basic level of rural organization should be a 'solidarity team' in which land, but not the means of agricultural production, should be collectivized."[50]

THE EXECUTIVE ORDER

By the end of 1979, although Cambodia was still far from peace, and famine was already exacting its toll on the people, the semblance at least of administrative order had been restored. On 16 August 1979, the Central Administration Commission issued a report which explained the arrangement of ministries and provincial departments within the provisional government of the PRCK.[51] The report explained the sources of cadres at the time that had to be relied upon: those cadres who attended the [first] congress of the Front in November 1978 and those who took part in the [third] party congress of January 1979, the cadres who had returned from political courses in Thu Duc, Ho Chi Minh City, and who were currently engaged in concrete work, and some sympathetic former intellectuals of the Sihanouk and Lon Nol regimes. The Ministry of the Economy was now split into five separate ministries, the provincial and municipal committees, both party and government, were strengthened, and ambassadors were named to a number of countries. Ros Samay was given a special cabinet portfolio, that of minister for "*Vimean Protean Roddh*" (Special Minister of State) to assist the president in resolving matters of government. In that position he was responsible for international economic cooperation, jurisdiction and courts, Buddhism and other religions. Other appointments were:

- Ministry of Industry: Meas Samnang, minister, Sar Ret, vice minister;
- Ministry of Agriculture and Forestry: Men Chhan, minister, Phauk, vice minister responsible for forestry and fisheries,

Kong Sam Ol, agricultural engineer as adviser to the minister or as specialist with duties in technology;
- Ministry of Commerce: Taing Sarim, minister, Chan, vice minister (responsible for food and utensils);
- Ministry of Finance and Banking: Chan Phin, minister;
- Ministry of Communications and Transport: Khun Chhy, minister, Kim Sak, vice minister (engineer for Posts);
- Ministry of the Interior: Chea Sim, minister, Mat Ly and Sim Song [sic], vice ministers;
- Ministry of Foreign Affairs: Hun Sen, minister, Keo Prasat, vice minister, Hor Namhong, adviser to the minister;
- Ministry of Education: Chan Ven, minister (and we will choose someone from within the Ministry of Education to act as vice minister);
- Ministry of Propaganda, Information and Culture: Keo Chenda, minister; Soriya, History Department of the University, knows French and Russian, vice minister;
- Ministry of Health: Nou Beng, minister, Chey Khan Nha, vice minister;
- Preparatory Committee for organizing a Ministry of Disabled Soldiers and Social Action: Neou Samon;
- Radio: On Dara, director;
- SPK: Chey Saphon, director;[52]
- *Kampuchea* Newspaper: Khieu Sengkhim, the younger brother of Khieu Samphan and director of the newspaper *Koh Santepheap* in the Sihanouk time, Khieu Kannharith, Bachelor's Degree in Literature now working on *Kampuchea*;
- Department of Government: Ung Phan, head of department, Say Kimchuon, chief of government office for increasing the harvest;
- Embassies/Consulates: Chea Soth (USSR), Van Sorn (SRV), Sar Pon (LPDR), Prach Son (Cuba).[53]

The Ministry of Defense, directly responsible to the party, was not listed and the document says only that the ministry was then carrying out fundamental rearrangements of military cadres in the provinces. "Banh" (probably Tea Banh) was named military chief for Koh Kong province and Bu Saroen was to be military chief for Siem Reap. Appointments to the special ministries and departments of the party, including the Department of the Party Center and the important central committee posts for Administration, Propaganda, and for the Front and its mass organizations were also listed, along with those to provincial and municipal party and administrative committees.

The errors made in this document with the names of these important state officials indicate that the architects of the new government were drawing on disparate sources and nominating people barely known to them. It is usually assumed that trust was of the essence in the early days of the regime when the lines between friend and foe were not clear. Therefore, the nomination of the brother of arch-enemy Khieu Samphan is surprising. Even more surprising were some appointments to provincial/municipal party and administrative committees where twelve of the twenty committees included members who had "changed over" from official military or political commissar positions within the DK to assume the same function in the PRK administration.[54] Some of them named in this document had "just changed over." Koun Ren, for instance, the member of the Prey Veng committee in charge of politics had been the KR political commissar in Takeo; he was a "former and current party member" who had fought against the French in 1949. Mom Sauphea, the committee member responsible for politics in Kompong Cham, had been deputy chief of provincial politics there in the DK regime.

The ease with which former political and military officers of the DK entered the new PRK administrative regime may seem hypocritical in view of the welter of anti–Pol Pot propaganda that came out of Cambodia after 1979, but this was still the brotherhood of the struggle (*cholena dasu*) and the Koun Ren case is a reminder of the long ties of camaraderie reaching back to the years of struggle for independence. Old comrades, even if they were temporarily on the other side, were more trusted than newcomers, their histories were well-known, and they belonged to the same faith. Most of all, the new administration needed them. The pool of educated human resources was both small and shallow at the beginning of 1979 and it would take several years to develop the requisite skilled administrative personnel. More worryingly, the party had had to admit people into the highest ranks of its administration, particularly its provincial administration, who lacked even the basic political credentials. How was the work of extending ideological hegemony over the masses going to proceed in these circumstances? This was a new regime which was revealing its political nature by readily reintegrating into the system of government representatives of the detested former regime. Moreover, the presence of Vietnamese troops and advisers, though welcome while the situation was so desperate, would, given traditional animosity towards Vietnam, someday wear thin, and the new regime would be blamed for Vietnam's prolonged occupation. The new leaders had to grasp the fleeting popularity they had with the masses in order to win their consent to be governed and to motivate them to accept the basic tenets of socialism. Unfortunately, but realistically, there simply were not sufficient cadres with the will and the competency to fulfill the task.

THE CONSTITUTION OF THE PRK

The most important task of 1980 in terms of building the structure of the regime's administration was writing the new constitution. On 10 January 1980, the People's Revolutionary Council created a Council for the Draft Constitution. The head of that constitutional council was Ros Samay. Four months later, on 11 April, he presented the first draft to the People's Revolutionary Council. In a covering report, Ros Samay explained how the constitution was compiled:

> In January, I organized to bring together lawyers and important documents such as the constitutions of fraternal socialist countries, e.g. the constitutions of Vietnam, USSR, GDR, Hungary, and Bulgaria and other documents—the Constitution of the Kingdom of Cambodia, the Constitution of the Khmer Republic and the Constitution of Democratic Kampuchea. In February, even though the number of people on our

legal staff is small, the secretariat started to write the draft of the constitution according to the possibilities it had. In April, we made alterations and finished it definitively on 7 April 1980.[55]

He proceeded to give a synopsis of the draft constitution that contained a preamble, eleven chapters and 106 articles. Ros Samay concluded his report by explaining that the secretariat had "reflected on words which were easy to read, easy to understand to take and weave them together as a text" and it only used difficult words when there was nothing easier. It was, he recommended, "an appropriate form based on the customs and thinking of the people and the eminent country of the PRK . . . a constitution of the people, for the service of the people."[56]

The PRCK accepted the draft, submitted it to the politburo "to improve and finish it" and then printed a number of copies which were distributed to various government agencies around the center and throughout various provinces for them "to study and reflect on the matters of the draft constitution for strong and weak points."[57] On 28 May 1980, these agencies were asked to report on the ideas and opinions which arose from discussion. By then Ros Samay had been stood down from his posts. There were slanderous rumors about "immorality" and "official corruption" and suggestions that he was under house arrest in Phnom Penh. Paul Quinn-Judge reported that he "faded out of the picture early in 1980. He irritated the Vietnamese with his draft of the new regime's constitution, which was quickly scrapped."[58]

On 8 August 1980, Ros Samay's replacement in the role of secretary general of the Draft Constitution Council at the Ministry of Justice, Uk Bun Chhoeun, referred to the PRCK Decision No. 179–80 issued on 28 July for the printing and public dissemination of presumably a second draft constitution "which the meeting of 21 July 1980 unanimously approved and agreed to" for the holding of study courses and subsequent reporting.[59] Pen Sovann recalled that in August that year, the Vietnamese presented him with yet another finished Cambodian constitution, written in Vietnamese, which he refused to accept.[60] In September 1980, Vietnam adopted a new constitution of its own, concentrating administrative power in the Council of State rather than in the hands of the Council of Ministers, and it was speculated that Cambodia would follow suit.[61] In other words, both countries were redefining their national identities at the same time and as the alterations to the draft preamble of 1980 indicate, there must have been a lot of pressure from Vietnam on Cambodia for a uniformity of viewpoints on (revolutionary) history, if not for constitutional specifics. The Cambodian constitution struggled for its independence.

By the end of February 1981, the final draft of the Cambodian constitution seemed to be ready for publication. There was no doubt about the ideological significance of this effort. It was "to let the Cambodian people understand the essence and basis of the constitution in order to increase their trust and love for the regime of the People's Republic, to resolve to defend and build the people's state authority, to expand the reputation of the PRK, and to further reveal the faces of Sihanouk and Son Sann with Pol Pot."[62] The plan agreed upon was that from one week to ten days after the PRCK's announcement of the draft constitution, there would be a meeting of the ambassadors of all Indochina countries, followed by an announcement by radio and in the Front's newspaper, *Kampuchea*. Heng Samrin would explain his ideas, the constitution would be read over the radio, and there would be editorials in the national press. Press conferences would be held, the media would present texts congratulating the draft constitution, and there would be question-and-answer sessions on the radio. All this was to be achieved before 5 March.

On 4 March, the PRCK announced the circulation of the draft ("definitively completed") in booklet form among all government agencies and institutions, so that "cadres, staff, workers, and youth serving in the Kampuchean People's Revolutionary Armed Forces as well as all the people throughout the country can discuss and make contributions to this Draft Constitution."[63] On 10 March, according to Raoul Jennar, the text of the constitution was presented to ten thousand people assembled in the Olympic Stadium in Phnom Penh.[64] Two days later, Uk Bun Chhoeun held a press conference to explain the constitution to local and foreign media representatives. The Front gave its stamp of approval in mid-May:

> All we cadres and staff of the office of the central committee of the Front seek support for the splendid draft constitution which has a national spirit and is appropriately proletarian according to the pure revolutionary leadership. With heart and soul overflowing with joy, we ask that this constitution be born quickly in order to be of great benefit to us all.[65]

The draft constitution was presented to the first session of the first legislature of the National Assembly of the People's Republic of Kampuchea and unanimously adopted on 27 June 1981.

The writing of the PRK Constitution caused serious strains in the top levels of the Cambodia-Vietnam relationship. Ros Samay was an early victim, down but not yet out, and after this Pen Sovann appears to have taken an increasingly intransigent stance. What were the major points of contention with regard to the constitution?[66] The final version had fewer articles (93) than the first draft (106) but that was often an editing issue rather than one of change. There were changes in wording and emphasis and in details such as the duration of maternity leave or the length of time given for notice of general elections. The real and fundamental differences, however, related to property, to law and the treatment of suspects, and to the position of the chairman of the Council of State.

The preamble to the 1980 draft constitution referred to the Communist Party of Kampuchea three times (always in tandem with the Front) including: "The leadership of the Communist Party of Kampuchea and the FUNSK is a true element coming from the working and farming class and is the one correct and lawful representative of the Kampuchean people." The preamble in the adopted version of the constitution referred just once to the party, as in "the clear-sighted political line of the party", and then, in Article 4, referred to the Kampuchean People's Revolutionary Party as "a force that takes direct leadership of the entire revolutionary task of the

PRK", using the new party name adopted at the fourth party congress on 26 May 1981, one month before the constitution was adopted on 27 June.

The preamble to the PRK Constitution was lengthy and stolid, lacking both the lyricism and penmanship of Khieu Samphan's preamble to the DK Constitution and the enthusiasm and nationalist flavor of the 1980 draft. Instead of the draft's celebration:

> 7 January 1979 is the glorious day when the Communist Party and the FUNSK created a new page in history to build our beloved country of Kampuchea according to rightful desire and truth to find genuine independence, peace, happiness and solidarity with the international proletariat,

the final version was a disheartening expression of gratitude due to others:

> Thanks to the clear-sighted political line of the party, the close unity within the FUNSK, the sincere assistance of the people and army of Vietnam, and the support of the fraternal socialist countries and peace-loving countries in the world, our people definitively overthrew the genocidal regime on 7 January 1979.

Under Vietnamese pressure, the adopted preamble thus paid lip service to the notion of the common struggle of the "three Indochinese peoples" as having won independence for Cambodia, and castigated the DK regime for having "continued to bow down to and follow the orders of the reactionaries in the Chinese leading circle, to send armies to commit aggression against Vietnam's borders and to massacre the fraternal neighbors who have shared with us the same trenches . . . " and claimed that by "heroically struggling in unity and close co-operation with the Vietnamese and Lao peoples . . . [Cambodian people] are a powerful force for achieving victory."

Article 20 of the earlier draft constitution adopted a strictly Marxist approach to the nature of property:

The property of the citizen is based on his labor; Property in the form of things for daily use, conveniences, food equipment and utensils, tools for the family economy, money from the profit of work can be considered private; The property of citizens and the right of inheritance are protected by law; The citizen has the right to use the land allotted by the state to practice other economies, to have orchards, vegetable gardens and raise animals and to build a house. The citizen must use the land allotted by the state properly; The citizen can make use of arable land and land which has not yet been cleared according to an area of open land fixed by law, in accordance with the characteristics and quality of the land in each region; The citizen cannot use private property or assets provided by the state in order to make a profit which is not created by labor or in a way which affects the interests of the society; A law will determine the people's place of abode.

In the final version of the PRK Constitution, the people had the right not only to use land allotted by the state for a house, for kitchen gardens and orchards but also to inherit that land (Article 15). Moreover, a farmer could apply to the state to borrow "an extra plot of land on which to produce seasonal foodstuffs according to his ability to work"; the farmer had the right "to keep the product of that work" (Article 16) and "the private ownership by citizens of work income, other legal incomes and legal goods is protected by law" (Article 18). Perhaps this simply reflected the trend in the countryside by 1981 towards more liberal patterns of land use and production, necessitated in part by the famine of 1980, or perhaps it was consistent with the view held by Vietnam since the 1950s that the Cambodian economy was still far too undeveloped to assume socialist characteristics.

The rights of Cambodian citizens before the law were severely affected by changes to the 1980 draft constitution. The draft provided for a People's Supreme Court, the local People's Court and the Military Court (Article 90) and for an attorney-general attached to the Supreme Court who would be appointed by and be responsible to the National Assembly (Article 97). The adopted constitution abandoned the Supreme

Court and the attorney-general; these institutions were not established until a decree-law (No. 34KrJ) was ratified by the Council of State on 26 August 1987 when the People's Supreme Court was declared to be "the highest legal institution of the People's Republic of Kampuchea" (Article 1). The final version of the constitution also rejected those clauses from Article 36 of the draft which made "coercion, violation of the person, or any other punitive act compounding the penalty or torture of prisoners" absolutely forbidden. In the draft, the defendant was innocent until the court definitively found him/her otherwise guilty and confessions given under "compulsion by cruel physical or psychological methods" were unacceptable as proof of guilt and if "accusation is based solely on suspicion, the defendant should be acquitted." Crimes against individuals "causing anxiety . . . in order to force the giving of information" were also forbidden by the draft (Article 94). The legal and penal codes which were based on the final PRK Constitution were harsh and the use of torture to extract confessions was reported to be common, as was lengthy imprisonment without trial.[67]

The most significant difference, apart from the preamble, was the dropping of Article 68 altogether. That article stated that "the President of the Council of State is the Supreme Commander of the Armed Forces and is the Chairman of the National Defense Council." The final PRK Constitution did not mention either of these roles. The State of Cambodia Constitution of 1989 did and it would also make the President of the Council of State the "Head of the State of Cambodia." The PRK constitution made no mention of a Head of State, but then neither had the earlier draft. It is possible that this position was to be reserved for Sihanouk.[68] The battle over the wording of the constitution did sour relations between the PRK regime and Vietnam, that much is evident, but when questioned on this point, Pen Sovann simply said: "The constitution was prepared and the Vietnamese insisted on changing some clauses that they didn't agree with."[69]

The majority of Cambodians were unaware of the behind-the-scenes struggle over the wording of the constitution. Many of them, however, were directly involved in the group discussions where they must have felt they were making a direct contribution. Hand-written notes attached to the document entitled *The Plan for Disseminating the Draft Constitution of the PRK* dated 28 February 1981 give an idea of the opinions that emanated from these discussions.[70] For instance, Article 24 of the draft declared that "the state awards scholarships to young men and women deemed capable of pursuing their studies in tertiary and technical education at home and abroad." One participant, presumably male, wanted "women" to be deleted from this article, although there was no dispute over several articles guaranteeing social equality of men and women. Practical questions were posed, such as: "Do monks have the right to stand as candidates and if so, do they have to leave the order first?" and "Land is property which the state shares out but can it be sold and can the owner exchange it if he wants to?" In the report of the chairman of the committee for the draft constitution presented to the first session of the National Assembly in mid-1981, Uk Bun Chhoeun said:

> All our brothers throughout the country, all the mass organizations from the center to the base, schools, enterprises, and military bodies have pooled their many ideas into making this constitution. They have all congratulated the essence of the draft constitution which has answered the needs of our people throughout the country . . . it will raise the morale of the people to fulfill their work in the cause of defending national independence and building the motherland while advancing towards socialism. The new constitution has declared and united the duties of the People's Republic of Kampuchea on the international stage.[71]

The year-long drafting of the constitution coincided with preparations for and holding of both local and national elections to provide the new regime with another valuable ideological tool.

74

ELECTIONS AT ALL LEVELS

Whether in preparation for elections or for purely administrative purposes, the government carried out a population count in 1980. Jerrold Huguet notes that this was described as "a general population survey, but it was probably more of an administrative count, with communes reporting their population to districts, districts to provinces, and provinces to the national government."[72] Seng Soeurn of the Cambodian Department of National Statistics who participated in the count spoke however of the hardships of collecting information in the eastern highlands of the country at that time. He said the count started in January or February of 1980 and took three months to complete.[73] The population recorded by that count was 6.4 million.[74] Some demographers challenged the figure, arguing that the local officials may have inflated the figures to increase their share of resources; others suspected it of undercounting the population in order to exaggerate the damage caused by the DK regime. Irrespective of these contradictory arguments, Huguet notes, the official total was adjusted to 6,590,000 as of the end of 1980, "perhaps to include some unreported groups."[75] The figures showed that there were 3,049,450 males and 3,540,504 females. The discrepancy between the sexes was entirely within age groups above sixteen years.[76]

Kershaw claims that the commune and *sangkat* elections and the national elections of 1981 were in response to a United Nations resolution calling for UN-supervised elections in Cambodia:

This chapter in the short history of the PRK opens, therefore, some time in mid-1980 when Hanoi became aware that the latest ASEAN/PRC[hina] "package" in the run-up to the Cambodia debate in the 1980 session of the United Nations General Assembly, was to include a call for internationally supervised elections. Suddenly, as if a hasty, impromptu response to these stirrings in the hostile camp, the ruling Front of Cambodia, the Kampuchean National United Front for National Salvation (KNUFNS), and the government, the Kampuchean People's Revolutionary Council (KPRC),

announced without commentary that elections would be held
by the beginning of 1981.[77]

Kershaw based his argument on a Radio Phnom Penh broadcast, on 13 September 1980. However, if this were the case,
then the standard of preparedness by the end of September was
nothing short of miraculous for a small and inexperienced
administration. On 30 September, Uk Bun Chhoeun, minister
for justice and permanent member of the Committee for
Preparing and Guiding the Election, sent a memo to Ung Phan
at the Department of the Central Committee inviting him to a
meeting to discuss the draft decree-law for the election "which
I sent you on 9 August 1980. When the committee for preparing the election meets, we will introduce the decree-law of the
election to the committee of the FUNSK for further approval
and when the Front has approved it, we will seek approval from
the PRCK."[78] That note was accompanied by a table specify-
ing the number of nominated candidates by election center
(that is, province or municipality). There were, at this point,
160 candidates for the 112 (later to be increased to 117) positions of deputy to the National Assembly. Diagrams showing
dimensions and design of ballot boxes, including mobile boxes
"for taking votes from people who can't come to the booth" as
well as pro forma voter identification cards and cards acknowledging successful candidates for the election were attached.
    The original plan for local elections included the district
level as well as the commune. *The Draft Table: Budget for the
Election of People's Revolutionary Committees of Sangkat and
Damban* made provision for a total of 8,059 polling stations for
the 141 *damban* or "districts" (seven of which were in Phnom
Penh), and 1,337 communes (including twelve *sangkat* in the
capital, and a further four in the other municipality of
Kompong Som).[79] The documents make no further reference
to district level elections and they did not occur. Why the
district (*srok*) level of administration between province and
commune remained so weak and poorly defined throughout
the PRK period is not clear, but the decision not to hold
district elections does help to highlight just how thinly spread
the party was in 1981. The communes were important because

they supervised the villages, and especially because they were supposed to implement and monitor the decisions and circulars relating to the *krom samaki*, the solidarity production teams of collectivized agriculture. The provincial level was directly responsible to the center and therefore the main channel of information to the countryside. The district level between commune and province was important, but in view of the scarcity of loyal party representatives, it was here that sacrifices could be made when necessary. The consequence was that the provincial governors, most of whom held both positions of secretary of the party committee and chairman of the people's revolutionary committee, were able to accrue considerable power and influence. The extent of that influence became more evident in the post-1985 period of the PRK, as the documents testify. The elections for the people's revolutionary committees of the commune/*sangkat* were scheduled to take place during February and March 1981, before the National Assembly elections. Because of logistical difficulties and problems created by the security situation, these local elections were staggered and some of them were still not finished at the time of the national elections. The local elections were a vitally important test of the new government's administrative capacity. A telegram from Bou Thong, vice-chairman of the National Election Committee, on 17 February 1981, to the provincial/municipal people's revolutionary committees made the ideological purpose of these elections very clear:

> The elections at the base represent a mobilization of the masses. Therefore, we must arrange for the people to study and discuss well within the solidarity groups for increasing the harvest in the countryside and the people's groups of the *sangkat* within the city about the victories during the previous two years, about the rebuilding of the economy of the PRK and about the destructive ruses of the enemy in order to let the people understand clearly towards strengthening their trust in the new regime . . .[80]

The Study Document for the Election to Choose People's Revolutionary Committees for the Commune and Sangkat prepared by the Central Propaganda and Education Commission was undoubtedly intended for cadres and representatives of the mass organizations whose job was mobilization of the people at the base.[81] It explained that the election was "a way to show that the PRK is a genuinely democratic regime of the people":

> After the genocide, our people had two proper goals: one was to have a sustainable life in order to carry out their lives as usual, the second was to have a firm state authority to ensure the protection of their lives and to wipe out the traitorous reactionaries who destroyed the revolution and the normal lives of our people. The election to choose members for the people's revolutionary committees of the commune/*sangkat* is a very important task for building the state authority according to the desires of the people and is an activity according to the democratic rights of the people also.[82]

The document continued that "if there was not a good state authority, it would make our lives unsustainable and there would be no bright future, our children wouldn't go to school. The destiny and fortunes of our people would be increasingly at risk . . . We want to increase the harvest, we want to strengthen our security system, we want to have houses that are cool, we want to study, to relax happily [and] if we don't have a good state authority then the reactionaries will not let us live sustainably and do our work as usual."[83] It urged the monks who were "citizens with rights and obligations like other citizens" to preach and make clear three things to the people:

> You must not listen to the propaganda of the enemy;
> You must go and vote together;
> You must choose good candidates to vote for.[84]

After studying the documents, each base was required to send its list of nominated candidates to the local party committee for approval and following the elections, the elected people's revolutionary committee of the commune/*sangkat* had to arrange for an occasion to show themselves to the people and swear before the masses the following three points:

1. To be honest with the motherland of Kampuchea, to be determinedly opposed to the enemy, to care for solidarity both internal and international, primarily that solidarity with Vietnam and Laos;

2. To serve the people wholeheartedly without oppressing or intimidating them;

3. To fulfill actively all the duties which are handed over and to implement them thoroughly according to each policy of the Party, the Front and the People's Revolutionary Council of Kampuchea.[85]

The people's revolutionary committees were advised to avoid two kinds of mistakes: "personal views or time-wasting. Both these mistakes will cause the loss of good opportunities and result in giving the enemy the advantage."[86]

Sau Phan, who chaired the election committee for the commune/*sangkat* elections, gave interim voting results during a cadre training course for the national elections that were held in Phnom Penh from 2–6 April:

> In the whole of the PRK, there are 1279 communes and by 1 April 1981, we had received 50 percent of the election results.[87] The number of people who went to vote was between 90–100 percent. Three percent of the vote was invalid and 0.05 percent was informal. Kandal province has completely finished and various other provinces have finished 20–30 percent ... The proposed budget is 20 million *riel* for expenses in this election. The elections to choose state authorities in the commune and *sangkat* must be finished before 15 April 1981. However, if they are not, they must resume after the elections to choose deputies to the National Assembly.[88]

The commune/*sangkat* elections were interrupted from 15 April until 1 May, the latter date set for the general elections, so that preparations for selecting deputies for the National Assembly could proceed. They may have resumed after the national elections, although the documents make no further mention of commune election results. The first quarterly report of the Revolutionary Women's Association of Kampuchea, however, claimed that at the time of that report 870 commune/*sangkat* people's revolutionary committees had been elected nationally which, if accurate, was roughly a 70 percent completion rate based on Sau Phan's figure given above.[89]

The decree-law concerning the general elections was issued on 3 March 1981. It declared that the elections "must be prepared and carried out within the first half of 1981."[90] According to this decree-law, the 117 members of the National Assembly "are chosen by the people according to each electorate, that is to say province and municipality." The number of deputies per electorate was determined by the number of people within the electorate, with allowances made for the two municipalities and for provinces with a large population of ethnic minorities "in order to give workers and ethnic people a sufficient number of representatives."[91] Each of the twenty electorates was divided into electoral offices with a minimum of 500 voters each, except for those in outlying regions. Hospitals which had more than fifty voters could organize an electoral office. Separate offices were set up for the army. The bodies responsible for the election were the Election Council at the center, the Election Committee at the electorate/provincial level and the Election Commission at the electoral office/base level. The Election Council was established fifty-five days before the election day, consisting of representatives of the central committee of the Front and representatives of the mass organizations at the center. The election committees and the election commissions were set up forty-five days and thirty days respectively before the election. They had a composition similar to that of the Election Council. All three electoral bodies were warned that they "must not propagandize or induce the voters to vote for any one candidate" (Article 17). Voter registration lists closed fifteen days before the election and "the people have the right to protest (about mistakes or omissions) in writing or by oral report" with the district people's revolutionary committee having the final say (Article 22). The candidates were nominated at the election center and they were barred from membership on the Election Committee or the Election Commission at his/her own center. Fifteen days before the election the candidate list had to be made public and any protests had to be resolved within three days. "Starting from the day of closing the public broadcasting of the list of candidates at the election center up to the day of the election, election propaganda can proceed freely. However, the propaganda should not affect the honor and reputation of the nation" (Article 29). Proxy or postal voting was not permitted, but if a voter was "sick, elderly or handicapped and asks to vote at home, the Election Committee must organize to send a ballot box to the home of the voter to give that person a ballot" (Article 32). Absentee voting was permitted and strongly encouraged. The voter had to cross off the unwanted names. Voting was to be absolutely secret but illiterate voters were assisted.[92] Counting began immediately after the election.

The candidates, two voters as scrutineers, journalists, photographers, film-makers, and radio broadcasters all had the right to observe the counting of votes. In cases where "two candidates or several receive the same number of votes, the older candidate should be declared the winner" and if an insufficient number of candidates was successful, further elections could be organized "on any Sunday within thirty days after the day of the first round" (Articles 45 and 46). After all the results were in, the PRCK "must summon all the deputies of the National Assembly in order to open the first session sixty days after the election" (Article 49). The final article advised that "citizens have the right to criticize any misdeed or illegal act that occurs during the election [and] anyone forbidding or seeking revenge on the accuser will be sentenced for up to three years in prison." Almost 30,000 copies of this decree-law were printed and disseminated. The question of allowing "Chinese aliens and Thai and Lao ethnic minorities" to stand for election and to vote arose at the 2–6 April cadre training course, referred to previously. The minister for justice advised that this matter had not yet been clarified by law and that this would be a matter for the future National Assembly to decide. Given the sensitive nature of the issue of ethnic Vietnamese and more recently arrived Vietnamese "residents" which was unstated but implicit in that question raised at the cadre training course, it should not be surprising that the matter of Cambodian citizenship was never resolved by the PRK regime.

The preparation and training for these elections, both local and national, exhibited military precision. The training of cadres and the election committees and commissions took place throughout March and the propaganda work at the base commenced on 18 March.[93] All the administrative sub-districts were responsible for monitoring progress. The electoral offices were urged to respect the need for constant communication with the center. A March document said that on the day of the election, each base had to report to the higher level three times, at ten o'clock, two o'clock and again at five o'clock and "we must use every possibility, every means which we have at the base such as telegraph and telephone in order to report in good time. When the provinces and towns receive the reports, they must telegram through to the center."[94] The results had to be tallied quickly: "At the district and province, they ought to use statistical staff members or accounts staff and calculators if they have them in order to help with the tally. However, whether there are calculators or not, you must check and recheck many times to get the real count."[95]

Eight of the eleven members of the Election Council were present at the meeting to approve unanimously the results of the elections.[96] The number of candidates who stood for election to the 117 seats was 148. Of the total number of 3,280,565 people with the right to vote, 3,209,583 or 97.83 percent exercised the right. Only 0.05 percent of ballots were rejected as informal and a further 0.36 percent were spoilt or invalid. No election center had to stage a reelection. The candidates who were expected to succeed did succeed. Heng Samrin and Pen Sovann polled 99.75 percent and 99.63 percent respectively. There were to be seventeen women deputies in the National Assembly (including a former princess, Peou Lida), as well as one monk, the Venerable Tep Vong.[97]

The 1981 national election was generally derided by foreign commentators. Certainly this was not a liberal, multi-party election. It was never intended to be. The candidates who stood for election had been pre-selected by the Front and by the party and their names were placed at the head of the ticket. To this extent, the result was a foregone conclusion. Just as importantly, it was a major nation-building, ideological exercise for the party/state. Nayan Chanda reported the election as "a consecration ceremony for the new rulers, and most voters fulfilled their obligation to vote with a shrug."[98] He added that, unlike the previous two elections of 1972 and 1976 "the latest one was made into a festive occasion: Phnom Penh was decked with flags and streamers and polling booths were decorated with coconut leaves, red flowers, flags and portraits of Heng Samrin and Pen Sovann."[99] Security, he reported, was very good. The national election was undoubtedly a major achievement and a source of great pride for the young administration. The heavy workload and the extent and detail of the organization for the election proved its worth. No doubt the Vietnamese helped. The report on the cadre training course in early April mentioned that thirteen Vietnamese experts had been invited to provide "opinions" in the conduct of the election. Battambang had three experts, Siem Reap had two, and eight other provinces had one each. Twelve years later, twenty-two thousand UN troops and civilian administrators with fleets of new cars, satellite communications systems and a US$2.8 billion budget would achieve essentially the same result. The 1981 elections did not allow for more than one party to contest them but the documents do show that in 1993, Cambodians did not have to learn from foreigners how to run a free and fair election.

THE NEW LEGISLATIVE AND EXECUTIVE BODIES

The National Assembly, under the presidency of Chea Sim, held its first session in late June within the sixty-day limit specified by the new constitution, which it unanimously approved and then proceeded to appoint all the new state organs. The Council of State and the Council of Ministers replaced the provisional People's Revolutionary Council. A Ministry of Planning with Chea Soth as minister was created, along with a monitoring committee for state affairs headed by Sim Ka, and the National Bank of the Kampuchean People which was "a state institution equal to a ministry as well as being an organization doing business in foreign currency."[100]

Heng Samrin became president of the Council of State whose function remained largely ceremonial. The Council of State ratified the decree-laws, treaties and agreements which emanated from the Council of Ministers, and received diplomatic credentials. Thus Heng Samrin was, in effect, head of state, whether or not that title was officially bestowed on him. Say Phouthang became vice president of the Council of State. Executive power remained within the Council of Ministers and Pen Sovann was the first chairman or prime minister of that body which met for the first time on 3–4 July. The vice chairmen were Chan Si, minister for defense, and Hun Sen, minister for foreign affairs. When Pen Sovann was stood down as prime minister on 1 December 1981, Chan Si was appointed to that position; his place as deputy prime minister and minister for national defense was taken by Bou Thong. Later, Chea Soth, minister for planning, became a third vice chairman.[101]

The law promulgating the organization and activities of the Council of Ministers was approved at the second session of the National Assembly on 10 February 1982. Further to this law, the permanent commission of the Council of Ministers at its session of 20 March agreed on its own working arrangements. The council met as a collective once a month while the permanent commission, which included the chairman, all the vice-chairmen and the minister responsible for the Cabinet of the Council of Ministers (Ung Phan), met once a week on Thursday "to discuss and exchange opinions about the measures for implementing all the decisions, all the major principles and policies of the politburo of the party center, of the Council of Ministers or the National Assembly—concerning directions, duties and big and important measures concerning the state plan and the annual state budget . . . concerning all the principles and actual policies on the side of economic management and state management."[102] Chairman Chan Si had the usual responsibilities of a prime minister and had particular responsibility for the ministries of the interior, justice, monitoring state affairs, industry, communications and posts, and for Phnom Penh. Bou Thong, apart from his role as minister for national defense, maintained his close relationship with the party's Central Propaganda and Education Commission and all media institutions, and was responsible for the ministries of propaganda, education, health, and the Commission for Social Action. He also took responsibility for all provinces in the northeast. Hun Sen was minister for foreign affairs while maintaining a close relationship with the Foreign Relations Commission of the party center, the Front center and all the mass organizations at the center; he was responsible for Kompong Cham and Kompong Som. Chea Soth, minister for planning, also had responsibility for the ministries of agriculture, commerce, finance and the national bank; he was responsible for Battambang and Prey Veng. Ung Phan was minister responsible for the cabinet of the Council of Ministers.[103] The lower administrative levels remained as before, with one exception for the administration of the municipalities. A 1983 law, *Concerning the Organization of the People's Revolutionary Committee at All Levels,* made provision for the *khan* which was at the administrative level above that of the *sangkat* in the towns and municipalities.[104] This law was passed by the sixth session of the National Assembly on 10 February 1984.

STRAINS WITHIN THE ALLIANCE

By the end of 1984, therefore, the structure of the administration was in place. There were constitutional amendments and boundary changes in the ensuing years, in particular the creation of a new province of Banteay Meanchey, but the new regime had established itself and its reputation within the country, if not abroad. This did not mean that everything was proceeding smoothly. The arrest and imprisonment of one prime minister, Pen Sovann, and the death under very suspicious circumstances of another, Chan Si, indicated that there were serious undercurrents within the power structure itself, and between the new administration and its Vietnamese mentors.

Both Pen Sovann and Chan Si were part of the Khmer Viet Minh/Issarak who had fought against the French for Cambodia's independence and who regrouped in North Vietnam after the 1954 Geneva Accords. Pen Sovann was then just eighteen years old and Chan Si was twenty.[105] Both had rural, peasant backgrounds; one was born and raised in Takeo Province and the other in Kompong Chhnang. Asked in a 1980 interview when he had joined the communist party, Pen Sovann avoided a direct answer, saying: "If revolutionary experience is counted as age, I am 20 years old," while according to his official biography, Chan Si also joined the Khmer People's Revolutionary Party in 1960 when he was working in Vietnam as an "electrical trades cadre."[106] In both instances, the date no doubt refers to the second party congress of 30 September that year when the party's existence was officially announced. Both men returned to Cambodia after the March 1970 *coup d'état*. During the civil war of 1970–1975, they worked for Voice of the United National Front of Kampuchea in Hanoi under Khieu Thirith, Minister for Social Action of Democratic Kampuchea and wife of the deputy premier and foreign minister, Ieng Sary.[107] Pen Sovann was a major in the Vietnamese army; Chan Si was a technician. In the first wave of party purges that followed the withdrawal of Vietnamese forces from Cambodian territory after the signing of the Paris Peace Accords in January 1973, Chan Si was imprisoned by the Pol Pot forces for five months. His biography then states simply that "he left the traitorous organization in order to gather the forces to fight against Pol Pot." Pen Sovann also escaped back to Vietnam in late 1974 or early 1975.[108] Both took part in the 7 January 1979 victory over Democratic Kampuchea. Pen Sovann was named secretary-general of the party, vice president of the People's Revolutionary Council and then prime minister of the Council of Ministers, minister for national defense and commander-in-chief of the Kampuchean People's Revolutionary Armed Forces.[109] Chan Si was the political commander of the KPRAF. In 1980 he was appointed deputy minister for national defense.

The relationship between Pen Sovann and Chan Si was long and trusted. "We were," Pen Sovann said, referring to the Khmer Viet Minh returnees, "a very close group."[110] In fact, that he had formed his own "group" was one of the surmises for his dismissal; other suggestions were that he was arrogant, could not cooperate with the Vietnamese, had leanings towards the USSR and so on.[111] Whatever the real cause, by mid-1981 there can be no doubt that there was serious friction between Pen Sovann and the Vietnamese.

From 24 to 29 November, Pen Sovann led a high-ranking delegation to the northwestern provinces of Battambang and Pursat.[112] At Samaki commune, Battambang, in an ironically prophetic speech to the people he said:

> When drinking water we should think of its source. When picking fruit to eat we should be thankful to the person who planted it. Our liberation was made possible by our Vietnamese brothers. Our Khmer saying teaches us to be grateful. Our country practices Buddhism. We believe in the law of consequence. If we commit a good deed, we will obtain a good result. This you understand . . .[113]

On 1 December he was removed from office and in the evening of the following day, the third anniversary of the founding of the FUNSK in which he had played a pivotal role, he was arrested.[114] Pen Sovann's explanations for incurring Vietnamese displeasure are nationalistic rather than political. When negotiations were being held concerning the setting up of the Front in September 1978, Le Duc Tho, for the Vietnamese government, had promised not to interfere in the internal affairs of Cambodia. However, almost immediately after liberation, he claimed, Le Duc Tho started to break this promise.[115] He referred to border markers being moved inland in Takeo, to Vietnamese monopoly of administration at Kompong Som port, to the stationing of PAVN troops on Puolo Wai, and to intransigent responses to his requests for supervision of cross-border traffic and unchecked Vietnamese immigration. "When I wanted to create our own army of five regiments, the Vietnamese didn't agree and Le Duc Tho went to the USSR to complain," he said. All of the above no doubt were compounding factors, but there must have been a trigger cause and given that his first cousin and close friend, Ros Samay was arrested just one hour after Pen Sovann's arrest, Ros Samay surely must have been complicit in that cause. Ros Samay, was charged by the arresting (Cambodian) security officers with betraying the nation and colluding with the Thai military on the northwest border.[116] Ros Samay was incarcerated in a southern Vietnamese prison for six years and Pen Sovann was kept in Ha Dong prison near Hanoi until 1988 and then under house arrest in Vietnam for a further three years. Bui Tin claims that the removal of Pen Sovann was "the work of Le Duc Tho acting together with Le Duc Anh."[117] On their recommendation, he claims, the politburo in Hanoi accepted an "appeal" from several members of the Cambodian Communist Party.[118] After his return to Cambodia, Pen Sovann told interviewers: "I have said who is responsible for my imprisonment: Hun Sen, Say Phouthang."[119] From his cell in Hanoi, Pen Sovann sent a letter to the central committee in Phnom Penh complaining of his arrest. The reply from Say Phouthang was said to have been: "Don't ask anything of the central committee . . . Your criminal act should be clearer to you than to anyone."[120]

The people were told nothing of this at the time. As one woman recalled, she asked her teacher why Pen Sovann's portrait had been removed from the classroom and was advised not to be so curious; another who worked in the SPK photo library was told by the resident Vietnamese technical adviser to "cross out" Pen Sovann's face from photographs in the collection, and if that was too difficult just to throw the photographs away.[121] The whole affair almost went unnoticed. However, the death of Pen Sovann's successor, Chan Si, which will be discussed later, was a cause for alarm and public grief.

Chan Si was a popular prime minister who is remembered with genuine affection by ordinary citizens in Phnom Penh and elsewhere in Cambodia. When he was sworn in as chairman of the Council of Ministers in February 1982, he inherited an administrative structure that was efficient, although the work undertaken was often slipshod. In March 1983, the minister for agriculture, Kong Sam Ol, sent a memo to Ung Phan at the cabinet of the Council of Ministers in which he set out some of the progress and some of the problems in the "system of work."[122] He explained that uniformity (*aikepheap*) in the relations between the various departments within his ministry was not yet complete. Some departments (*nieyukedan*) often sent correspondence to the leadership level of the ministry without going through the *munti* (senior department), so that the *munti* did not grasp the situation. He thought that the relationship between the ministry and the provincial departments did not operate well and that the whole line was not clear. Not all the problems were bureaucratic ones. By 1984, some of the bad habits of officialdom of the former Sihanouk and Lon Nol regimes had resurfaced: petty corruption, bribery, extortion of extra 'charges' for government services, illegal checkpoints and surcharges, negligence, and bullying. These habits were considered to be an affront to revolutionary morality and detrimental to popular support for the regime. Acting Prime Minister Chea Soth issued a circular on 31 January 1984 in which he admonished that "there are some cadres, staff, workers, security police and our soldiers who have not yet understood clearly about their duties and obligations in serving the revolution, serving the people and they have used their role and rights of authority to create difficulties and display behavior lacking in morality, lacking good breeding, [using] authoritarianism to oppress the people in order to get money, confiscating goods without proper conditions and breaking the law, creating many phenomena making the people unhappy and causing them to lose faith in the party and in the revolutionary state authority, opening the way for the enemy to increase activities of psychological warfare, propaganda to break solidarity between the revolutionary state authority and the people, and causing the energy of the revolution to diminish."[123] He wanted to make a bridge between the people and the state institutions by instructing them all to "arrange to have a room for receiving the people and to assign a representative and assistant staff to resolve all the requests of the citizens in good time."[124] This room should display public notices informing the people of their rights and obligations as citizens and the laws concerning the inspection and resolution of protests and denunciations of citizens, directives for implementing these laws, etc. Relevant information and exhortatory slogans (about not taking bribes or having a "quarrelsome attitude") should be posted at checkpoints along the roads concerning the inspection of travelers and goods. He advised cadres to respond to the people's requests for copies of official

89

documents within two days, and for the cadres to have "polite relations with the people," and they "should not accept money or materials outside of the money for preparing petitions according to the fixed price."[125] Had the party's cadres paid heed to these simple directives, perhaps Cambodian society could truly have been transformed.

Chapter 5

REBUILDING THE ECONOMY

THE DESTRUCTION OF the Cambodian economy had begun in the late 1960s and it was exacerbated by the war and the bombing of the Lon Nol period. The extremist policies of the Pol Pot period shattered the remnants of the economy. Most of Cambodia's later economic woes were blamed on what happened during the DK regime, but despite nostalgic memories Cambodia had never been a Shangri La. It is true that Phnom Penh was praised by its neighbors as the "Pearl of the Orient" but beyond the suburbs, life in rural Cambodia had always been hard, and despite the much-touted occasions during the 1960s when Cambodia produced a modest rice surplus for export, reality for almost all Cambodian farmers was that for two to three months per year there was no rice left in their storehouse and they had to resort to secondary crops or send their men to the city to do dirty manual work or push a pedicab or *cyclo* for the city folk.

The output of the year 1968, when the harvest finally reached the magical figure of three million tons of paddy, including both wet and dry season crops, was the target that the post-1979 government yearned for.[1] That harvest was produced on 2,457,200 hectares. Rubber production that year was 49,060 tons off 50,975 hectares. There were eleven state-owned enterprises for cement, glass, tires, textiles, wood and paper, sugar, fish-canning, a distillery, a company for exporting precious stones and gold, and a tractor company. "Mixed Economy Enterprises" or joint state-private ventures operated in jute, petroleum refining, phosphate, cigarette manufacture and oxygen and acetylene. The private sector was not large. In 1968, by far the largest private enterprise sector was rice-husking and polishing with 1,468 mills at work. The other main private enterprises were sawmills, charcoal kilns, brick and tile kilns and "factories producing aerated waters, syrups, ice cream and ice for domestic consumption." Imports in 1968, overwhelmingly from Japan, cost more than 2.2 million *riel*, which was markedly down on previous years. The value of exports was 1.2 million *riel*.

The downturn after the 1970 coup was dramatic and by 1974 very little of the economy outside the KR-controlled liberated zones in the countryside remained. Damage to economic infrastructure during the fierce civil war was massive. Ney Pena claimed that "four-fifths of the factories, two-thirds of the rubber trees, and between seventy and eighty percent of roads and railways were destroyed," especially by the American bombing.[2] Hildebrand and Porter explained that "an analysis of the total resources used by the government of the Khmer Republic to remain in control of Phnom Penh and a few provincial enclaves shows that by 1974 domestic revenues accounted for only 2.2 percent of these resources, while 95.1 percent came from US assistance," the remainder coming from other foreign assistance.[3] They further claimed that the Lon Nol regime did nothing to prevent massive deaths from starvation; "as a popular Phnom Penh student slogan ran, 'Corruption + Incompetence = The People's Hunger.'"[4] The sense of social service was "so alien to the Cambodian governmental elite that the few foreign-sponsored efforts to provide relief simply put more money in the pockets of wealthy officials."[5]

The economy of Democratic Kampuchea never developed beyond the agricultural, barter-based economy which it established in the liberated zones before 1975. A huge rice harvest was predicted by foreign sources for the 1978–1979 wet season crop. Given the concentration on the paddy crop by the leaders and the massive labor force involved in its production, this should not be surprising. However, as so many witnesses have testified, previous heavy crops disappeared on the back of trucks, perhaps to pay China for the regime's arms purchases or to feed the large DK army.[6] Desbarats says that "gross domestic product, which was around US$3.1 billion in 1968 had fallen to about one-quarter of that level by 1980."[7] That figure would double by 1988 when it reached $1.56 billion, but per capita income in 1989, that is at the end of the PRK, was still less than 75 percent of its 1968 level.[8] The near-zero starting level, ongoing war and security threats, the embargo on credit and trade which it shared with Vietnam, the lack of competent managers, skilled technicians and tradespeople as well as erratic weather conditions all played their part to defeat the best efforts of the PRK regime. At play too was the age-old resistance of Cambodian farmers to pressure applied by the center to work in ways which were alien to them and the failure of efforts by the party to win their consent to change.

THE ECONOMY AT THE BASE

The first crisis which confronted the Phnom Penh government in 1979 was famine. The bumper wet season crop, only partly harvested when the Vietnamese troops invaded, was either fired by the retreating Khmer Rouge troops or left to rot in the fields as the people, newly liberated from the terrible oppression of the later DK years, packed their few remaining possessions and set off in search of their former lives. On 17 February, China's People's Liberation Army forces launched a massive attack against the northern border provinces of Vietnam and captured Lang Son and several other key locations "to teach Vietnam a lesson" for its invasion of Cambodia and to give the KR time to regroup. Tens of thousands of Vietnamese and Chinese are thought to have been killed before the Chinese pulled out on 16 March. Whole PAVN divisions were recalled to defend their country but most Cambodians remember only that the Vietnamese soldiers left "to celebrate Tet."[9] During that month, the Khmer Rouge resurfaced throughout much of the countryside and massacred many villagers in fierce reprisal attacks.[10] By the end of May when the situation had settled down, when few people were left roaming the highways and the Vietnamese had restored security, the country was confronted with the reality of famine.

There were no stores from the previous harvest and even the seed rice had been consumed. The fields which were usually plowed and harrowed with the first of the season's rains were largely untouched and while the rivers and lakes teemed with fish, there were no nets to harvest them.[11] Cambodia was a nation in deep shock and severe emotional depression and few people may have had the energy or will to stave off death. Demographer Ea Meng Try calculated that "throughout the country, 5–10 percent of the population, amounting to 325,000 to 625,000 people may have died of starvation in 1979 . . . food shortages continued in 1980."[12] In 1979 and 1980, according to Desbarats' figures, 137,894 and 43,608 Cambodian refugees respectively were admitted to UNHCR camps on the border with Thailand.[13] Immediate relief was provided by Vietnam as Hun Sen acknowledged:

> In this situation, the support of the Vietnamese people was of great importance. The party and the government of Vietnam provided urgent assistance in the form of food, medicine, equipment and materials to the Kampuchean people who were in need. In addition to the assistance of the government, we saw the assistance of the people of Vietnam whose families sent tens of thousands of parcels to the Kampuchean province twinned with their own province. Some parcels had perhaps one kilogram of milled rice and perhaps one gram of salt; other parcels had a lot more, including clothes . . .[14]

The newly installed government in Phnom Penh sent a request to all the people's revolutionary committees on 7 April 1979, which began, "At present there is starvation in a number of regions" and urged all the provincial committees to take "quick measures to avoid death from starvation."[15] It referred to an earlier circular instructing the army, cadres, workers and staff to be thrifty in the consumption of food, and set quotas of thirteen to sixteen kilograms per month for those engaged in factory production, and nineteen to twenty-one kilograms for the combatants and those doing heavy labor. The rest would receive seven kilograms per month "when salvation gifts

94

allow."[16] "When we see people are short of food, we must hurry to organize cadres to go down immediately to places where it occurs and solve it . . . we must have popular movements in the villages and *sangkat* to help solve the problem together. Districts which have good supplies of food must help districts with shortages."[17]

The chaotic conditions of those early months, and the demands made on the small administration by the emergency created by the famine, delayed the official implementation of agricultural collectivization until 26 May. A circular of that date ordered all cadres to organize the planting of the rice crop following the method of collective labor:

> Village, commune and district committees must organize production groups sharing labor appropriately according to the state of affairs of each region. Draught power, agricultural equipment and rice seed in the village must be shared among the production groups, making use of all village rice land area and securing the highest possible harvest.[18]

To encourage production and no doubt to win favor with the farmers, the circular noted, "the People's Revolutionary Council of Kampuchea will not collect rice or tax the people this year or impose other levies. The rice and precautionary vegetable planting which the people produce is to get a harvest."[19] The people's revolutionary committees were told to "divide up the essential food appropriately according to the situation, by democratic discussion, helping each other and knowing solidarity . . ."[20] At the time of that circular, more than two million people or one-third of the population was short of food, particularly in the eastern provinces of Kompong Cham, Prey Veng and Svay Rieng which had taken the brunt of the fighting in 1978.[21]

In the last week of July there was a conference of the People's Revolutionary Council, the central committee of the Front, representatives of all central ministries and departments, of the armed forces and of all provincial state authorities to assess achievements and to set goals.[22] The conference reported that a wet season crop had been transplanted on 875,000 hectares. By then, "tens of thousands of tons" of aid rice had been distributed to the hungry:

> The government and the people of Vietnam have supported our people with 10,000 tons of rice seed and 20,000 tons of milled rice as aid, 9,000 tons of fuel and 5,000 tons of things to trade and they are continuing to provide other assistance. The governments and people of other countries including the USSR, Laos, GDR, Hungary, Bulgaria, Poland, Czechoslovakia, etc. have provided us with basic assistance . . . Many international organizations have expressed warm support both materially and spiritually for our people.[23]

The emergency relief effort during the first two years of the PRK was vital for millions of Cambodians but the government was always aware that it would end and that Cambodians would have to feed themselves. The most important task for independence was to strengthen the agricultural production groups, "the solidarity groups for increasing the harvest" (*krom samaki bongor bongkaun phal* and hereafter *krom samaki*). Because of the emergency situation, the *krom samaki* were organized on an *ad hoc* basis in 1979, more as a practical response to the desperate plight of many people than for any deliberate political motives. An evaluation survey was conducted following the start of the harvest of the 1979–1980 wet season rice crop. It noted that the system of mutual support had positive value, but the size of the groups (then from forty to fifty families per group) was too large for the competency of the cadres who were required to manage them, and that harvest sharing and distribution was still very confused. As a result, in December 1979, a circular was issued to reduce the size of the *krom samaki* to between fifteen and twenty families each. A confidential report on the work achieved in the first half of 1980 estimated that this adjustment had increased the number of groups from 54,952 to 74,374.[24]

An early 1980 document entitled *Distributing Agricultural Produce within the Solidarity Groups for Increasing the Harvest* admitted that the freedoms allowed in that first season had created problems.[25] Referring to the distribution of the harvest, it noted that "because we didn't encourage it clearly, the distribution that has been done was done according to this method here, that method there and that has not ensured the raising of morale of labor and mutual support into the future. In some places, the distribution is not yet equitable and not yet appropriate and this is causing jealousy among the people."[26] The document set out future guidelines. It advised that "good practice" would make the distinction between the Pol Pot regime and the new regime very clear, that "under our new revolutionary regime, the farmers are masters of increasing the harvest and together with this, are masters of its distribution also. Those who work are those who receive a harvest."[27] The distribution of agricultural production within the *krom samaki* was to be transparent, equitable and reasonable. "Those who do a lot should receive a lot; those who work little should receive a little of the harvest. The elderly, children and those without the strength to do labor receive a portion of food also in order to guarantee their livelihood."[28] Most importantly, the sharing out of the harvest "must be understood by every member of the group and agreed on in democratic meetings . . . Every cadre, group, village and *sangkat* must respect all these democratic rights."[29] The full-time laborer was taken as the measure for calculating shares. "One day's work by a full-time laborer is equal to one 'part' . . . The elderly, the handicapped, those who have lost their strength for labor, widows who have lost their strength for work, orphans and the insane who have no one to depend on are to receive a portion equal to 50–60 percent of the number of working days of the laborer who does the most work in the group."[30] Newborns would receive the same portion as other dependants. The village militia would be paid at the same rate as full-time laborers for the days they drilled. *Krom* leaders were expected to do labor the same as the members in the group and they were expected to receive the same portion as other full-time laborers. The owners of the draught animals were paid at the rate of full-time labor for themselves and either part or full-time rates for the animal. Oxen and water buffalo were in such short supply by 1979 and so important for the agricultural economy that there were separate policies concerning their use.[31] Despite these prescriptions, the people's revolutionary committees were still warned to "be appropriate" and to practice compassion for special cases. They were reminded that "through practice and time we will gain experience and the work of distribution will get better and easier."[32]

In June 1980, Heng Samrin sent a telegram to the key ministries and all the provincial committees noting with relief that "at the commencement of this year's wet season, the weather was kind and gave us rain from the beginning of the year."[33] He urged them to use all means and all their efforts to resolve the problems of the *krom samaki* in order to ensure a good harvest and to double the harvest of the previous year. The center made plans to buy rice from the farmers and to sell the farmers essential manufactured goods at the end of the 1980–1981 wet season harvest. The objectives of this plan were three-fold:

> To make the farmers happily strive for the production of staple food items in order to have commodities according to their needs and to guarantee their livelihood at the same time; To start the circulation of the *riel* to make it widespread in the countryside; For the state to have the staple food items in order to provision the army, the cadres, staff and to serve other urgent requests.[34]

There was, theoretically at least, no compulsion to sell to the state: "the farmers have the right to sell, exchange, transport and use all those products freely, keep for use in the family or sell in order to get money to buy other things according to their own needs, without anyone having the right to force them."[35] The farmers were free to sell in the free market or to sell to the state and the document promised that "the state will buy according to the market price and will hand over money immediately."[36]

The state planned to buy 100,000–110,000 tons of paddy and corn from that 1980–1981 harvest.[37] Each province was advised of the quota to be purchased; for instance, Battambang was to purchase 15,000 tons, Siem Reap 12,000 tons, Kompong Cham 10,000 tons, and so on. Eighteen commodities were to be on sale, including sugar, milk, cooking oil, salt, alcohol, cigarettes, cloth and clothes, soap, pots, pans and eating utensils, paraffin, tires and inner tubes, batteries, and flashlight batteries. The total retail value of these goods amounted to 171,665,000 *riel*. For this plan to achieve success, it required the full cooperation of the ministries of commerce, agriculture, industry, finance and banking, communications, and propaganda/information/culture. Each ministry was advised of its role. The role of the Ministry of Propaganda was crucial for providing "important definitions and essential meanings of the principles of the Front and the People's Revolutionary Council in the purchasing of staple food . . . and the selling of manufactured goods to the farmers (as well as) the duty of all state authorities for the cause of defending and building the nation at the present time."[38] Specific tasks were enumerated for the provincial and local people's revolutionary committees.

To motivate the farmers to increase the harvest and particularly to win the farmers' active support for the new regime, the family economy was encouraged and promoted. An undated document, probably drawn up late in 1980 began: "At present and in the future also, the expansion of the collective economy is the duty of farmers and workers and the leadership which must progress towards socialism step by step."[39] However, in view of the inevitable difficulties that the farmers would face in the time ahead, "in order to diminish all those difficulties, the Front and the People's Revolutionary Council of Kampuchea have issued correct principles for the expansion of the family economy in order to complement the collective economy."[40] It noted that early policies had produced good results. Those policies included:

1. Sharing the land to allow each family to build a home and to make gardens for families to plant fruit trees or early crops;
2. Lending families extra land, that being the land which the village group and the *sangkat* cannot use or do not yet use for a harvest;
3. Organizing the clearing and use of formerly cultivated

land by groups and families on large areas of land which have been fallow for a long time.[41]

The family economy had played an important role in defeating the famine and it was useful for helping to develop fallow land and for encouraging the planting of diverse crops, as well as for animal-raising, but it was necessary to give the system some uniformity. Land allocated to families for private use, that is for the home and the family garden, was to be from 1,500 to 2,000 square meters, where possible. Families were allowed to retain their former family plots, regardless of size, except where "conditions are cramped." Should late-comers contest the land allocation, "get the two parties to negotiate with each other in order to avoid a situation that would break their solidarity."[42] Families or small groups of two or three families could borrow land which was not being worked by the *krom samaki*, on the understanding that the land would be returned to the *krom* when it needed to work that land. The borrowers should guarantee to undertake production on land before borrowing it. The local committees were urged to develop traditional craft occupations such as weaving, making pots and pans, carpentry, etc. The document explained that the collective economy and the family economy had mutual benefits. "Therefore each group member must strive hard on both sides not to let the family economy stand in the way of the collective economy and not allow the collective economy to stand in the way of the family economy either."[43] The *krom samaki* brought both aspects of the village economy together "by providing seed, technical guidance, giving farmers time to do labor to serve the family economy and by lending basic equipment, etc."[44] With regard to the family economy, "whatever a family produces, that family takes all that produce . . . The state does not tax or buy the produce of the family economy but if a family wants to sell to the state, the state can buy that produce according to the free market price."[45] The target was to have two million hectares of arable land under production as soon as possible. By the end of 1980, less than half the target had been reached. The family economy was supposed to help achieve the target.

Many of the policies introduced by the Cambodian government at this stage seem to have been experimental and to have had little in common with Vietnam's rural policy, although that was also in flux. Full collectivization was obviously impossible without a lot of coercion by the state authorities but, in the immediate post–Pol Pot situation, state coercion was both unwise and impractical. There simply were not enough cadres to enforce and then manage full-scale collectivization. Rural cadres, many of them illiterate and poorly educated in socialist principles and practices, were also inexperienced in management and administration. At the center, relations between line ministries were unclear, uncoordinated and frequently uncooperative.[46] In any event, after the catastrophe of the DK's efforts to impose collectivization, the farmers undoubtedly would have resisted such attempts which would have weakened the economy even further. The PRK therefore proceeded with agricultural collectivization very cautiously.

Given the lack of experience of central cadres and local leaders, mistakes were inevitable and the people's patience was sorely tried at times. What appears to be the text of a speech prepared by the Ministry of State Commerce and delivered at the start of the 1980–1981 harvest describes some of those slips between policy and practice in the matter of buying rice and corn from the farmers during that first good season.[47] Some of the purchasing offices did not receive money from the center in time to exchange it for grain with the farmers, and the business of weighing was so confused that some people had to wait for two or three days before they could weigh their corn and then another day, usually two, to get their money. In some districts, "the people became annoyed" with the lack of proper management.[48] The purchasing offices also became credit agencies as the government introduced its rural credit program. In Kandal, for instance, the commune chiefs were responsible for this. Some communes lent rice while others lent money. Manufactured goods were also given on credit. The people agreed to borrow and promised to repay in paddy to the state. The writer noted that "lending money is easier" because lending paddy involved difficulties with weighing, bagging and transport but warned that, in the matter of financial credit, monitoring was essential and there had to be "enough cadres" to do it.[49] The rural credit scheme had the aim of extending the circulation of the new *riel* and of increasing the provision of essential commodity items to the farmers. As the document/speech explained, "This is a policy to help the farmers at the end of the month to have money to buy staple food, to buy essential things to guarantee their livelihood and to take care of the growing rice."[50] Determining the correct price for purchasing rice was difficult but it had "important political and economic meaning."[51] If the price was correct, the farmers would be happy, and would produce a lot and sell a lot to the state. If the price was too low, the farmers would neglect production and if it was too high, it would affect the cost of living, "making life difficult for the people. It is also inter-related with state savings."[52] Cadres had to note the market prices, consult with the people and be familiar "with the ideas of all sides."[53] Districts should have just one price, provinces could buy for one or two prices but the price had to follow the conditions and be appropriate. Storehouses or granaries were another matter because "in the work of buying paddy, apart from the preparations of having enough money to do the buying, you must prepare enough storehouses for stocking it . . . The repair of storehouses and the building of new storehouses is not something you can do in a morning or an afternoon. Therefore, after this conference ends go back and start work immediately."[54]

The next wet season harvest was a disappointment. Flood and drought took their toll by actually reducing the cropping area by almost half of one percent (to a total of 1,350,000 hectares); the yield was lower than the previous year by approximately 350 tons. Despite this, state purchasing of rice showed that the lessons of the previous year had been well learned: "The purchasing of rice this year was fast in settling the money to the people and in many places the people were happy, not grumbling like last year."[55]

In fact, on 15 April 1982, the Central Commission for Buying Rice could announce that they had bought 166,732 tons of rice which was 50,000 tons over the plan.[56] This was declared "a huge result for both politics and the economy" being due to "the leadership and guidance from the party and the state authority at all levels from the center to the provinces, districts, and communes . . . "[57] The commission noted that the pricing policy was appropriate and raised morale, while the preparations ranging from organizing the cadres to preparing the bags were done with "mastery and in good time." Some of the weak points included debt recovery, irregularities in the buying of seed rice and "the weighing hasn't been organized yet, the sorting out of money to give to the people is slow and the people have to wait a long time so the businessmen take advantage to buy cheaply and sell expensively to the state."[58]

In June 1982, the Ministry of Agriculture reported that it planned to begin intensified rice production on 100,000 hectares in eight provinces of both dry and wet season crops and "as for regions where the people do not have faith in intensification, the ministry has sent agricultural technicians to go and cooperate with the regional state authority. . . "[59] However, many problems and shortages remained. Intensification could not proceed without fertilizer, especially phosphate, and the state could guarantee only 20 percent of requirements. Despite the problems, this new policy suggests growing self-confidence on the part of the administration. On the other hand, the PRK leaders were still anxious about perceptions of their regime's legitimacy and sensitive to outside criticism of dependency on Vietnam. Even a simple economic transaction with Vietnam, for example, had to have the people's approval. On 13 November 1982, prime minister Chan Si announced that the increase in agricultural production had ensured the people a good livelihood.[60] In fact, there was a surplus in the state granaries which threatened to spoil. The politburo and the Council of Ministers had therefore decided to exchange paddy with Vietnam for some essential items such as cloth, nets, corrugated iron, bags, et cetera. "This is a necessary duty in economic cooperation especially with Vietnam in order to serve the advantage of our people throughout the country."[61] Chan Si, however, was fully aware that "in this exchange, the enemy can take advantage among the ranks of the people in order to propagandize and twist the facts about our Kampuchean revolution."[62] Therefore, he urged the state authority at all levels to "organize measures to extend to all leading cadres in the provinces for them to mobilize the people to understand clearly about the principles of the party and our government in eliminating all the ruses of propaganda of the enemy in the above matter."[63]

Constant concern with how outsiders might judge the regime, and anxiety about winning popularity within the country, allowed contradictions between theory and practice to flourish. These contradictions were already apparent within the economy. Chea Soth, minister for planning and chairman of the Central Commission Responsible for State Purchases of the Farmers' Paddy, in summing up the achievements of 1982, and announcing the goals of the 1983 state plan, praised the economic achievements of the base claiming, "We say our state can ensure staple food for cadres, staff and state workers as well as the troops, including the Vietnamese troops."[64] He made the obvious point, however, that while the *krom samaki* were supposed to be the basic building blocks of the collective economy, in fact, very few characteristics of the collective economy existed. He noted that the private economy had "regained its shape [and] among workers, laborers and businessmen, there are some who have started to become capitalist businessmen already."[65] This early trend was never reversed.

At the seventh plenum of the central committee, 19–22 December 1983, Chea Soth presented a report which summed up the situation of the *krom samaki*.[66] There were then 102,500 groups, consisting of 1,340,000 families, participating in the various models of *krom samaki*. On average, the *krom* represented ten to fifteen families and from twenty-five to thirty workers on a land area of fifteen to twenty hectares. "However, because the situation and the conditions of production and the management capacity of cadres and the consciousness of the people in each region and each base is different, the *krom samaki* have various forms of management."[67] In general, he explained, there were three types of *krom samaki*. The first type was the model collective: the *krom* directly managed all the riceland, the draught animals were kept for use within the group, and the *krom* leader was responsible for sharing out production work from sowing to harvesting, and also for the distribution of food within the group. According to the second type, the *krom* managed the riceland but the group divided itself into smaller teams of three to five families, and those teams assigned the labor for themselves and also shared out the food according to their own team (*puok*). Each *puok* had at least one ox or buffalo. The *krom* leader acted as overseer. In the third type, the *krom* worked some of the land collectively but other areas were handed over to families to work separately or according to mutual assistance practices (*provas day kinear tveu*). Within this third type there were many variations. For instance, in Battambang and Siem Reap, the *krom* worked the rice fields collectively but families worked their own gardens (*chamcar*) individually. However, in the northeast and highland forested regions, the *krom* worked the *chamcar* collectively, but grew their own rice. The methods of sharing food were also numerous. Chea Soth reported that some *krom samaki* had started to create rice funds to pay the collective work expenses of the *krom*, to support the poor in the village, or to sell to members of the *krom* when they were hit by natural disasters. Some regions were actively engaged in intensification practices and in intra-group competitions (*bralong branang*) to vie for 3–4t/ha yields per season. Some *krom samaki* were actively engaged in local crafts such as smelting, carpentry, making ploughs, weaving mats, scarves, and mosquito nets.

According to this document, which provides a very detailed analysis of rural conditions, the first type of *krom samaki* had the preferred socialist characteristics but it suffered from poor management by inexperienced or incompetent cadres. Its style of food distribution caused jealousy and friction "between families who have many mouths to feed and those with few mouths to feed, between those who work actively and those who are lazy" and this had negative effects on the morale of "those who are active in labor."[68] The *krom* leader was usually disgruntled about receiving a share only equal to that of other full-time laborers. By the end of 1983, perhaps no more than 10 percent of all the *krom samaki* operated according to the collective method. The second type which relied on mutual support (*provas day kinear*), accounted for about 50 percent of the solidarity groups and had "management appropriate for the competency of the cadres of the *krom*, appropriate for the aims of most of the people and is liked by the masses."[69] The report noted that "in fact, many [of this type of] *krom samaki* have become private enterprises" because when a farmer works a piece of land for his family "it becomes as though he is working for himself."[70] The ownership or lack of draught animals in this second system of management was already causing inequalities within the *krom samaki*. The third type was, in effect, private enterprise, and the *krom* chief was responsible only for organizing political study, buying materials and goods for the people in the *krom*, and protecting security. Production was on an individual basis or performed according to village traditions but the *krom* managed the land. The goal was to turn this type three into type two and do away with type three altogether.

The report noted that the family economy, that is, the allocation of plots of land for families to work privately, had made the countryside new again. Families had made protective fences, planted vegetables and fruit trees, dug fishponds, and so on. "Farmers not only have paddy for eating; they also sell tens of thousands of tons of paddy to the state each year. All families have the possibility to buy goods for the family, agricultural equipment, clothes and commodities for their children's schooling, et cetera."[71] The constant, nagging problem, however, was the level of culture and management capacity of the cadres, and "there are some places where the state authority does not strive to mobilize the *krom samaki* and does not cooperate closely in guiding, supporting and strengthening the *krom samaki* and the family economy."[72] Many of the cadres and group leaders could not read or write, so keeping a tally of days worked by individual members of the *krom* was beyond their capacity. Under those circumstances, it was virtually impossible to practice the collective system of management in a fair and democratic fashion, even if the political will of the cadres had been strong. The report noted, "According to the experience of the *krom samaki* that work well, this is because there are *krom* cadres doing the job with good morality who strive hard in the work together with the *krom* and, generally speaking, they have received upgrading in management and the study of policy."[73] Recommendations were for developing the capacity and potential of the cadres and the people within the *krom samaki* for setting out "the function and the concrete duties of the chief and the deputy chief of the *krom* and the secretary with the job of general organization. The chief and deputy chief should know how to make a plan for regular production, how to manage the labor force, share the food, and share out the general work within the *krom*. The state must set down a system of bonuses for *krom* cadres in order to make them happy in their work."[74] The report ended:

> We should educate and guide the people to understand deeply and clearly that only when there is organization to increase the harvest as a collective can we eradicate the shoots of oppression and make all the people equal, happily supporting each other in increasing the harvest and the livelihood of all the people. Then all families will eat to their fill and have happiness.[75]

In 1984, it was decided to expand the intensification program to fifteen provinces on a total of a quarter of a million hectares (of the 1.7 million hectares then under production). The early season rains were good, which promised a bountiful harvest and there had been a satisfactory increase in the number of draught animals. However, the state was still having difficulty buying agricultural produce other than paddy from the farmers. This was the fault of the local authorities who neglected to buy industrial crops, "letting businessmen play with the prices, competing to buy with the state in times when the state has fixed low prices."[76] The delivery of manufactured items to the rural areas was inefficient, made worse by fears of enemy attacks as the security situation throughout the country became increasingly complicated. Even worse, this report continued, "there are some cadres with responsibility for commercial work (in the provinces and in the center), who take advantage and collude with the issuing of state goods to businessmen in order to make a profit, particularly when the price in the free market is very different from the state price. The workers have to buy from the businessmen at high prices.

Some goods are twice the price of the state. This has a detrimental effect on the purchase of agricultural and fishery produce and on the state also."[77] This black marketeering was akin to treason, "taking the goods which we make and putting them into the hands of businessmen to act like a gun to fight us."[78]

In 1984, the government introduced agricultural taxes for the first time. The "patriotic contribution" was a farming tax on the amount and quality of land farmed rather than on production.[79] The minister for agriculture, Kong Sam Ol, is reported to have said that only rice fields producing more than one ton per hectare per year would be taxed. The rate was to be 100 kg per hectare in the fertile plains region and 60–80 kg in coastal regions. The family economy was not taxed, and "as an incentive for military service, taxes will be reduced for families of soldiers or security forces, whether they are still in active service, disabled or dead."[80] The government moved very cautiously in introducing what Hiebert noted could become one of the regime's most sensitive policies: "It has tried to win the support of peasants by showing it is different from its draconian predecessor. Three years ago, I asked a group of farmers in the southern province of Takeo how the present authorities were different from the Sihanouk or Lon Nol governments of the 1960s and early 1970s. 'They don't collect taxes,' the farmers responded with obvious approval."[81]

On 3 August 1984, the central committee issued a decision, the aim of which was to make the management and use of agricultural land "improve in an orderly fashion according to socialist objectives which are:

> 1. The leadership is that of the People's Revolutionary Party of Kampuchea which is pure, proper and splendid;
> 2. The land is the property of the state; the management and use of the land is appropriate, ensuring its good quality and building new relations of production according to objectives advancing towards socialism."[82]

This important document stipulated precisely how the land was to be used and managed for its various purposes, and who had the right to decide on its allocation. It concluded by stressing that "the center has a need for key people and cadres in all sections, at all levels to understand [this decision] sufficiently and to extend [it] widely among the masses in order to increase the management and use of farming land, to promote production, to build a firm revolutionary force, to build a new countryside, to raise the awareness of the masses towards eliminating each destructive trick by the enemy against the revolution of our country."[83] To this end, in September, the government created a National Committee for Guiding the Movement to Strengthen the *Krom Samaki*, with Kong Sam Ol, minister for agriculture, as chairman of its central commission. The committee's job was to arrange courses in the work of leading and mobilizing movements to strengthen the solidarity groups; that is, to train cadres at the base in their management role.

According to Viviane Frings, in 1984 and 1985, propaganda missions were organized and state employees were required to spend three months in the countryside encouraging the peasants to work collectively and engaging in social work.[84] Hun Sen described his own experience of this policy when he went with "more than one hundred cadres" from the Ministry of Foreign Affairs to a commune on the outskirts of Phnom Penh to transplant rice:

> I was transplanting with about twenty people . . . After a while, I had a conversation with them. First, I asked them what kind of *krom samaki* it was. The answer came that it was a No. 1 *krom samaki*. Then I asked how many families there were. They replied that they were not sure but perhaps there were twenty-five families. I asked again how much land these twenty-five families had. There was no answer. Then a talkative "older sister" replied that they didn't know, it all depended on what "they" told you to go and do and you went and did it. I was surprised that the farmers hadn't yet taken mastery over the land or their work.[85]

Hun Sen claimed that some cadres on the base falsely reported that they had organized No.1 *krom samaki* "as if they were very proud of this type of *krom samaki*," or because they were afraid of criticism "for not leading the people towards socialism."[86] Other cadres at the base, he said, became anxious about the whole notion of private property, "of the matter of land and the means of production and distribution" and implemented policies of rotating land among the families in the *krom samaki*, which destroyed the farmers' incentive for improving the land they worked or for clearing new land. The whole policy of agricultural collectivization appears to have been poorly understood and consequently mismanaged and incorrectly applied. When it did appear to work, the results turned out to be merely window-dressing, as in the case of the model villages.

Hundreds of model villages were created in 1984 and 1985 to encourage collectivization. In theory, Frings says, they were supposed to be "close to roads and easily accessible so that other people could benefit from the experiment and see the advantages of working collectively."[87] In practice, however, as a senior official of the Ministry of Agriculture admitted to her, the choice of village was made according to family ties by staff of the ministry's Department of Political and Economic Management, or on the suggestion of the local authorities "who were not more objective."[88] Those villages chosen by the Ministry of Agriculture to act as models received rice mills and water pumps, adequate fertilizer and high quality seed rice, all provided by foreign assistance. For the most part, however, the designation of "model village" was meaningless "since the central government lacked the resources to support so many villages and the *khum* (commune) were not able to do anything by themselves."[89] That there were hundreds of them, Frings argues, was because "the criterion to be considered to be a model village was the production results of a given village" and had nothing to do with state assistance or methods of production.[90] Without some form of agricultural collectivization, the PRK leaders could hardly claim that they were advancing towards socialism so, to this end, the solidarity production groups, the *krom samaki*, were the very wheels of the revolution. By the end of 1984, they had served a useful purpose in helping to restore normalcy to the lives of Cambodian farmers. They had also provided important means of social welfare and support for the thousands of widows, orphans, and the debilitated created by the Pol Pot regime, and they had helped to bring order to the countryside. Once this was achieved, the *krom samaki* had little further benefit and therefore no longer made sense, because the real purpose of the *krom samaki*, collectivization of agriculture in the name of social revolution, meant nothing to the rural people. In many parts of the country even the pretence of collectivized agriculture had disappeared well before the end of 1984. About half of the female respondents in a qualitative research study conducted in 1995 in villages throughout the country reported that the *krom samaki* system lasted less than a year, while one-third reported that it ended in their villages in 1983.[91] Most farmers expected that "normalcy" meant a return to life as it was lived before the war and they appear to have had very little interest in advancing towards socialism or any other goal dictated by foreign ideas. Thus, quite obviously at this point, without large-scale propaganda efforts and the unstinting honest efforts of the party's cadres, the revolution was going to capitulate to the will of the peasantry: in the words of the commonly used analogy of the PRK leaders, "the tail was going to wag the dog."

The sharp irregularities in the way the *krom samaki* operated throughout the country by the end of 1984, with only 10 percent of them practicing anything resembling a collective economy, did not augur well for the revolution's goals. The failure by the government to provide the essential incentives of traction power, fertilizer, seed, et cetera, made the whole notion of collectivization meaningless once the food emergency had passed. Moreover, by the end of 1984, as Chea Soth had already admitted, corruption, greed and malpractice were already creeping back into the administration system. Theory and practice were diverging, and instead of extending its ideological hegemony, the PRK government seemed to be satisfied with maintaining its popularity with the masses through low taxation and rural credit schemes.

THE ECONOMY AT THE CENTER

The Pol Pot regime had abandoned the domestic market. There was no exchange of goods and no official currency. In 1979, the victors found stacks of freshly printed notes which the DK must have planned to use but finally rejected. They had also operated a few factories and plants in Phnom Penh, but they destroyed the machines before they withdrew. Many of the engineers, technicians, and skilled workers of the previous regimes had been killed, the survivors scattered or fled abroad. Hun Sen wrote with admiration of those who came back to work the factories:

> Workers who were left from the killing and who were scattered in distant places came back to their native villages and their true native village was the factory where they used to work before the Pol Pot era had scattered them. Even though the factory was not yet producing, they came to live beside the factories and came together to protect the factory. In many places, the workers collected spare parts and repaired the factories even though they did not yet have organization from the state authorities.[92]

Vietnam sent engineers and specialists, as well as spare parts and raw materials, to start production again. According to Hun Sen, they worked alongside the Cambodian workers to get the power stations and the waterworks of Phnom Penh functioning and continued to work in other factories to get them operating also.

In the first chaotic year, markets quickly revived on the basis of private exchange. The main medium of exchange was rice, measured in empty condensed milk cans. More expensive items were paid for in gold which the people had kept on them throughout the DK regime, or which they had buried before they were evacuated from Phnom Penh in April 1975. The Vietnamese *dong* and the Thai *baht* were also used as currency. There was no attempt to regulate the market at this stage, because there was urgent demand for essential items which the state could not provide. Gold was used to import goods from

Thailand through Koh Kong, Battambang and Siem Reap, and also from Vietnam. In fact, this amounted to state-sanctioned smuggling by petty traders, who crossed the country on bicycles from border to border. Later, large-scale smuggling by a handful of powerful *towkay* (Chinese business owners) in Koh Kong and Kompong Som would give the government problems, but in the early days the smugglers fulfilled an important economic function. The urgent task for the government was the introduction and circulation of new currency, the *riel*.

The document, *A Number of Matters Concerning the Clarification of the Value of Money and the Price of Goods in Kampuchea in the Time Ahead* declared, "Now we are going to circulate revolutionary money, even if it is still called the *riel* as before."[93] Value was the important thing; the revolutionary task was to "change the awareness of this and make this very clear":

1. Money must be a means for the easy exchange of goods between producer and consumer in the various components of the economy within the society;
2. Money must show the strength of the socialist economy which is still rebuilding itself and will spread out rapidly.[94]

Because rice had already established its purchasing power, it was decided to determine the value of one *riel* as equal to one kilogram of milled rice. "Compare it to various foreign currencies. Take the American dollar . . . and we see that the value of one ton of milled rice is equal to one thousand *riel*. The value of one ton of milled rice on the international market is currently equal to $250. Therefore, one *riel* equals twenty-five cents or one dollar equals four *riel*."[95] The document discussed the need to develop an industrial base, but "in order to change and develop industry, we have to have capital to build the whole base again, we have to have skilled workers, and we have to expand exports in order to import machines, spare parts and raw materials. Therefore, for a long time, industrial production for the people will not achieve sufficiency and the price of goods will be high."[96] It warned that the situation would be difficult for everyone until agricultural sustainability was reached, so "we must explain to all the people that even if this is the case, if we compare the situation to former regimes, living standards are actually better because before the farmers had to put up with the aggression of inspectors, money lenders (extorting severe interest) and businessmen (who bought cheaply and sold expensively). Nowadays, all these acts of aggression have been erased by the revolution and farmers can keep their own harvest after making their contribution to the cause of building the nation."[97]

The setting of prices followed this theorem: If one kilogram of paddy is equal to 70 percent of the price of milled rice, then considering the cost of transport, milling and storing, one kilogram of paddy is worth 55 percent of one kilogram of milled rice, that is 0.55 *riel*. All other agricultural produce and industrial crops such as kapok, jute, sugar cane, coffee, tobacco, as well as the product from raising animals, could be estimated. "For instance, one kilogram of pork is equal to seven kilograms of paddy, et cetera."[98] Motivation factors were added in. Corn kernels were worth 1.1 kg of paddy, to encourage farmers to grow corn "for the raising of pigs for meat and for fertilizer in order to plant more crops later and to get higher results than from planting paddy and other crops."[99] Pepper was priced to guarantee an export advantage, but kapok was priced higher than international markets for reasons that are not explained. The text ends with advice for the state about savings, and "don't allow import activities to develop into a private economy; don't allow profiteering."[100]

The *riel* was put into circulation on 20 March 1980. Around that date, there was a conference chaired by Pen Sovann, vice-chairman of the People's Revolutionary Council. An undated document outlines the agenda of that conference in a series of questions around two topics. The first was "Concerning the principles and measures for collecting and changing Vietnamese currency and forbidding the use of foreign currencies in Kampuchean markets towards strengthening and uplifting the *riel* which is the one and only legal currency in Kampuchean markets" and the other was "Concerning pricing and commercial activities." These were important issues which included buying paddy and other produce from the farmers, pricing goods in the state retail outlets, and guaranteeing the livelihood of combatants, cadres, workers, and staff, in the state employ. The fast and efficient exchange of *dong* for *riel* (three for one), and the successful introduction of the *riel* into the market was considered to be a "substantial achievement for us, following on from achievements in the harvest to overcome hunger and in showing our fighting strength as well as the occasion of the festival to commemorate 7 January."[101] The document noted that the circulation of the *riel* was still very small because the people's purchasing power was very small and there were not many goods in the market to buy. The author warned that if the free market price for some essential items dropped below that of the price in the state outlets, the state should not follow the market: "Any goods, any place and any time that the market has better goods, cheaper prices, then we let cadres and the people buy them at the market."[102]

Care had to be taken to ensure sufficient provision to cadres of seven goods: rice, salt, cooking oil, sugar, soap, cloth, and fish. A circular issued on 25 March announced that the state would sell essential goods and foodstuffs to its cadres and staff at fixed prices which "should ensure solidarity and expand awareness of dealing with problems together between cadres at the higher and lower levels."[103] Ministers and others at the salary level of 230 *riel* per month were entitled to four kilograms of meat or lard, eight kilograms of fish, two kilograms of sugar, and two liters of fish oil or fish paste (*prahok*), per month. Deputy ministers were paid 200 *riel* with commensurate quantities of the same. Chiefs of department, deputy-chiefs, and cadres with a salary level of 140 *riel* and less than 200 *riel* received two kilograms of meat or lard, five kilograms of fish, one kilogram of sugar, and two liters of fish oil or paste. Those cadres earning less than 140 *riel* per month were entitled to only half a kilogram of meat or lard and half a kilogram of sugar.[104] The ministries for commerce and finance were responsible for setting the prices of those commodities but "if necessary, the state can supplement the cost in order to take care that the selling price is appropriate and sustainable."[105] Some other items such as soap, cigarettes, flour, et cetera would be shared among the ministries/departments, factories and enterprises, for sale to cadres and state workers at guaranteed prices. "For other goods, cadres, workers and staff must buy them as the people do."[106] The circular was effective from April until the end of 1980.

Goods for sale in the Phnom Penh markets were expensive in comparison with civil service salaries. According to the *Revised List of Sale Prices for Goods on Sale in Phnom Penh Markets*, a boy's white school shirt cost 13 *riel*, the common blanket made of mixed kapok thread cost 80 *riel*, a bicycle inner tube was 24 *riel* and a pair of rubber sandals cost eight *riel*.[107] The high prices reflected the short supply in the market, but "if we decide on cheap retail prices, within just a short period, we will sell everything and the living standards of the people will still be unchanged."[108] In its first year, between 400 and 450 million *riel* went into circulation; 250 million for salary supplements and 100 million to the farmers as payment for their paddy and as loans. The government had to back this spending with a quantity of goods with a value of between 350 and 400 million *riel*. These are intricate calculations, balancing anticipated demand with supply and then quantifying the demand; for instance, ten million meters of cloth at eight *riel* per meter, one hundred thousand kettles at twenty *riel* each, five million rice bowls each costing one *riel*, and three thousand tons of soap at twelve *riel* per bar. Reading the documents, one senses that in introducing the money economy the government was crossing a river by stepping on the back of crocodiles. The lives of the people were generally wretched and they regarded all government action with well-deserved suspicion, if not distrust. In return for their cooperation in selling their produce to the state, the farmers expected a worthwhile return in consumer items and agricultural equipment and supplies. The free market was an essential supplier of many of those goods and therefore had to be tolerated. On the other hand, the government could not allow the merchants and middlemen untrammeled access to the farmers' produce and thus allow them to control or manipulate the price of agricultural produce, particularly staple foods. This would have had serious effects on the living standards of the army and the civil service and, consequently, on their loyalty to the regime. Whichever way it steered the economy, the government saw only dangers. The dilemma is explained in a document from early 1980 which wisely states:

> Awareness is the basis of policy: high class and low now join fortunes together because what we produce is still not sufficient for our food needs. Our country is poor, the people are in a difficult and miserable state, lacking food and still dependent on aid at every level. The army and the families of combatants need to improve their lot a little. Have compassion for intellectuals and don't oppress them too much for this will create confusion. We need to do more research into the matter of old cadres. We should have financial assistance for cadres at commune level and the militia shouldbe cared for by the state (budget for national defense).[109]

The 1980 state budget was declared a success. Total expenditure was 294,546,000 *riel*.[110] Revenue "from the base economy of the state, revenue from taxation and revenue from international assistance" was only 25,477,000 *riel*, which admittedly created "a large deficit."[111] The report explained that this was because the government had decided not to tax the people yet, "because it wanted to give people's living standards sufficient sustainability first."[112] The 1981 budget which was being implemented at the time of that report represented a five-fold increase with estimated revenues of between 1 billion and 1.2 billion *riel* (70 percent from international assistance) and expenditure between 1.4 billion and 1.6 billion *riel*. "This (1981) state budget can achieve balance if taxation is implemented but up until now the People's Revolutionary Council of Kampuchea understands that this is a special time and we should wait for the People's Assembly to examine the matter and make a decision."[113]

Cambodia desperately needed revenue sources. Rice production would not reach the point of reliably meeting the people's basic needs until 1986, let alone providing a surplus for export. Taxation was unpopular and the government was very reluctant to spend its very small political credit on forcing people to pay tax. Rubber was seen as a potential export earner. In his book on the period, *Dap Chhnam ney Damnaeur*

Kampuchea 1979–1989 [Cambodia's Ten-Year Journey], which was published in Phnom Penh in December 1988, Hun Sen mentioned that the DK regime had practiced some rubber exploitation, but many of the rubber technicians were killed, and "after liberation it was as though we had nothing left apart from the rubber trees and areas of land full of mines which the Pol Potists had laid before they left."[114] On 13 December 1980 there was a working meeting of the People's Revolutionary Council concerning restoring the rubber plantations.[115] The meeting was chaired by Heng Samrin, and among the seventeen participants were three Vietnamese experts and an interpreter. The minutes record that of the 50,000 hectares of rubber plantations, only 5,000 hectares had been redeveloped by then; the Chup factory was 62 percent repaired and by the end of 1980 it had produced 1,200 tons of rubber. There were many problems and the living standard and health of the plantation workers was very poor, much lower than that of farmers in neighboring regions. All ministers were given special requests to fulfill in order to meet the needs of restoring the rubber industry and helping to relieve the suffering of the rubber workers.

At the second session of the Council of Ministers (28–29 July 1981), prime minister Pen Sovann expressed some of his frustration over the management of the rubber plantations. He accused some workers and cadres of stealing the rubber to sell it in Vietnam. The lives of the rubber workers, he noted, still had not improved:

> The life of the rubber workers is very difficult but since 1979 it hasn't radically changed. Nevertheless, their awareness/attitude is good and there are some workers with long experience of rubber exploitation; there are a few 65 year-olds still working . . . They work very hard; some stand soaked in stinking water the whole day but they don't have enough food to eat. Some months they do and some months they don't. They don't have enough salt, let alone *prahok*. They don't have enough clothes. Their housing is inadequate, their children don't have clothes and, in truth, they have to struggle for everything. They don't demand much, just work tools and protective work clothing (gum boots and hats).[116]

He added, "Our state considers rubber to be an important source of exports. Therefore, if the living standard of the rubber workers remains like this, we cannot achieve [our goals]."[117] The government was aware that the non-refundable assistance which had been provided by the fraternal socialist countries since January 1979 was drying up. It needed industrial crops like rubber to pay for its increasing debts. Other export sources were fish and timber and in 1983, the government formed *krom samaki* for both fishery and forestry exploitation, and initiated regulations to boost production of export commodities. By the end of 1984, however, the three export sectors had achieved poorly and many problems remained to be solved.

In an effort to curb imports and also to raise state revenue an import tax was introduced according to a decree-law issued on 27 November 1982.[118] By the first week in February the following year, it had contributed eleven million *riel* to the state coffers but it was a difficult and dangerous exercise. Chan Phin, minister for finance, submitted a report on 15 February 1983.[119] The "big" smugglers were the first challenge. In Kompong Som there were about twenty businessmen with a lot of capital and large boats illegally importing between two and three million *riel* worth of merchandise in each boatload. In Koh Kong also there were a lot of smugglers, "but almost all the important activities have fallen into the hands of two or three big businessmen only."[120] The smugglers were highly organized and skilled in tax evasion. The minister noted that "the management of collecting import taxes has not had a bad effect on the political value of the state and has not had an effect on the living standards of the people. So far, prices in the market of some essential goods such as cloth, et cetera have not changed significantly."[121] All the problems, he said, came from the attitudes and activities of the businessmen which caused "confusion and difficulties for management and made it easy for them to cheat on incoming goods and evading tax."[122] He warned, "If we don't have a proper level of support, tax collection won't have a good result and income will diminish along with the system . . . some people rely on arms to threaten taxation staff and bribe them . . ."[123] He estimated that in one month the state lost at least ten million *riel* on cigarette smuggling by rail alone. When state officers had intervened, "they were pushed and shoved by armed groups and received threats at the end of a gun from others."[124] When smuggling by road, the businessmen used military license plates and had military riding on the trucks and they refused to stop at the inspection posts. "These things happen every day . . . we have to open the barrier because if we don't they will clearly smash it to bits and there will be major disputes."[125] Vietnamese troops were actively engaged in smuggling cigarettes and cloth from Kompong Som. In one incident, a Cambodian soldier who tried to inspect such a vehicle "was slapped with a gun and there were some threats."[126] Civilian tax officers who tried to do their job were told, "Civilian units do not have the right to inspect military vehicles."[127] The minister thought that the problems were vast and that his department had achieved only 30 percent of its goals. The tax rate was increased starting from 1 April 1984. There were no longer exemptions for essential items. Goods were taxed at rates between 5 and 60 percent.[128]

State planning commenced in 1982. Until 1986, these were annual plans only. Chan Phin submitted his *Report on The Financial Situation and the Proposed State Budget for 1984* to the sixth session of the National Assembly.[129] In March 1983, he explained, the Council of Ministers had handed over the management of income and budgetary expenditure to the ministries and provincial/municipal state authorities. All these sections had developed their own plans under the guidance of the Ministry of Finance. The minister noted that "this work has great importance in the work of economic and financial management at present, and we should praise the model of the industrial sector which has implemented the system of financial self-reliance in almost all of its enterprises, along with starting to pay money into the state."[130] Despite the improvements made, he warned that Cambodia was still heavily dependent on borrowing. Financial aid and borrowing from abroad would amount to "perhaps 650 million *roubles*/dollars" in 1984.[131] Almost 30 percent of budgetary income would be from printing money. "Generally speaking, in the past few years, aid and loans and the printing of money have amounted to more than 90 percent of our total income which shows that our economic base does not yet have normalcy, and this feature will be protracted if we don't all pay attention to it."[132] Deputy prime minister Chea Soth's lengthy report, *Concerning the Situation of the Implementation of the Duties of Defending and Building the Country in 1984 and Objectives for Duties in 1985*, describes an economic structure that, despite its weaknesses, had made great recovery under exceptional circumstances.[133] The hopes for a good harvest in the 1984–1985 wet season, however, were once again dashed by unfavorable weather and the harvest levels actually dropped below those of the preceding year. The problems of management remained, and he admitted that "the organization and distribution of goods is showing signs of liberalism and theft."[134] Prices in the free market were rising and the state still could not guarantee the supply of specific items to its cadres, staff, and workers, which was having a bad effect on their living standards. State expenditure still exceeded income and that income still relied heavily on credit and aid. Some bases were not implementing the state plan well and displayed "a lack of high responsibility for the party and the state."[135]

The economic recovery made by the PRK regime in the period 1979 to the end of 1984 should not be under-estimated. The massive infrastructural damage caused by the civil war and the American bombing between 1970 and 1975, the mismanagement and neglect of the economy during the DK years, the exodus and slaughter by the DK of those with the skills and knowledge needed to revive the economy, the famine of 1979–1980 and the chaos that reigned during that year virtually destroyed the Cambodian economy. That normalcy was restored so quickly and with so little state coercion is testament to the political will and determination of the young regime and its Vietnamese advisers. Within this short period, it should not be surprising that the economy was still dependent on aid, credit, and the printing of money. The economic trends which were already evident, however, were cause for genuine concern.

The most serious concern for the government, both in practical terms and in terms of extending its ideological hegemony, was the upward trend of free market prices. The government knew that it could not revive the economy without the help of the petty bourgeoisie. The government lacked both the capital and access to large-scale credit which it required to develop even light-scale industry. It was therefore virtually at the mercy of the free market to supply consumer demands, which increased commensurately with economic recovery. The free market was already dictating the price of agricultural commodities. The government had stipulated that farmers would not be forced to sell their produce to the state, so, in order to meet procurement targets, the government had to pay farmers prices which were determined by the free market. Increasingly, the state could not afford to compete and procurement levels fell far below what it needed to support the living conditions of its own cadres, state employees and the army. Failure to satisfy these basic needs cost it dearly in terms of the loyalty and enthusiasm it needed to implement its socialist objectives. The state could have extracted a surplus from the farmers by imposing agricultural taxes, but for obvious practical reasons it was not prepared to do this. The "patriotic contribution" which was imposed on farmers at the start of 1984 allowed for so many exemptions that as a form of taxation it gave minimal returns. Other internal revenue sources were desperately limited and, as the period after 1985 would show, attempts to raise revenue through exports of rubber, timber, and fish were effectively sabotaged. Smuggling, black marketeering, state employees colluding with profiteers, and poor management at every level and in every sector all played a role in hampering the PRK's early efforts to develop the economy in its preferred fashion. The more the new regime tried to win popular consent and support for its ideology, the more opportunists conspired to take advantage of its goodwill.

Midway through its period of power, it must have been obvious to the PRK leaders that the economic gains their regime had made were at the expense of its ideological principles. Even in the early history of the economic development of the PRK there was little which was attributable to socialist-inspired policies, in fact, quite the reverse. When the government met economic difficulties which threatened its popularity with the masses, it found a liberal economic solution. These solutions were populist ones. Pen Sovann and Chan Si both believed that if the people loved them, the people would follow them—advancing step by step towards socialism. These essential and unresolved contradictions and confusions between theory and practice, policy and implementation, popularity and hegemony, private practice and mastery ultimately destroyed the PRK's attempt to revive the Cambodian revolution.

Chapter 6

POLITICAL SOCIETY

WITHIN THE SOCIALIST system, the public function of the state is performed by its cadres, that is the vanguard elite and trusted functionaries of the party, the military and the security officers. In a normal revolutionary situation, these combined forces would have been developed and their skills honed throughout the period of struggle prior to taking power. The Cambodian revolution developed differently. The Pol Pot phase of the revolution had murdered most of its own trained cadre force and following the *coup de force* of January 1979, what remained of the skilled and experienced fighting force of the revolution had retreated with the leadership to the sanctuaries along the Thai border. The Memot Congress, the third party congress, of January 1979, was attended by just sixty-two out of perhaps two hundred surviving party members who were loyal to the new regime. This number was supplemented by defectors as the PAVN/FUNSK forces swept across Cambodia in the final days of 1978 and in early 1979 but the numbers were ragged, stitched together from groups of different revolutionary experience and "true party lines" as well as a lot of political opportunists, all under the guardianship of the Vietnamese. This small band of party affiliates was spread thinly throughout the early administration. Hun Sen noted that "in some places at the center and in provinces and towns there were almost none . . . In some central institutions there were no party members and many institutions were without party branches which were necessary to organize other branches and establish a *chivepheap* (routine system) for building the party."[1] Nevertheless, during the early period to 1981, the party did build its forces so that there were nine hundred members by the time of the fourth party congress that year. By the fifth (and final) congress of the People's Revolutionary Party of Kampuchea in October 1985, there were 7,500 members.[2] Hun Sen thought that "in this period, the party was like a party of cadres because most of the members at that time were important cadres around the center or around the province/municipality. At the district level, most were district cadres, and if there were any at commune level, most were leaders or deputy commune leaders."[3] He said that it often happened that if cadres at the higher level had not yet joined the party, then no matter how qualified lower level people were, they could not join the party before their leaders did. He thought that this was a mistake. A bigger mistake, in his opinion, was neglecting to build the party at the base, where the gains of the revolution had to be fought for and defended.[4] By the fifth congress, all central institutions had party branches and almost all provinces had provisional party committees. By the end of 1988, the figure he quotes for party membership was 22,000. "Examining this number, if we compare it with the number of people, we see that the proportion is low, but if we compare it with 1979 when we had just over 200 party members, it seems that this number has increased a lot."[5] This number did not include the core groups and the youth alliance which he described as "the seed bed of the party" but the communist party of Cambodia in its various manifestations throughout its history was never very large.

The core groups and youth alliance may have been the "seed bed" but the real recruitment ground of the party was the army, as it had been in Vietnam. The Kampuchean People's Revolutionary Armed Forces (KPRAF) originally consisted of some thirty rebel battalions from the eastern and northeastern regions and from Koh Kong in the southwest, whose commanders were relatively low-level military officers. However, according to Carney, "immediately after victory the army seems to have undergone a crisis, with massive desertions and uncoordinated efforts at expansion . . . The end of 1979 and the beginning of 1980 seems to have marked a turning point, a fresh start toward creating a military establishment."[6]

It was difficult to find willing recruits for the KPRAF, particularly when so many men had been killed and the labor of men in the family was vitally important for the recovery of agriculture. The strengthening of the resistance forces along the border with Thailand, particularly after the formation of their Coalition Government of Democratic Kampuchea in 1982 meant that military conscription became inevitable by 1984 and general mobilization by 1985, which severely eroded popular support for the regime. Civil war is a miserable and shameful affair for any national army, but in Cambodia's case it was made more difficult by the relentless propaganda of the combined resistance forces, which accused the KPRAF of deliberately helping the *yuon* (Vietnamese) to swallow Cambodia. Morale was generally low and desertion rates stood as high as 50 percent.[7] There were no Lei Feng paragons as in the Chinese PLA mythology, or heroic victories like Dien Bien Phu for the Vietnamese PAVN, to inspire Cambodia's new army, and 7 January 1979 had really been a hollow victory. Ith Sarin had spoken of the revolutionary army's unstinting efforts to help the people with the harvest, and in times of personal hardship, during the nine months he spent in the maquis in 1972–1973. However, this never seems to have happened, or even to have been encouraged, during the PRK.[8] Whether because of their poor conditions of pay and living or because it had always been so, the foot soldiers of the Cambodian army often employed their arms and uniforms for brigandage and extorting illegal tolls from travelers on the highways. The KPRAF never seems to have been a source of either pride or inspiration for the citizens of the PRK. The cadres and the military/security forces were the public face of state power. They were the acolytes and torchbearers of the state's ideology. They should have been the vanguard of the revolution, with a long period of theoretical training and practical experience. Instead, they were patched together from remnants of the Pol Pot catastrophe and were unequal to the huge task of mobilizing, leading and protecting the masses and defending the gains of the revolution during those ten difficult years of rehabilitation and reconstruction.

STRENGTHENING THE PARTY

Guidelines for building the party were set out in a decision of the central committee of the Communist Party of Kampuchea, dated 17 July 1979, arising out of a central committee plenum (*sonnebat mechhem*) which commenced on 25 June.[9] As mentioned previously, the party that reconvened at Memot in early January 1979 represented two broad strands of the revolution's history. The survivors of the Khmer Viet Minh who had gone to North Vietnam after the 1954 Geneva Accords, with party experience dating back to the founding of the Khmer People's Revolutionary Party and anti-French resistance, had a lot of theory but little practical experience of revolution within the country. The group that had rebelled against the Pol Pot clique's control of the party and had escaped into Vietnam before December 1978 certainly had experience and understood the internal situation well, but many of them were lacking in political theory or had received theory from the "incorrect" political line of Pol Pot. By the time of the party plenum at the end of June, other old party members had broken with the Pol Pot clique and joined that faction of the party now in power in Phnom Penh, either as full or provisional members; they were strong in hatred for the Pol Pot clique but often lacking in political education. The training of cadres to meet the urgent need of establishing control over the country began immediately. A document referring to a joint government-Front conference that commenced on 24 July 1979 mentioned that political courses had been held "for more than 600 cadres at the primary level in various provinces, for 350 to be *bongkorl* (focal point) cadres around the center, and for 200 intellectuals and students in the capital."[10] Various provinces were said to have already held education courses of between five and fifteen days for cadres at the primary and intermediate levels. It should be noted that a cadre (*kammaphibal*) was not necessarily a party member at this stage, nor even a declared candidate for membership; on the other hand, not all civil servants were *kammaphibal*. The designation of "cadre" seems to refer to people within the administration, units and institutions of the state at all levels who had received specific types of political training. The high level cadres received further training and upgrading in Hanoi and other centers in Vietnam, particularly at Thu Duc in Ho Chi Minh City. Lower level cadres were trained in-country, usually with support given by the Vietnamese advisers.

According to the 17 July 1979 decision above, the most important factor for the party to stress was solidarity. It observed that some places practiced it well but that some other places did not. It suggested that "some places have the characteristics of factionalism, regionalism and nepotism; some places want to celebrate the individual but the most severe problem and the one which we must pay most attention to is the problem of factionalism, not respecting the leadership and the organizational discipline of the party, suspecting each other, not knowing when enough is enough, not listening to each other until there is hatred for each other."[11] This was a warning with obvious reference to the experience of the Pol Pot years. The author advised that solidarity was the party's strength and "breaking solidarity will make the party weak until the revolution is utterly destroyed."[12] The members were ordered not to bend the system, "making another system," and to avoid at all costs the sentiments of "factionalism, sectionalism, and regionalism on the matter of leadership and the principles of the party."[13] Group democracy and cooperation were advised to combat individualism but, wisely, "we must ensure the conditions for the organization and discipline of the party, that the leadership is good and that the selection and organization of our cadres will not lead to division and factionalism."[14] The attitude (*attachoret*) and morality (*selatoa*) of cadres and party members in their work had to be close and trusting and "if there are quarrels they should be brought into the open for the parties to come together and resolve the suspicion."[15]

Differences of opinion had to be raised and solved honestly in order to find consensus. "Any place which shows signs of breaking that solidarity must do monitoring and criticism and self-criticism to search for the cause and take measures to change the situation."[16]

The document noted that the center had already stipulated many methods for the selection of cadres, but it raised some more points. It warned against "rely[ing] on sympathy and having a desire for revenge, of [deciding on the basis of] having a debt of blood or not having a debt of blood (*chumpeak bomnol chiem*), or having a tendency or not having a tendency (*ninniekar*), in order to examine and reflect."[17] From the Pol Pot regime, it explained, anyone who had sorrow had a reason for revenge. This was "very complicated because under the Pol Pot regime there were some people who had acted in person, and there were some who acted at a distance, and there were some with a heavy debt of blood and others with a little, some who were forced to act and others who did it willingly . . . some people with the debt of blood in the end were mistreated and punished by Pol Pot and they rose up to fight against Pol Pot– Ieng Sary and developed the skills of a revolutionary."[18] The author warned against generalizing. The question of "tendency" (*ninniekar*) was also complicated. This referred to family background. "Within a family group, there may have been relatives who were lackeys of the Lon Nol or Sihanouk era, but there were also members in that family group who joined the revolution to fight against the French and the Americans, or who are now fighting the Pol Pot regime, just as there are families with some members who 'joined hand and foot' with Pol Pot and others who struggled against Pol Pot . . ."[19] The quality and the competency of the cadre him/herself were the main criteria, plus a determination to serve the revolution. The central committee had decided on six concrete criteria for selection:

1. Sincere in serving the cause of the revolution unconditionally;
2. Operating precisely according to the leadership of the party, the government and the Front within the country and abroad and respectingthe organizational discipline of the party and the revolution;
3. Having close relations with the masses, having the love and esteem of the masses and their trust;
4. Living cleanly;

5. Having the competency for the work of the party, the government and the Front which is given to them;
6. Having a clear biography.

If someone suited all the above criteria but was known to have killed in the Pol Pot era, that person was to be assigned to work in a place where there would not be much contact with the people. This was "to protect the cadre and his family from revenge, as well as preventing the enemy from twisting the facts about the good qualities of the revolutionary state authority and [it] avoids the masses finding fault with [us] leading to bad influences on their faith in the revolution."[20] With regard to provinces in the eastern part of the country which had suffered greatly and which had a long history of rebellion against the Pol Pot–Ieng Sary clique, "the cadres and the people . . . except for a small number of bad people . . . are good people and for this reason we must train all those cadres in order to let them become good cadres of the party. However, it is not as though we strive for this one region and forget about the other regions."[21] Representatives of ethnic minorities, intellectuals and monks were to be trained "to use them in order to build the nation in a proper and genuine way" while guarding against the reactionaries among their ranks.[22]

As for the cadres who had served the DK regime and who had broken ranks and surrendered to the new regime, "we have educated them and approved for them to go and be reunited with their families to live a normal life."[23] This group was considered to be a valuable resource. "Now that they have come back, they see the situation clearly. Their families were smashed to bits or their relatives were killed and for this reason we must strive to attract them back to the revolution, to receive training and education and use them in proper work according to the guidance of criteria set down by the party. But their selection must be precise, taking precautions against people who are only pretending to want to join or who are using the policy of two faces among the cruel and stubborn groups whose leaders still resist the revolution."[24] There were also 100,000 people who had gone as refugees to Vietnam starting as early as 1970. "Among this number are many good people but there are also some bad people and the enemy have persisted in attracting these people to burrow into our ranks."[25] The job of selection and training, monitoring and evaluation, had to be precise and constant so that the bad elements could be expelled quickly.

The work of cadre selection, training and appointment, was to be done within the ministry/department, institution or mass organization, by its own staff. When doubts arose, appointments were to be termed "acting" until the center could make a formal decision. The party committees in the provinces were severely understaffed. Each was supposed to have between five and seven people. If there are not yet enough party members with good points as full rights members of the party committee, that province must supplement the number with candidate members."[26] This was to be done only after "the opinion of the masses" was sought. This was the responsibility of the Front organization in the province. Biographies of all party committee members had to be submitted to the center for inspection.

All ministries/departments at the center and in the provinces were supposed to have organized party branches by mid-1979. The branch had the job of expanding the party in its own area of work. In fact, few branches existed at this point because there were so few party members. The gap was filled by the core group (*krom snoul*) of three to five politically trained cadres who held meetings "just as for party meetings" in order to extend circulars and decisions of the party.[27] The core groups then had the task of passing on that information to all the mass organizations. The core groups were "like seedlings in the time before we have party branches."[28] When a core group member was seen to have all the good points, that person could be accepted as a party member, and if all the group members qualified, the core group could be recognized as a party branch. Finally, for those cadres returning from long periods of stay in Vietnam or Laos where they had joined the local party, their party age (*aayu pak*) was to be estimated from the day that they were declared as full rights party members of those countries. For those defecting from the DK, two party members who recognized them could act as witnesses while the provincial (party) committee inspected their right to join the new party organization.

The party needed more members, but it was concerned about both political and intellectual quality. Only 15 percent of the nation's intellectuals, doctors, engineers, educators, et cetera, remained in Cambodia by 7 January 1979.[29] Many had left the country before the Khmer Rouge entered Phnom Penh in April 1975 and many others were murdered in the killing fields or had died of starvation and neglect. After liberation, many of the surviving intellectuals chose not to return to their professions, either because they did not want to support the new regime with its Vietnamese backers, or because civil service salaries and conditions were so poor. During the 1960s, under Sihanouk, these professionals had formed the middle class. They had been relatively highly paid and had become accustomed to status and privilege. The PRK regime needed them but could not support them in the former style. On 22 November 1979, Pen Sovann, as party secretary general, issued a circular *Concerning Increasing the Work of the Propaganda and Education Movement for our Brother Intellectuals.* He was concerned that "we still have some wrong tendencies which we must change and make appropriate. For example, in some places, they do not understand clearly the important function of intellectuals in the ranks of the revolution."[30] He outlined four points:

1. Gather together all brother intellectuals who are left in the country as a matter of urgency;

2. Provide political education and consciousness-raising to make all our brother intellectuals understand the state of affairs and their duties—understand the leadership and policies of the party, the Front and the People's Revolutionary Council and the duties and responsibilities of intellectuals for the motherland;

3. All levels must prepare to use all the brother intellectuals appropriately, according to their competency and capacity in their skill or profession;

4. Give them material support, awareness and means of work . . . We must have an attitude of respect for them and

absolutely avoid improper or careless attitudes and looking down on them as intellectuals.[31]

Pen Sovann was concerned that "old" cadres were looking down on new ones, and that friction existed among the three general "types" of cadres: the Khmer Viet Minh, the ex-Khmer Rouge who escaped and defected prior to 7 January 1979, and those party cadres who rebelled against the DK regime and joined the PAVN/FUNSK forces as they swept across the country after 24 December 1978.[32] There was suspicion, distrust, scorn and derision on all sides and all three, it seemed, looked down on the cadres newly admitted from among the mass movements, "considering them to be non-revolutionary."[33] He referred again, to "the depressing lesson of the Kampuchean revolution" which was that factionalism weakens and defeats.[34] He argued strongly that "raising movements to build the ranks of cadres from among the masses at the base is most urgent."[35] The habit of admitting cadres "who are chosen by ourselves" had sometimes been careless "until there are some places with bad types who have a debt of blood and this has soured relations between the party and the masses."[36] There had to be thorough checking and investigation. It was important to wait for the ideas of the masses, but not to act "according to the 'tail' of the masses . . . if we do not investigate clearly and thoroughly, there will be bad elements, opportunists, who will burrow themselves into the state authority of the village and the commune."[37] Referring to the problem of admitting those with "the debt of blood," his ideas seem to be less forgiving than those of the author of the central committee document referred to above. While acknowledging the role played by cadres, party members and the masses who rose up to overthrow the Pol Pot–Ieng Sary clique, it was important to admit that "there are some who . . . killed with their own hand or they issued commands to kill cadres and the people, or they made lists of cadres, party members and people and reported to the higher authority in order for them to be killed. Almost all cadres within the security section have the debt of blood. As for those with the debt of blood, the political program of the party makes it clear that they cannot join the party committees or important ministries of the party."[38] He explained:

> For the cadres and party members within the leadership of the party and the state authority of Pol Pot who changed over after the day of liberation, at present they are the object of the masses' hatred and severe anger . . . we cannot use them in the leadership of the state authority nor in the committees of the mass organizations.[39]

This strong argument was based on the principle that "our party always takes the bond between the party and the masses to be the life of the party. If the party moves far from the masses, the party will come to grief."[40] Because the Chinese hegemonists were as much the enemy as the Pol Pot–Ieng Sary clique, he decided that "we do not choose ethnic Chinese or train them to be cadres or use them in jobs in enterprises either."[41] Nor would he allow certain elements—"police, spies, security, military leaders, provincial governors, district governors . . . "—of the Sihanouk and Lon Nol regimes to work for the new regime. If they had already been admitted, they were to be expelled and "sent to increase the harvest as farmers."[42]

The third plenum of the party central committee which was held in 1980 announced that "we have more than two hundred party members, most of them in the armed forces."[43] Throughout the country there were only thirty-three party branches. The core groups, however, were expanding quickly. The report on the plenum claimed that ten thousand new cadres had been trained and that "half of them are in core groups, the majority in the provinces."[44] However, the core groups lacked guidance because the party branches were still disorganized and had not yet established their *chivepheap*. Consequently, the core groups were organizing themselves slowly and "the ministries/departments around the center are weaker than the provinces."[45] In fact, there were only three core groups around the center at this stage.

The plenum called on all state authorities and institutions to work hard in organizing the youth groups. The Communist Youth Alliance of Kampuchea had been formed in 1979 and its

statutes were in order.[46] The youth alliance branches throughout the country were regarded as "the right hand of the party
. . . a major force in our socialism."[47] The core groups had
responsibility for selecting young people between the ages of
eighteen and thirty for these groups and "on that basis we will
then have easy conditions for expanding the party because the
source of expanding the party comes from the Kampuchean
Communist Youth Alliance itself."[48] This document expresses
concern about existing weaknesses within the party, noting
that "we are weak in both quantity and quality."[49] The author
judged that while internal solidarity had strengthened over the
course of the year, he was concerned that some cadres had lost
"all their feeling and their revolutionary nature and have fallen
into libertinism, getting excited by females and materialism,
not being honest with the revolution and not considering the
well-being of the masses, causing the masses to look down on
them . . . some other cadres only think of themselves, living
every day to gather lovely girls to come and serve them and
forgetting about their revolutionary stance."[50] There had been
instances of careless selection: "Some other comrades choose
the enemy to come and work in their ministry or department.
Therefore, the phenomenon arises of state assets being
destroyed or stolen and taken to the forest and internal
solidarity is destroyed."[51] In the provinces, instead of cadres
helping the people, "they chase the people away to look for
materials by themselves and take one or two extra wives."[52]
The author warned that these bad habits would destroy both
the internal solidarity among cadres and between cadres and
the people as well as giving the propaganda advantage to the
enemy.

The party needed "active members who can analyze and
think clearly and have good relations with the masses and who
are determined to operate according to the principles and
policies of the party."[53] Therefore, "we should not run after
quantity only."[54] In order to be admitted to the party, one had
to be nominated or sponsored by two full-rights party
members (penh seth) "but not necessarily a full-age members as
before." (A member of the Committee of the Communist
Youth Alliance needed only one sponsor). Approval was given

by a two-thirds majority of full-rights members of the party branch and this had to be ratified by the higher level of party administration at the base. When a new member was admitted, he or she had to undergo a period of preparation, which was six months for "workers, farmers and poor people in the city," and nine months for "Kandal farmers, students, intellectuals and those in various other moneyed classes."[55] A "dignified and harmonious" ceremony was held to admit the new members who took the oath:

> I volunteer to serve the Communist Party of Kampuchea and the working classes all my life; I am determined to overcome all obstacles in order to change myself into a good communist, honest all my life with the Party and the motherland and will sacrifice my life for the cause of communism.[56]

This circular also called for the recognition of membership of former members to be speeded up. This referred to those former party members who had taken part in the rebellion against Pol Pot–Ieng Sary. The concern with checking the credentials and sincerity of new members is understandable in the special circumstances of the party in those early years, but the rate of admission as full rights members does seem to have been inordinately slow. For example, a party document dated 28 September 1980 says that "so far only three new party members have been introduced."[57]

THE FOURTH PARTY CONGRESS

The most important event for the party in 1981, that year of many significant political events, was the fourth party congress which was convened from 26–29 May. Prior to the congress, Pen Sovann prepared a study document called *Building the Strength of the Marxist-Leninist Party is the Key Factor in the Success of the Cambodian Revolution* which clarified the party line.[58] In the first point, he noted: "Our party was born on 19 February 1951, originating as the Khmer People's Revolutionary Party. Our party is one that holds fast to pure Marxism-

Leninism."[59] Pol Pot had "snatched power and made our party deviate from Marxism-Leninism and destroyed the attitude (*attachoret*) of the party. The Pol Pot party betrayed Marxism-Leninism, betrayed the goodwill of the people and turned them into objects to serve the hegemonistic ambitions of the Chinese power-brokers in Beijing over Indochina and the whole of Southeast Asia . . . Our party was gathered up, rebuilt and given new life at the congress on 5 January 1979."[60] The second point states: "Our party is the vanguard of the Cambodian working class . . . Our party uses every possibility to lead the Cambodian revolution towards socialism, along with leading it to a life filled with happiness for all people and expanding and protecting the foundations of national independence. This is genuine socialism which is totally different from the so-called socialism of the reactionary Pol Pot group."[61] Pen Sovann argued that the party had to establish the clear relationship between pure patriotism and international proletarianism; "separation from international proletarianism leads us towards narrow nationalism."[62] Thirdly, "our party is an alliance of solidarity and consensus which is strong in political awareness and organization." He counseled all members "to act always as a model and meticulously implement the leadership of party policy and state laws."[63] The fourth party congress was attended by 162 Cambodian party representatives and it had "the participation and warm congratulations" of party delegations from Vietnam, Laos, USSR, Bulgaria, Cuba, East Germany, Hungary, Mongolia, Poland, Czechoslovakia, and Afghanistan.[64] The congress noted the achievements of the previous two years, and declared that "these vast victories come from the victory of national and international solidarity, especially solidarity with Vietnam."[65] The key decisions of the congress were:

    1. The victory of 7 January 1979 is a victory of national solidarity and international solidarity;

    2. Defending the country is a frontline task of all our people. Building and strengthening the defense of the country is the task of the whole party and all the people;

3. Developing and expanding the economy and the culture is a step towards socialism, to a life of harmony and happiness . . . We have to start from agriculture and take agriculture as the core . . . At the present time, the basis of the economy of our country is of this kind: the state economy, the collective economy and the private economy;[66]

4. The solidarity of all the people—expand the strength of the people to defend and build the motherland. The revolution is the cause of the masses . . . The party is also a member of the Front and is a core leader of the Front. All organizations of the party, all cadres must consider the work of mobilizing the masses as an important strategic task. In mass work, we must unite closely the three sections: education, administration and revolutionary activities.[67]

It was at this congress that the name of the party was finally resolved. There had been some confusion about the name at the hurried third congress at Memot, which was interrupted by news of the liberation of Phnom Penh on 7 January 1979. At the fourth congress it was declared that "in order to make a clean break with the reactionary party of Pol Pot, in order to show and continue the glorious tradition of the party, the congress has decided to take the name, People's Revolutionary Party of Kampuchea."[68] The statement of congress resolutions ended with the rousing call for "all party members and cadres to form firm ranks, to strive to turn the decisions of the congress into truth, to increase the alliance of the three countries of Indochina, to defend strongly the beloved motherland, to rebuild the nation, to produce a life of harmony and happiness for the people, to unite actively the parts in the cause of world revolution."[69]

The congress chose a new central committee of twenty-one members.[70] The politburo which doubled in size, now comprised Pen Sovann, Heng Samrin, Say Phouthang, Chea Sim, Bou Thong, Hun Sen, Chea Soth, and Chan Si, while the seven-member secretariat was Pen Sovann, Say Phouthang, Bou Thong, Hun Sen, Chea Soth, Chan Si, and Chan Phin. With the exception of Pen Sovann and Chan Si, these men remained at the helm of the PRK leadership and guided Cambodia into the post-Cold War era. They represented both major strands of the party's origins and the party's internal disputes, when they occurred, were carefully kept out of the public gaze. The only reference in the documents to the dismissal of Pen Sovann, Ros Samay, and some other key party leaders in December 1981 is made in the *Summary Report—First Quarter, 1982* of the party central committee which noted:

> A number of individuals and a number of phenomena which caused blockages in the process of revolution have been expelled from the ranks of the party, making our party increasingly united and pure and firmer than before. Up to today, we have 974 party members and 100 party branches.[71]

The party continued to grow steadily throughout the first six years of the People's Republic of Kampuchea. However, the quality of party cadres remained a serious concern. Chea Soth, writing in 1982, acknowledged the expansion of the cadre ranks but, "along with that, there are not a few cadres who still nurture bad habits of the former society. These groups take advantage of times when our economic management is still short of bolts and because of [our] negligence, use the rights of their position to take bribes, collude with evil businessmen, steal public assets . . . [and their] behavior causes the faith of the people in the revolution to be diminished."[72]

The whole decade of the PRK was plagued by this sort of opportunism and self-centeredness on the part of some cadres. The habit of corruption, traditional notions of power and merit, and the ingrained customs relating to patron-client patterns of social organization were largely unaffected by the revolution which, for the most part, remained something external to the individual's regular behavior. The revolution did not require every Cambodian citizen, or even every party cadre, to be expert in the major doctrines of Marxism-Leninism, but it did require that the cadres at least have sufficient faith in and knowledge about the belief system to consider it to be worthwhile and to behave according to those principles. If the cadres could not take the lead in teaching the people about the value of the new system, in raising the consciousness of the masses, how was the party's hegemony going to be established? Even an observer as sympathetic to the regime as Michael Vickery was led to comment, "Many new PRK cadres at all levels were sent to Vietnam after 1979 for courses . . . but I never met anyone who had a clear idea of what Marxism-Leninism is, or who cared."[73]

Anecdotes from various sources about people who went to study political courses in the early 1980s suggest that the problem lay in learning itself, that attending the courses usually became, as one student described it, a matter of "in one ear, out the other, and back to the teacher."[74] Learning occurs when new knowledge is successfully incorporated into the learner's own existing knowledge and belief structure. If the new cannot fit the old structure, or be explained so that it can fit, it will be discarded. New political notions of a classless society, democracy and social justice, obviously did not blend well with firmly held traditional beliefs that status, power and wealth derive from merit and karma, most especially when the learner was, or was about to become, a member of the ruling elite with expectations of the benefits that accompanied such position. For most, the new learning offered no direct personal benefit, therefore did not make sense, and was thus rejected. Moreover, while spartan and puritanical habits were expected of the Vietnamese cadres, the same lifestyle in Khmer terms was an affront to hospitality. A middle-ranking cadre, for example, declared that he would rather sell his trousers than offer a guest the poor fare that his new father-in-law, a notoriously honest and upright minister, had provided at the post-nuptial family dinner.[75] That there were committed and honest party cadres must be acknowledged and respected, but there were too few of them to make the difference that was required to change Cambodia. The failure to raise the critical self-consciousness of the cadres themselves was partly a pedagogical failure, and largely a reflection of the deeply conservative nature of Cambodian society. Without this crucial step, however, the catharsis essential for genuine social transformation would never occur and the revolution would fail.

By the end of 1984, Hun Sen claimed, all the central institutions had party branches and almost all the provinces had provisional party committees. Some districts had party branches, some communes had party members, and a small number of communes had party branches or affiliated party branches. The *chivepheap* was clearly delineated and although there were recurrent criticisms in the following years of the personal behavior of individual cadres along the lines of those comments made by Chea Soth above, the party had established itself as a relatively disciplined, organized force. Despite its claims to the contrary, however, it was not a mass-based organization. Its size was too small and its nature far too secretive to have had much effect on the lives of ordinary Cambodian citizens. Moreover, the economic and security situation was too demanding for the cadres to pay attention to political training and consciousness-raising among the villagers, and the Pol Pot era "meeting" had given the ordinary people well-developed skills in polite indifference to all forms of political propaganda. The quality and standard of political education among the cadres themselves remained very poor. The rhetoric came easily but comprehension and practice remained another matter.

DEATH OF THE PRIME MINISTER

Both internal and international solidarity took another heavy blow in December 1984 with the death of prime minister Chan Si. He was fifty years old and in apparent good health. According to information provided by the official biography, "in 1979, he accepted the duty of supreme political commander (*protean akke snangkar noyorbai*) of the Kampuchean People's Revolutionary Army."[76] He was also deputy minister for national defense in 1980, became a member of the politburo and of the central secretariat in 1981, a vice chairman of the Council of Ministers and a member of the National Assembly. In December 1981 he was named acting chairman of the Council of Ministers after the dismissal of Pen Sovann and during the January–February 1982 session of the National Assembly, he was named prime minister.

Written speeches and circulars signed by Chan Si reveal a warm and generous personality and, in fact, he is remembered with genuine affection, even by people who were then adamantly opposed to the regime. His sudden death in Moscow, which was formally announced on 31 December 1984, shocked and angered the people, who blamed it rather predictably on the Vietnamese.

On 28 December, the national news agency SPK reported that Chan Si was seriously ill. However, the documents indicate that he died on or before 27 December 1984. On 20 December, a decree of the Council of State signed by Heng Samrin handed over the rights of acting chairman of the Council of Ministers to Hun Sen "in order to substitute in the Council of Ministers, resolving all the daily work during the time that Chan Si . . . is taking a rest and receiving treatment for illness."[77] Exactly one week later, in an extraordinary meeting of the politburo, Hun Sen was named chairman of the Council of Ministers, the decision to be formalized at the eighth session of the National Assembly in January 1985.[78]

Rumors circulated throughout the city that Chan Si had been given a lethal injection while in Hanoi en route for Moscow.[79] Official explanations varied from liver damage, leukemia, heart failure, to the effects of Agent Orange (*plieng krahom*). This confusion only served to confirm the people's suspicions. The body lay in state in the former royal palace before the cremation, which took place during the first week of 1985 in the *viel men*, the traditional site for the burning of the bodies of Khmer kings. The motive for Chan Si's "murder," if that is what it was, is generally attributed to his reluctance and possibly even his refusal to cooperate in the K5 Plan for a major civilian effort to build a strategic defense barrier along the Cambodia-Thailand border, which began before the commencement of the 1984–1985 dry season offensive against the combined resistance forces. The K5 Plan, to be discussed in detail later, was responsible for the deaths of thousands of Cambodian civilians.

On 26 April 1998, Sam Rainsy, Cambodian opposition party leader, issued a statement containing a number of serious accusations of wrong-doing against Hun Sen. These accusations allegedly were made during "a long meeting" that Sam Rainsy had held with Pen Sovann the previous day. The second point of the statement read:

> Hun Sen assassinated Chan Si on 22 December 1987 [sic] at a reception given at the Chamcar Mon State Palace in Phnom Penh in honor of the Vietnamese Army. Hun Sen poisoned prime minister Chan Si who died on the same day. But the authorities claimed he was ill and under intensive treatment. His death was announced only on 31 December 1987. National funerals were organized for him. Shortly after, Hun Sen became the new prime minister.[80]

During an interview with *The Cambodia Daily* on 28 April 1998, Pen Sovann acknowledged that he was the source of this information, "[but] he said he did not authorize public dissemination. 'We had a private conversation,' he said."[81] A senior Hun Sen adviser, Muth Khiev, dismissed the allegations against Hun Sen and was reported to have said "the CPP [Cambodian People's Party, successor to the People's Revolutionary Party of Kampuchea] and its leaders from all generations have never had any problems with each other or any violence [amongst themselves]."[82] The unstated exception was the long-running feud between Pen Sovann and Hun Sen and it is knowledge of this feud which casts serious doubts on these allegations. Pen Sovann was in prison at the time of Chan Si's death, so he could not have known the details. His confusion over the date and place of death also detracts from the veracity of these allegations.[83] Prime minister Chan Si was suffering from a severe stomach complaint the day he left Phnom Penh by plane accompanied by his Vietnamese physician, Dr Lam.[84] This complaint could have been the result of any number of causes.

By 1985, although key Khmer Viet Minh members remained very influential, party and state power was largely in the hands of that group which had defected from the Khmer Rouge before 1979. They were led by Heng Samrin, Chea Sim and Hun Sen. Following the dismissal of Pen Sovann, the top party role of secretary general was given to Heng Samrin who was also president of the Council of State. Chea Sim was president of the Front and president of the National Assembly. Foreign affairs minister Hun Sen was chairman of the Council of Ministers. These were experienced revolutionaries and they understood the situation within the country very well. That experience had left them with few ideals. They tended to be less impatient with the overlordship of the Vietnamese in Cambodia which is not meant to suggest that they were either more "pro-" or "anti-" Vietnamese than the 1954 group had been. They were simply more pragmatic. Furthermore, Vietnam experienced severe economic problems after 1985, and may have reacted more leniently towards Cambodia's growing independence in formulating policies which diverged farther from socialism as the decade progressed. Certainly some warming of relations between the two countries occurred after 1984 when PRK leaders accepted the fact that without proper defense and security systems, both the revolution and their own hold on power would be lost. That meant not only accepting but welcoming full-scale support from the PAVN.

THE KAMPUCHEAN PEOPLE'S REVOLUTIONARY ARMED FORCES

The soldiers of the FUNSK constituted a very small part of the huge military force that overthrew the Pol Pot regime in 1979, the thirty or forty battalions of dissidents quoted earlier by Hun Sen being organized into three or four brigades.[85] Immediately after the liberation of Phnom Penh on 7 January, Carney claims, "the army seems to have undergone a crisis, with massive desertions and uncoordinated efforts at expansion."[86]

Towards the end of 1979 and early in 1980, the new administration turned its efforts towards creating a military establishment including both air and naval arms, although the emphasis remained on building up the infantry forces.

Building the forces was not just a matter of numbers. With a PAVN force averaging between 160,000 and 180,000 stationed within the country, ordinary Cambodians probably did not understand the need for an armed force of their own while they were struggling to feed themselves and there were tendencies, as Carney notes, for men "to drift away from the forces to less disciplined and dangerous pursuits, simply letting the PAVN do the dirty work."[87] The work of building consciousness and loyalty towards the new regime among the people so that they would volunteer to defend it was the task of the party and the Front. The development of the armed forces was crucial for the new regime, not only because the Vietnamese troops and advisers would remain in Cambodia as long as the Cambodian armed forces were inadequate for the task of national defense against the perceived Chinese menace and the Khmer Rouge "lackeys of Beijing" but also because, as Carney says, "without a military force of their own, the Heng Samrin authorities could not credibly claim legitimacy internally."[88]

The presence of Vietnamese troops on Cambodian territory was legitimized by the *Treaty of Peace, Friendship and Cooperation Between the Socialist Republic of Vietnam and the People's Republic of Kampuchea* which was signed during the first summit meeting of both governments held in Phnom Penh from 16 to 19 February 1979. The treaty was valid for twenty-five years. Article 2 of the treaty stated:

> the two parties undertake to wholeheartedly support and assist each other in all domains and in all necessary forms in order to strengthen the capacity to defend the independence, sovereignty, unity, territorial integrity and peaceful labor of the people in each country against all schemes and acts of sabotage by the imperialist and international reactionary forces. The two parties shall take effective measures to implement this commitment whenever one of them requires.[89]

General headquarters of the PAVN in Cambodia were at Chamcar Mon in Phnom Penh, under the day-to-day command of General Le Duc Anh. Cambodia was divided into four military regions, each corresponding to a distinct front. The northwest under the command of Front 479 with its rear headquarters in Siem Reap town was the most sensitive and most heavily manned region (Region 4), being closest to the border with Thailand.[90] The other sensitive region, Region 3, which included other western and coastal provinces, as well as Kandal and Phnom Penh, was under the command of Front 979 based in Kompong Speu. A third region (Region 1) stretched across the northern and northeast border from Preah Vihear to Mondolkiri, and the fourth included the provinces of Kompong Thom, Kratie, Prey Veng, Svay Rieng and Kompong Cham (Region 2). The Special Military Administrative Zone formed an inverse triangular corridor bounded by National Route No. 5 and No. 6 and Lake Tonle Sap with Phnom Penh at the apex. The logistics and supply lines to the western fronts passed through this corridor which "constitutes a strategic axis of the Vietnamese occupation forces in Kampuchea."[91] Each of the four fronts was twinned with a military region in Vietnam.

Front 479 with its main headquarters in Siem Reap was said to have had the command of three infantry divisions, eight autonomous brigades and two technical units at the time of that report. The technical units were "civic action units" or "units of propaganda and education," one based in Battambang province with 2,500 men, and the other in Siem Reap province with 2,700 men. "Consisting mainly of Vietnamese experts, these units serve primarily to administer and govern . . . to maintain internal security, while providing the Vietnamese authorities with intelligence about the local situation. Second, their basic task is to build up the local infrastructure of the Phnom Penh regime."[92] The report noted that "in their pacification tasks, the PAVN operates jointly wherever possible, with the KPRAF whose military performance is still very modest. Unified commands have been set up at all levels."[93]

Defending itself against the very real threat of the return of the Khmer Rouge was the constant and urgent task of the PRK regime. In its first six-monthly report, the PRK leadership declared that in the past dry season "42,000 of the enemy were wiped out, broken up and surrendered . . . [However] the dispirited enemy split into small groups and came back into densely populated regions on the plain and into towns. They burrowed into our bases to implement their ruse of creating state authorities with two faces, to fight against us and to gather their forces in order to continue a secret and protracted war."[94] Confronted with the reality of what he realized would be a long and bitter civil war, Heng Samrin called on all parties to strive to build the army of all three types: regular, regional and the militia. The task of the army, he said, was a heavy one:

> Our cadres and combatants not only have to sweep out the enemy, they must join in the building of the state authority, care for the security system, help to care for the people in increasing the harvest, solve the problem of hunger and treat the people's diseases. Therefore, our armed forces must be strong in all sections and in particular they must improve the political quality of their cadres.[95]

The development of the armed forces had to be achieved "through struggle and through building the masses."[96]

The *sonnebat mechem*, the plenum of the central committee, held some three weeks before the joint congress at which the above report was delivered, described problems within the Cambodian forces, some of whom "have run off with the enemy" which was using all kinds of incentives to attract them.[97] For this reason, "we must have a plan to build the armed forces according to a system from top to bottom and we must have a system of contact between our army and the army of our friends."[98] As for Khmer Rouge defectors, "they must lay down their arms and receive education, register their names according to exact administration and not be allowed to go about oppressing and intimidating the people again."[99] Those with the 'debt of blood' were to receive one or two years of reeducation, but those showing genuine remorse and whom "the people in that place agree can reform themselves," would be given permission to do so.[100]

Carney notes that 1980 was a key year in the formation of large infantry units staffed by volunteers but that "the draft began in earnest in 1981,"[101] In June 1981 an agreement was signed between the Ministry of Defense of the SRV and the

Ministry of Defense of the PRK *Concerning Vietnam's Assistance to Kampuchea for the Upgrading of Training of Commanders, Cadres, Staff and Technicians.*[102] According to Article 1 of the draft agreement:

> The PAVN agrees to assist the KPRAF in training and upgrading the level of its political armed forces and the skills of its commanding officers to the 'intermediate' level and cadres to the 'primary' level. It is necessary for some to go to institutes for training cadres of the PAVN. The PAVN accepts to train some cadres and skilled technical staff to the 'intermediate' level and staff to the 'primary' level, according to the request of the KPRAF.

The PAVN agreed to assign teachers to military training schools in Cambodia. Representatives of both parties would consult annually to review both the numbers and the period of training. On 30 June the following year, with reference to this agreement, prime minister Chan Si sent a letter to prime minister Pham Van Dong, requesting among other things an increase of experts in a number of units of the KPRAF, as well as help for training 728 cadres in army schools in Vietnam, and a further 200 skilled technical staff.[103] A draft agreement attached to the June 1981 agreement above, valid for five years and also signed by both countries' defense ministers, was entitled *Concerning the Distribution of Troops and Military Cooperation Between the PAVN and the KPRAF.*[104] Noting that the armies of both countries were already working together "at the land border of Kampuchea and Thailand and along the coastline . . . on the chain of the first battlefield," Article 1 of the agreement states:

> In future, all the divisions, brigades and regiments of the Kampuchean army will guarantee to accept the task of striking at the enemy, one step at a time, to defend the border at the first line of defense and defend the coastline of Kampuchea. All the Vietnamese military volunteer forces will be distributed along the second line of defense and will act as mobile alert troops on call in order to help the Kampuchean armed forces in the frontline of battle.

This would take many years to fulfill. In fact, it was not until the 1987–1988 dry season offensive that the Vietnamese forces acted as support rather than frontline forces.[105] It does prove, however, that the Vietnamese intended to develop the KPRAF into a genuine fighting force from very early in the history of the PRK.

The document accompanying that agreement set out the planned *Distribution of Vietnamese Military Experts in Kampuchea.*[106] This document reveals the administrative structure of the Cambodian Ministry of National Defense.[107] In all, there were 138 experts: nine "political and military experts" including the counterpart to the minister, fifty-eight experts for all areas of command under the Senior Command, thirty-five under the Senior Political Command, twenty-two under the Senior Logistics Command, and fourteen experts at the Ministry of National Defense (for finance, foreign relations, the air force and the ministry office). There were cadre training schools for general infantry, logistics, communications, for army doctors, technicians and drivers. There was a school for "military culture" and a finance school. There were five regional political army schools, each school with three experts and ten to fifteen teachers per school. Experts were based in the army's factories for producing and repairing armaments, for motor vehicle repairs, the sewing factory and the pharmaceuticals factory at the rate of two experts per factory plus a number of technical experts depending on Cambodia's requests. The same number of experts was placed in the various types of warehouses. The army hospital had eight experts as well as doctors and staff on request. There were also regional medical teams of eight experts per team. There were fifteen experts in each provincial military office and two per district office. Twenty-seven experts were assigned to each infantry division and experts of various kinds for each lower level. Along with the experts came research cadres, translators, guards, drivers, cooks, et cetera. In such conditions, the KPRAF must have felt almost redundant.

ENEMIES OF THE STATE

Apart from the Khmer Rouge, internal security was threatened by an assortment of "reactionary groups" which were generally called the *Khmer Serei* (Free Khmers) although they banded together under many different colorful names and banners.[108] The term *Khmer Serei* had been in use since the mid-1950s; small, armed gangs of criminals and smugglers operating in the Thai-Cambodian border region had applied this term to themselves.[109] In 1975 they were joined by remnants of the Lon Nol regime troops who had managed to escape the Khmer Rouge net but, in general, they lacked the means and the leadership to cohere into a genuine military or political force. They later formed the backbone of the Son Sann/KPLNF forces, formed in October 1979; other bands of them joined Sihanouk's Front, the FUNCINPEC, which was formed in March 1981. Meanwhile, they caused mischief in the towns and denigrated and undermined the new regime with rumors and propaganda.[110] The party leaders called for them to be arrested and punished but with a warning:

> The arrest of reactionaries must depend on clear proof, must be investigated and monitored in detail. Don't make impulsive arrests without obvious cause which would result in panicking the masses. When you arrest someone don't use torture to extract confessions.[111]

There is sufficient evidence to show that this latter admonition was often ignored in the first half of the PRK. In late 1984 and early 1985, two fact-finding missions by the Lawyers Committee for Human Rights, assisted by Stephen Heder, examined the human rights practices of the PRK and the conditions within the areas administered by the Khmer People's National Liberation Front (KPNLF), and Democratic Kampuchea (DK). The missions were not given permission to visit Phnom Penh or other parts of Cambodia. Their findings on the PRK practices were drawn solely from accounts given by recently arrived refugees to the Thai border camps. These findings were informed by "various sources of official policy, particularly government broadcasts and decrees."[112] The report gave numerous accounts of torture of those arrested on suspicion of political crimes and the majority of those accounts gave identical details of treatment during interrogation and imprisonment and of detention without trial. Michael Vickery's critique of the report observed that "there is a suspicious lack of detail about the location and modalities of the interviews" and that derogatory reports given by refugees in KPNLF camps, in particular, "are *de rigeur*, and . . . any hint of moderation toward the PRK is considered an indication of treachery to the KPNLF or DK."[113] As reliable foreign observers, notably the International Committee of the Red Cross (ICRC), were not permitted to review Cambodia's penal system until after the United Nations-sponsored election in 1993, reports of maltreatment of prisoners cannot be corroborated. However, some clarity is provided by the *Report of the United Nations Fact-Finding Mission on Present Structures and Practices of Administration in Cambodia*, 24 April–9 May 1990 which states:

> It was reported that, before the enactment of Decree-law No. 27 of 1986, cases of imprisonment by the police without a trial were numerous and concerned especially members or suspected members of the resistance forces. This situation is supposed to have been remedied by the new legislation, even if the powers of the police in matters of detention remain quite wide. In order to solve the many pending cases of detention without trial, the Council of State in 1986 established a special central committee in Phnom Penh and a sub-committee for every province. The mandate of these bodies was to review the cases and, if necessary, to demand the release of detainees. This network of committees is still in place and, apparently, cases of detention without trial have not yet been entirely resolved.[114]

In all the 1979 documents, there is stated awareness of the vulnerability of the revolution and the realization that the new administration was not coping quickly enough to deal with the threats that came from every quarter. "There is insufficient alertness and there is a serious level of negligence within the ranks of cadres and soldiers and among many of the people . . . When they meet difficulties and complications among the people, the ministry of the *nokorbal* [i.e. the Ministry of the Interior] at all levels cannot find measures to solve them definitively, looking as though they do not know which way to go and this just creates further problems."[115]

THE PUBLIC SECURITY FORCES

As in other socialist states, the Cambodian public security forces (*nokorbal*) were as important as the military for the protection and defense of the state. During the Pol Pot regime, they were the most feared and loathed of the party's cadres. After the overthrow of that regime, it was presumed that most of them bore "the debt of blood" and defectors among them were not permitted to join the new administration. Consequently, the Ministry of the Interior commenced its duties in 1979 with a serious lack of trained and experienced staff.

Because the Khmer Rouge started to infiltrate the administration almost as soon as it was established, there was an urgent need to build the public security forces, particularly at the base. The party decided that "we should choose from among the masses those active people who have been through movements and who we have seen are honest and revolutionary and trusted by the people to build core groups to act as security (*nokorbal*) for the villages and communes, reporting to cadres in the districts."[116] At the same time, the party and the Front had to engage in the struggle to raise the consciousness of the masses, "raise awareness of taking care of the revolution, defend it actively" so that the masses would regard themselves as "masters" of the situation, willingly striking down the enemy and denying the enemy inroads to the new administration.[117]

In view of the threats to the new regime and the lack of trained local staff, it must be assumed that for the first three years at least, the Vietnamese directly managed public security work in Cambodia. Then, on 20 November 1981, prime minister Pen Sovann issued a decision according to which the Ministry of the Interior would have full responsibility for the administration and training of the *nokorbal* ("just as the Ministry for National Defense manages all three kinds of army").[118] This decision applied to all the security forces throughout the country. In the countryside, the Kampuchean people's security sector would cooperate closely with the revolutionary state authorities at all levels and with the army, mass organizations and the people "to defend unceasingly the gains of the revolution."[119] The sub-decree *Setting out the Duties, Rights and Organization of the Ministry of the Interior* was not issued until 11 January 1983.[120] In this document, the people's security forces, the *nokorbal*, were described as "an important armed force of the party and the state of the People's Republic of Kampuchea . . . to protect political security and care for social order, in the goal of protecting and caring for the revolutionary state authority, protecting the armed forces, protecting state assets and collective assets, protecting the assets and the lives of the people by actively bringing together the parts in the cause of defending the nation and building the motherland, pushing ahead the cause of the Kampuchean revolution, marching step by step through time of conflict to socialism."[121]

By the time of that sub-decree, however, the *nokorbal* had already received a lot of training and support from Vietnam. A *Convention and Agreement of Cooperation* was signed by the ministers of the interior ministries of the SRV and PRK on 26 June 1980 which guaranteed mutual support in five areas: political security, social order, the provision of experts and "cooperating fighting forces," the training and upgrading of cadres, and logistics.[122] After signing, Vietnam sent 258 experts to the Cambodian ministry, including "70 to the center, 21 in the capital city, 51 experts in all the provinces and 116 experts were assigned to 26 important districts in 11 provinces and municipalities."[123] Apart from helping to set up an administration system, the experts "exchanged experience in the work of mobilizing the masses, the work of protecting the security system, struggling against criminals, the work of expertise in managing statistics, managing the traffic, managing arms and explosives, et cetera."[124] Short-term experts were sent to help train cadres to manage the border access points, airports, shipping ports, and so on, and to train cadres in the techniques of photography, breaking codes and the issuing of identification cards. More than five hundred cadres of the Cambodian ministry went to Vietnam for short-term skills training in 1982–3, while twenty-two students, "most of them children of martyred combatants" were sent for long-term study at the training school for public security forces in Vietnam.[125] Vietnamese teachers and curriculum experts were sent to help establish a training school in the Cambodian ministry.

The 1981 *Annual Report* of the Ministry of the Interior provides detailed information about the security situation in Cambodia and the three year-old regime's ability to cope.[126] It is almost dismissive of the various movements, parties and fronts of the right-wing dissidents loosely grouped under the leadership of either Son Sann or Sihanouk. The Khmer Rouge (KR) guerrillas, however, were another matter. In December 1980 Pol Pot had "retired" from the position of leader of the government of Democratic Kampuchea and Khieu Samphan had replaced him as prime minister, thus paving the way for the creation of a coalition of the resistance groups.[127] The report expressed some concern over the impact that a proposed united front of the three main factions in the resistance would have on international opinion but the more worrying concern was over the KR's relentless covert activities to undermine the regime. Some former high-ranking officers of the KR had changed their identities to get menial jobs in Phnom Penh or had "burrowed" into the state authorities from the center to the base, including the security and military forces, "until the time is right."[128] Their psychological warfare had attracted cadres, staff, soldiers and ordinary people "to carry out political activities against the communication routes, the railroads, the waterways, and they have exploded grenades in the city and in gatherings, killing gentle people."[129] Despite employing heavy intimidation, the KR had failed to upset the national elections and in revenge "they used propaganda ruses saying they had liberated Phnom Penh and for the people to come together and do looting. That . . . resulted in some people from Takeo, Kompong Speu and Svay Rieng, et cetera, who do not yet have high revolutionary awareness, without firm revolutionary attitudes, coming to Phnom Penh on oxcarts and bicycles with knives, axes and staves in the hope of gathering loot according to the propaganda of the enemy."[130] They started rumors which caused panic and hoarding in the capital and constantly stirred up anti-Vietnamese sentiment with stories that the Vietnamese put poison in food to kill Cambodians. Elsewhere the KR tried to woo the people with gifts of medicine, cloth, radios and even dollars and gold. "As for the psychological warfare which is the most poisonous, it is the propaganda which says that Khmer do not kill Khmer, they only kill Vietnamese."[131] The security police were the most vulnerable to this kind of propaganda and several had been arrested for cooperating with the KR or had run away to Thailand. By the time of this report, there had been 352 defections by PRK cadres and staff of state authorities in Phnom Penh and 405 from among just eight provinces.[132]

Interior minister Khang Sarin reported that there had been increased military activity in almost all provinces, and particularly in the northwest in Battambang, Siem Reap/Oddar Meanchey and Preah Vihear. The enemy were using typical guerrilla tactics including "raids, armed attacks, laying mines to kill the people and laying mines to destroy roads, bridges, railways, transport vehicles, and so on."[133] He said that the Pol Pot forces were placing arms all along the length of the border with the aim of moving into Cambodia to cut National Route No. 6 and to move south of Siem Reap to attack Pursat province."The activities of the KR enemy sent into Siem Reap are consistently larger in number, as they are in Preah Vihear," he said.[134] In the northeast, the KR were acting jointly with the FULRO forces of the Montagnards of Vietnam while in Kampot and Takeo they were cooperating with "soldiers left from Thieu Ky," ARVN troops.[135] He reported that in 1981, the Phnom Penh to Battambang railway line was hit fourteen times; nineteen people were killed and 113 injured in the raids. In all, in the first ten months of 1981, there had been 1,285 attacks and raids on the village and commune militias in the eight most severely affected provinces resulting in the deaths of 145 militiamen. Twenty-seven families or 243 people had been "snatched." The raids and intimidation were affecting agricultural production, he claimed, because people were afraid to go far from their homes to grow rice.

Reporting on the state of security and public order in the towns and provinces throughout the country during that period, Khang Sarin admitted there had been 742 acts of armed robbery, of which 182 had been committed in "uniforms of the Kampuchean military or of the security forces."[136] He added that "sometimes they were people masquerading as military to carry out robberies."[137] On the whole, however, he was pleased with the work that his ministry had done and with the attitude of most of his cadres and staff. The total number employed by the Ministry of the Interior as of the end of October 1981 was 611 in the central ministry and 2,160 in nine provinces, their provincial centers and districts. He reported that there were one thousand two hundred people employed in the commune security forces. In all, there were only fourteen party members in the Ministry of the Interior by the end of 1981 although five more were preparing to be members (*triem*). There were 138 core group members and ten more preparing to be members of core groups. He considered that relations with the Vietnamese experts were "clean and close . . . building an effective working system and preparing a complicated department."[138]

This lengthy report helps to put the problems of the new regime into clear perspective. The relentless propaganda campaign waged against them, particularly that of denigrating the PRK leadership as the *yuon* (Vietnamese) head on the Khmer body, was very difficult to combat and as corrosive as the highly effective guerrilla war. Their own propaganda could only appear to be defensive. And, as Khang Sarin admitted, the real enemy was within. As long as party cadres, state authorities and the troops themselves lacked commitment, the people's faith in and loyalty to the regime could never be assured:

> We have opened people's courts to try these traitors, making our people realize how bad they are and to understand the ideas of the enemy, but we still have a few weaknesses in that

we do not yet work hard in raising popular movements with enthusiasm to join in exposing the enemy who are buried among the people, and our state authorities do not yet use competency in our popular movements to note clearly the ideas of the enemy. While we have cadres and staff and combatants who are not good, operations to destroy the revolution's leadership, the wild and terrifying raiding, shooting, capturing and killing of the people will affect our political influence.[139]

KHMER ROUGE ACTIVITIES

The 1981 wet season witnessed a consolidation of Khmer Rouge activity in eight key provinces. A report by Chan Seng, chief of command of C80 Combat Force stationed somewhere in Siem Reap province, highlights some of the frustrations and fears of a conventional army fighting against sparrow war tactics.[140] The author describes the people in the area as being totally in the hands of the KR. He says, "The enemy have taken hold of and manage the people according to Pol Pot methods, by building a number of cooperatives in the battlefields which they control" and they controlled corridors from those bases to the border. He listed four points which were almost impossible to combat:

- Since the beginning, the unknown enemy have been erratic in defeat. They divide their strength, hide, move, evade in order to defend themselves and keep their strength intact and make plans to strike us from behind, hitting at our careless points and striking to destroy the communication routes;
- in disguise, they wait for a chance to mock the revolution;
- they use their strength in groups to grab villages and communes, to make contact with the bases to get food to take to the forest;
- they use their forest bases to snatch our cadres and write letters to threaten the people at the base.[141]

Chan Seng continued that the people were terrified, so that "in many places where our forces have entered, the people have fled from their homes, taking refuge in the forest until the time is good and in some places they still haven't come back."[142] The people knew who the enemies were in the local administration "but the enemy takes revenge so the people do not dare point and tell."[143] During August and September, the KR forces had overrun a number of villages and communes, so that members of the state authorities, armed forces and mass organizations who survived were now, in fact, turn-coats who "still pretend to work for and serve our revolution and every month they still come to the district to collect their salary as usual."[144] They had made some progress ("54 killed, 152 arrested, 293 defections, 83 arms taken . . . and we have cut off the source of food and contact between the enemy and the people") but the prognosis was bad, because "we still do not understand the enemy. We haven't grasped the enemy or evaluated the enemy clearly. Occasionally we catch a glimpse but then they shrivel away, daring not to come out and operate openly. We still do not know them because they bury themselves among the masses."[145] The more important reason for failure was that "the work of mobilizing the masses is still weak and not united."[146] The author thought that his men were not close to the people, "they don't yet understand about the will of the people" so "the measures aren't appropriate and the practice is not strong . . . none of them have yet got close to mobilizing the masses as the core task, the essential strategy of the battle. Therefore, we haven't grasped the essence of the task."[147] The task was not essentially a military one, it was "gathering, assigning and pushing hard the mass movement [as] the core task of the second step of the battle. The need [is] to destroy the influence of the enemy over the people, to encourage the people to dare to speak the truth, to speak clearly about the enemy, to change [their] activities and strike at the enemy, to work hard at all important communes."[148] The confusion and fear among the people at the end of 1981 in this part of Siem Reap could hardly be more graphically illustrated.

Throughout 1982 and 1983, however, the internal security situation deteriorated further, prompting Carney to report:

The KPRAF, after four years of effort, including receipt of modern Soviet arms and artillery and training of large numbers of officers and men in Vietnam and the USSR, remains inadequate to cope with the resistance, even in an auxiliary role. The SRV does not have confidence in the loyalty or discipline of KPRAF mainforce units. The KPRAF, considering its resources, has failed to develop as well as the non-communist resistance. This powerful evidence undercuts notions that the Heng Samrin regime is succeeding in consolidating its hold in Cambodia. The resistance continues to view the KPRAF as a potential source of converts rather than as implacable foes.[149]

In the same vein, Jacques Bekaert reported that "the PRK armed forces collapse almost as fast as they are built. Khmers are just not anxious to fight against Khmers. The rate of defection is high. Combativity is minimal. Incidents between the PRKAF and Vietnamese troops have been numerous since the early days of 1979."[150]

The turnaround in the resolve of the PRK government to take charge of its own defense is dated from a political seminar led by Le Duc Tho in Phnom Penh in January 1984 which focused on "the imperative need for a definitive solution to eliminate the Khmer resistance movements."[151] The Council of Ministers agreed to begin conscription at a meeting on 10 March that year.[152] The decree-law *Concerning Military Service* was ratified by the Council of State in March 1984, conscripting citizens between the ages of 18 and 25 to two years military service.[153] Conscription was an admission of the PRK's failure to mobilize the masses to defend the new regime by other means. It was also a recognition of the seriousness of the threat coming from the combined resistance forces of the Coalition Government of Democratic Kampuchea (CGDK), representing the Khmer Rouge, the royalists and the republicans, which was formed in June 1982 at the prompting of ASEAN and with the backing of China and the USA.

Chapter 7

CIVIL SOCIETY AND SOCIAL ACTION

IDEOLOGICAL HEGEMONY DEVELOPS most thoroughly and least obviously through the agency of civil society, that is, the media, the religious bodies, the schools, trade unions, sporting institutions, artistic and cultural organizations and displays, and various other types of social association. It is in this essentially private sphere that public consent for state direction and control is fashioned. The more willingly consent is granted, the more efficiently hegemony is established. The work of rebuilding and defending the new regime, starting from a very low base, necessitated unpopular decisions on the part of the party and the government. It was the role of the FUNSK to convince the people that supporting the new regime was in their own best interests. The Front had a pseudo-religious function in the new secular state; it had to gather, inspire and motivate the people to acts of selflessness. Heng Samrin explained the Front's role in these terms:

> In order to help the people at all levels broaden, deepen, intensify their love of nation, to depend on themselves, to support themselves, to have awareness of mastery over their destiny and the country, to increase solidarity and consensus in activities to push ahead the revolutionary movements of the masses, to implement every policy of the government and the Front with success in these new times, the Central Committee of the Front must open wide and gather the important people, intellectuals, patriotic monks into the Front in all the provinces; it must organize this in good time . . . to defend national independence, to save the nation and the society of the people recovering from genocide.[1]

In July 1979, the party central committee issued a circular "Concerning Expanding the Central Committee of the FUNSK, Organizing a Front Committee in all Provinces and Towns, and Increasing the Work of the Front in the New Situation." It decided to increase the size of the fourteen-member Front central committee by a further thirteen or fourteen people "from the milieux of dignitaries, intellectuals, monks and representatives of ethnic minorities." The original committee consisted of Heng Samrin (president), Chea Sim (vice president), Ros Samay (secretary general) and eleven members: Mat Ly, Bun My, Hun Sen, Mean Soman, Meas Samnang, Neou Samon, the Venerable Long Sim, Hem Samin, Chey Kanh Nha, Chan Ven and Prach Sun. These members represented the Cham and ethnic minorities, the clergy, and the mass organizations for youth, women, the trade unions, the farmers and intellectuals. That four of those eleven members represented the Intellectuals' Association is perhaps indicative of the new regime's urgent need to recruit cadres from their ranks. In the provinces, the party committee of each province assisted the mass organizations in electing a nine or ten-member committee of the Front for that province. The central committee met every three months and the provincial committees met monthly. Their specific task was to popularize government policies through propaganda and mass movements. Mass organizations were established in every ministry/department, enterprise and provincial center.

The second congress of the FUNSK was held in the meeting hall of the former Chinese Embassy in Phnom Penh on 27–28 September 1979, attended by 157 representatives. The chairman of the organizing committee for the congress was Yos Por, a member of the 1954 group, whose most recent public task had been advocate for the defense in the trial of Pol Pot and Ieng Sary which had been held in August. In his opening address, Pen Sovann called the Front the "rudder" of the revolutionary movement:

In his notes on culture and social affairs, Pen Sovann compared our culture to something which has crossed over and come back. He said that the Sihanouk time adopted the corrupt culture of America and the West and spread it throughout the society. In the time of Pol Pot–Ieng Sary, people had blind eyes and deaf ears. Culture clearly comes from education, tradition and art. After liberation, the people had the right to freedom and resisted having any pressure put on them. The first light which the Front shone brightly on them was culture. Now children aged seven or eight do not walk around picking up cow dung in the rice fields. There are more than 200,000 children in school even if the equipment is far from enough. In every province in Cambodia, in every place with a school, children go to study in clothes of all colors; they are well-behaved children with teachers. The children have pieces of paper pinched together to make books, they write in the dirt or use sap to paint on wood and they study day and night. Therefore, we see that black clouds will melt near the sun . . . This is our future.[2]

Pen Sovann paid homage to the doctors who were restoring the health system throughout the country saying, "We have science and if we have science then our society will progress. The despicable Pot said if there was water and rice there was everything but, on the contrary, his great leap forward was just towards a bowl of rice gruel."[3] On the second day, Heng Samrin announced that the leadership of the Front had been increased by twenty-one members, making a total of thirty-five in the central committee.

The challenges confronting the new state and its key agencies, particularly the Front, with regard to the most fundamental needs for reconstructing society were practically overwhelming during that first year. Cambodia was like a person without a skeleton. Hoang Tung, editor of Vietnam's official daily newspaper *Nhan Dan* explained the analogy in these terms:

Three million people were killed. And they were some of the best human resources they had. The mass killing of the people was like removing the skeleton from a person. The intelligentsia was killed, the skilled were killed, the economy destroyed, and society thrown into disorder.[4]

The essential building block for the restored society was considered to be the family and then the village and so on but, as Hoang Tung continued, "Everything has to be provided—even clothes, household goods and medicines." Foreign assistance, notably from Vietnam and the USSR, was essential, but political will and personal endurance were even more important. Heng Samrin made note of the slim but important gains made during the first six months following the overthrow of the Pol Pot regime in a *prakas* issued in July 1979.[5] Despite the obvious hardships and shortfalls in equipment and standards, thousands of children were back at school, hospitals and clinics were functioning, cultural and historical artifacts were being cared for, art troupes were entertaining the people, and "young men and women have the rights and freedom to choose a spouse and marry according to our national traditions." Cambodians had regained their "right to travel, to hold ceremonies, to make a living, and rebuild the lives of their re-united families." He lamented that "we haven't yet achieved many results" and that many people were still hungry and debilitated by disease. Nevertheless, the real gains he listed were "the pride and the joy of our people. And we must try hard, with all our capacity, to do more. With the experience of other countries in the world and the assistance of countries who want to help us redevelop our country quickly, we can do it . . . " The most pressing needs were for education, health, and social action for disabled veterans and other vulnerable groups. Religion, the arts, and cultural preservation, were also issues which the new regime addressed, in accordance with the promises made at Snoul in December 1978 to restore the Cambodian society. The efforts were huge and the achievements were even more remarkable, given that Cambodia was struggling with war on two fronts: sabotage, subversion and guerrilla raids waged by the "resistance" forces, as well as the diplomatic war in the international arena, which effectively served to isolate Cambodia politically and to maintain the embargo on credit, trade, and aid, which Cambodia needed to rebuild itself.

In 1981, after the holding of the general elections, the opening of the National Assembly, the staging of the fourth party congress, and recognition that its original eleven points had been realized, the Kampuchean United Front for National Salvation renamed itself the Kampuchean United Front for the Construction and Defense of the Motherland (KUFCDM). Heng Samrin's speech making the announcement on the second day of the third congress of the Front, (21 December 1981), declared that the new Front "continues and expands the glorious revolutionary tradition of the FUNSK, holding to the cause of solidarity for building and defending the motherland, acting as the sacred goal in order to gather the strength of all the people . . . "[6] The new Front called on the people to fulfill seven tasks. These were related to building the armed forces, strengthening the state authority and the administrative and mass organizations of the Front, developing the economy and the culture, expanding the systems of general education and health, and increasing international solidarity. The speech concluded: "The revolution is the cause of all the people. The building and defense of the nation is the special cause of all citizens who genuinely love the nation . . . The cause of the revolution is endowed with justice for our people, so it must win."[7]

The third congress of the Front, attended by 430 full rights members and a further 314 observers, including representatives of mass organizations and the army, as well as members of the diplomatic corps who were invited to participate, was held on 20–22 December 1981 in Chatomuk Hall in Phnom Penh.[8] The whole month of December had been set aside to celebrate the third anniversary of the Front, with *bralong branang* movements (competitions) throughout the country for increasing productivity, thrift and combat readiness, with ceremonies to commemorate the victims of the Pol Pot regime and to respect the graves of Cambodian and Vietnamese soldiers, and with special media broadcasts and cultural exhibitions. The congress itself was preceded by a meeting of the Front's central committee which was attended by twelve of the thirteen members of the steering committee, Heng Samrin being absent.[9] Chea Sim was the new president of this central committee, and on the final day of this preparatory meeting he named the eighty-seven candidates who would hold leadership positions on the National Council of the Front. They included the president, a seven-member steering committee and seventy-nine members. Vice presidents were Bou Thong, Chan Ven, the Venerable Tep Vong and Men Chhan. The secretary general was Yos Por, assisted by Chem Snguon, Vandy Ka'on, Khieu Kanharith, and Min Khin. The congress adopted the new statutes of the Front and its ten-point program of activities.

EDUCATION

Schools are key instruments of state hegemony in every society, but in socialist revolutionary societies, education deliberately serves the long-term goal of transforming the society's values and morals, and creating the new socialist man and woman. Although primary schooling commenced almost immediately after 7 January 1979, the system of education was not standardized until the decree-law concerning the system of general education was ratified by the Council of State on 20 November 1986.[10] Article 1 of the law stipulated:

> Schools for general education should stand under the management of the state and should practice the general objectives of training students to become good workers with the pure spirit of loving the nation allied with the solidarity of international socialism, with proper conduct and revolutionary solidarity, with basic knowledge, with competency of labor, with bounteous health in order to fulfill tasks well in the future in an occupation towards serving the needs of defending and building the motherland.

The curriculum was based on "political consciousness, revolutionary morality, basic knowledge for competency in modern labor skills, production, agriculture, craft, and industry appropriate for the real situation of the Kampuchean revolution" (Article 6). Article 7 advised that education should follow the principles of theory tied to practice, education tied to labor and production, and schools tied to the society; schools had to expand revolutionary awareness, "awareness of being forged, persevering and being active in battle." The directive of the Council of Ministers for implementing this decree-law recommended that "we should strive to ensure a balance between quantity and quality by relying on needs and concrete possibilities, avoiding running after quantity only, and we should have a clear and appropriate plan for education."[11] Education was not compulsory but "we should ensure that all the pupils study to the end of grade five," that is, the end of primary school.[12] The target was to have all primary school graduates continue to level 1 secondary within five years (by 1992) but "it isn't necessary for everyone to continue to level 2."[13] State authorities and the mass organizations at all levels were required to have measures for employing high school graduates, either in the production units at the base, in the armed forces or for sending them to do short-term vocational skills training. All schools were supposed to have production bases of their own such as "timber or metal workshops, sewing or weaving . . . vegetable gardens or ricefields for serving the work of practice and research" and to have "clean relations" with nearby production units for the purposes of work experience.[14] On the principle that "The State and The People Unite in order to Build," the authorities and the masses were to ensure that every school had "classrooms, desks, chairs, a library, a laboratory, a room of 'traditions,' a workshop, trial rice fields, sportsfields, et cetera."[15] Many of these demands far exceeded both the means and the ability of the local people, the administrators and the teachers. Nonetheless, the efforts and sacrifices of communities and teachers were vast throughout this period. The directive referred to the slogan, "Every Teacher is a Revolutionary Fighter" and teachers were urged to "educate themselves and forge themselves according to the needs of progress and development."[16] Their finest contribution was to the campaign to eradicate illiteracy.

National literacy figures are notoriously difficult to discuss because the term "literacy" is variously defined. However, accepting Banister and Johnson's definition of "illiteracy" as "unable to read or write", 57 percent of Cambodia's population above the age of ten years were illiterate at the time of the 1962 census.[17] Modern education made considerable progress under Sihanouk's *Sangkum Reastr Niyum* (Popular Socialist Community) and with American assistance during the Lon Nol period. Teachers then had been relatively highly paid, and accorded high social status, but one doubts that they moved far from the capital and the provincial centers. During the Pol Pot regime, intellectuals were derided and murdered, and while some children in some places were taught the Khmer alphabet during that time, there was little that could have been called an education system. The PRK realized far better than the DK that public education has political benefits. They also respected the fact that science was essential for economic development. Like all socialist regimes, the DK apart, the PRK gave education generally, and literacy in particular, high priority.

The Campaign to Eradicate Illiteracy commenced on 18 June 1980. In his speech to announce the commencement of the campaign, minister for education, Chan Ven, stated unequivocally that the purpose of the campaign was "to raise a movement of study for all our people as a factor to push ahead the duty to build leaders, to defend the country effectively and to advance quickly towards socialism."[18] The task was given to the ministry's Department of Adult Education and by the official commencement date for the campaign, it had already started classes for 61,242 students ("cadres, staff, soldiers, workers, farmers and youth") in 1,365 classes with 1,516 volunteer teachers. The minister announced that the Central Pedagogy Faculty was operating again and provincial teacher training institutes were preparing to reopen (Battambang and Kandal had already begun). The Curriculum and Textbook Writing Center had put together and printed books for primary education and for adult students for all grades. The curriculum for level 1 secondary school adult students had also been prepared. Bulgaria had provided assistance and educational material to establish a senior high school for cadres, staff, soldiers, factory and state enterprise employees throughout the country to finish their schooling in Phnom Penh; this "complementary" school had been operating since 17 March

1980. Complementary schooling was primarily for young adults, whose primary and post-primary education had been interrupted by the DK regime. Right throughout the 1980s, young workers attended early morning or evening classes in order to finish primary school, to study for the *diplome* (level 1 secondary certificate) and some even for the *baccalaureat* (level 2 secondary leaving certificate). These classes ensured that there was no "lost generation" of Pol Pot adolescents, as occurred in China after the Cultural Revolution. Many of the next generation of Cambodian leaders owed their good fortune to the opportunity provided by complementary education. This was a fact that the young people appreciated at the time. Even after the University of Phnom Penh reopened in 1988,[19] many of its students still attended complementary secondary school classes in their free time in order to get their senior high school certificates because "otherwise the old people will think we are not educated."[20] Complementary school enrolments peaked in the 1985–1986 academic year when there were 243,121 in the preliminary level ("for all targets, [i.e. civil servants, youth, ethnic minorities] and for cadres from ethnic minorities"), and 22,791 in the general education program.[21]

The minister stated the goals of the three-year plan for adult education:

- 1980 is the year . . . (for) building a model in order to experiment and extend. Each village should have at least one literacy class. We should gather at least half of all illiterate people to study. We must get 100 percent of cadres, staff, workers, soldiers, and youth and organize for those of them who can read and write already to complete their study at the village school. Each province should have one school for complementary education.
- 1981 is the year for pushing the movement hard to top level . . . In districts and communes we should open complementary classes.
- 1982 is the year of striving to achieve the campaign to eradicate illiteracy. Step by step, we should end the campaign province by province in order to work towards achieving the

goals with stability throughout the country and along with this to open more complementary classes.[22]

Heng Samrin's speech on that occasion explained that

> Socialism places high value on knowledge. According to this point of view, the education of adults is really a basic means for building the economy and for defending the nation. Our people will practice new techniques in increasing the harvest if and only when they study this technique themselves . . . Cadres, staff, workers, soldiers, the people, all classes must have a high level of science and then we can build our nation and develop well and abundantly . . . Rebuilding the educational infrastructureand revolutionary education which has the characteristics of democracy and pure socialism is the vast task for creating a generation of people to be good citizens and a courageous army to serve the construction and defense of our beloved motherland and to advance towards socialism.[23]

All cadres and state employees under the age of thirty were required to complete their primary education and all the people, males aged forty-five and under, and women aged forty and under, had to attend literacy classes. Heng Samrin added, "As well as this, we must raise a vast movement among the masses in order to eliminate illiteracy among ethnic people . . . with many teaching methods appropriate for the place . . . Those who know teach those who do not; those who know a lot teach those who know a little."[24]

In August 1982, the permanent committee of the National Literacy Campaign held a meeting to sum up and evaluate the results of the campaign as it drew to the conclusion of the first three-year plan.[25] According to its statistics, Cambodia had 1,025,794 (adult) illiterates and 72.51 percent of them had taken part in the campaign; more than a quarter of those participants had already graduated.[26] As for complementary education, 281,995 people were studying grades two to eight in fourteen schools specifically for that purpose in eleven provinces, as well as in two military complementary schools and the Central Complementary School. Heng Samrin was president of this committee, which indicated the importance and value that the government placed on giving the people access to the education which had been denied them during the DK years. He said he regretted the lack of materials and the many other demands on people's time, including the newly implemented public labor scheme for tree-clearing as part of the national defense plan, political study sessions, et cetera which had interrupted the literacy campaign. Natural calamities had also caused personal hardship, and the worsening security situation in the border provinces had placed the people's priorities elsewhere. If the plan could not reach the full target, then all ministries/departments, provinces/towns and all mass organizations should ensure at least that all illiterates in the civil service categories were "liberated."A second three-year plan to fight illiteracy was initiated by a government directive on 31 January 1984.[27]

The first campaign involved 33,597 "teachers" and claimed a success rate of 55.29 percent.[28] The mobilization of volunteer teachers employed the skills not only of trained teachers and students but also of cadres, civil servants, monks and ordinary citizens:

> Many of the volunteer teachers endured difficulties to fulfill their duties actively to liberate hundreds of illiterates. Some other teachers overcame all difficulties until they sacrificed themselves in the time of teaching. Many thousands of our people took part in building the base for the movement such as building literacy classrooms, tables, chairs, blackboards, providing books, chalk, pencils, paraffin oil . . . As well they helped to support the livelihood of the teachers with rice, money, et cetera. The monks participated with propaganda to raise the morale of the students to go and study. The mass organizations at the center as well as in the provinces/towns participated in the movement.[29]

The second campaign "decided to eradicate illiteracy among 435,031 people, or 85.65 percent (compared with the 507,908 of newly counted illiterates)."[30] Together, the two campaigns claimed to have "liberated" about one million illiterates. Recidivism was recognized as a real possibility in the countryside where there was little to read and few opportunities to maintain newly acquired literacy skills. Ten years after the end of the literacy campaigns, in 1997, the National Institute of Statistics reported an adult literacy rate of 68.7 percent; the adult female rate was only 58 percent.[31] Nevertheless, the statistics show that rural women who were targeted by the campaign (under forty years of age in 1980) had fared well in comparison with groups on either side of their age cohort.[32]

HEALTH

Cambodians who were weakened by starvation during the DK regime were very susceptible to diseases. Cholera was a major fear in 1979 and malaria was almost endemic; less life-threatening but no less debilitating conditions such as beri-beri among the children and enervating, chronic depression exacerbated by untreated gynecological problems among the women, hampered recovery and restricted productivity. Medicine and provision of medical treatment was a priority second only to food production during that first year, but it was a priority which was virtually impossible to meet because there were few doctors or other trained and qualified medical staff, and little in the way of medicine or other supplies. In the countryside, in the absence of a healthcare system, the focus was placed instead on a public health education program, self-reliance, mutual support, and traditional medicine. By the end of July, twenty-five hospitals had reopened throughout the country, five of them in Phnom Penh. A foreign journalist who visited one of these Phnom Penh hospitals in December that year reported that there was just one doctor to attend to the needs of the four hundred people who came for outpatients' treatment each day; "his chemist supplies contained in one glass cabinet are pathetically small."[33] By then, however, some relief had been provided by international aid supplies. The provision of health care developed in 1980. By mid-year, eighteen provincial hospitals and one hundred district hospitals were operating, while half of all communes had built clinics and birthing centers.[34] The total number of health cadres was 7,000, among whom were seventy-five doctors and twenty pharmacists. The Science Faculty had recommenced courses in January 1980, and 606 students were enrolled in medicine and pharmacy. One thousand basic medical staff were studying in the provinces. Apart from Vietnamese experts who were based in all the hospitals, assistance was also provided by experts from Cuba, GDR, Hungary, Poland and the USSR. Mortality rates had dropped greatly since the previous year and vaccination programs had recommenced. The birthrate soared. Jacqueline Desbarats notes:

> The sharp drop in fertility induced by the atypical political and economic conditions of the second half of the 1970s lasted only as long as those conditions endured, and with the return to more normal conditions in the early 1980s, the crude birthrate rebounded to a higher level than had ever been recorded before, peaking perhaps as high as 50 per 1,000 or even higher ... the rate of natural increase reached at the beginning of the decade is believed to have been the highest ever documented for the country.[35]

The following year, 1981, was very much a year of consolidation of the new regime in all spheres. In health, too, there was cause for pride in the statistics: 1,225 health bases, one university faculty and three pharmaceutical factories.[36] The National Blood Transfusion Center opened that year, which helped to ease the severe lack of blood and plasma for transfusions. Of the 11,231 medical staff, however, only thirty-five were university trained, and eighteen of them were new graduates. Public healthcare continued to focus on the prevention of communicable diseases and immunization programs were already being practiced. Mobile teams were organized to go down to the base and inoculate the people in areas where there were disease outbreaks. The report for 1981 claimed, "We have treated 1,849,478 people." A total of 956 tonnes of medical equipment had been received from fraternal socialist countries and from humanitarian aid organizations, but the Ministry of Health regretted that the poor power and water supply had hindered the production of drugs in state pharmaceutical factories, and the medical needs of the people were still not being met. It also admitted that "the service and care of patients is still weak."

Developments in the health sector continued steadily throughout the regime, but the lack of qualified staff and the restrictions imposed on it by the persistent shortage of drugs and other medical supplies meant that healthcare provision was severely restricted throughout the whole decade of the 1980s. At the beginning of 1985, as Hun Sen took over the reins of chairman of the Council of Ministers, and as the full cost of the border defense work in terms of public health began to bite very hard, Say Phouthang released a circular for the Party's Central Committee Secretariat *Concerning the Work of Health in the Time Ahead*.[37] He acknowledged and praised the genuine achievements of the sector, but admitted that many weaknesses remained, namely: "the perspective on the goals of socialist health is not yet very deep or strong, the organization of the health network is not yet firm, the ranks of the cadres are still lacking in quantity and quality, the people's lifestyle and environment does not yet have appropriate hygiene, all the major debilitating diseases are still rampant, the distribution and use of drugs is not yet appropriate, the attitude of doctors towards the sick in some places is not yet good, the work of protecting the health of the people is not yet good or thorough enough, and the sector lacks the full force of the various other ministries to participate in these movements." He called for stronger efforts to implement a public health education campaign, including encouragement of sports and other active measures to prevent disease and for times to be set down "to organize all the general hygiene work in order to resolve the problem of rubbish, to clean up the water system, and to cut down trees. Raise up the building and management of all hygiene structures to defend against disease such as toilets, bathrooms, wells, enclosures, and animal pens . . . It is important that all health units, education and sports units, propaganda and culture, radio, and newspapers, should cooperate to accept responsibility in the work of propaganda and education for understanding about everyday hygiene for our people in order to protect their own health."

According to this circular, "Health is a productive force. Health is weak both on the side of form and awareness . . . " Realistically, however, the demands that crowded in on the small regime after the decisive dry-season offensive of 1984–1985, meant that the health sector would remain over-taxed and under-resourced, and therefore unable to implement these very practical recommendations, until the settlement of the civil conflict in 1991.

SOCIAL ACTION

While the whole society was in desperate need of support in January 1979, it was the thousands of orphans who first came to symbolize the tragedy that Pol Pot's attempt at social revolution had wrought. These were the children, thin and swollen-bellied with beri-beri and parasites, whose parents had died or who had lost their parents, perhaps as early as during the confused evacuation of the city in April 1975 or later, due to enforced separation, and who could no longer remember their parents' names, or even their faces. Some of them were "Pol Pot's children," socialized into an alien, totalitarian culture, who defied the state's attempts to "re-school" them after 1979. Later in the decade, their prominence would be eclipsed by thousands of amputees, mostly disabled veterans who were victims of landmine explosions while defending the northwestern border from rebel incursions.

The People's Republic of Kampuchea was a socialist state but acute, abiding poverty, and a severe shortage of trained and qualified personnel throughout its rule, put social welfare benefits which were equivalent to the people's needs far beyond its capacity to provide. Confronted with the scale of the people's suffering, Heng Samrin called on his party's cadres to encourage the ancient tradition of mutual support:

> Raise awareness of self-reliance, supporting oneself. Raise awareness of mutual respect and helping to care for each other. Share food together; save each other from disaster in this time of shortages. As well as this, we must take every pos-

sibility of assistance from the international community. We must organize in order to ensure that the distribution of aid gets to the people and is not spoilt or lost or falls into the hands of the enemy. The distribution must ensure justice and appropriateness. Strive to get it to the revolutionary families, the families of cadres, and those who have no means of support, and the orphans.[38]

Orphans did receive aid. Initially this came from Vietnam, its PAVN troops inside Cambodia and then from those provinces which were "twinned" with Cambodian provinces. Each member of the Women's Association, RWAK, reportedly cared for an orphan.[39] International humanitarian aid organizations, notably Oxfam, raised awareness of the plight of the children throughout the Western world, and the public response to their campaign was vitally important for the children's recovery. A British aid worker had said of the children in Phnom Penh's Orphanage Number One in August 1979, "Many of the children are too weak to stand. They will die if food is not got to them soon."[40] Just four months later, an Australian delegation commented on the positive changes that had occurred among those same children: "We are cheered by a group of them who march in filing order up to our car."[41] Other fraternal socialist countries provided long-term assistance, particularly Hungary which built and resourced the Kampuchea-Hungary Friendship Orphanage on the outskirts of the city at Prek Phneu, and provided technical teachers and trainers to develop vocational skills training courses for the orphans.

While orphans received urgently needed support and the sick and elderly were primarily cared for by family, it was the acknowledged duty of the government to support its disabled veterans and the families of combatants who were killed or incapacitated on the battlefield. This work was the responsibility of the Commission for Social Action, headed by Neou Samon, which was established in accordance with a decision of the provisional government of the PRCK in October 1979. Until 1985, the achievements of the commission seem to have been at best haphazard, and responsibility for its work was spread over so many different agencies that neglect of the disabled and their families was more or less guaranteed. Prime Minister Chan Si issued a circular in October 1982 *Concerning the Administration of Practice according to a Number of Points in the Policy for Martyrs and Disabled Veterans and Army Families*.[42] It was the duty of six separate ministries, the Front committees in all provinces, and the Commission for Social Action to enact the stipulations. In essence, the circular offered no direct material assistance to the veterans or their families. One of Hun Sen's first official acts was to request the Council of State to dismantle this commission, because "it can no longer effectively manage" the work it had to do.[43] He called for the creation of a Ministry for Disabled Veterans and Social Action, which would assist the Council of Ministers "to research and build in order to send to the Party Central Secretariat and the Council of Ministers, to extend all the principles and policies and methods . . . concerning the work of disabled combatants, the families of killed combatants, the families of combatants, elderly people, children and orphans without support, the disabled who have lost the power of labor, those suffering because of war . . . to administer and guide the implementation properly according to all the principles and policies." Mom Sabun was awarded the portfolio of the new ministry. Ironically perhaps, in view of the increasing need for welfare provision as the civil war worsened, Mom Sabun was faced with declining international humanitarian assistance. In 1984, that assistance was measured at a little over 556 tonnes, less than the previous year. By year's end, almost all of it had been distributed. The Council of Ministers report for 1984 showed that the number of children's centers actually fell from thirty-five the previous year to twenty-eight; and with re-education efforts "we have reformed 229 vagabonds and 172 prostitutes. As well as this, we have placed 128 orphans in *krom samaki*, 104 to serve various [army] units, given seventy-four orphans technical skills training, put thirteen in teacher training, fifty-four in the army and forty-five have gone to study abroad. To October 1984, there were 4,753 orphans, 113 [abandoned] babies, 235 amputees, 329 vagabonds and 226 prostitutes."[45] Three years later, the Council of Ministers reported "good practice of all policies for disabled veterans and martyrs as well as families who have merit and skill for the revolution."[46] The number of disabled veterans in just eleven provinces was reported as 4,000 which was a huge increase over the 235 amputees recorded at the end of 1984. Even so, the higher figure was probably just the tip of the iceberg. The official report also noted that "leg prostheses manufacture has expanded and increased and 101 people have artificial legs."

The Ministry of Disabled Veterans and Social Action was given an extra brief in 1988 to care for the offspring born in Vietnam of Cambodian soldiers and Vietnamese mothers. On 7 August 1986, Men Samon, head of the Central Administration Commission, presided over a meeting where two representatives of the Foreign Relations Central Commission of the Communist Party of Vietnam presented a report concerning the children and wives of some of the Khmer Viet Minh who had regrouped in North Vietnam following the signing of the Geneva Accords in 1954. Of the original 1,015 Khmer Viet Minh, more than half or 557 of them had married Vietnamese wives. After 1970, the CPV had supported a total of 878 dependants according to a pension scheme, and as children of martyred combatants, their sons and daughters were given priority for entering schools and universities. The specific concern of the delegation, however, was for "fifteen Kampuchean comrades now working in Kampuchea, who have sixteen wives and fifty-six children living in Vietnam." While the children had been granted provisional support from the state, the sixteen wives received no assistance. "All those widows," the delegates reported, "have requested that if they cannot come and live in Kampuchea, they would like their children to come. In fact, at present, there are twenty-two orphans, and there is only one who is in an orphanage. The rest live with grandparents and aunts and it is the wish of all of them to come and live in Kampuchea. Each child now receives thirty *dong* per month, but they have a lot of problems because the *dong* is falling and prices are rising. Therefore, we ask Kampuchea to help with measures and principles."[47] Men Samon thanked the delegates and promised to take the matter to the leadership. She added, "Where are those fifteen comrades now? They have wives and children in Vietnam, but they probably have other wives in Kampuchea . . . We are concerned about these sixteen women and their children, and we will ask comrade for more details later." The matter took some time to resolve but it was not forgotten. On 1 June 1988, prime minister Hun Sen issued a decision on *Specifications concerning the Policy for Family Groups of Martyred Combatants who died in Cambodia (Mother Vietnamese, Father Cambodian)*. Those children who chose to live in Cambodia would receive one-off support in the form of a package of money, clothing, a mosquito net and bedding; they would be provided with a place to live and assistance with studying literacy in the Khmer language. The abandoned children, and their mothers, who remained in Vietnam would receive a monthly pension at various rates, including 1,500 *dong* for orphans, and the same amount for mothers who were not in state employ or who had retired. For dependants who were no longer children and who were living alone, the Cambodian government would provide half of that level of financial support for which they were eligible as children, as well as a clothing allowance. This detailed directive served as a compassionate and dignified conclusion to one small chapter of the Cambodian revolution.

RELIGION

The new regime moved very cautiously on the matter of allowing the restoration of religion. Under Pol Pot, all religions had been banned and the practice of religion outlawed. Monks of the majority religion, Theravada Buddhism, had been defrocked and some had been forced to marry. Of all the traditional institutions of Khmer society, perhaps religion suffered the gravest harm during the years of totalitarian rule. Religion had provided neither shelter nor solace to the masses during those Pol Pot years, and most of the former religious leaders and teachers had gone abroad, were defrocked or otherwise discredited. In the declaration of the eleven-point program at Snoul in 1978, the new regime had promised religious freedom, but that freedom, in practice, was always limited by its own claims, based largely on political expediency and the need for social control.

On 5 December 1980, Heng Samrin signed a circular of the People's Revolutionary Council entitled *Concerning the Implementation of the Policy on Religion*.[47] Referring to the Front's eleven-point program, the circular stated that "since the day of liberation achieved victory on 7 January 1979, freedom of belief has been guaranteed by the revolutionary state authority. The policy of democratic freedoms and freedom of belief of the FUNSK is appropriate for the desires of all the people."[48]

The freedom to practice religion was shepherded by four principles listed in that circular:

> 1. We must discuss all the matters to be resolved democratically together within the Front and the decisions must have the approval of the revolutionary state authority;
> 2. The law to protect the freedom of belief of all religions must be implemented according to the law;
> 3. Depend on the people and the masses in order to help block and scatter all the ruses of the enemy which use religion as a means to endanger the united cause of the people and the masses;
> 4. Clergy or religious organizations do worthwhile activities for the nation and the people. Those clergy or religious organizations are protected. Any clergy or religious organization operating illegally, doing activities contrary to the advantages of the people and the nation must accept the responsibility of the law.[49]

The Buddhism which was restored was "solidarity Buddhism, without sects." This, in effect, referred to the Mohanikay sect; the Thammayut sect which had been introduced from Thailand in the mid-nineteenth century and which had maintained close links with the court was not restored until after the king returned to Cambodia in 1991. Permission to enter the monkhood and the administration of the *wat* depended on the consideration and approval of the central committee of the Front. The circular planned to set up a Department of

Religion within the Front Central Committee, "to help the secretariat to investigate the matter of religion and guide the implementation of all the policies and circulars of the Front and of the government concerning the matter of religion."[50] This department would be under the direct management of the secretary-general of the Front. The religious leader throughout the PRK regime was the Venerable Tep Vong, an original member of the central committee of the Front, and also a member of the first session of the National Assembly which was elected in May 1981.

Another circular, *Concerning the System of Entering the Buddhist Monkhood*, issued on 5 June 1981, explained that early in the regime some people had abused their rights of religious freedom by entering the monkhood and donning the robe, without the recognition of the state authority.[51] To bring some order to the system, in September 1979 the state had invited abbots to come from Kampuchea Krom to consecrate seven former monks at Wat Unnalom in Phnom Penh so that they would be able to establish and provide proper training for novices. "Then," the circular continued, "the state became interested in arranging religion with proper consensus and appropriate [form]." A provisional Ministry of Religion was created, and a circular issued by the government in November 1979 setting out the approved system for entering the monkhood had been practiced "with excellent results." In fact, the circular had produced such good results that the monks at the center entrusted with the supervision of the novitiates had been overwhelmed with work. Consequently, the June 1981 circular explained, "The central committee of the Front and the People's Revolutionary Council of Kampuchea agrees with the monks at the center to create a *sangha* in all provinces in order to meet the needs and wishes of the people."

The provincial *sangha*, practicing strictly "according to the precepts issuing from the discipline of the *pitaka*" would supervise the selection and training of candidates for the monkhood according to their biographies and also according to the law.[52] The chief abbot of the provincial *sangha* was responsible for the novices in his own province only, "and cannot ordain monks in another province and cannot guide anyone from other provinces to enter the monkhood in his province."[53] A certificate of recognition had to be issued and given to the state authority at the base for agreement when the period of monkhood was completed. The circular indicated that "restoration" rather than development was the aim. It ordered, "We must choose to take the former monks who were violated by the unbelievers . . . and who do not have families or wives and who have not caused any harm to the revolution."[54] By 1982, 700 of the 3,000 wats which had existed in Cambodia before the war had been restored, housing approximately 3,500 monks, "that is, nearly one-twentieth of the clergy at its peak."[55]

Just one week before the People's Republic of Kampuchea transformed itself into the politically neutral State of Cambodia, the Front president, Chea Sim issued a definitive circular on the freedom of religious practice, at least for Buddhists.[56] Chea Sim reminded the reader of the many policies, circulars, decisions and directives which the party, the state, and the Front had issued concerning respect for the practice and discipline of Buddhism. He noted that two conferences of monks had been held "to examine and reflect collectively" on the management of *wats*, on respecting the practice and discipline of the religion, and on the right to genuine freedom of religious belief of the masses "in accordance with Article 6 of the Constitution of the PRK." From the date of the circular, 24 April 1989, "all citizens who have pure and clean faith in Buddhism can enter the monkhood according to their own desires without specified ages." The other stipulations which required authorization from both state and Front authorities from the level of commune to district, or *khan* in the case of a municipality, remained in effect. Like many of the circulars which were issued just prior to the dissolution of the People's Republic of Kampuchea, this one was merely recognizing what was already a *fait accompli*, a retrospective acknowledgement of what the people had already decided was politically tolerable to the regime. Its acknowledgement represented, nevertheless, a compromise, and one intended to win favor with the masses in the dangerous days and years not too far ahead when external forces would impose different standards and values on the Cambodian political system.

PROPAGANDA, CULTURE AND THE ARTS

Propaganda (*korsanakar abrum*) was an essential tool of the regime. In fact, it was so important that there was a special party commission, headed by Bou Thong, which existed solely for its purpose. This commission had the role of developing the "correct" attitude among the party's cadre force, as well as conducting propaganda work among the masses and on the international stage. Bou Thong was also a vice-president of the Front and there was a close alliance between the party commission, the Front, and the executive body, the Ministry for Propaganda, Culture and Information.

This ministry, headed by the popular former Khmer Viet Minh, Keo Chenda, was regarded as a key ministry in the early years of the PRK. Already in 1979 it had thirteen sections covering art (i.e. dance, drama and music), the fine arts school, film, sport, mobile propaganda, the National Museum, the Tuol Sleng Genocide Museum, the National Archives, the National Library, the printing house, tourism, radio broadcasting, and the Front's newspaper, *Kampuchea*. In 1980, these sections were organized into ten departments and extended to the provinces. The *Annual Report* for 1980 claimed a total staff of 1,777 people with forty-five of them educated to university level.[57] The report suggests an outstanding degree of activity and great enthusiasm for the task. For instance, "Since January this year, the Department of Art has achieved very wonderful results. This makes the work of art feel incomparable delight. Apart from serving their political duties, all art has tried hard to restore dance, which is the heirloom and the tradition of the nation . . . "[58] During 1980, this department had performed for foreign guests, other ministries, the public in Phnom Penh and several provinces, in Laos, Vietnam, GDR, Poland, and Czechoslovakia, for a total audience of close to one million people. The report regretted only that "in 1980 we did not have the possibility to research our ancient music in the collection of 700 pieces of music, because that music is buried in the remote regions, and those who know music who are left from the killings of the traitors are very old and for that reason we cannot do the research."[59] The mobile film unit had made 230 trips to the countryside "for an audience of 345,000 people."[60] The Cambodian film delegation had already participated in five international film festivals and "in Tashkent, we received an award from the committee that prepared the festival."[61] Apart from all the other pursuits, the ministry was busy planting crops and raising animals, (180 chickens, 70 ducks, 15 rabbits, one goose, one pig, two fishponds, and two shrimp ponds).[62]

In 1981, the government announced that it had signed a contract with India, which remained the only country outside the socialist bloc which formally recognized the legitimacy of the People's Republic of Kampuchea, to give three-month training courses in restoration work at Angkor Wat, that core symbol of the nation. Three years later, prime minister Chan Si set up a special committee, chaired by Chan Seng, party secretary and head of the People's Revolutionary Committee of Siem Reap/Oddar Meanchey, to design strategies for the repair and care of the Angkorian temples. According to the decision of the Council of Ministers, "enemy ruses have been used to cheat some of our people in Siem Reap to dig holes under the temples and big trees, with the aim of destroying our national cultural wealth."[63] Specifically, the high-ranking, inter-ministerial committee was to fill in the holes, replant trees, and "do whatever is necessary to ensure orderliness and restore the area to its original beauty." Actual work was supposed to commence on 15 March 1984, the day before the decision was signed. This was obviously a mass campaign and involved the volunteer labor of teams of civilians, because Article 4 of the decision stated, "We should ensure security and provide for the livelihood and the treatment of disease of all types to the people who have come to fulfill their duty in this campaign."

The allocation of the national budget towards social services, including education, health, culture, and social action, was tiny throughout the decade of the PRK. In 1984, for example, this budget line which was called simply "causes" was allocated between 430 and 460 million *riel*. Total budgetary expenditure that year was estimated to be as high as 3,982 million *riel*, while total income would be 3,123 million *riel*.[64] Nevertheless, the

Ministry of Propaganda managed to contribute thirty-nine million *riel* to the national coffers that year.

RESEARCHING THE CRIMES OF POL POT

The new regime accepted responsibility for the health, education, and welfare of its citizens. It also accepted the duty of care for the emotional well-being of Cambodians. The efforts of the new leaders to come to terms with the personal tragedies bequeathed by the Pol Pot era cannot be dismissed as a cynical propaganda ploy. The trial held in Phnom Penh in August 1979 to hear the crimes of Democratic Kampuchea, and which found Pol Pot and Ieng Sary guilty of genocide and sentenced them to death *in absentia* may very well, in part, have been a "show trial" intended to legitimize the new regime and the continued presence of Vietnamese troops and advisers in Cambodia. The majority of Cambodians, however, knew and cared very little about how their plight was being portrayed internationally. After all, the world had shown little concern for them while Pol Pot was in power. The records of that trial and the testimonies of victims will always stand as proof of unfathomable pain which individual people suffered, and the trial proceedings must have acted as genuine catharsis for at least some part of the general population.

The Cambodian countryside was littered with mass graves. These shallow pits were gradually unearthed over the first couple of years, often accidentally. The Australian delegation in December 1979 reported on the last day of their short visit:

> On Sunday the government called on the population to give half a day of socialist labor on their Sunday holiday to clean up the streets for the forthcoming anniversary celebrations. However, during one of the countless trips to the dump, a new mass grave was discovered. In a ditch about 200 yards long are the bones and skulls—some still with hair attached—of probably 50 to 100 adults and children. Ragged clothes and shoes are in amongst the bones.[65]

These graves represented a public health risk. In 1981, Chea Soth signed a circular concerning the treatment of corpses recovered from these graves.[66] The circular begins:

> Having observed that recently some of our people, on their own account, have dug up the graves where the traitors Pol Pot, Ieng Sary and Khieu Samphan killed the people so savagely, in order to search for gold for their own advantage, and have thrown the bones of those corpses to the mercy of the wind and rain;
>
> In order to respect the memory of the corpses and as clear proof to our Khmer children/descendants in the future, and to demonstrate to our international friends the savage crimes against the gentle people of Kampuchea, whereby millions were killed so tragically in the genocidal regime; In order to avoid contagious diseases from the remains of the corpses and all dangers to the health and well-being of the people who live nearby the graves, especially the people who live lower than the graves where seepage can enter their water supply;
>
> Having observed that on some bases people are not yet paying exact attention to the care and protection of the corpses . . .

Provinces and municipalities where bones had already been disturbed were required to build pavilions to store those bones already dug up, and when further bodies were uncovered, their bones were to be placed in these pavilions. Local authorities were encouraged to adopt measures to forbid the people from disturbing the graves further and "for any individual who fails to respect this request, the local state authority must have measures to educate and use strict discipline." Before the peace settlement, it was rare to approach any district center where these small wire-meshed pavilions containing human remains did not exist.

On 5 October 1982, the National Council of the Front issued a decision to organize a commission "to accept responsibility to research the crimes of the Pol Pot regime, lackeys of the expansionist Beijing Chinese clique, in the period when it controlled the Kampuchean society, 1975–1978."[67] The six-member commission was headed by Min Khin as acting secretary general of the Front Council. Its mission was "to compile the crimes throughout the country and bring together all the documents for extension throughout the country and outside."[68] Their report was presented on 25 July 1983. In the course of nine months, they had made "contact with people of all classes, party organizations, state authorities and mass organizations from the center to the base" and received nineteen reports from provinces and municipalities (Ratanakiri province and ten districts in six different provinces had not handed in reports at the time of totaling the figures) "which are documents about the crimes against all classes of the people in all bases, towns, provinces, districts, communes and villages throughout the country."[69] A total of 1,166,307 people had made accusations.[70] The commission calculated that 2,746,105 people had died, and unidentified bodies discovered in pits as well as "missing persons" amounting to a further 568,663 people took the total to 3.3 million.[71] Of that larger total, almost two million had been farmers; 25,268 monks had died, as had 488,359 members of ethnic minorities.[72] The report commented on the horrible forms of killing: "they died like animals without kindness from anyone." The Pol Pot regime had left more than 200,000 orphans and many widows.[73] The report was presented to the permanent committee of the national council of the Front on 3 August. Exhausted by their efforts, the meeting decided to end the investigations and not to wait for figures from Ratanakiri and ten districts to complete the statistics. They proposed a day of commemoration which "can be profitable in two ways: on the side of politics and on the side of psychology."[74] Many dates representing significant revolutionary anniversaries were suggested: 25 May, 27 September, 17 April, 27 May, 24 May. The meeting asked the president, Chea Sim, to decide. He thought that "the matter of this day of commitment to anger (*chang komheng choe chap*) with the genocidal regime of Pol Pot is a very complicated matter."[75] Finally, there was no consensus and "the meeting decided to take the designation of a day of commitment to anger with Pol Pot, the crime statistics, the report, the motions, and the decisions to the National Assembly and the party politburo for a decision."[76] The day of commemoration, usually translated into English as "National Day of Hatred," was finally set as 20 May.[77]

The third conference of the National Council of the Front was held 15–17 December 1983, celebrating the Front's fifth anniversary. "The conference body took joy in realizing that the victories over the five years which our revolution fought for have led to progress in all sectors . . . each person has enough food, has appropriate clothing, the children go to school, there is the right to freedom of religious belief, sick people receive care and treatment. Phnom Penh these days has 500,000 people . . . "[78] There was just cause for their pride. The Council of Ministers' report *Concerning the Situation of the Implementation of the Duties of Defending and Building the Country in 1984 and Objectives for Duties in 1985*, dated 5 December 1984, describes a society which, if not affluent, was provided for with most essential social services.[89] School enrolments were already large and increasing. It was claimed that 66.83 percent of all illiterates had been "liberated." Local state authorities and parents' associations were repairing and constructing schools around the country. There were seven more commune clinics than there had been the previous year and 481 students were studying to become doctors. They claimed to have reformed 229 vagabonds and 172 prostitutes. The court system was being strengthened and upgraded.

So much effort had gone into the gains of these first six years. However, quality suffered in the rush to restore the fabric of the society. Teachers were sometimes barely literate themselves, but class sizes and the urgent need to provide an education system meant that there was no time for in-service training and upgrading of teaching skills. Doctors and nurses were also too hastily prepared for their roles and the concept of patient "care," rather than simply "treatment," remained generally alien to the hospital system. In any case, materials and equipment were so scarce that education, health, and other social services remained rudimentary, right throughout the regime. Poverty remained the main cause of ignorance and ill-health. Grinding poverty compounded the risks associated with change of any kind, which remained the root cause of the farmers' reluctance to cooperate with the system of collectivized agriculture. In these circumstances, it was, as Hun Sen said, impossible to raise the people's political consciousness and awareness when they were too hungry to pay heed:

Theory is easy but practice meets many difficulties because
. . . until we end poverty, the aim of socialism cannot be achieved either. Old habits teach us that you cannot advise children when they are hungry; they cannot hear us. For the people it is the same; we cannot take theory to teach them about advancing towards socialism when they do not have enough to eat, when they do not have clothes to wear. The important points are firstly to have a full stomach, clothes, mosquito nets, homes, means of transport, their children at school, time to celebrate, et cetera, and then they can proceed to socialism. These are socialist objectives, not capitalist ones . . . The problem of socialism in Kampuchea is something that makes people afraid, not about private ownership of land and assets, homes, factories, enterprises, and various other means; what makes people afraid is poverty which is never-ending, until the people lose faith in the leadership of the party and the state and join the enemy in striking to overthrow the party and the state.[80]

Between 1979 and 1984, the party and the state had kept faith with the people. The eleven-point program of the Front which Heng Samrin had promised to fulfill at Snoul on 2 December 1978, had been fulfilled to the utmost ability of the small band of revolutionaries who committed themselves to those objectives. That the results of their efforts had produced few rewards in terms of improving the material conditions of the people, should not detract from the efforts which had been made. Hun Sen's analysis was correct. Structurally, Cambodia was not ready for revolution, and revolutions cannot be made, or even re-made as in the case of the PRK, when the most fundamental economic and cultural conditions do not exist, because despite all the goodwill in the world, the people, most particularly farmers who rely on the output of their labor for their very survival, will not persist with schemes where the risk factor is excessive.

Throughout the first six years of the PRK, Cambodian society gradually healed, and lives returned to the degree of normalcy allowed by ongoing war and the Vietnamese presence. The institutions of civil society, however, particularly those most characteristic of socialist states, remained as ornaments attached to the state rather than as integral and essential components of the state. The mass organizations, for instance, such as the Cambodian Federation of Trade Unions and the Communist Youth Alliance, were only minimally effective in mobilizing popular support and raising the consciousness of the masses.[81] Organizations such as these were too alien to Cambodian culture to be of real value to the state. Of them all, only the Women's Association appears to have been sincerely adopted, perhaps because it was organic, because village women had always organized themselves to give mutual assistance in times of need. The Buddhist *Sangha*, most particularly its leader and spokesperson, the Venerable Tep Vong, was loyal to the new regime, and despite the close supervision of religious practice, there was no state-sanctioned religious persecution as occurred in other socialist regimes in the region. At the same time, the freedom of religious expression which the Front promised in its eleven-point program was not genuine freedom, and the people were well aware of this. Religious festivals had always provided the rhythm of seasonal life for Khmer villagers. Constraints on the celebration of their religion compounded the sense of loss caused by the absence of their king. Essentially, in 1979, Cambodians wanted their old society back. Given the levels of violence and pain they had suffered in the period 1969–1979, this should not be surprising. Restoration of the past, however, was not an option. In this situation, the new state could only ever be a poor substitute for the real or imagined past, and one the people hoped would be transitory. Winning ideological hegemony was therefore both vitally important and very difficult to achieve.

Midway through the PRK regime, there were two major threats to the revolution. The obvious one was the ever-growing danger posed by the guerrilla war and behind that, the propaganda campaign waged by the sponsors of that war,

China, the USA and the countries of ASEAN. The other even more intractable problem was the failure to build a cadre force which was imbued with socialist principles and the desire to carry out the revolution. There were too many corrupt, incompetent, lazy and self-serving cadres at all levels of the administration who corroded the revolution from within, just as the KR attacked it from without. On the other hand, the history of the PRK in its early years does reveal a small core of leaders who were genuinely revolutionary. Their numbers, however, would prove to be too small to effect the necessary changes to societal structures that revolution demanded.

At the end of 1984, the scenario was one of worsening economic and security problems, which could produce only negative political effects; cadres who were being trained in greater numbers for the necessary administrative tasks but who could not be relied upon to provide genuine ideological support for the revolution or to raise the consciousness of the masses; and severe external pressure from the powerful backers of the tripartite coalition of Khmer resistance forces as well as from Vietnam who was demanding that the PRK play a greater role in its own defense. State coercion may have been an understandable response to these conditions. From 1985 onwards, the state did exert its power with far more force than had been applied in the previous six years. At the same time, however, it would appear that state force, when it was applied, most blatantly for the purposes of conscripting civilian labor for military and defense work, was tempered by tolerance, even encouragement of popular democracy in the public arenas. The battle for hegemony was not yet lost; it merely adopted new strategies.

Chapter 8

RESTRUCTURING THE REVOLUTION

THE CREMATION OF the body of Chan Si on the *viel men* on 5 January 1985 dramatically marked a major turning point in the history of the PRK and of the revolution itself. The lighting of the funeral pyre symbolized the end of the rule of the "old guard" of committed socialist revolutionaries who had struggled for national independence from the French and furthered their political training in North Vietnam after 1954. In the months that followed the National Assembly's endorsement of Hun Sen's appointment as prime minister in January 1985, the leadership of the party and the state underwent major restructuring and young technocrats, especially new party recruits without revolutionary backgrounds, rose quickly to positions of prominence. A new urgency had entered the revolution, the urgency to construct and defend the motherland, or risk losing all in the battle with the powerfully backed resistance forces.

Between 1981 and 1984, the economy had grown quite strongly from a near zero starting point. The growth rate then leveled out, however, and the economy stagnated.[1]

Recurrent prolonged dry seasons followed by severe floods plagued the whole decade of the PRK but the 1984–1985 wet season rice harvest was particularly disastrous. In addition to hard-hit harvests, the state had to cope with difficulties in developing light industries, which were hamstrung by insufficient power supply, obsolete and rundown machinery, and persistent shortages of spare parts and raw materials. In these circumstances, the state failed to produce the goods demanded by the farmers in exchange for their paddy, and the state could not afford to pay the farmers even the recovery cost of their produce. Without subsidized rice, however, the state feared it would lose the loyalty of its poorly paid civil service and army. Private traders exploited this situation, to the point where the private economy became an "objective reality of history" which the party and state had to recognize, if only in order to obtain revenue by taxing it.

As the period from 1979 to the end of 1984 showed, the PRK regime had deservedly won a fair measure of popular goodwill: many parts of the country were quite secure and the horrors of the DK period were beginning to fade there. Normalcy had returned with the establishment of markets, currency, schools, hospitals, and clinics, and an administration which was not always efficient and may even have been officious and frequently corrupt but which, in the Cambodian context, was also more or less accepted as the norm. The 1981 general elections and the literacy campaign had been very positive examples of what mass mobilization could achieve. On the other hand, buying popular goodwill had been very expensive for the state: taxes were far too low and state revenues were insignificant compared with the budget deficit, debts were only reluctantly called in, the private sector was vigorously exploiting the gaps that the state commercial sector could not fill and, most importantly, as long as the people were prepared to let the Vietnamese volunteer forces fight their battles for them, the prospect of full independence from their Vietnamese mentors seemed more and more unlikely. The post-1985 period would prove to be a crucial test of the regime's legitimacy. Highly unpopular decisions had to be made to protect the sovereignty of the state, still fragile and unsure of the degree of hegemony it had secured, and to fashion an economy which could at least guarantee the people's livelihood.

The events of the period 1985–1989 were very much dominated by prime minister and minister for foreign affairs, Hun Sen. Circumstances that put tremendous strain on the economic viability of the nation and which threatened national security required him to chart a course which was radically different from that of his revolutionary predecessors. As an economic innovator, an astute political strategist and a gifted negotiator on the diplomatic stage, Hun Sen won the admiration of many international observers. Domestically, however, this was a difficult and dangerous transitional period, when hard decisions that had to be taken by the party ultimately cost the PRK a large measure of the loyalty and support it had won from the people during the preceding years.

POLITICS AND GOVERNMENT

The eighth session of the National Assembly's first legislature which commenced in January 1985, elected 32-year old minister of foreign affairs and deputy prime minister, Hun Sen, as prime minister of the People's Republic of Kampuchea. The fifth party congress of October that year confirmed his rank within the party as number three in the politburo, after Heng Samrin and Chea Sim, and number two in the secretariat, behind Heng Samrin. Such concentration of power in one person was inconceivable without the full consent of the Vietnamese. On the other hand, this was no meteoric rise. Hun Sen had held considerable power since 1979, and he had proved to be a very efficient administrator and a clever politician. In an administration where the average age of its ministers was only middle to late forties, his youth was not an issue. It is possible that the Vietnamese considered his youth to their advantage, just as the French had thought that a young Sihanouk as king would make the Cambodian monarchy more compliant to their wishes. History proved the French wrong and in negotiating the peace settlement, Hun Sen disproved the *ayong yuon* (Vietnamese puppet) tag that was so often applied to him by his enemies.[2] After 1985, he used both his executive power and his party status to effect changes to the administration which would make it easier both to institute liberal economic reforms and to conscript the people for border defense work.

Following a politburo decision, on 5 February 1985, prime minister Hun Sen submitted a memo to president of the Council of State, Heng Samrin, requesting the issuing of a decree on the appointment of Mom Sabun as minister of a newly created Ministry for Social Action and Disabled Veterans (replacing the former Commission for Social Action) along with those of seventeen other cadres in what amounted to sweeping changes to the executive.[3] Two sub-decrees naming eight high-ranking transfers and ten promotions within the Ministry of National Defense were issued on the same day. During the February cabinet reshuffle, Khmer Viet Minh veterans, Chan Phin, Taing Sarim, and Khun Chhy, were moved from the key ministerial posts of finance, commerce, and communications, and were replaced by the younger, technically-trained and experienced Chay Than, Ho Noan and Tea Banh, respectively. In the aftermath of the fifth party congress in October that year, the veteran Khang Sarin lost his interior portfolio to the young governor and party secretary of Preah Vihear, Ney Pena. Radical changes continued throughout 1986 and 1987, most notably the transfer of responsibilities for defense and planning from the party "venerables" Bou Thong and Chea Soth to technocrats Koy Buntha and Chea Chanto. Another major cabinet reshuffle occurred in August 1988, when eleven ministers were ousted or transferred. Ministers Mom Sabun and Meas Samnang, former Khmer Viet Minh, were retired at that time. Foreign commentators rather predictably ascribed these changes to the apparent trend since 1981 of removing the influence of the Khmer Viet Minh from important decision-making positions within the party. As Tim Huxley, for instance, noted, ". . . the available evidence seems to suggest that during 1986 the balance of power within the PRK leadership tilted further towards former Khmer Rouge members, 'independent communists' and technocrats lacking a pre-1979 communist background."[4] As the foregoing paragraph shows, the old guard of Hanoi-trained cadres did lose most of their direct, executive power after 1985. Nevertheless, they remained influential while they maintained their party status. When they lost party support, executive position counted for nothing. Say Phouthang, Bou Thong and Chea Soth retained that status and remained as revered party elders. Others, such as Khang Sarin, Soy Keo, Lim Nay, and Lay Samon were dropped from the central committee at the fifth party congress and thereafter soon lost their high-ranking executive positions as well. It is wrong, however, to attribute these "waning stars" solely to the theory that the former Khmer Rouge systematically set about reducing the influence of the Khmer Viet Minh. Some of those who returned from exile in Vietnam, in fact, were not sufficiently competent for the high posts given to them, while others were in poor health. Minister for industry, Meas Samnang, for instance, was terminally ill with cancer when he retired from office in 1988. By the latter half of the 1980s, the regime had a new pool of skilled expertise to draw on, thanks to scholarships for Cambodian students that had been provided by Vietnam and the Soviet bloc countries.[5] In these circumstances, it was fitting that more qualified personnel should be appointed to executive positions. With the obvious and notable exception of Pen Sovann, however, the party never discarded anyone. Party loyalty was a two-way affair and this was how factionalism, the scourge of Cambodian politics, was avoided. Frequently, when removed from ministerial office, these older party leaders were moved "sidewise and upwards." Khang Sarin, who became president of the People's Supreme Court, is a case in point and Chan Phin who became chairman of the Central Commission for Economic Research is another. Former minister for national defense, Bou Thong, became supreme political commander of the KPRAF and first deputy secretary of the Central Military Party Committee.[6] He and Chea Soth remained as deputies to the prime minister until the end of the regime.

There was much more to these sweeping changes than a perceived factional tussle within the party. These changes in the executive were made for both political and pragmatic reasons, most especially the need to improve the economy. The Cambodian communist movement was not alone in the region in attempting liberal experiments to energize its economy after 1985. China, for instance, was implementing its new policy relating to the household economy and Vietnam and Laos were moving in the same direction. The Cambodian economy was desperately in need of new initiatives and the party showed that it was prepared to experiment in order to find workable solutions. As one official reportedly said, "Many cadres who are ideologues are being moved. Before, if you understood Marxism-Leninism and were a good speaker, you were chosen. Now you have to show that you can produce."[7] Kong Sam Ol, the former minister for agriculture until the 1985 reshuffle, at the time was "interpreted as indicating that Hun Sen . . . was 'establishing direct personal control over crucial sectors of the economy'."[8] There can be no doubt that Hun Sen was strengthening his hold on the day-to-day management of the economy by placing young technocrats without strong political bias in key executive posts. At the same time, it must be admitted that young technocrats without strong political bias were not very useful for advancing his own political ambitions. Hun Sen never managed to win majority support within the party. The membership of the central committee was always weighted in favor of the more conservative left-wing "faction" whose generally acknowledged leader was Chea Sim. Hun Sen's failure to control the central committee acted as a brake on his sometimes impetuous drive to change the Cambodian economy. As the prime minister and a high profile minister for foreign affairs during the protracted peace negotiations, Hun Sen received a lot of attention from the foreign press. Within the central committee, however, he was a member with the same voting rights as other members and was subject to the same party discipline.

THE FIFTH PARTY CONGRESS

The key political event of 1985 was the staging of the fifth congress of the People's Revolutionary Party of Kampuchea in Phnom Penh from 13 to 16 October. The 250 delegates represented the party's 7,500 members.[9] Heng Samrin's political report addressed the weaknesses in the party, which he listed as follows: resolutions, policies and options did not match reality and implementation was slow and lacking depth and responsibility; ideological work was lagging behind the needs of the revolution and had not taken deep root among the workers and peasants of the state enterprises and farms; the liaison between party members and the masses was weak and the masses had not been really mobilized to take part in party building; and the then current contingent of cadres

suffered from a serious shortage of numbers and strength.[10]
Heng Samrin told the congress that it was "imperative to continue to build the party into a solid Marxist-Leninist party with
a correct political line and a pure and firm political, ideological and organizational basis to make the party a vanguard
detachment of the Cambodian working class animated by a
heroic fighting will, absolutely loyal to the interests of the
working class and laboring masses of Cambodia . . ."[11] He
listed eight concrete measures for party-building work and
advised that there were two key tasks: "Vigorously build and
consolidate the bases of the party. Form at all costs a contingent of cadres sufficient in quantity and quality to meet the
needs of the new revolutionary stage while attaching priority
to the formation of a nucleus of cadres at the central and
provincial levels."[12]

Subsequent to the decisions on party-building at the fifth
congress, the party grew rapidly. Nayan Chanda noted that
"the KPRP was reported to have 10,000 members in 1986. An
additional 50,000 were selected to be candidate members."[13]
By the third quarter of 1988, the membership had increased to
"more than 22,000 who have *chivepheap* (routine system) in
nearly 3,000 party branches and among that number there are
more than 1,000 party branches in communes and almost all
districts have a branch."[14] Hun Sen claimed that party-building after 1985 was relatively easy because by then the party
administrative organizations were scattered widely throughout
the country, making the checking of biographies much easier,
which allowed for quick decisions about admitting and pro-
moting candidates. The membership drive focused on the
base—factories, enterprises, hospitals, schools, state farms, the
commune level, and all levels of the armed forces:

> All the gains were achieved at the base because the base is the
> battlefield for defending the people, protecting the people,
> protecting the revolutionary gains; it is the place for gather-
> ing the people against whom the enemy is struggling, fighting
> against the base, the village, commune and the revolution.
> Taking lightly the building of a force at the base for a long
> time was a big mistake of ours.[15]

Prior to the fifth congress, as noted previously, party growth had been very slow because, in time-honored Khmer fashion, subordinates in government positions would not aspire to party membership before his/her superiors had joined the party. Despite the comparatively rapid growth in numbers after 1985, however, the strict rules and training for membership, and the rigorous checking of credentials, remained in force, at least until the end of 1989.[16] During the PRK period, the party maintained the fragile balance between quantity and quality of party membership quite well and party discipline and unity never seem to have been threatened. That conditions for membership did not necessarily transfer to proper behavior in the field as active role models of social reform, or to genuine understanding of the ideological principles which were supposed to underpin the party, continued to be the party's main weakness. Heng Samrin's admonitions at the congress to consolidate ideological work among the masses appeared to fall on deaf ears, and ideology counted for less and less as the decade progressed. At its final session, the congress made public the results of the elections to leading organs of the party. A new central committee with thirty-one full members and fourteen candidates was elected, with Heng Samrin once again secretary-general. Only five of those thirty-one members were from the Khmer Viet Minh group: Say Phouthang, Bou Thong, Chea Soth, Chan Phin and Kim Yin, director of the national radio who had been named as a candidate at the fourth congress. To outsiders it seemed, with good reason, that Say Phouthang lost much of his very powerful party influence at the fifth congress.[17] He fell from third to fourth place in the politburo and lost his membership on the secretariat. His appointment as chairman of the Party Central Monitoring Commission, seemed to be poor compensation for the loss of his role as chairman of the Central Administration Commission which went to Men Samon. In spite of appearances, however, Say Phouthang, in fact, lost neither prestige nor power at the congress and his influence on party decisions remained very strong.[18]

PERESTROIKA

The first legislature of the National Assembly should have ended in June 1986. Article 47 of the PRK Constitution allowed: "In the case of war or under other exceptional circumstances, the National Assembly may pronounce the prolongation of its term of office." Citing that clause, the National Council of the Front proposed a motion requesting an extension of the National Assembly's first term of office.[19] The Council of State met to discuss the matter and decided that preparations for elections would "cause blockages to our urgent and unfailing core work at the present time."[20] Moreover, it considered that the fifth party congress had stipulated the duties for the revolution in the period from 1986 to 1990, and that the most important task of the National Assembly was "to gather the forces of the people as well as our assets in order to expand the victories which have been achieved and implemented successfully for the important objectives" in the ensuing five years.[21] On the basis of these two arguments, the Council of State acceded to the Front's request and extended the National Assembly's first term until 1991. This decision was approved at the tenth session of the National Assembly in January 1986. During this extended term, the National Assembly passed important legislation which had a direct bearing on the fate of the Cambodian revolution, in particular those amendments to the constitution recognizing the private economic sector and changes to land entitlement. In April 1989, this legislature also accepted a new constitution which formally replaced the People's Republic of Kampuchea with the State of Cambodia. Other significant laws passed by the National Assembly between January 1986 and April 1989 included the family law bill, the law on military conscription, and the recognition of a new province, Banteay Meanchey.

It would be wrong to assume that the decision not to hold general elections in 1986 represented a tightening of the party's control. In fact, just the opposite appears to have been the case. After 1985, the PRK seems to have trialed its own *perestroika* with not only economic restructuring but also toleration, even encouragement of the people's criticisms of the state. The documents relating to National Assembly sessions during this period illustrate that there was lively, free debate on the issue which most closely threatened the revolution, that is, the careless and even abusive treatment of the people by arrogant and corrupt officials. They also prove that the law *Concerning the Inspection and Resolution of Accusations, Protests and Denunciations of Citizens*, which had been approved by the National Assembly in the July session of 1982, was being upheld, if only by the outspoken deputies of the National Assembly.[22] This law granted the people the right to *pdeng* (accuse in the court), to protest against and to denounce the misbehavior of cadres and staff working in state institutions, organizations relating to the economy, culture and social action, as well as the armed forces "who harm the state, the collective and the rights and proper benefits of citizens."[23] The official memo accompanying the draft of that law explained:

> This draft demonstrates Article 2, Article 30, Article 32 and Article 39 of the Constitution of the PRK to make it easy for citizens to participate in state management, in social management, and to monitor each activity of the various state institutions and of the cadres, workers and state staff and to struggle against each infringement of policy.[24]

According to the report to the tenth session of the National Assembly on activities carried out in the interim between the ninth and tenth sessions, that is, the latter half of 1985, "our people increasingly dare to participate in exchanging opinions with our deputies and dare to raise requests and matters, as well as using the right to denounce and protest as citizens against individuals who serve the work in the state organizations and the social organizations which affect them, or cause harm to the people's legal rights or benefits."[25] There were nine protests in 1985, two of them relating to the Ministry of Interior and another to a local state authority. The deputies' task was to check the citizens' protests and to pass them to the responsible institutions for action. However, the author complained that "there are a few institutions, ministries and departments that remain silent and do not give information about their solutions, such as the Phnom Penh People's Revolutionary Committee, et cetera."[26]

In the absence of a workable justice system, the National Assembly's deputies performed the important role of conciliator in disputes between citizen and state. The development of the justice system under the PRK was slow and haphazard. The decree-law defining the organization and the activities of the Supreme Court and the attorney-general's Office (*moha ayakar*) attached to the Supreme Court was ratified by the Council of State on 26 August 1987.[27] As the highest legal institution of the PRK, its purpose was described as "strengthening the legal system, strengthening the social order, protecting the advantages of the society, protecting the rights and freedom and benefits in law of the citizens, and ensuring the laws are implemented properly and uniformly throughout the country in all types of courts, as well as having the aim of educating the citizens to have awareness of sincerity for the motherland and the popular democratic system, to respect precisely and properly the constitution and the laws of the state, to respect the discipline of labor and public assets, the rights of freedom of others and the standards of living within the society" (Article 1). However, the UN fact-finding mission of 24 April–9 May 1990 found: "The Supreme Court is still at an initial stage of its activities and has not yet issued any judgment."[28] The UN mission found instead that "extrajudicial conciliation has established itself as the main form of settlement of disputes, mainly in the civil field but also for criminal matters such as involuntary manslaughter."[29] The conciliation function, the mission noted, was exercised by the head of practically any institution but "there are also proper conciliation bodies at the province and district levels, where conciliation is administered within the local people's committees. Also tribunals attempt conciliation before instituting proceedings."[30]

The report on activities between the fourteenth and fifteenth sessions, that is, the first half of 1988, recorded forty-five requests for compensation and two of denunciation, and observed that in the past years, these requests had increased significantly:

Even though some of the petitioners don't know about the office of the Assembly, because of their unbearable suffering, they move heaven and earth to come to Phnom Penh to look for justice. Moreover, they tell us that the local authorities warn them strongly that it is forbidden to take complaints to the central authority as it undermines the honor of the local authority.[31]

The author explained that the National Assembly had appointed several delegations to carry out investigations into the causes of the conflicts, "for example, conflicts originating in solidarity groups and which spread over several villages and communes, or when there are three or four conflicts at the same base," but the Assembly was never informed of the outcome of resolutions: "we have been apprised only of measures for their resolution . . . they volunteer nothing and keep absolute silence."[32] The author warned that this was a matter that demanded close attention, because "if the citizens come regularly to follow up their affairs, we can appreciate that they still have confidence in our party and in our state but if they keep silent without coming to inform us about what measures we should take, how can we serve them?"[33] The report strongly advised the relevant authorities to go back and study Article 45 of the constitution, which stipulated that "the National Assembly is the supreme organ of the people's power," not merely "something which appears on page twenty-five of the constitution."[34]

The National Assembly deputies continued to denounce incompetent authorities for not heeding and following-up the people's complaints. In the report to the last assembly before the PRK transformed itself into the State of Cambodia on 30 April 1989, the author listed the essence of some of the sixty-two complaints received between the fifteenth and sixteenth sessions. They included violation of the rights to own land and homes, murder, illegal behavior of individuals in the local state authority, improper and slow implementation of laws concerning the checking and resolution of the citizens' protests and denunciations, and protests by the collective against individuals who used their official status to commit crimes of corruption and misappropriate state property.[35] Only seven of these new cases had been resolved, plus nineteen among the backlog. The author praised the people for their courage in coming forward with complaints, and told the National Assembly that "because of intervention from individuals with roles and rights of authority, or sometimes because of this or because of that, the process is very slow, which makes the people complain about the lack of concern, and they are not satisfied with resolutions which do not comply with the law."[36] S/he warned again that "our cadres and key people must be vanguard people in respecting the process of the law, and should dare to overcome the difficulties, dare to do away with family sentiment or personal benefit in order to give the people truth and justice, avoiding doing anything which causes the people to lose faith in our new regime."[37] The report referred to "the crime of oppression" and explicitly accused some cadres of deliberately dragging out the resolution of protests, despite the fact that "that period is set out in the law."[38]

The top levels of leadership were only too well aware of the selfishness and corruption of some cadres at the base, and of their abuse of the legal process. Khang Sarin, president of the Supreme People's Court, told the ordinary session of the Council of State, 1–2 February 1989, that "the court and prosecutors frequently meet barriers causing difficulty in the implementation of the law, because sometimes the court and prosecutors see that it is a serious crime, but the party committee issues a principle to overrule the crime as in the case of Kompong Thom. If the court and the prosecutors do not act according to [the demands of the party committee] but work according to the law, they have to leave that place of work."[39] It was Khang Sarin's opinion that the court would never be independent while the cadres of the court and the prosecutors were under the authority of the government, "under the authority of the party committee and the provincial/municipal people's revolutionary committee, because if they are footballs and whistles [i.e. on a string, like a ship's whistle] they cannot hold to a position."[40] He argued that the public prosecutor and the head of the provincial court should be appointed by the Council of State and not by the local people's assembly. President Heng Samrin agreed and thought they should examine the situation and see if they could "separate the line" because "the party and our state authorities have violated some of the rights of the courts and the prosecutors."[41] Vice president Say Phouthang pointed out that leaders and experts were different sorts of people: "The court organizations have legal experts, but whether they like it or not, their appointments have to go through the party committee at each level."[42] To this, Secretary general Chan Ven responded that "we have to make a distinction between the work of leadership and the work of a profession, in order to avoid confusing the head with the tail."[43] For Heng Samrin, "the party has the leadership role in all spheres but the party has to respect the conditions of the law."[44] To this, National Assembly president Chea Sim pointed to the reality, which was that the provincial courts had preceded the Supreme Court so "whether we like it or not, they still have an inescapable influence."[45]

This frank exchange by members of the very top level of the party/state leadership reveals that they understood the real situation very well, but they were not prepared to interfere with the authority of the provincial governors. In this way, they squandered the goodwill of the masses. The people may not have understood the finer points of law, but they most certainly recognized injustice when it applied to them, and the "whether we like it or not" attitude on the part of some of their leaders did not endear the party to the people.

THE NATIONAL ECONOMY

The severe drought during the peak growing period of 1984, followed by torrential rains, left withered crops rotting on thousands of hectares of ricefields in the important cropping regions of Battambang, Prey Veng, Svay Rieng, Kompong Cham, Kandal, and the provinces bordering Lake Tonle Sap, by the end of the harvest in February 1985.[46] These natural conditions also caused crop diseases and destructive pests, which reduced the yield even further. The government feared that the harvest would not meet the coming year's needs; some parts of the country were reported as already facing food shortages.[47]

The Council of Ministers' 1985 annual report coincided with the holding of the fifth party congress in mid-October.[48] It admitted that the weather was only part of the problem with agriculture. The agricultural labor supply was suffering from the demands of the border defense work and many of those laborers returned ill and were unable to work the fields; many tractors were broken, and some regions still lacked traction power. The work of storing and distributing agricultural supplies was not meeting requirements. If the better weather held until the end of the 1985–86 season, it was hoped farmers could meet between eighty and ninety percent of the plan for cropping 1.7 million hectares, the same target area as the previous wet season. A statistic which must have been cause for alarm in this report was that state purchases of paddy, as of 10 September 1985, represented only one-third of the planned quantity, or 22.5 percent of the same period in the previous year. Even worse, because the management of state purchasing had been so poor, the price per kilo paid to the farmers fell below free market prices. The same was true for corn prices. State purchases of other produce (pork, dried fish, timber, rubber, raw cotton, and tobacco) were far below the plan. The state commercial network was hampered by corruption "because some of the goods fall into the hands of businessmen first, and then into the hands of the consumers later."[49] That year, exports were worth 11.77 million commercial *roubles*/dollars, while imports were 58.8 million. Income for the first nine months of 1985 was 3,248.3 million *riel* (more than half of total domestic income came from state enterprises; tax and patriotic contributions together earned just 179 million *riel*). Total expenditure for the same period was 3,126.6 million *riel*.[50] Defense costs were not given. The report was confident that "generally speaking, we can guarantee the supplies of rice, food and some commodities to ensure the livelihood of cadres, staff, workers and the armed forces."[51] Of great concern, however, was the rapid rise in the price of rice, construction materials and manufactured goods, coupled with the poor management of state commerce and the market in general.[52]

The squeeze on food prices for the urban population led to a twenty percent salary increase for cadres and government employees (forty percent for those in remote and malarial districts and the rubber plantations) which only added further to inflationary pressures.[53]

In the political report to the fifth party congress in October 1985, Heng Samrin acknowledged the real nature of Cambodia's economy:

> . . . we still have several economic components operating simultaneously and that is an objective reality of history. The responsibility of our party and state is to build a national economy in conformity with the conditions of the country, reorganize production in the direction of socialism, in which the state-run economy and collective economy are the main components of the national economy. In order to correctly utilize the existing possibilities and the capacities of production and to mitigate the weaknesses of the state-run sector, we advocate the development of our economy encompassing four components: economy of the state-run sector, collective economy, family-run economy, and private economy.[54]

Heng Samrin made reference to the first five-year program of socio-economic restoration and development (1986–90). The first and most important objective, he said, was "to stimulate to the highest point agricultural production" by identifying four spearheads: rice, rubber, timber, and fisheries. Rubber production was singled out for special comment: "make this branch into a real spearhead in the national economy." By 1990, rubber production was expected to have regained its pre-war status of 50,000 hectares, producing 50,000 metric tons of latex. Production of staple foods would have to increase at the rate of seven percent per year to keep pace with a 2.8 percent population growth rate; timber production would reach 200,000 cubic meters and fishery output would be 130,000 tons. Small and medium-scale industrial bases, "appropriate with the country's situation," were to be restored and developed; there would be investment in basic infrastructure, including waterworks and communication lines; exports and thrift would be stressed.[55]

In line with the decisions made at the congress, Hun Sen sent the draft law concerning changes to Article 12 of the constitution to the National Assembly on 1 February 1986, with the explanation that "in order to utilize the level of possibility and capacity of production which we have at present and to fulfill and increase the state economic base which is still weak, the Council of Ministers asks the National Assembly to define the composition of our economy as follows: state economy, collective economy, family economy, and private economy."[56] The private commercial sector, resourced by smugglers, had been operating vigorously since 1979, with the tacit acceptance of the state, which was unable to balance consumer demand with supply. However, if the government's hope was that a legal private sector would invest in production, first it had to provide the incentives of basic infrastructure including regular water and power supply, and guaranteed supplies of raw materials and spare parts. The international embargo on trade and credit with Cambodia ruined any chance of providing those guarantees. Moreover, the manufacturing base was small and not appropriate for production needs. For example, of 11,000 "exploitation bases" (*moulithan achivekamm*) in Phnom Penh in the first quarter of 1985, almost seventy percent of them were in commerce, food or services, not in production.[57] In mid-1986, "over forty percent of the country's pre-1975 factories remained inoperative, and the operations of those that have reopened were seriously hampered by shortages of raw materials and spare parts. Interruptions in electricity supply also damaged productivity, which was reportedly as low as twenty-five to fifty percent of capacity in the cigarette, soap and tire factories."[58] The leading textile factory at Tuol Kork, for example, was reportedly idle three days a week, because of power interruptions and the erratic supply of yarn.[59]

Taxation remained very reasonable and was not a disincentive to private enterprise. In 1986, taxes were levied for the first time on profits, rents and utilities from private businesses. Depending on annual profits, the tax rate was levied on outlets with a monthly income above 400 *riel*.[60] The "exploitation" (*achivekamm*) tax system was "from eight percent to twenty-six percent of annual profit for fisheries, construction, forestry and transport; and from twelve percent to forty percent of annual profit for commerce, food and service work."[61] Given an official exchange rate of thirty *riel* to the dollar (compared with the more commonly used standard unofficial market rate of 130 *riel*), "a woman selling fruit drinks in the market pays 100r a month tax and another 100r rent for her stall. A silver shop downtown [Phnom Penh] pays 2,000r in tax each month and another 200r each for rent and electricity."[62] There was no personal income tax. As an indication of wage levels, however, a car mechanic employed in a private business at the time earned approximately 8,000 *riel* per month.[63] By comparison, a government employee earned only 200–300 *riel* per month.[64] In 1987, the government adjusted the official exchange rate to reflect more realistically the value of the *riel*, which was then worth just one US cent.[65] By way of incentive, remittances in foreign currency from relatives and friends living abroad earned a bonus of between five and fifteen percent.[66] Even so, state salaries were minimal. They were subsidized, however, by the provision of essential items, which consisted of the following (per person each month) as at 30 September 1987:

1. Rice
   - cadres and staff   16   kg
   - workers   19–21   kg
   - children   10   kg
   - dependants   8   kg
2. Soap   0.5   kg
3. Paraffin   5   lt
4. Salt   1   kg
5. 'Liberation' Cigarettes   5   packs
6. Cloth
   - cadres, staff, workers   5   meters per year
   - children   3   meters per year.[67]

In addition to these goods, depending on supplies, state employees were entitled to one kilogram of white sugar, one can of milk, and 0.7 kilos of dried fish each month. When the state could not provide them, salaries had to be supplemented accordingly. This became a very complicated system and was obviously open to abuse. Free market prices escalated so far above the fixed state prices that civil servants were induced to sell their salary provisions to traders, so that state subsidies ended up further profiting those who were already exploiting the situation. In civil servant households in Phnom Penh, it was virtually the norm by 1989 that if the husband worked for the state, his wife was a small market vendor and he moonlighted as much as his regular job allowed. In this way, ends could meet but state worker efficiency declined markedly. In February 1989, the government changed the state salary system again: rice and paraffin were provided as usual, but the differences between the real cost of the other goods and the free market prices were computed and added directly to salaries. Moreover, when prices rose on average ten percent, the Ministry of Planning was required to announce how much had to be added to salaries and support, according to that rate of increase.[68] To recoup the cost of increased salaries, the Ministry of Industry was supposed to produce more and the Ministry of Commerce was supposed to increase sales.[69]

The system was obviously unsustainable. As Hun Sen explained, "Over the past ten years, in Kampuchea, we have created two markets and three prices: they are the state market and the free market, prices for provisions, prices to ensure livelihood and prices of the free market, [a situation] which has created severe difficulties for market management."[70] His stated objective was "one market, one price."[71] He did not speculate on who would determine the outcome. In October 1988 the government issued a decision granting virtual self-management rights to factories and enterprises.[72] According to the terms stipulated by the decision, "salaries and wages of workers and staff depend on the effectiveness of production and exploitation of the enterprise and the results of labor of each in the enterprise."[73] Worker rights were supposedly protected by "an annual conference of workers and staff or a conference of representatives of workers and staff in order to participate in decision-making about policies and the duties of production and distribution of enterprise income."[74] This annual conference elected a workers' "Enterprise Council." On 26 July 1989, three months after the People's Republic of Kampuchea had become the State of Cambodia, the Council of State ratified a bill to allow foreign investment as joint enterprises, foreign enterprises or "cooperation and exploitation on the basis of contract," with tax payable of fifteen to twenty-five percent of total profits.[75] The de-socialization of the economy was complete.

This surrender to the free market system was only partly in deference to terms and conditions that were being negotiated as part of the peace settlement being imposed on the warring factions in the Cambodian civil war by the international community. The Cambodian economy was in severe recession, and it could not have survived as it was without the ongoing support of the Soviet bloc partners. The USSR's deliberate steps towards *rapprochement* with the People's Republic of China and, in particular, president Mikhail Gorbachev's Vladivostok statement delivered in July 1986, made that support seem dangerously weak and transitory.[76] As John Pedler, consultant for the NGO Forum on Cambodia, reported in April 1989, "the fears of refugees, emigrés and ordinary residents of Cambodia that the USSR will 'drop Cambodia like Afghanistan' cannot be altogether dismissed."[77] These economic reforms undoubtedly represented abandoning ideological principles in favor of pragmatic solutions. Realistically, however, they were based on the expediency of economic survival.

The four spearheads of the 1986–90 socio-economic plan were food staples (*spieng*), rubber, timber, and fish. In August 1986 the government announced its targets for the second year of the plan, 1987: staples would provide 2.5 million tons of paddy (wet and dry season total) and 70–80,000 tons of corn (20,000 tons for export); rubber production would expand to 40–42,000 hectares tapping 35,000 tons of latex (25–27,000 tons for export); the target for timber was 150,000 cubic meters, of which 35,000 cubic meters was for export, exclusive of "cooperative exports" between the twinned provinces and the SRV Ministry of Forestry's own exploitation in the northeastern provinces of Cambodia; the targeted quantity of fish was 90,000 tons.[78]

The previous wet season harvest of 1985–86 had been a good one and the government had anticipated purchasing 300,000 tons of paddy. By the middle of 1986, however, less than one-third of the target had been reached.[79] These shortages fueled inflation and state employees went for months without receiving the rice provisions which supplemented their meager salaries. Recurrent failure to reach procurement targets was partly due to the incompetence of the state commercial network. In September, the government issued a decision to expand the network urgently, because "the network of purchasing and sales at the base from the province down to the commune and the village is still weak, so the people wanting to trade meet barriers and there are a lot of quarrels; the movement of goods does not go from production to consumption and economic relations between the state and the people, in general, the farmers say, are not very good."[80] The prime minister fell back on the socialist moral argument of mutual obligation that "the state should make sure that the people have the essentials for their livelihood, including food, clothing, shelter, education, travel, and medical care. And the people, for their part, especially the farmers, should sell their rice and agricultural products to the state in order to serve industry and exports. We should bring production and consumption together and be determined to erase all the middlemen who are not necessary."[81] It was left to the Women's Association to mobilize efforts and to maintain the state trading depots from every *sangkat* in the city to every *krom samaki* in the countryside.

Corruption, mismanagement and poor weather conditions aside, the real problem with rice procurements was that the state could not afford to pay the farmers what it cost them to produce their rice. The state eventually managed to meet half of its 1986 target for rice purchases, in part by barring merchants from moving rice across provincial borders, but "farmers complain that the government's price of 2.5r/kg is less than it costs to produce the rice, and that the state has too few goods, such as fertilizer, cloth and soap, to exchange for their products."[82]

In July 1987, the National Assembly's Commission for the Economy and the Budget presented its report to the thirteenth session of the National Assembly. In the previous six months, its members had investigated the target sectors of the economy to understand why results were so far below the plan.[83] With regard to food staples, "the people complain strongly that at the market the price of goods is going up out of reach. While the state knows only how to increase the price of state goods, the price of the people's produce remains the same. The state acts as if it is not very concerned about the livelihood of the people. This problem makes it difficult for our state to purchase paddy."[84] The commission urged the government "to check the price of state goods and the prices of farmers' produce and do whatever is necessary to make a balance."[85]

Timber production was developing rapidly, but not for the state's benefit. Kompong Speu was singled out for special mention:

> . . . the illegal cutting of timber and the illegal transportation is still going on. The province has measures to stop it but it is as if they have no effect. If this chaos continues, some day our country will meet severe difficulties because now our commission has checked and seen some places where there used to be a lot of forests but now they have become cleared fields. Before, we used to say that it was the activities of the enemy which caused us to meet difficulties in cutting and protecting the forests. However, in reality, we see that the people who can cut the trees know only how to continue cutting without stopping.[86]

Precious timbers like *korki* were being destroyed for firewood. The commission called this "national destruction" and argued that "our tree-planting is still only in principle and actually we are not implementing it well at all."[87] There was "chaos" on the fishing grounds also, "especially when the fish are spawning and when fishing is prohibited."[88] According to the commission's report, "the fish stock in Kampuchea has dropped by more than fifty percent and some fish have almost disappeared. From ancient times, our country has not had to raise fish. However, if this anarchy continues, and we have no firm measures, then one day Lake Tonle Sap will have no fish at all."[89] The laws were in place, but implementation was careless. The most important economic spearhead, the rubber industry, was victim of "pillaging by transporting rubber out of the storehouses as if they have no respect for the laws of our state at all."[90] Many rubber workers had abandoned their jobs. The commission reported on bad management, maladministration, negligence in the storage of export produce and graft and petty corruption, particularly the taking of bribes and illegal tariffs at inspection posts.

Minister of health, Yit Kimseng, warned the government of the dangers caused by negligence and illegality in the supply of drugs and medicine.[91] The minister calculated that a population of 7.8 million Cambodians needed a budget of nine million *roubles*/dollars for drugs, materials and medical equipment, but in 1986, the ministry had to function on less than twenty percent of that amount: "Therefore, we can say there are no drugs for treatment and the doctors make the patients buy the drugs."[92] Private businessmen, he said, were very active in supply through illegal border trade with both Thailand and Vietnam; there was the added problem of drugs sent through the post by relatives living abroad. The minister feared that this unsupervised trade was having a bad effect on the health and the lives of the people. Due to difficulties in importing raw materials from socialist countries and because of the very small amounts of "free" currencies held in 1987, the factory for producing drugs within Cambodia met only half of the proposed output for 1986. The minister advised that this would be further reduced in 1987.

When the prime minister presented the Council of Ministers' annual budget report in October 1987, he noted that forestry and fishery production were on target, although saltwater fishing was very weak.[93] Rubber, however, achieved less than half of the targeted output of 35,000 tons of latex, which was a serious blow to export sales. The prime minister admitted to serious problems in the rubber industry: sand was being mixed with the latex which affected its export quality, the work of tapping was carelessly done, workers were stealing a lot of the product, and management of the industry was poor.[94] In food crops, the country achieved its highest dry season rice yield since 1979 of 2.3t/h; 121,000 hectares were harvested.[95] However, estimates for the 1986–1987 wet season crop were very bad; area harvested would meet only half of the plan, partly because of drought, but largely because of poor management and low motivation. Total area planted to corn was only fifty percent of the plan, and "measures for expanding land area and increasing the yield for assorted and short-term industrial crops have progressed very little. The seed experiment station for vegetables works very slowly. Cropping methods still haven't changed, there still isn't development in agronomy, which should be acknowledged. Many of the regions for these kinds of crops are near the river but from year to year they still suffer from a lack of water. Fertile land is left idle . . . "[96] Moreover, competition from the private sector was proving to be too strong for the state procurement network. The prime minister noted, "The situation of prices in the free market has fluctuated a lot . . . In general, the price of foodstuffs and commodity items has increased, on average, 50 percent compared with the same nine months for 1986 . . . We must at least ensure supply of fresh fish and vegetables for the cadres, staff and workers of the city and provincial centers, especially Phnom Penh, the Kampuchean armed forces and our Vietnamese friends."[97]

From this report made by the prime minister at the end of the third quarter of 1987, it is obvious that the farmers were not producing according to state targets. This amounted to an admission of the failure of the *krom samaki* system of cooperative agriculture. There was never an official closure, no decision or directive which marked its end;[98] it was rather a slow process of attrition which led up to constitutional changes and the law passed in February 1989 giving citizens "full rights to own (*kan kap*) and use (*brae bras*) land and the right to bequeath and inherit land which the state gives them for living on and exploiting" as enshrined in the new Article 15 of the PRK Constitution.[99]

Because some form of collectivized agriculture is central to the definition of a state experiencing social revolution, the failure to maintain that essential structure, not once but twice in the history of the Cambodian revolution, implies gross maladministration, and not simply the farmers' unwillingness to cooperate with the state. Serge Thion offers an interesting point of comparison with the agricultural cooperatives of the DK period:

> By 1978, and possibly earlier, the cooperative system appeared to be a failure. The lack of an efficient local and central bureaucracy made any control over cooperatives purely formal. It has been said by members of the 1980 DK government that by 1978 the central authorities had only vague ideas about what was happening in more than half of the country's cooperatives.[100]

In fact, Thion asserts, "at no time between 1975 and the end of 1978 were the central authorities close to having complete control over the national economy, the state power system, the army, the party, and possibly even the state security office, S-21. All of these were riddled with political factions, military brotherhoods, regional powers, personal networks, all contending for influence and the purging of rival forces. The state never stood on its feet."[101]

The PRK, by contrast, was not faction-ridden. There most definitely were groupings within the leadership, but probably to an extent no greater than in any labor/social democratic party in a modern Western democracy. The center admittedly had problems asserting its authority over the provincial party secretaries and governors, but there was never the problem of regionalism that had plagued the DK; and while there were always desertions and even defections from the national army to the resistance, the loyalty of the KPRAF leadership to the center never seems to have been in doubt. Questions about the extent of the PRK's administrative reach were, however, valid ones. Peter Schier claimed that "even the economic planners in Phnom Penh do not have a precise overview of the economic situation and . . . no or only insufficient information about some areas."[102] This was true. The gaps between production targets and eventual outcomes were vast by the end of the PRK period, and suggest the paucity of worthwhile information that was being relayed from the base. On the other hand, Tim Huxley's argument that "throughout 1986, the PRK regime's control over much of Cambodia remained essentially nominal," is an exaggeration.[103] No regime, not even the French, ever had administrative control over 100 percent of Cambodian territory. Persistent guerrilla warfare, however, really necessitated a sound administrative network throughout the country. That the PRK was able to survive ten years of both overt and covert war surely attests to the broad sweep, if not the thoroughness and depth, of its control, both before and after 1986. The proximity of the KR resistance bases made the northwest border region extremely dangerous for permanently-based PRK officials before 1986. To help ease the problem, in September that year, the government sent the draft of a decree-law to the Council of State, requesting its ratification to set up the new province of Banteay Meanchey by taking five districts from Battambang and one from Siem Reap/Oddar Meanchey.[104] Most importantly, the new province was designed to rationalize the supervision of the Cambodia-Thailand border; the new province would have 185 kilometers of that border, Battambang would have 165 kilometers and Siem Reap/Oddar Meanchey would have 150 kilometers. The creation of Banteay Meanchey proved to be crucial for the maintenance and supervision of the K5 border defense system. The population of the new province was only 325,000, similar to that of Svay Rieng province bordering Vietnam in the east, although Banteay Meanchey had an area three times larger. Sparsely settled population inevitably made for less thorough administration.

The function of the district (*srok*) administrative level, the link between the province and its communes, was clarified only in the latter half of 1986, even though provision had been made for it in the 1981 constitution and it had had a nominal function since 1979.[105] The district's role was mainly an intermediary one between the provincial center and the most important base, the commune. The commune (*khum*) was always the mainstay of the administration and of the party's relations with the village masses, its legitimacy having been established with the commune elections of 1981. The commune's chief duty was to oversee the work of expanding agricultural production through the *krom samaki* (solidarity production groups).

The responsibilities of the commune people's revolutionary committees were redefined in a government circular dated 17 March 1988. These responsibilities applied to all aspects of village life and security. The first of them was to "specify a plan and measures for production, to administer guidance for all assisting institutions, all villages and *krom samaki* to implement the plans and the measures such as those for developing the land and building hydrology structures, increasing the rice-growing season, practicing intensified rice production, performing rice trials, encouraging the use of natural fertilizers and manures . . . "[106] The *khum* committee had to ensure that farmers paid their patriotic contributions, sold their produce to the state, and repaid their debts.

That the farmers were only very reluctantly selling their produce to the state has already been discussed. Some farmers, moreover, were not repaying their debts to the state either. Just four days after issuing the circular defining the duties of the commune committees, the government issued a further circular about debt collection.[107] The circular explained that from 1981 onwards, the farmers had gathered satisfactory harvests. In emergency situations, provincial authorities had given food support and seed on loan conditions. In the calamitous 1984–1985 season, the government had given materials, equipment, fertilizer, rice seed and food rice, on the clear understanding that the accounts would be settled. In May 1986, decisions were issued about settling accounts for fertilizer and for plowing by payments in rice. The new circular complained that "implementation has not yet been thorough enough, so that now we must face severe difficulties in the problem of getting debts back from the people."[108] Some loans had not been witnessed, some debts had been passed on to descendants, "most families have a poor livelihood and have no possibility to repay while some families have the possibility to repay but do not agree to repay," and "some state authorities at the base have taken the debts back from the people already, but do not agree to pay it back to the relevant institution and they take it to use for wrong reasons."[109] In fact, the government had little hope of recouping its losses. At a Council of State meeting in February 1989, Men Chhan, who had been the PRK's first minister of agriculture, forestry and hunting in 1979, admitted:

> Reclaiming debts is a complicated problem for the livelihood of the people, especially for some bases where the people cannot grow much rice and do not have [enough] rice to eat. The people say that when they have no food left, they go and borrow from the businessmen and when they have a little, they beg to keep some to pay back the businessmen first because when they are hungry they can go and borrow money from the businessmen immediately. Regarding this problem, if we do not look for a solution, in the days ahead our people will never finish paying back the businessmen.[110]

The fact that such deep rural poverty still existed ten years after liberation from the Pol Pot regime, and ten years after the restructuring of the cooperative farming system and that the people's last resort was still the rural moneylender whose interests rates were, as they always had been, from 12 to 15 percent per month, was an admission of policy failure on the part of the government, and thus of the failure of the socialist revolution in Cambodia. To their credit, the PRK leaders blamed only themselves. At that Council of State meeting, Chan Ven said, "Apart from their obligation to sell a certain number of kilograms to the state, the people do not sell to us because we do not have goods to sell to them."[111] The meeting also discussed the matter of wastage. Because state trucks lacked fuel, and because state depots for rice purchases lacked shelter, seven thousand tons of the season's paddy from Prey Veng spoiled before it could be transported. Chan Ven said it was a common story and that "those with responsibility should accept the blame because our cadres, staff and workers have eaten rice of poor quality for too many years already."[112] President Heng Samrin added, "Before, when the businessmen bought the paddy, it didn't spoil . . . In the past, we just said that the state does not make a profit; but how can we make a profit if we act without responsibility? . . . In Kamchay Mea the people brought a lot of paddy to sell to us, but we did not buy it because we lacked [storage] bags and money."[113] Heng Samrin thought that the core problem was poor management, because while the decree laws were sound, their implementation was far too easily blocked.

Poor management may have been one of the problems of the *krom samaki* system. The core problems, however, were more fundamental. In her analysis of the PRK's failure in agricultural collectivization, Viviane Frings lists seven causes:

1. Economic factors, including the lack of incentives within the distribution system, as well as the absence of state support in the form of high-yielding seed varieties, fertilizers, pumps, fuel, spare parts and tractors which would also have provided incentives to the peasants;

2. Lack of competent cadres to administer the *krom samaki* which compounded the management problem;

3. Lack of cadres who believed in the system to implement it;

4. Lack of efforts from the government whose objective was to increase production rather than to develop the socialist forms of production;

5. Little Vietnamese influence in this field;

6. No coercion. "The government could not afford to alienate the population so when the peasants realized that they would not be punished if they did not work collectively, they stopped doing it. And the government could do nothing to prevent this."

7. And, in any case, lack of cooperation from the people who did not want to work collectively: absence of solidarity among Cambodian peasants and DK legacy.[114]

In sum, these factors account for the half-hearted efforts on the part of the government to make the *krom samaki* system work, and all, it would seem, revolved around the third factor, "Lack of cadres who believed in the system to implement it."

While incompetence, attributable to the absence of literacy and numeracy skills among those farmers who were put in charge of the solidarity groups, plus the failure by the higher levels in the administration to give them adequate training and guidance compounded poor management at the base, at the upper levels, Frings believes, the more abiding problem was that few of the cadres in the relevant departments of the Ministry of Agriculture, if any, were genuine "communist believers":

> If these people, whose job was to go to the villages to check if the peasants were working collectively and to encourage them to do it, did not believe in collectivization, how could they have persuaded the peasants of the advantages of working collectively? And if the cadres in Phnom Penh were not communist, how likely is it that the cadres at lower levels were?[115]

Moreover, the Department of Political and Economic Management of Agriculture, which was responsible for the administration of the *krom samaki*, was located in a building outside the Ministry of Agriculture [compound] which was "an indication of the little importance the government attached to it."[116]

From 1984 on, there is little reference in the official documents to the *krom samaki*, other than as an agency for rice provisions to the state, or as the smallest administrative unit when militia troops or civilian labor were needed for defense work. Plans for the full collectivization of agriculture according to form-1 of the *krom samaki*, as defined by Chea Soth at the end of 1983 were never referred to again. As agronomist Francois Grunewald noted in 1990, "almost imperceptibly, the emphasis has moved from support of form-1 of the *krom samaki* to recognition of the importance of form-2. Form-2 allows the advantages of a certain degree of community management of means of production still in short supply, it allows a certain amount of government assistance, and, most importantly, it ensures that the final crop harvested actually goes to the person who did the work."[117] The form-1 system of full collectivization, which involved rotating property among the *krom* members, hindered land investment and proper maintenance of embankments and the hydrology system. Under the *krom samaki* system, farmers had the right to borrow land which had not been apportioned to state production but, as Hun Sen observed, these areas were too small to motivate the farmers, and far too much land was left idle:

> In this matter also, we kept aside hundreds of hectares of salt fields in Kampot, and thousands of hectares of rubber plantations in Kompong Cham, Kratie, and Kompong Som were kept free for the state even though the state did not have the possibility of exploiting them. This was a cost we bore for a long time until 1986–87 when the state handed over the salt fields and the rubber plantations to the people to exploit.[118]

In Hun Sen's analysis, the *krom samaki* should have served a purely utilitarian purpose, without specific form: "The fundamental need was to examine the concrete possibility of the forces and the means of production, and what possibility that might have for letting us arrange a system for exploitation within the *krom samaki*."[119] For him, the best case scenario was "letting the people decide together . . . then arranging the relationship of production appropriate for the level of competency of the labor force. It was not a case of the party and state abandoning its function of leadership; they had to lead, but the leadership had to examine the real situation and the genuine possibility of our people. We had to understand that the aim could not surpass the genuine possibility."[120]

According to the party's revised analysis of the economic situation in 1985, the aim, he claimed, was not socialism.[121] Pen Sovann and Chan Si, he argued, had made the error of not respecting "the norm of objectivism"; by adhering to orthodox Marxist-Leninist policy rather than acting in conformity with the [real] means of production and the forces of production, "[in their time] we did not think of the demand to boost our production," and it was for this reason, he said, that he instituted the land reforms of February 1989.[122]

Viviane Frings maintains, however, that "boosting agricultural production surely was not the main aim of the government in February 1989. The principal aim of the government was political."[123] She claims the constitutional reform was only "the legalization of an already existing situation, given that in most places land had been distributed for good [sic] several years before."[124] In her view, the reform was "a desperate attempt to rally popular support prior to the withdrawal of the Vietnamese volunteer forces in September 1989" and to compensate for other unpopular measures such as increased conscription.[125] Furthermore, as Frings correctly points out, Article 14 of the PRK constitution (and Article 14 of the SOC constitution which superseded it at the end of April 1989) remained unchanged in that "Land, forests, the sea, rivers, the lakes, natural resources, economic and cultural centers, national defense bases, and other state constructions constitute state property." Therefore, what Cambodian farmers got from the February amendment was "some kind of usufruct rights for the people who cultivate the land, with all the land theoretically remaining the property of the state.[126] They did, however, appear to have secure rights of tenure and the land could not be distributed. Whether it could be reappropriated by the state, and in particular by the military, remained a moot point.

The *krom samaki* survived the land reform as "mutual aid production teams (*provas day kinear*), the nature of which had more to do with traditional forms of agricultural practice in Cambodia than with advancing towards socialism, and, in fact, most of the *krom samaki* had been functioning in this fashion at least from the beginning of 1984. Nevertheless, they had served their purpose well as a linchpin in the reconstruction of Cambodia's economy, and as an essential safety net for the most vulnerable survivors of the Pol Pot years. As Frings says,

> However ineffective the *krom samaki* became, in the first years of the PRK, they succeeded in keeping the people in the countryside and in helping them to restart normal lives and agricultural production. The policy of collectivization that the PRK government advocated during ten years, if only in theory, succeeded in keeping order and limiting abuses in the Cambodian countryside. After the theoretical framework was abandoned in 1989, inequalities became larger, abuses more

frequent, and the disadvantaged people were left without any-thing to replace the social security provided by the *krom samaki*.[127]

The competency demands of a centrally planned economy ultimately proved far too difficult for the struggling PRK government to meet. On 13 May 1989, a group of eight key planners and economic policy makers met at the Cabinet of the Council of Ministers to discuss a long-term socio-economic plan for the period 1991–2005.[128] Referring to their first five-year plan, Chea Soth believed, "We only had an eco-nomic program, not a five-year plan, because the provinces did not provide sufficient information for us to make a balance, and up to the point of implementation we only knew rough estimates."[129] Hun Sen agreed that "we do not yet make five-year plans well and if we have to make ten- or fifteen-year plans, the quality will be even lower. We call them long-term economic plans because the USSR has them, but they have a sufficient material and cultural base . . . We should change the words 'economic strategies and long-term planning' to 'long-term development objectives for the economy and for social action' . . . [but] how can the party congress dare to accom-plish only a program if the [Soviet] politburo uses the word 'plan'?"[130] Referring to the Soviet *perestroika* "where they are restructuring a planned economy to a socialist market economy," Hun Sen felt that "in this transition, we do what-ever is the least not yet done. Our market prices cannot hold, the political and economic issues are not yet stable . . . "[131] At the end of the third quarter of 1989, the government acknowl-edged that prices in the free market, most worryingly the price of food items, were rising at the rate of 10 percent each month.[132]

The abandoning of ideological principles for guiding the economy appeared to be a realistic response to the needs of the concrete situation in Cambodia by the end of the PRK's term of office. What mattered most, Hun Sen explained, was growth in the material and spiritual well-being of the people and "for me, I do not see a big difference between revolution and reforms."[133] The real argument, however, lay not in the response to the situation, but in its cause. After all, social revolution, in Marxist terms, was supposed to be the best guarantee of that very "growth in the material and spiritual well-being of the people" and, as Frings pointed out, for the most vulnerable groups in the countryside after February 1989, the liberal market reforms represented regression rather than benefit. Surely the main reason for abandoning Marxist-Leninist principles for economic development was that almost no one knew what they entailed, and cared less about their implementation. Socialist principles for economic change had simply become irrelevant by 1989. There were some genuine "communist believers" at the top level, and Hun Sen himself understood those principles better than most. These top leaders, however, failed to educate and to motivate those cadres below them to act in accordance with socialist principles. Implementation of economic policies remained slipshod and half-hearted right throughout the PRK. On the other hand, the power that the centrally-directed system gave to some officials was easily and readily translated into personal gain. Corruption and other abuses inevitably cost the regime its ideological hegemony and forced it into adopting pragmatic solutions. Failure to socialize agriculture and implementation of the K5 Plan for border defense provided the clearest illustrations of the PRK regime's failure to achieve hegemony.

Chapter 9

DEFENSE AND WAR

THE PRK MIGHT have wrestled with its economic problems, and might even have been able to accommodate a private economic sector within the socialist economic system, if it had not been for the escalating civil war. After the PAVN/KPRAF's resounding victories in the 1984–1985 dry season offensive which destroyed the resistance camps along the northern and western borders and pushed the rebels and their followers inside Thai territory, the guerrilla campaign against the PRK fractured into smaller and smaller units which burrowed deeply into the interior of the country, spread pernicious rumors and propaganda, staged terrifying raids against district and commune headquarters, confused the people and divided their loyalties to the new regime. The K5 Plan of border defense, which began in advance of that dry season offensive, required the efforts of thousands of civilians.[1] The human and economic cost of the K5 Plan in particular, and of the war in general was too much for the people, and thus for the regime and the revolution, to withstand. Rapid and marked changes to the international power balance towards the end of the decade eventually forced the four warring factions to accept a negotiated settlement so the revolution was bartered for peace. The Paris Peace Agreement was finally signed on 23 October 1991. Well before that, however, by the time the Vietnamese volunteer forces completed their withdrawal at the end of September 1989, there were few revolutionary gains left to trade.

DEFENSE STRATEGIES

In December 1984, General Le Duc Anh, one of the architects of the 1978 invasion and commander of the Vietnamese volunteer forces in Cambodia, outlined five key points which formed the strategic framework of the Vietnamese military efforts towards the defense and consolidation of the Cambodian revolution:

> 1. Indochina was a single theatre of operations so a threat to the independence of one of the three countries was a threat to all;
> 2. The success of the Cambodian revolution would be decided by the Cambodian people themselves;
> 3. The people at the base had to be mobilized according to the principle that strength in national defense required the combined strength of the entire population;
> 4. Mastery had to be achieved on two fronts, on the Cambodia-Thailand border and in the interior of the country and while both were important, the latter was decisive;
> 5. Building the KPRAF was "an urgent strategic demand" of the Cambodian revolution.[2]

Five years after the establishment of the PRK, bases housing some 230,000 Cambodian civilians and several thousand resistance fighters controlled by the Khmer Rouge, the republican KPNLF and the royalist FUNCINPEC (and at least one FULRO base of the Montagnard rebels) stretched along the full length of Cambodia's border with Thailand, from the junction with Laos to the southernmost part of Thailand's Trat Province.[3] The full force of the 1984–1985 dry season offensive commenced in mid-December, when an impressive offensive force of more than 30,000 Vietnamese troops, equipped with Soviet-type heavy artillery and tanks, and supported by several thousand PRK auxiliary troops, were sent into action."[4] By the end of that dry season, there were no bases left on Cambodian soil. Peter Schier claimed that "in most cases, positions that fell into the hands of the Hanoi troops had already been evacuated, and human and material losses by the resistance groups were thus limited."[5] However, Phnom Penh's

Ministry of Foreign Affairs Press Department, claimed otherwise (see Appendix).

THE K5 PLAN

The 1984–1985 dry season offensive was the most aggressive in the PRK's short history and its success was due in very large part to the preparatory work done by thousands of Cambodian civilians according to the K5 Plan (*phaenkar kor pram*).[6] Robert Karniol, a Canadian journalist who spent three weeks with resistance forces inside Cambodian territory in 1986, suggested that the name of the plan referred to five "phases" within "Vietnam's blueprint for ending the Cambodian conflict."[7] These phases, he explained, involved the destruction of the border bases, sealing off the border with Thailand, mopping up resistance units in sweep operations, consolidation of the PRK regime, and the withdrawal of Vietnamese troops from Cambodia by 1990.[8] While these were the logical steps in the overall strategy for national defense, in fact, K5 referred specifically only to the second phase which Karniol listed. By definition, "*kor*" (the first letter of the Khmer alphabet) referred to the initial syllable of "*kar karpier*" (defense). K5 was therefore the fifth defense plan, which was the plan for the defense of the Cambodian-Thai border.

From 1979 to 1984, the Vietnamese forces had borne the brunt of the defense of Cambodia's border with Thailand.[9] At the same time, PAVN forces were heavily engaged in protecting Vietnam's own northern border against the very real threat of a second "lesson" from China. After five years, Cambodia was reasonably expected to shoulder its fair share of the burden. In January 1984, Le Duc Tho chaired a political seminar for the PRPK central committee and the Council of Ministers, which focused on "the urgent task of consolidating the grassroot infrastructure of the PRK regime, the imperative need for a definitive solution to eliminate the Khmer resistance movements, and the all-round integration of Kampuchea into the Indochinese Socialist Bloc."[10] This workshop was most probably the genesis of K5.

A defector from the PRK later reported that the K5 program of border defense work was initiated in "March 1984 under the supervision of a committee headed by Foreign Minister Hun Sen and comprising a senior Vietnamese adviser and vice-ministers from each of the ministries . . . "[11] The committee he referred to was the Central Leadership Committee of K5 (*kenna kommatikar doeknuam mechem kor pram*). However, Hun Sen denied that he was the head of this committee:

> K5 started in 1984 before I became prime minister. K5 was under the responsibility of the Ministry for National Defense. Responsibility was allocated to the provincial authorities, along with the [military] division stationed in that area. The recruiting of new forces or the sending of the people to participate in the Plan had to be determined by sub-decree or a decision of the Council of Ministers.[12]

The documents relating to K5 rarely refer to its leadership. They refer often to the fact that final responsibility for K5 belonged to the party secretariat and the Council of Ministers and, implicit in Hun Sen's statement above, the chairman of the Council of Ministers was the nominal chief of the Central Leadership Committee of K5. The permanent deputy chief was in charge of its day-to-day affairs. Thus leadership was provided by the Central Leadership Committee of K5 made up of party officials and vice ministers, and within that, by a Permanent K5 Commission. Soy Keo, chief of general staff and a vice minister for the Ministry of National Defense was the permanent deputy chief of the K5 Committee,[13] until his dismissal as chief of staff following the fifth party congress of October 1985, when Nhim Vanda took over his K5 role.[14] Chea Dara was referred to as a vice chairman of the Permanent K5 Commission in April 1986, and an early 1987 document refers to comrade Khvan Seam in the same role.[15] That same April 1987 document specifically names Nhim Vanda, "Vice minister of the Ministry for Planning and Permanent Deputy head of the Central Leadership Committee of K5"; in February 1989, Lt. Gen. Nhim Vanda was the head (*protean*) of the Permanent K5 Commission.[16] All official documents relating to K5 refer to a decision of the politburo, No. 228SRMCh of 17 July 1984, by which it can be assumed that the K5 Plan was officially adopted by the party and the state on that date.

The plan for sealing the Cambodia-Thailand border, to prevent the infiltration of resistance troops and supplies into the interior of the country to support their guerrilla bases, consisted of the construction of a barrage, "a long fortification structure composed of a 700km canal, doubled with a wall. In the form of a strategic arc, it will follow 10 km inside the land border from Laos to the maritime border in Koh Kong province. It will be completed in regular intervals by small forts, which are not unlike the Great Wall of China."[17] The concept may have been similar, but the K5 barrage resembled nothing like the Great Wall, nor even a "Bamboo Wall" as it was often referred to. Jacques Bekaert witnessed part of it under construction near Pailin and described it as being about two kilometers wide, with first a 500 meter strip of clear terrain, then a fence, a mine field, another fence and more clear terrain.[18] Its construction was more or less detailed and complex depending on the terrain, and also proximity to the main corridors used by the resistance forces.

Soy Keo's report of 4 July 1985 to the ninth session of the National Assembly gives a thorough description of the barrage and of the construction process.[19] In the last two months of 1984, almost 50,000 laborers were cooperating with the KPRAF and the PAVN troops "in important duties such as repairing roads, making roads, cutting down trees along the side of the road, making storehouses, making camps, first-aid stations, digging ponds, dykes, exploiting stone, timber, et cetera."[20] During that dry season, a total number of 90,362 laborers were involved in the first stage of building the defense line "starting from the border of the three countries (Kampuchea, Laos, Thailand) down to Hill 199 (Koh Kong), with a length of 829 kilometers of the Kampuchean-Thailand border" in the shape of "a line of trenches, a line of barriers, patrol paths and security structures."[21] The workers were assigned to the three strategic areas which had formerly provided the enemy with easy entry points to the interior. They were in Military Region 1, from the Lao border point to Anlong Veng; Military Region 4 which included the important areas of Tatum, Ampil, Poipet, and Phnom Malai where the three resistance forces had their main bases; and Military Region 3 which extended south to Hill 199 (the border of Koh Kong). By mid-1985, they had already completed 293.9 kilometers, which far exceeded the season's target. In the course of that first season's work, almost four hundred thousand mines were laid, more than one and a quarter million metal spikes were put in place, and roughly four hundred kilometers of patrol paths were prepared. Apart from the barrage itself, Soy Keo reported, laborers and troops were busy upgrading key roads in the border region, specifically six routes which led north to the Dangrek Escarpment and west to the Cardamom Mountains. New military routes were opened and bridges were repaired and constructed. In the first season, five hundred square kilometers of forest were cleared on either side of the roads. All of this work and the ongoing work represented a huge human effort and required a massive levy of civilian manpower. The government justified these levies by citing Article 9, Chapter 1 of the PRK Constitution which read: "The PRK adopts the principle that the people as a whole participate in national defense."

Mass mobilization efforts for national security were not new; only the scale and the urgency of the K5 Plan were novel. On 9 November 1981, the prime minister, Pen Sovann, issued a circular for the mobilization of "all the people led by the people's revolutionary committees of provinces/municipalities and the high command of the KPRAF" in manual labor (*komlang pulakamm*) for "cutting down all the trees along the communication routes, repairing roads which are in disrepair, helping to provide food, transporting food and ammunition to the battlefields, and using all means and materials of the base for the building of the campaign, such as making trenches."[22] M. A. Martin confirms this early phase of mobilization by noting:

> Beginning in 1982 the government levied peasants for 'socialist labor' in the collective interest—constructing or repairing

public buildings (schools, hospitals). Non-peasants participated in the rice harvest within a production team, and
individuals levied could pay others to labor in their places.[23]

During the Chan Si years, 1982 to 1984 inclusive, the sever-
ity of the levy was lightened by the institution of a series of
mass movements under the general term of *bralong branang*,
which were contests or competitions of skill and effort among
teams of workers, soldiers, farmers, and students, who com-
peted with each other in defense- and nation-building activities and received praise and rewards in the form of cash payments, pennants and flags. This *bralong branang* movement, or
series of movements, was announced with a stirring call to
revolutionary effort in a circular of the party secretariat on 2
October 1982.[24] The circular begins: "Revolution is the cause
of the people (including cadres and the army). Therefore it is
necessary for the people to participate actively in movements
and to practice well." The essence of this first *bralong branang*
of "Loving the Nation" was listed as:

- to attack the enemy cleverly,
- to produce a lot,
- to work well,
- to fulfill the obligations of the state,
- to have high awareness of caring for, defending and con-
   serving the assets of the state and the assets of the people.[25]

A special Department of *Bralong Branang* was established in
the Cabinet of the Council of Ministers and a special *Bralong
Branang* and Rewards Council was set up to deal with specific
tasks. The department and the council later worked in con-
junction with the K5 administration to help mobilize and
motivate the people in the border defense work. In fact, the
system and procedures of the K5 *corvée* were a continuation of
these early mass movements. Chan Si believed that each
bralong branang was an opportunity "to educate the cadres and
the people in a genuinely concrete way, letting the people
realize more and more the function of self-reliance for the
cause of the revolution, as well as developing their own revo-

lutionary potential."[26] He thought it would also cause his cadres to respect the revolutionary potential of the people, and by reflecting on this "[begin] to serve the people and to search for all means to rid themselves of the diseases of individualism, authoritarianism, mandarinism, et cetera."[27] At the same time, he warned that this was "a new, young and complicated issue" for cadres at all levels, and he urged caution.

The first *bralong branang* exercise was a short trial from October until the end of 1982. Perhaps the result of this initial effort was a disappointing sign that the people were not enthusiastic about volunteering their efforts in the cause of revolution, because on 21 February 1983, the Council of Ministers issued a decision for the provincial committees to levy "a sufficient labor force, not divided into men or women . . . to serve the needs of the campaigns of the army and to build the defense of the country . . . The period of labor levy (*komnaen komlang*) of the people for national defense will not exceed sixty days per person per year and each can be called upon once or many times" (Article 1).[28] Noting that the economic situation of the people had stabilized and that living standards had improved, the government decision required that all the people assist with rice provisions for this people's defense force (*komlang pracheachon karpier chiet*). The costs of transport, medicine and expenses for materials and essential tools were met by the provincial military units who employed the people's defense forces, and those same provincial units cooperated with the provincial people's revolutionary committees to supervise the levy, assign workers to various units and provide the cadres, health staff, cooks, and so on. Overall responsibility lay with the Ministry of National Defense in cooperation with the line ministries, especially communications, health, finance, and interior.[29] Martin now observes that what she melodramatically and inaccurately calls "the second brutal phase of Vietnamization" began:

> The frequency and the difficulty of the levies increased. The work involved cutting swathes in the forest and erecting strategic barriers around villages. The first clearing seems to have taken place in the park of Angkor in late 1982. They then

occurred almost everywhere in the country for the purpose of destroying the guerrillas' sanctuaries, situated in the dense forests of the mountains and plains.[30]

The 1983–1984 dry season offensive showed disturbing signs that the resistance forces were not only stronger in numbers but were more concerted in their attacks. In his report of 22 May 1984, Campaign Commander Men Vanna estimated the resistance forces at 12,500 men, compared with 11,000 in the previous year; he noted that "they are strengthening all their bases on Thai territory and the territory bordering both countries" and that "they continue to carry out destructive activities (striking at all communications routes, at district and provincial centers, ministries and departments, granaries, markets, etc.) as well as using psychological warfare."[31] These figures for the resistance forces are either deliberately set low or they account only for active combatants encountered during the offensive. Referring to resistance force sizes at the time of that offensive, Rodney Tasker reported, "The Khmer Rouge has about 25,000 tough guerrilla fighters . . . But the KPNLF appears to be growing both militarily and politically."[32] Son Sann had claimed that his KPNLF army "now had 12,000 fully armed fighters, with an additional 8,000 trained but still without weapons"; the Sihanouk faction, FUNCINPEC, had fewer than 5,000 fighters.[33] In summing up his report, Commander Men Vanna declared, "This dry season offensive has shown strong evidence that our revolution has the possibility to attack major bases of the enemy on the border . . . "[34] To this end, the party implemented the slogan, "Every Citizen is a Revolutionary Fighter," and by the third quarter of 1984 there was a massive mobilization of civilian defense labor.

A foreign medical worker in Cambodia at that time, Esmeralda Luciolli, notes that the requisitioning of civilians began in September 1984:

> Two or three times per year, the province recruited a contingent of laborers called 'volunteers' for a period of three to six months, according to a quota proportional to its population determined by the central government. The provinces, in

turn, determined the quotas for each district, the districts did the same for the communes and the communes for the villages. In principle, only men aged seventeen to forty-five could be requisitioned but often women or adolescents took the place of others within their families. For the whole country, each departure gathered at least 100,000 to 200,000 people.[35]

Part of her claim is borne out by a Council of Ministers decision of 28 September 1984, which handed over the duties for the implementation of the K5 Plan to the provinces/municipalities, and to the relevant ministries/departments.[36] The specific task covered by this decision was to construct roads. Luciolli's figures for each tour of duty, however, are exaggerated. The total number of workers per year for two years was fixed by this decision at 32,000, with quotas relevant to the population size of each province. However, this official target also proved false. During the first two tours in the latter half of 1984, a total of 90,363 workers were deployed (47 percent of the total K5 Plan for approximately 200,000 workers); the following year, 26,000 laborers were requested.[37] The 1986–1987 dry season report claimed a total of 20,304 workers over two tours (plus 15,231 militia and 2,864 cadres and state employees).[38] The following year there were only 8,814 workers (plus 1,431 militia, 3,071 regional troops, and 815 state workers).[39] Workers continued to be conscripted, but the construction of the barrage itself was practically finished by the end of 1985. Militia and state workers may have brought the total number of civilians employed on K5 to 380,000, or equivalent to the number of souvenir certificates for Labor to Defend the Motherland (*pulakamm karpier mietophum*) that were ordered by the government in February 1985.[40] The total number of people conscripted into the army during this period is not recorded although the documents indicate that numbers were consistently below target and they do not account for desertions.

Accompanying Document No. 1 attached to that 28 September 1984 decision noted that the budget approved for the K5 Plan was 200 million *riel*, eighty million of which was set aside for expenditure in 1984. The cost of heavy machinery and road-making equipment was not included in that budget total; the medical budget was also separate. Of the total budget outlay, 120 million *riel* was for capital works (including road construction, the manufacture of metal spikes and tools) and eighty million *riel* was to pay and provision the workers (including their transportation and the making of shelters).[41] Short-term workers were paid 140 *riel* per month; laborers who worked more than six months, depending on "the real situation at the base and each construction site" were paid 180 *riel* per month in addition to one set of clothes and materials.[42] The militia were paid at the same rate. The provinces were responsible for drafting their own budget proposals, which were forwarded to the Ministry of Finance. As noted previously, expenditure on defense was not quoted in the state budget, but an amount of eighty million *riel* represented less than four percent of domestic income for 1985, which was a high but not an unbearable cost.[43] The machinery, materials and drugs were supplied by the USSR. Bekaert quoted the *Economist Intelligence Unit* (EIU) figure of a thirty percent increase in the value of USSR exports to the PRK in 1984, bringing Cambodia's trade deficit with the USSR to 71 million *roubles*.[44]

Soy Keo's report to the National Assembly in July 1985 acknowledged that the highly successful 1984–1985 dry season offensive was due in large measure to the better access to the border provided by new and upgraded roads, which had been built as part of the K5 Plan. He claimed a further victory, the successful mobilization of the masses:

> . . . all the people, all the forces have high determination and the revolutionary atmosphere of the masses throughout the country is bubbling over and [this] has become a great and wide revolutionary movement with organizations of all categories. The people throughout the country go to the border with joy to unite the building of the motherland by repairing and building roads, building defense shelters, building a line of barriers . . .[45]

Some people did volunteer to take part in K5, but the great majority of them were conscripted. On 4 September 1985, the Council of State ratified a decree-law which, in effect, mobilized the whole of the able-bodied population.[46] Male citizens between the ages of eighteen and thirty had to serve in the army, while "citizens of both sexes between the ages of sixteen and fifty-five (for women) and sixty (for men) must serve in the militia or the self-defense units" (Articles 2,3). The period of military service was five years. The following January, the tours of duty of "brothers who have had the honor of serving in the forces before and who are now fulfilling their obligations in the army" were extended indefinitely.[47] If the people went to the border "with joy" in the early tours of K5 duty, many of them returned to their villages so ill with malaria and other diseases that later worker contingents virtually had to be press-ganged.

The mountainous and densely forested regions of the border defense work sites were notorious for their particularly virulent strains of malaria. The plains regions, on the other hand, until then had been virtually free of the disease, or its spread had been contained. The laborers from the plains were thus particularly susceptible and they took the disease back to their villages. Luciolli claims that "eighty to ninety percent of the volunteers returned sick. The mortality rate was very high, in the order of five to ten percent. In Kandal, of 12,000 laborers, there were 9,000 cases of malarial infection and 700 deaths. In one district of Takeo, of 1,100 participants, there were 900 cases of malarial infection and fifty-six deaths."[48] Taking the figure of "at least one million participants" in the K5 Plan between September 1984 and the end of 1986, she calculates that there were 50,000 deaths due to malaria alone. However, as noted earlier, her excessive figures for participants cannot be substantiated.

The border region was also literally peppered with mines which had been placed there by all parties to the civil war, and the mortality and mutilation rate among the construction workers was high. Luciolli notes that in 1985, the prosthesis center in Phnom Penh received a minimum of sixty new amputees per month but, she argued, this number was just "the tip of the iceberg," as most amputees went directly back to their villages.[49] Other accidents occurred during jungle clearing. The workers were unskilled in tree-felling techniques and the huge trees, their canopies intertwined with lianas, bounced and swung as they fell, smashing back into the cutters. A young medic from the Pursat provincial hospital who did two tours on the border defense work, recalled finishing work every day covered in the blood of injured and dying workers.[50]

From 18–27 December 1985, a delegation of the Central K5 Leadership Committee led by Chhea Thang, vice minister, Ministry of Health, with representatives from the ministries of planning, propaganda and culture, industry, agriculture, and communications visited parts of Region 3 and Region 4 which were located in Battambang Province. The report on that visit states the following alarming statistics:

> Up to 20 December 1985, the number of workers was 2,956 out of the planned number of 3,150. Of that number of 2,956:
> - 745 were in hospital (among them were 52 wounded workers)
> - 602 were sick and receiving treatment
> - 32 had died on the battlefield
> - 144 had deserted
> - and of the 1,433 left, a number of them were also sick but were receiving treatment while they were still working.[51]

The reasons for sickness were attributed to shortcomings in the system of providing food, because "the wet season this year was longer than usual, which slowed down the transportation of food, and many of the workers did not receive sufficient supplies [according to the report, some workers lived on rice with salt] and this made the workforce susceptible to various illnesses, especially malaria."[52] Another cause was poor hygiene:

> Adhering to good hygiene practices such as cutting down the trees around the camps, sleeping with nets and drinking clean water are necessary for reducing the sickness rate. This year,

the state has a system of providing nets to all the workers but, in fact, some of the workers are still without nets to protect themselves against mosquitoes.[53]

The report noted that the Vietnamese soldiers working alongside the Cambodian workers had a much lower sickness rate, because they observed better rules of hygiene and "they raised animals and grew vegetables in order to provision themselves."[54]

A flurry of reports and correspondence in February 1986 defended the Ministry of Health's efforts to supply adequate drugs and treatment to the workers on the border while admitting that the opening of its stores of drugs in the 1984–1985 dry season had, in fact, resulted in some drugs falling into the hands of private traders. As a result of the delegation's report, active measures were taken to treat and combat illness among the workers, including a *bralong branang* movement from the end of 1986 to December 1987, which set goals stressing "good assurance of livelihood . . . ensuring that each person has sufficient food in good time . . . " and "good prevention of disease and combating malaria, good hygiene, especially for combating malaria . . . "[55] Each ensuing annual report on the K5 Plan reported diminishing rates of disease and accidents. For instance, the Council of Ministers' report to the National Assembly in July 1987 claimed a 23 percent reduction in sickness compared with the previous year.[56] The report to the permanent committee of the Council of Ministers in August 1989 stated, "The total number of deaths and injuries during K5 in 1989 was forty-four people, low when compared with 1988 when it was eighty-nine people."[57] Care has to be taken with these figures, however, because the size of the workforce peaked in 1985 and the figures are not really comparable.

The K5 Plan was a dangerous wager by the PRK regime. That the conscription it necessitated was hugely unpopular was testified by the sudden increase in the number of people seeking refuge in the Thai border camps. According to statistics provided to Jacqueline Desbarats by the Bangkok offices of the UN High Commission for Refugees, after 1980, the number of refugees admitted to UNHCR camps had dried to a trickle;

in 1983 no refugees were officially admitted.[58] In the two years, 1984 and 1985, UNHCR camps accepted 12,335 refugees. The conscription drive also provided further opportunities for wealth creation by corrupt officials, who collected monthly payments from families who were desperate to keep their sons out of the army.[59]Officials could also be bribed to conscript someone else in the place of the one named by the K5 authorities; this bribe was popularly called *si chnuol chuol mnuh*.[60]

If the border barrage was intended to keep the enemy out, it was also meant to keep the citizens of the PRK in. On 12 November 1984, prime minister Chan Si issued an order which forbade journeys across the border to Thailand without permission and official passes.[61] The use of firearms and mines for hunting in the border regions was forbidden; boats had to be properly registered and their movements had to be reported to the authorities in advance; comings and goings within families were to be reported to the commune security forces. As part of that system of increased general surveillance, later that month, acting on a politburo decision of 11 June, a sub-decree was issued to create a Commission for the Movement of Bringing Back the Misled (*kenna cholena chun vongveng phlouv*) at each level of the administrative system.[62] The central committee of the movement, which represented the Central Propaganda and Education Commission, the ministries of defense, interior, education, and propaganda and culture as well as the Front, the mass organizations, and the People's Radio, was led by Bou Thong. The Movement for the Misled was intended to consolidate the gains of the 1984–85 offensive and to fend off the counter-offensive by the resistance, which more and more took the form of extremely dangerous psychological warfare. In April 1985, the party secretariat issued a directive "[to] make the people understand clearly that this wet season is the opportunity to strike politically to make the enemy collapse, especially the enemy inside the country . . . We should not let the enemy have the chance to reorganize and develop the awareness of their routed forces. We should do whatever [we can] for the enemy to defect and to reveal themselves in 1985 in every region twice or two and a half times more than in 1984."[63] This mass movement was most critically important in those districts situated in the forest and mountain regions beside the border, and in the Lake Tonle Sap region. Say Phouthang advised:

> Organize the women and families of the enemy military forces and the commanders to act as a core force. We should strive more than before for the families who have contact with the commanders of the small groups of enemy units who are carrying out activities in their own regions in order to attract all those commanders. Create conditions to make the enemy units collapse.[64]

He suggested that monks and state authorities write personal letters "to attract the enemy, et cetera, in order to diminish their numbers or make them reflect on the weak situation of the enemy at present and to stop their crimes."[65] Meanwhile, provincial authorities "should strive to cause disputes between the enemy soldiers and their commanders in order to create confusion within the enemy's internal solidarity (*ptey knong*)."[66] Propaganda was an important tool, especially when delivered by defectors; "and don't be afraid of sham defectors or be hesitant in using them in order to strike politically at the enemy. On the contrary, if the defectors whom we suspect have only pretended to defect, then we should always use them in order to put pressure on them to show their [true] attitude."[67] The reeducation of defectors was the responsibility of the *krom samaki*, with monitoring provided by the commune. The commune authorities had to explain "the policy of compassion endowed with humanitarianism for all those who come back to the people and the genuine revolution" but those who took improper advantage of this policy were to be punished: ". . . we must lead those people to an open-air court in order to get the support from the people . . . "[68] The directive warned that the enemy's ruse was to use the people as a shield, making the people provide provisional caches for arms and supplies "as well as serving them in various other work." When it was necessary to make a military strike, "the battlefield commanders must grasp the situation clearly and search for means to attack appropriately . . . to lower the level of damage to the people."[69]

Between military conscription and forced labor levies where the great part of the burden, as always, fell on rural Cambodians who did not have the financial or other means to escape them, the stricter enforcement of restrictions on freedom of movement, and the harshness of this directive about flushing out the enemy, the Cambodian countryside had become a very threatening place by mid-1985. The Movement of the Misled was, on its own terms, rated a success. The government report on the first nine months of its implementation in 1985 claimed "3,454 brothers who lost the way with the enemy have woken up to the truth and come before our revolutionary state authorities, bringing their arms (1,962 weapons) and a quantity of other materials. Among them, 1,992 were Pol Potists and 1,462 were from *Sereikar* and *Moulinaka*.[70] If we compare this with the same nine months of 1984, the number of defectors has increased 2.75 times."[71] The government also provided cash incentives for defectors, which were undoubtedly more persuasive than the propaganda. Paul Quinn-Judge reported that "defectors who perform an 'outstanding feat' before leaving coalition ranks, such as killing their commanders, qualify for rewards of up to 2,000 *riel*."[72] To outsiders, this was a foolhardy policy and one unlikely to attract genuine defectors. Nayan Chanda noted:

> The practice of allowing defectors to return to their native villages without having to go through re-education or screening is not welcomed by the Vietnamese, but it is accepted with resignation. "Maybe this is the way the Khmers will achieve reconciliation," a source said. The notion that Cambodians are tired of war and would like to see an end through compromise is gaining credence.[73]

In the years that followed, reports on the movement claimed great success until the beginning of 1989, when defections virtually ceased. Hun Sen's report to the seventeenth session of the National Assembly in July suggested this was because "they won't come out before a political solution is reached because they are afraid of losing their role and status."[74] There can be no doubt that the increased momentum of the peace process following the 17 August 1987 declaration of a policy of national reconciliation by the PRK government, and the meeting between Prince Sihanouk and Hun Sen in France during the first week of December that year, had a direct bearing on the strategies of the Khmer Rouge.[75]

The huge cost of conscription to the PRK's popular support had to be recompensed by greatly improved security, so that the people could concentrate on their economic tasks. To this end, the border barrage did significantly hinder border incursions; for the remainder of the PRK period there were no major dry season offensives after that of 1984–1985 and the "hot" war on the border reached a stalemate. Nevertheless, the security situation inside Cambodia remained dangerous. Foreign journalists reported that KPRAF troops often aided and abetted their resistance counterparts by allowing them to pass through the border barrage.[76] Once inside the country, however, it was difficult for them to return, so the guerrilla bases in the interior grew stronger and spread more deeply into the countryside. The Vietnamese forces were stretched to defend the length of the barrage that had been constructed, leaving the interior thinly defended. It seemed that this was exactly what the KR wanted:

> The way the Khmer Rouge assess the situation, the border is only of secondary priority. More important in their calculations is the broad operational belt around the Tonle Sap lake, which it has penetrated with a considerable degree of success. To the guerrillas, success in combat is a matter of what proportion of the 40–50,000-strong fighting force is inside the country, not control of frontier bastions.[77]

In view of that, a government directive of 19 April 1985 set down strict guidelines for the management of the Lake Tonle Sap region, that is, the provinces of Siem Reap, Battambang, Pursat, Kompong Chhnang and Kompong Thom.[78] The Ministry of the Interior monitored the compiling of statistics on people living on the lake, of fishery units and collectives, of state transport and communication facilities. Anyone fishing on the lake had to have all the proper permits, and all movements on the lake were strictly supervised. The second main area of guerrilla activity was around Phnom Penh. Just as worrying as the terrifying armed raids of the KR on commune and district offices, and the sabotage of the main communication routes, was the strength of its psychological warfare. A report to the National Assembly on the military situation up to October 1986 expressed deep concern over the effects of this psychological warfare "until sometimes these tricks cause our cadres, staff, workers, combatants, militia and the masses in all units and bases to feel unsure about who is friend and who is foe, and numb their will for battle and fulfilling duties . . . "[79] The author admitted that within the country, "the enemy's strength is still unknown so we dare not send our infantry to remote border regions and regions where the revolutionary movement is still weak in order to support and encourage the mass movement . . . " Moreover, because "many of our cadres and administrative organizations do not yet pay heed to building and strengthening the villages, the three revolutionary movements in the village have developed slowly and in some villages the enemy still come in and out regularly."[80] The militias were functioning at the commune level, if only to defend the commune offices, but villages often lacked a militia, because the local authorities did not appreciate their importance. The report also expressed concern about methods used to levy troops for the regional armies: "some places selected troops according to methods of compulsion until some people were arrested in order to make them join the troops according to the methods of the former regimes, doing whatever to get enough troops to achieve the state plan."[81] All of this played easily into the hands of the KR propaganda machine.

KR propaganda was not only aimed at the central government's policy. It also played on the fragility of the government's hold over the northern and northwestern parts of the country, by enticing the people away from their normal productive tasks with promises of easy wealth. The consequences were highly disruptive to the local administration. In this way, the KR taunted the government into employing ever more coercive means of authority, which would further weaken the tenuous support it had managed to create in those parts of the country. The extent of the effectiveness of this sort of enemy propaganda was revealed in the contents of a circular of April 1989 which made the startling claim that many people, troops, *nokorbal*, cadres, staff, and state workers had given up "their duties to increase the harvest, to defend security and the social order, to serve the work within the government and productive units of the state to go and do various occupations including digging for gems and gold."[82] Hun Sen had referred to this situation in June of the previous year, when he blamed the enemy for tricking the people to go and dig for gems and gold in Pailin and Phnom Chi, in order to "resolve the getting of forces and food in those places and to create other difficulties and complications for us."[83] According to the circular, the situation had become extreme in the Battambang region, where "some people have given up growing rice and farming, and between ten and twenty percent of cadres, staff and workers in the departments and units of the province have given up their state jobs, their military units, and district duties; the village and commune militias are lacking fighting force, some schools and hospitals have closed their doors, and they have all gone to dig for gems, creating a confused situation throughout the province."[84]

By early 1989, guerrilla activity was widespread throughout the country, "uniting armed activities and political activities (but mainly political)."[85] The KR were using the strategy of "Scatter 2 and Build 4": scatter the state authorities at the base, scatter the armed forces at the base, build the state authority of Democratic Kampuchea, build the armed force, build the genuine political force, and build the core force through individuals and families.[86] As the Vietnamese troops withdrew, the KR were testing the strength of the PRK and they had plans, the minister of interior warned, to expand their operations widely on the eastern side of the Mekong and across to the Vietnam border. Already by then they had carried out attacks in Kompong Cham, Prey Veng, Kratie, Stung Treng, and Ratanakiri, but they were also active in Kompong Speu and Kompong Chhnang, and "attacking deeply into the region of the belt around Phnom Penh."[87] The heightened level of insecurity bit deeply into agricultural production, not only because farm labor had to be diverted to the war effort, but also because vast tracts of arable land became dangerous no-go zones. In Kompong Speu, for example, forty percent of the province's cultivable land was reportedly out of production in 1987 because of insecurity, and the governor of Battambang told a foreign journalist in 1989 that "roughly half the rice fields in his province have been forced out of production during the past decade of fighting."[88]

In May 1988, Vietnam announced that it would withdraw 50,000 troops from Cambodia by the end of the year.[89] The following month, Vietnam withdrew its military command and most of its advisers.[90] The remaining force of 40,000 Vietnamese soldiers was nominally placed under KPRAF command and pulled back thirty kilometers from the Thai border. In fact, during the preceding dry season offensive, PAVN troops had already retreated twenty to thirty kilometers from the border, thereby acting as support rather than frontline forces.[91] At the ceremony to celebrate the tenth anniversary of the 7 January 1979 victory and the foundation of the PRK, Nguyen Van Linh, secretary-general of the CPV announced, "Vietnam declares its complete unanimity of views with the People's Republic of Kampuchea and decides to withdraw all its remaining volunteer troops by September 1989."[92] This promise was contingent on a political settlement to the Cambodian problem. Following the Jakarta Informal Meetings (JIM 1 and JIM 2) of all conflicting parties in July 1988 and February 1989, decision was reached on a basic agreement on the substance of a settlement of the Kampuchea question:

> . . . linking closely the withdrawal of Vietnamese volunteer forces from Kampuchea with the prevention of the return of the genocidal Pol Pot regime, with the cessation of foreign interference, the cessation of foreign military aid to all the Kampuchean parties, and with the prevention of civil war, the setting up of an effective international control mechanism for the implementation of the above-mentioned provisions, the convening of an international conference to guarantee the independence, neutrality and nonalignment of Kampuchea and

the agreements reached. The People's Republic of China and several other countries have solemnly declared their complete cessation of military aid to all the Kampuchean parties concurrently with the total withdrawal of Vietnamese forces from Kampuchea.[93]

Vietnam completed the withdrawal of its troops on 26 September 1989. "And who," a young male student of the University of Phnom Penh demanded angrily that afternoon, "will protect us now?"[94] The Vietnamese left the defense of the PRK in the hands of 40,000–50,000 KPRAF troops, including both regular and regional forces, backed by a district and commune level militia force, trained but ill-equipped, of somewhere between 100,000 and 220,000 men and women.[95] It was time for Cambodians to defend themselves. To this end, and in the belief that in "people's war" the local people were the best defenders of their own territory, local defense was turned over to the district and commune militias, and many formerly regular military units were transferred to the command of their own provincial officers.[96] The Khmer Rouge were thus kept at bay until the UN Transitional Authority in Cambodia arrived to prepare for the May 1993 general elections.

In retrospect, the K5 Plan was broadly successful in terms of having achieved its main goals, and it is fair to say that the PRK regime would not have survived the withdrawal of the Vietnamese volunteer forces without it. However, it panicked the people and turned the goodwill that the regime had earned into bitter and long-lasting resentment over the methods used to recruit labor and conscript troops. In this way, the PRK played easily into the hands of its detractors. For instance, a propaganda tract circulating in Phnom Penh in 1996 accused "the group of Mr Hun Sen" of "creating policies to kill pure Khmers by methods which are called K5":

> The group of Hun Sen, Heng Samrin, Chea Sim, Men Samon, Sar Kheng conscripted the strength of young and mature men from month to month and silenced the villages. In each village, there were only the old to do the work, the newly born

and the widows. If a country does not have the strength of its youth, then where is the future?[97]

The resistance forces turned K5 against the PRK regime, by employing political propaganda to win over the people's sympathy and turn them against what they could claim, with obvious justification but no apparent irony, was an oppressive regime that overtaxed the physical and emotional capacity of its citizens. In February 1985, at the height of the massive 1984–1985 dry season offensive which destroyed the resistance bases, and when the K5 program of civilian defense work necessitated the most intense propaganda drive by the PRK authorities, John McBeth reported:

> Perhaps giving the lie to the widely held belief that they alienated the entire Cambodian population during their brutal three-and-a-half years in power, the Khmer Rouge rely on local villagers for food and also to act as porters in a now well-organized network that relays supplies into the interior.[98]

Of course it could be argued that the villagers were forced, tricked or even paid to provide food and labor, and no doubt some were. On the other hand, McBeth's comment deserves some credence. A further telling report was that which quoted a Vietnamese soldier who explained, "In Cambodia, people act like family. If Pol Pot troops come, people let them stay overnight."[99] The obvious fact was that in many instances the guerrillas *were* "family" and family obligations naturally took precedence over obligations to the state. In a civil war, all boundaries are blurred and state loyalties are hard fought and narrowly contested.

Most of the foreign journalists reporting on the Cambodian situation at that time had far better access to the resistance forces than they did to the KPRAF, and their accounts reflected this bias. The Canadian journalist who spent three weeks on patrol inside Cambodia with the KPNLF in 1986 observed that the resistance had created small mobile bases in the interior, and that "political action, such as helping villagers with medical care and crop harvesting, increased."[100] The

Khmer Rouge, he said, were recruiting inside Cambodia and "establishing firmer roots in the villages by marrying off its soldiers to local women." During the time he spent with the resistance, he noted that "the KPNLF had no trouble purchasing food supplies from the villagers. They also appeared to have good intelligence sources, among them villagers and local militia."[101] The Khmer Rouge, meanwhile, "appeared well supplied and highly organized. Its troops were confident while passing through its territory, and villagers encountered on the march seemed relaxed in the presence of the soldiers."[102] Prince Norodom Ranariddh, commander in chief of the royalist faction of the tripartite resistance, commented on the success of FUNCINPEC's propaganda work, where "Sihanouk's name helps immensely, not only with civilians but also Heng Samrin troops."[103] Confronted with these ploys and in a countryside that was so desperately poor that young men sometimes donned the uniform of the warring faction that offered the highest salary, ideals had little reward. Worst of all was the accusation that the KPRAF were killing brother Khmers at the command of the traditional enemy, Vietnam. All of this accounted for the bad report that the KPRAF soldiers received, which usually involved four criticisms: that they were "lacking motivation and discipline, ineffective and often desert."[104]

That the achievement of K5 was never celebrated as the great victory that in many ways it was, and that Cambodian people later hid their participation or spoke of it with embarrassment rather than with pride, is the most telling testimony of the PRK's failure to win hegemonic support for their struggle. The failure of agricultural collectivization, and the regime's inability to broker an agreement with the private market sector to support the state rather than compete with it, proved beyond doubt that the revolution had collapsed well before the end of 1989. Despite the withdrawal of Vietnamese advisers and troops in September that year, however, the party held strong, the impoverished administration continued to function and the beleaguered KPRAF forces and local militias managed to defend the state's sovereignty until the Paris Peace Agreement delivered a kind of peace in October 1991. These efforts, however, were related more to the stoicism of the Cambodian people and their capacity to survive great odds, than to their loyalty to either state or ruling party. Many foreign reports commented on the PRK/SOC's quest for legitimacy. Internationally, particularly in the diplomatic struggle over who should represent Cambodia in the UN General Assembly, legitimacy was a major issue throughout the decade. Within the country, among the ordinary citizens, however, as long as the People's Revolutionary Party of Kampuchea held power, the PRK ruled and the people obeyed. This was the direct antithesis of ideological hegemony. Despite its huge costs, the revolution changed Cambodian society very little, and illustrated instead the deep continuities that exist within Cambodia's history and culture.

Chapter 10

CONCLUSION

WHEN THE REVOLUTIONARY armed forces of the Communist Party of Kampuchea entered Phnom Penh on 17 April 1975, the ruling power of the traditional elite was forcibly transferred to the Khmer Rouge, who represented the social stratum of the peasantry, the vast majority of the Cambodian population. To this extent, in political terms, Cambodia underwent revolution. Those who led the movement and who had engaged in the struggle, firstly against European colonization and later against class-based injustices within Cambodian society, believed that they were making social revolution, that taking power was the means to their desired end of actual transformation of state and class structures which determined how that power was articulated. For many complex reasons, however, those efforts failed, and with hindsight, the Cambodian revolution can be judged as little more than a further violent episode in Cambodian history.

For Marx, a new society cannot emerge until all the productive forces within the existing society have exhausted themselves, and until the necessary and sufficient conditions for the new society already exist or are in the process of development. According to these criteria, Cambodia was not ready for the revolution that occurred. Despite the apparent popular support which brought the Khmer Rouge to power in 1975, theirs was not a genuine, class-based movement which grew inexorably out of objective structural contradictions inherent in that society's evolution. Certainly the old regime was in crisis in Cambodia prior to 1975, but that crisis was provoked by its own short-sighted agency and fortuitous events rather than by historical inevitability. The *coup détat* of March 1970 when the forces on the right under the leadership of General Lon Nol, and Prince Sirik Matak usurped the power of the king, sealed the fate of the privileged elite. In the eyes of the rural masses, the coup was a supreme act of blasphemy, an attack on the moral order, the divine essence of Khmer society. The traditional elite thereby lost the merit which justified their privileged rights as rulers. Their insatiable corruption, a vacuum of able decision-making, inability to perceive injustice or care for the suffering of the people, almost total dependence on foreign economic resources, as well as brutality and recalcitrance in the face of internal rebellion and foreign invasion all made a change of leadership in April 1975, if not "revolution," welcome. The decision made by the new regime immediately after taking power to evacuate the capital city and the provincial towns and to close all markets, at one stroke eliminated rural debt. Nothing was more likely to ensure peasant support for the new regime than this single act.[1]

Popularity, however, was insufficient to sustain revolution. There was form but no substance in Pol Pot's revolution. If Pol Pot's intention was social revolution, on what concrete, material basis was that revolution going to depend? Cambodia was virtually a pre-capitalist society in 1975 and whatever capital infrastructure existed, in the form of transportation facilities, factories and plantations, had been ravaged by bombs and warfare. Rice was the main commodity of the old regime, and apart from the rubber plantations which were worked largely by Vietnamese laborers, there was little existing capital investment and there were few natural resources to allow for further state investment of this kind. The only industry to speak of, apart from artisanal and village-based manufacturing and processing, was concentrated in a small urban manufacturing base whose few employees hardly constituted a "proletariat." The population was largely uneducated or educated only into the consciousness of the elite. It was therefore inevitable that without substantial foreign assistance, the new state would have to squeeze the surplus it needed from the farming population, which was a guaranteed way to lose the popularity it had won. Pol Pot's revolution, with its gross misinterpretation of the terms "mastery" and "self-reliance," as well as its poor choice of ally in China, at that time the pariah of the socialist world, was therefore doomed from the start. It is generally assumed that the Pol Pot clique spurned external assistance; it is more likely, however, that little was offered.

There undoubtedly were severe injustices within Cambodian society before 1975, but it is difficult to argue that they derived from irreconcilable contradictions arising out of a society evolving towards a new mode of production. Moreover, while an outsider may well have prescribed major changes for the good of Cambodia, within that society itself attempts at change were habitually met with well-practiced inertia. Certainly the regime of Democratic Kampuchea altered the lives of all Cambodians in drastic fashion. On the other hand, the persistent structures of the old society, those "levels of reality which exist beyond man's visible relations and whose functioning constitutes the deeper logic of a social system—the underlying order by which the apparent order must be explained" changed very little.[2]

In 1975, Cambodian peasants participated in the revolution for their own personal benefit, just as the peasants of France, Russia, China and other revolutionary states before them had done, initially "without being converted to radical visions of a desired new national society, and without becoming a nationally organized class-for-themselves. Instead they struggled for concrete goals—typically involving access to more land, or freedom from claims on their surpluses."[3] Various close observers, both foreign and Cambodian, have commented on the Khmer Rouge's successful efforts to collectivize property and to mobilize the farmers during the pre-revolutionary period. Considering the scale of the aerial bombardment which the Cambodian countryside bore between 1969 and the end of 1973, peasant cooperation with such schemes made sense. The very survival of isolated farming communities depended on the leadership, the organizational strategies and the hope that the revolutionaries gave them. Peasant solidarity and autonomy, however, were radical and perhaps even absurd concepts in the context of traditional societal structures. In Cambodian society, the patron-client dyadic pattern of ordered power relationships, which was justified by ideological beliefs in merit and karma, made for a highly fragmented society where notions of inequality and dependency were integral to the maintenance of social order. Solidarity, equality and autonomy could only disturb cosmic harmony. Theravada Buddhism provided the *dharma*, the law that guided the people's spiritual life and created order out of the chaos which constantly threatened to consume them. Everyday life, however, was directed by the *chbab*, separate laws for women and for men which, like the analects of Confucius, established rules for proper behavior and conveyed moral values that included unquestioning respect for those with higher social positions.[4] These laws shaped both behavior and thought. According to Chandler, "The world picture transmitted by the *chbab* is one where deference and fatalism take up more space than rebelliousness or hope."[5]

The DK regime exercised its authority through fear, excessive coercion, and by control over the most basic means of survival, food. The sudden rise to power of poor, uneducated, and, for the most part, male adolescents of peasant stock, Mao Zedong's "poor and blank" of his "cultural" revolution which Pol Pot strived to emulate, resulted in an easy return to traditional interpretations of power relations. In Cambodia, as in Thailand, "when a farmer, he acts as a farmer, but when he receives his insignia of office, he discards his rustic ways . . . To a greater extent than in the West, the insignia transform the person."[6] As eyewitness Someth May remembered:

> The weird thing about this peasant revolution was that none of the accumulated wisdom of the peasants went into it . . . Even when I was a leader I never heard a discussion about agriculture. It was as if the peasants who ruled us despised the fact that they had been peasants. They were choked with power. They had turned their backs on everything they knew for the sake of politics about which they knew nothing. And because they forced us to pretend that we knew nothing, nobody in the society knew anything. If a skilled engineer looking at what they were doing had laid down his spade and offered to design a wonderfully functioning reservoir, he would have been killed for not being a peasant. The whole society was working at maximum—and brutally enforced—inefficiency.[7]

Those who survived the regime adapted themselves as best they could to the conditions dictated by those who held power, neither resisting nor accommodating themselves, but simply absorbing the misery inflicted on them from above, from *angkar loeu*. In the words of one survivor:

> The suffering was because the leaders created it . . . According to my understanding, people seem like grass. The people are like grass because the grass accepts everything: rain, sun, cars driving over it, storms. It accepts all seasons . . . If we want to build a house, we have to take a big log out of the forest and move it over the grass. Compare this to the suffering of the common people. If the leaders need power to do something and the people get injured and killed, that is separate. This is [the case] since long ago up until now . . . The grass accepts all suffering and the people accept all suffering.[8]

Pol Pot's revolution, then, was the triumph of conservatism. As Chandler says, "The same values that made so many Cambodians reluctant to struggle for their 'rights' under the French, Sihanouk, and Lon Nol, has preserved many survivors of the 1970s from revolutionary transformations . . . Pol Pot and his 'organization' (*angkar*) were entangled and defeated not only by the Vietnamese and by their own ideas, but by the social behavior they set about to undermine."[9]

The Democratic Kampuchea stage of the Cambodian revolution, then, while purporting to be socialist, became simply an exercise in domination and control. Chandler notes that "Pol Pot and his colleagues were entranced by the exercise of power and by the praxis of prolonged and unrelenting warfare."[10] Had the revolutionaries coped with the transition to the new society smoothly and efficiently, the Cambodian people might well have accepted the revolution as a *fait accompli* and accorded the Democratic Kampuchea regime legitimacy. They did not, and because the revolutionaries were mere mortals, and worse, commoners with origins as humble as their own, the farmers withdrew their support for them as soon as the patrons could no longer deliver either material benefit or political favor to their clients. Kate Frieson's interviews with peasants in Kandal, Takeo and Kompong Speu provinces revealed that "the infringement on village autonomy and freedom was deeply resented by Khmer peasants . . . People were especially alienated from any sympathies they might have had for the KR over the issue of food."[11] She noted further that the regime's policies were never explained to the peasants in terms they could understand or appreciate.[12] The possibility remains, of course, that the peasants may have deliberately chosen not to understand or to appreciate what the revolutionaries were attempting to do on their behalf. The notion of revolution, of losing whatever continuity existed in their already chaotic world, may have been too terrible to comprehend. In Thion's words, "even the beneficiaries could not be led towards paradise."[13]

The corollary of excessive coercion, especially when that coercion appears to be unjustified and remains unexplained, is distrust. In the Democratic Kampuchea regime, that distrust was mutual. Chandler contends, "The balance of evidence and the document[s] suggest that the leaders knew very little about the 'people' and distrusted them *en masse*."[14] In Pol Pot's case, that distrust developed into fear and paranoia, causing him to search for "microbes" within his own ranks, which he purged with a thoroughness verging on frenzy. For any socialist regime, making the radical and permanent changes to cultural norms, beliefs and customs which the goals of revolution dictate, requires that a high level of trust be forged between the people and the ruling party. This is dangerous territory for the revolutionaries, the chasm where the revolution itself may come to grief. The bridge between the party's goals and the people's preferred habits has to be constructed and constantly renegotiated by the cadres, those "brokers between the little traditions of the village and the national revolutionary party."[15] In the process, state coercion may be necessary if the party is not to capitulate to the people's will entirely, but coercion is always an unsatisfactory option. Consent is obviously preferable because when consent is given, trust is implicit. If this trust is not established and if the party fails to achieve its goal of social transformation without resorting to excessive force, the consequences for the people and for the national economy will be disastrous. Ideology as hegemony holds the key to people's trust. For Gramsci, revolution was fundamentally and essentially something that occurred in man's own conscious reality of the world. If revolution was to be sustained, he argued, the people had to transform themselves, and come to see themselves as responsible agents of change. Establishing ideological hegemony, therefore, was the core duty of the party and its cadres. This is what Pol Pot and his regime failed to understand and thus to accomplish.

Pol Pot's additional failure lay not only in the mismanagement of the economy, but also in his inability to end factionalism within the party, and to command the loyalty of his own cadres. "[W]hat matters most," Skocpol warns, "is always the support or acquiescence not of the popular majority of society but of the politically powerful and mobilized groups, invariably including the regime's own cadres."[16] Given the rebellions engineered by party cadres, which began as early as September 1975, and the plots and vicious retaliatory purges after September the following year, this was not the case in the DK regime. There was also a lack of politically trained and committed cadres at the village level, which inhibited the extension of ideological hegemony over the masses. Noam Chomsky found the success of the Khmer Rouge was "all the more amazing when it is realized that they had few, if any cadres at the village or hamlet level . . . In most cases, there was no separate party existence nor were there political cadres at the village level or at any level below."[17] The party's social program was instead implemented by "locally recruited military units . . . as well as 'interfamily groups'."[18] This situation was hardly cause for commendation; rather, it indicated that what was happening at the village level had virtually nothing to do with socialism. During his visit to a liberated zone in 1972, Serge Thion observed a district level political training course (eight hours per day for two weeks plus two hours of review each evening) for cadres with responsibilities in the communes and villages, almost all of them farmers with very little primary schooling: "so the classes are given in simple, repetitive language, and the answers to the students' questions are aimed more at ensuring that they have assimilated the doctrine than at developing their intellectual curiosity."[19] This, then, was the caliber of those cadres who were in daily contact with the farmers and who were responsible for the political education of the masses at the base. It can further be assumed that the majority of those peasant cadres were not motivated to join the revolution out of a desire to alter society. Instead, they joined the struggle in order to restore it to its original, perhaps idealized form. Serge Thion believed that "the massive participation of peasants in the insurgency, schooled by their local monks and led by minor officials or intellectuals usually from rural backgrounds, can only be explained in terms of the highly symbolic political and even religious upheaval that was precipitated from outside by the *coup d'tat* of March 1970."[20] When the victory of April 1975 returned their king to his palace but not to the throne, the people lost interest in, disbelieved and distrusted the revolution that was supposedly being made on their behalf.

Evidence that the DK stage of the Cambodian revolution was marked by ruthless and constant purges, by starvation and neglect of the masses, and by gross incompetence and mismanagement is overwhelming. However, while it can be accepted that both the "new" people were relieved and perhaps even grateful to have been freed from DK slavery, this should not imply that the people therefore gave their trust and support to their liberators, the Vietnamese-backed regime of the People's Republic of Kampuchea. Even less should one assume that the Cambodian peasantry trusted the new regime any more than they had trusted the former one, or believed its leaders when they said that their revolution, unlike the false one of Pol Pot, was "pure" and "genuine."

The leaders of the PRK claimed to have returned the Cambodian revolution to the path advancing towards "pure" socialism based on proper Marxist-Leninist principles untainted by Maoist deviationism. In the first half at least of its decade of rule, the leadership was sincere in its commitment to social revolution. Although far from liberal, the PRK was generally a benevolent regime. There was undoubtedly harsh punishment for transgressors of its laws, particularly for those suspected of espionage and collusion with the resistance forces, especially the Khmer Rouge. At the same time, the very real threat that the Khmer Rouge might return to power with the backing of the People's Republic of China and the tacit and material support of the USA and ASEAN remained constant throughout the decade and was as much a threat to the Vietnamese revolution as it was to the dangerously weak PRK. State coercion was justified to the people in those terms. The state may have been fragile but, at the same time, despite the extent of destruction and loss of human lives and the consequent lack of experienced administrators and technicians, the government was surprisingly efficient.

By the end of September 1989, when the PRK had constitutionally metamorphosed into the politically neutral State of Cambodia, and when the Vietnamese advisers and soldiers had returned home, the party leadership could justifiably claim that it had kept faith with the people and had indeed fulfilled the program of the Kampuchean United Front for National Salvation to which it pledged its efforts at Snoul on 2 December 1978. The outcomes of the PRK stage of revolution were more substantial and certainly more beneficial and lasting than those of the DK had been, although they were not essentially "revolutionary gains," that is, in the sense of actual transformation of state and class structures. The National Assembly, for instance, was neither more nor less influential than pre-revolutionary assemblies had been *vis-à-vis* the power of the Council of Ministers. Nevertheless, it did perform its proper function as defined by the PRK Constitution and, as the documents dating from 1985 attest, its deputies were dedicated, hard-working and daringly outspoken in their support for small people who fell victim to the abuse of power by corrupt officials. There was a system of administration, not always thorough or efficient and frequently officious and corrupt, which reached from the center (the ministries located in the capital, Phnom Penh) to the base (the commune, village, factory, farm) over most of the nation's territory and brought a sense of order to the countryside and relief during times of natural disasters. The free market thrived, trading with the new national currency, the *riel*, whose value remained fairly stable throughout the life of the regime, despite the fact that the national economy did not prosper beyond the point of simple recovery, and the regime remained heavily dependent on external assistance. In spite of the security situation and the demands made on their time and energy by defense work, farmers gradually restored the rice harvests to their pre-1970 yields, and the rubber plantations resumed exports of dried latex. Schools and hospitals were opened all over the country and literacy campaigns claimed huge successes. Wats were restored and the practice of religion, while carefully supervised, was not forbidden. There was a national army and trained public security forces; there were properly formulated laws and people's courts in all the provinces. The PRK, in short, gave Cambodians back their lives. The people, in their turn, gave the PRK their tacit acceptance, perhaps even legitimacy.

Despite all its achievements, the PRK was not genuinely popular. At the same time, despite the overwhelming presence of Vietnamese troops and advisers, neither was it unpopular. Generally speaking, the Vietnamese "invasion" and the new regime it helped to establish was greeted with understandable relief, as one informant remembered:

At that time [January 1979], we were as if submerged under water. Someone came to us and held out a stick for us. We did not think at that time about who was holding the stick. We only knew that we needed to grasp the stick or we would die.[21]

As life slowly returned to normal, however, the majority of people remained indifferent to efforts which attempted to engage them in revolutionary restructuring, and evaded when they could the new state's best efforts to co-opt them into schemes for the construction and defense of the country. If memory can be trusted, it seems that this indifference sometimes stemmed from private judgments about the motives of those who offered development assistance. "We realized there might be some punishment," one official said; another confessed, "We knew that we would have to drink poison."[22] Almost fifteen years after the PRK was established, these officials claimed that they could recall the connection they had then made between the assistance they desperately needed and the hegemonic intentions of those who gave it: "By giving assistance, the Vietnamese and Russians spread socialist ideology," claimed one official, while another said, "Assistance was a means of expanding this ideology. This is very simple."[23] Among these urban, educated officials who offered their "detached observations" on the efficacy of what Clayton calls "this hegemonic *mission*," only a minority, he notes, "believed that some Cambodians genuinely accepted the tenets of socialism, becoming true communists . . . "[24] One informant claimed, "Our leaders of that period were so thoroughly communist that even their bones were black" while another viewed the apparent conversion of some Cambodian officials as blatantly pragmatic: "In communism, he who supports socialist ideology gets the high positions in the government, gets fancy cars, gets nice villas."[25] On the other hand, it should be noted that not one of Clayton's informants admitted to engaging in overt resistance to socialist ideology at that time.[26]

Attempts aimed at the collectivization of agriculture also fell prey to a variety of responses to the ideological message. Again, the dialogue was generally "silent" and whatever degree of resistance occurred was usually passive. The leadership of the PRK could hardly claim to be building socialism, however, if the nation's rural inhabitants were not participating. Unlike the foolish policy of the Khmer Rouge to abolish family plots, foolish in view of the absence of a strong rural infrastructure or political leadership, which exacerbated the people's hunger and galvanized their resentment and hatred for their regime, the PRK encouraged the family economy and made this the foundation of its rural legitimacy. At the same time, farmers were organized into solidarity groups, *krom samaki*, which, in theory at least, were supposed to work the ricefields collectively. The *krom samaki* system of collectivized agriculture failed for many reasons, including poor management and bad weather, but most especially because of lack of interest on the part of the farmers and lack of understanding and commitment on the part of the cadres who were supposed to guide its implementation. One farmer, a former *krom samaki* member, defined the *krom* system he remembered as "just a means for distributing food."[27] A former core group member recalled that her work with the farmers involved teaching them about hygiene and clean water and occasionally explaining a government circular, ". . . but we never talked about politics."[28] Coercion seems never to have been used by the PRK to fashion the *krom samaki* into anything other than "a [practical] means for distributing food" and political indoctrination, if that is what the *krom snoul* (core groups) of the party at the base were supposed to be doing, seems to have fallen very wide of the mark. In an interesting case of pragmatic accommodation to the ideology, one of Clayton's informants, graduate of a political course in 1979, who was sent to the provinces "to promote socialist ideology among the farmers" explained:[29]

> The farmers would not have wanted to listen if I had used the plan provided in Phnom Penh [which was very theoretical and not relevant for use with farmers]. So, I gave my opinion about what to do now. I explained that the farmers must have solidarity now because many people were dead, there were few draught animals, and there was no equipment. The farmers must band together into *krom samaki*. I also suggested that the farmers follow Buddhism. Buddha also supported solidarity and *krom samaki*, so it was an idea that had some merit according to socialist principles.[30]

The testimony above rings true as the sort of advice that a practiced survivor might give, but one wonders what he could possibly have absorbed during his political education course. The interesting point is that, for the most part, these young "propaganda agents" of the party, the *krom snoul* who were sent down to the village to carry out *kosanakar abrum* (propaganda) believed that they were doing the party's bidding and they did their best to help the rural folk whose lives were wretched for several years after the catastrophe of the DK regime. Like the informant who "never talked about politics," they decided that what the farmers needed was good hygiene or clean water or solidarity. It simply never occurred to them that they might be delivering the "wrong" message or that they might be punished for doing so.

Where the early PRK leaders, veterans of the anti-colonial movement, "erred," if that is what they did, in terms of sustaining revolution, it was generally on the side of benevolence and knowingly abandoning theory when confronted with the harsh reality of practice. In attempting, yet failing, to win the trust and support of the masses, they sacrificed the goals of revolution. After 1985, as the power of this group of veterans was gradually transferred to the dissident group who had broken with the Khmer Rouge during its reign of terror, the Cambodian revolution became more deliberately pragmatic. Even the stage of development of the revolution was revised, it being decided that the Cambodian revolution had not progressed beyond the stage of "people's democratic revolution." As the threat from the combined resistance forces worsened, the state offered more and more liberal economic and political reforms to the people, in exchange for their continued loyalty and perhaps in compensation for the coercion it had to expend in order to defend its sovereignty.

The PRK was harshly criticized for the force it used to counter espionage and, in particular, to conscript civilians to execute the K5 Plan. That a socialist state, or any state, should employ force to exercise its will is not unusual. In fact, the contrary is the case. Classically defined, "the state is an institution which possesses a monopoly of legitimate violence . . . Deprived of this force, the system of cultural control expressed in terms of popular consent would be instantly fragile."[31] Even for Gramsci, coercion had an important role to play in politics. After all, the struggle for hegemony involves a struggle for power, and while political society and civil society can be distinguished for the purposes of analysis, in fact it is within civil society that state hegemony is contested. Gramsci described civil society as the battlefield where the war of contending ideologies had to be fought, and where hegemony was won or lost. The important point was that state power is always more effectively exercised through civil society than through political society. Power exercised through ethico-political means, through ideological hegemony, is more likely to win the lasting, active consent and cooperation of the masses than repression through the courts, public security forces or the military. Therefore, Gramsci argued, intellectual and moral leadership was an integral attribute of political power.

The "stay in the corset,", the conceptual core of the state itself, was the "organic intellectual," the party cadre who emerged from and was organic to the working class, and who was engaged in the work of political education at the base, raising consciousness and the level of theoretical knowledge at the same time.

The PRK suffered desperately from a lack of trained and committed cadres. The Communist Party of Kampuchea, under whatever name, was never very large and it was always smaller than its membership suggested, because even in its heyday prior to taking power in 1975, many of its cadres were not genuinely imbued with faith in doctrines of socialism and barely understood its basic tenets. The "true believers" who returned from Hanoi exile to participate in the mass mobilization efforts after the *coup d'état*, were slaughtered in 1973 and then from 1976 to the end of 1978, thousands of other cadres were tortured in Tuol Sleng and murdered on the killing fields of Choeung Ek. As the documents attest over and over again, the intellectual poverty, moral ambiguity and lack of political awareness of its cadres was the constant, nagging concern of the PRK leadership. Without a genuine working class, it was difficult to build a genuine revolutionary force. The party had to look to peasant members of its mass organizations to fill the party ranks, but this was always an unsatisfactory alternative.

At the end of 1986, eight years after he had led the FUNSK forces to victory over Pol Pot's regime, Heng Samrin signed a decision of the party central committee concerning *Building the Working Class of Kampuchea and turning [it] into a Genuine Vanguard Class imbued with the Cause of the Kampuchean Revolution*.[32] He listed five major weaknesses of the Cambodian working class. The workers, he said, had very low levels of culture and technical skills; they still had "superstitious beliefs and feudal consciousness" as well as the fearful consciousness of the colonized, fear of "the big man." Secondly, "the level of revolutionary awakening of our working class is still low." Many workers lacked class consciousness, "do not yet understand about the function and the responsibilities of the working class, do not yet understand that the People's Revolutionary Party of Kampuchea is the political commissar of its own class, do not yet understand that the state of the People's Republic of Kampuchea is the state of its own class. Not only that, they are still afraid of the cadres of our party and our state." Thirdly, he admitted that many factories and enterprises had outputs that were actually lower than those produced manually. Fourthly, while the state of the PRK was truly a proletarian state, actual contact with the working class was not yet "clean." "Most cadres have origins as farmers or petty bourgeoisie of the city. The intellectuals have not received education and do not yet have working class consciousness. There are remnants of the influence of the consciousness of all former regimes." Finally, the *krom samaki* for increasing the harvest lacked awareness of their role within the "proletarian system." The fault lay, he argued, with the failure of the mass organizations to raise the consciousness of the people:

> . . . trade unions have not made building working class consciousness the focal point [of their activities] and have not realized their own huge responsibility in building the alliance of workers and farmers to act as the foundation of the revolution. The Kampuchean People's Revolutionary Youth Alliance is a youth organization of the working class. It is the righthand of the party but it does not yet have clear class consciousness either.[33]

He believed that the successful creation of a working class with proper consciousness had "life and death definition for the revolution of our country." A lengthy program of concrete duties followed, and the decision concluded with the advice that at the end of 1988, the party secretariat would evaluate the two years' implementation of the program and, on the basis of that evaluation, would build a further program to ensure good results.

By then, it was too late to reinvigorate the party or the revolution, and powerful external factors, including rapprochement between the USSR and China, the end of the Cold War, the pressure to end the conflict in Indochina, and to include its member states in the ASEAN marketplace, all finally put paid to ambitions of social revolution in Cambodia. Hun Sen's reassuring words to the interior ministers of the other

Indochina countries in July 1989, just two months before the final withdrawal of the Vietnamese volunteer forces, were probably no more than bravado on his part:

> Truly I have made a lot of changes to the form but they do not affect the strategic objectives. The Cambodian battlefield can be said to be exceedingly complex, demanding that we have many measures. Sometimes we wear a red shirt, sometimes we wear a blue shirt, but we ourselves must remain the same. We change our name but the important thing is that we should take care of the revolutionary gains . . .[34]

A little over two years later, the revolution was abandoned with the formal renunciation of socialism.

The People's Revolutionary Party of Kampuchea failed to sustain the revolution, but it ended the terror and gave the people the means with which to restore their lives. In these terms, the PRK was loosely comparable with the Thermidor reaction, that period of rule following the Jacobin Terror of the French revolution, which was one of moderate dictatorship under which order was restored, tensions eased and there was a return to normalcy, or near normalcy for the majority of the people. The PRK regime was fortunate to have been governed by three fine prime ministers, Pen Sovann, Chan Si and Hun Sen, and to have had in Heng Samrin, party leader and head of state, a practical "man of the people," devoid of personal ambition and motivated primarily by the needs of the people and the defense of his nation's sovereignty. There was one important intangible revolutionary gain. An entire generation of Cambodians was born and raised to adulthood without knowing their king, and without studying the deference that was demanded by those born into privilege. However, they were not consciously taught republicanism either. Their attitude could be summed up by the reaction of one university student, the son of Svay Rieng farmers, to the news that there were plans for Sihanouk to return to Cambodia: "I myself do not know the man but my parents say he is kind and that he used to give the peasants rice and blankets."[35] This generation had never learnt the special language reserved for addressing

their king and his entourage, or the associated rituals of behavior. They had lost their elders' deference, and the traditional elite had lost its mystique. The king returned to Phnom
Penh in 1991 as a constitutional monarch, one who reigns but
may not govern. This was the revolutionary gain which was
most closely guarded and defended.

Marx's comment that communist societies do not develop on
their own, but emerge from the past still stamped with the
birthmarks of the old society, is a reminder that the popularity
of a political system may have less to do with its ideology than
with its continuities. For Cambodians, their carefully nurtured
grudges against Vietnam and xenophobic conviction that alien
elements constantly seek to destroy Khmer culture and
language, have shaped their national identity. These sentiments may be said to be more generally shared than faith in
the national motto of "Nation, Religion, King." Cambodian
citizens, deeply conservative, are the product of their historical experience, and old habits carry over to influence new realities. Once the terror had passed and their lives seemed secure, how could Cambodians identify with a state, however
benign, which derived its authority from Vietnam? Gratitude
is, after all, an ephemeral emotion, and one that can irritate
old prejudices if played on for too long. It is dangerous to make
assumptions about Cambodians' reactions to the prolonged
presence of Vietnamese troops and advisers throughout the
PRK regime. For most of that time, at least, ordinary Cambodians seemed reassured by the strictly disciplined presence of
the *bo doi*, which intruded very little on the private lives of citizens. One spectator, for example, defending her tears at the
ceremony for the final withdrawal of Vietnamese troops on 26
September 1989, replied, "It is true that we Cambodians hate
the Vietnamese, but we love the Vietnamese soldiers."[36]
Nevertheless, many PRK leaders and administrators chafed
under the authoritative presence of Vietnamese advisers and
perhaps by resisting Vietnamese hegemony, they also impeded
the progress of their own.

In the absence, as yet, of findings by an independent, international tribunal on the nature and scale of the crimes committed by the regime of Democratic Kampuchea, 1975 to 1979,

the veracity of testimonies given by survivors of their direct experience and those recorded by witnesses immediately before, during and then after that brief regime has to be relied upon to provide an accurate, or at least acceptable and consistent history of what occurred during that time. If those testimonies and accounts are true, then it also follows that the contribution made by Vietnam to the subsequent reconstruction, in fact the renewed life of Cambodia, was practically incalculable. Cambodia's condition at the beginning of 1979 was like the drowning man in the analogy recounted above; everything had been swept away and Vietnam held out the stick to save him. Rescue entailed the recreation of the state in its entirety, as well as the economy and its infrastructure. Cambodians could not have done this by themselves because there simply were not enough people with the capacity and the will to do so, let alone the material and technical support to match the scale of the problems. International Cold War politics of that time ruled out any possibility of an international, United Nations–led initiative. For their part, the Vietnamese no doubt had various, even conflicting motives for their intervention. They helped to create a Cambodian state in the administrative mold of their own, which was a perfectly understandable response to the situation. It was a mold which happened to work and it continues to function almost twenty-five years later, with very little change in form. Then, as now, the mold provided the shape, but not the substance, of the new state. In fact, ideology had very little to do with the reconstruction of Cambodia under the PRK.

In September 1989, the Vietnamese made the final withdrawal of their troops with an almost audible sigh of relief. In the decade which has passed since then, the Cambodian state has gradually resumed its particular, indigenous characteristics. If there is a debt owed to Vietnam, whether financial or in the nature of moral obligation, the details are carefully kept away from public scrutiny.

During a visit to Phnom Penh in 2000 by Vietnam's deputy prime minister, Nguyen Tan Dung, the two countries agreed to an repatriation operation for the remains of ten thousand soldiers, dead or missing, from the decade-long "occupation" of Cambodia by Vietnamese troops.[37] A five-year joint plan of action was signed in May 2001 to recover the bodies of Vietnamese soldiers who fought with the Khmer Issaraks against the French in the war for independence, and again during the Second and Third Indochina Wars. As many as twenty-two thousand Vietnamese soldiers were reported to have been killed in action on Cambodian soil in the cause of the Cambodian revolution, over four decades of war.[38] The toll may seem insignificant compared to the tragic millions of Cambodians who died during that time, not to mention the millions of Vietnamese soldiers and civilians who died during their own revolutionary wars in the same period on their own soil. The debt of gratitude owed to Vietnam is too sensitive a political issue to be expressed openly in Cambodia today. In Vietnam, likewise, the issue of Vietnam's role in Cambodia's revolution, and particularly in Cambodia's reconstruction during the PRK, is still too sensitive to be debated publicly. It is thus reassuring to return to the archival documents and to record some of the words addressed to the Cambodian National Assembly in August 1983 by the then young foreign minister, Hun Sen, who expressed his gratitude in these terms:

Last May, the army and our people made the second nostalgic trip for the brave Memot heroes of the . . . division, a unit of the Vietnamese volunteer troops who went back to their motherland. All those comrades are sons of a heroic nation . . . They all left parents, wives, children, brothers and sisters and lovers, left their native village and their land to go and face death and give their lives for their ideal of internationalism. What praise should we give for that shining and pure spirit? There are still other good sons of the heroic Vietnamese people who have spilt their blood to forge our land, to give back its life. And there are other children of the Vietnamese people who have sent their bones to the depths of the earth of the western border region of our country to defend our beloved motherland. For the cause of the integrity of a fraternal nation, these friends have sacrificed everything. This offering will resound forever in the hearts of our people. Their honor will be preserved among the pages of the history of the restoration of our nation. In this world, there is nothing of value to compare with that loss. I ask permission to stop a while because I am too upset . . . and I ask the chair to give all comrade members of the National Assembly a few minutes to remember the merit of all the heroes who have sacrificed their lives . . .[39]

NOTES

CHAPTER I

1. Thomas Engelbert and Christopher E. Goscha, *Falling Out of Touch: A Study on Vietnamese Communist Policy Towards an Emerging Cambodian Communist Movement, 1930–1975* (Victoria, Australia: Center of Southeast Asian Studies, Monash University, 1995), p. 15.

2. Ben Kiernan, "Origins of Khmer Communism," *Southeast Asian Affairs 1981* (Singapore Institute of Southeast Asian Studies: Heinemann Asia), p. 163.

3. Kampuchea Krom refers to the areas in the lower Mekong Delta region with large Khmer ethnic populations which were absorbed by Vietnam in the eighteenth century.

4. Ben Kiernan, "Origins of Khmer Communism," p. 167.

5. Ben Kiernan, *How Pol Pot Came to Power* (London: Verso, 1985), p. 68.

6. *The Kampuchean People's Revolutionary Party Propaganda Document concerning The Fifth Party Congress of Representatives Throughout the Country* (Central Propaganda and Education Commission, Phnom Penh, 1985), p. 3.

7. Ben Kiernan, *How Pol Pot . . .* , p. 84.

8. From *Cambodge*, 26 July 1951, quoted by Ben Kiernan, *How Pol Pot . . .* , pp. 77–78.

9. This date is still celebrated as Independence Day. However, it is not clear when Cambodia's independence from France became final. Randle presumes that "the Geneva ceasefire agreement, together with the French declarations, were the instruments by which it achieved independence." See Robert F. Randle, *Geneva 1954: The Settlement of the Indochinese War* (Princeton: Princeton University Press, 1969).

10. According to Engelbert and Goscha, "Vietnamese military statistics claim they had regained control of around 43% of Cambodian countryside while another estimate puts Vietnamese resistance forces in control of around a third of Cambodia." See *Falling Out of Touch*, p. 43.

11. Robert Randle, *Geneva 1954*, p. 206.

12. Wilfred Burchett, *The China Cambodia Vietnam Triangle* (Chicago: Vanguard Books, 1981), p. 27.

13. Robert Randle, *Geneva 1954*, p. 488.

14. *Ibid.*, p. 501.

15. The figure of 1,015 is given in "Minutes of Meeting: concerning the matter of children and wives of Kampuchean cadres who gave their lives after coming back from northern Vietnam," attached to letter "Respectfully addressed to the Ministry of Disabled Veterans and Social Action," No. 864 JTMCh, for Central Administration Commission, vice-chairman, (signed and stamped) Ieu Samom, 12 September 1986.

16. Engelbert and Goscha, *Falling Out of Touch*, p. 47.

17. Sieu Heng, Nuon Chea and So Phim returned to Cambodia "after a few months." See Ben Kiernan, *How Pol Pot . . .* , p. 154.

18. Most remained in North Vietnam. However, Pen Sovann confirmed during an interview with the author, Phnom Penh, 22 August 1998, that some went to China, North Korea, the USSR and other communist countries. Chea Soth, for example, went to China after regrouping in Hanoi. Interview with Chea Soth, Phnom Penh, 12 January 2000.

19. Timothy Carney, "Communist Party Power in Kampuchea (Cambodia): Documents and Discussion," Cornell University SEA Program, Data Paper No. 106, 1977, p. 3.

20. Engelbert and Goscha, *Falling Out of Touch*, p. 49.

21. Dmitry Mosyakov, "The Khmer Rouge and the Vietnamese Communists: A history of their relations as told in the Soviet archives," DC-Cam web-site, p. 2. The footnote to the article notes, "An earlier version of this paper appeared in the Russian journal *Vostok* [Orient], No. 3, August 2000." English translation made possible through the support of Ben Kiernan and Yale University.

22. *Ibid.*

23. *The Kampuchean People's Revolutionary Party Propaganda Document*, p. 5.

24. Ben Kiernan, *How Pol Pot . . .* , pp. 190–91.

25. Nate Thayer, 'Am I a savage person?', *Phnom Penh Post*, 6, 21 (October 24–November 6, 1997).

26. Ney Pena, *Kar Duol Rolum ney Robap Praleypuchsar Pol Pot* [The Downfall of the Pol Pot Genocidal Regime] (Phnom Penh: Printery of Pracheachon Newspaper, 1991), p. 30. Corroboration of Ney Pena's story concerning Nuon Chea's dilemma is given by Engelbert and Goscha, *Falling Out of Touch*, p. 64.

27. Sara Colm, 'Pol Pot: the secret 60s', *Phnom Penh Post*, 7, 8 (April 24–May 7, 1998).

28. Engelbert and Goscha note that "[Saloth] Sar himself spent time in Vietnamese Offices 100 and 900 in liberated areas along the Vietnam-

Cambodian border in mid-1963 and 1964." See *Falling Out of Touch*, p. 66.

29. See map in Truong Nhu Tang, *Journal of a Vietcong* (London: Jonathan Cape, 1986), p. 169.

30. Engelbert and Goscha, *Falling Out of Touch*, p. 56.

31. Dmitry Mosyakov, 'The Khmer Rouge and the Vietnamese Communists', p. 5.

32. Engelbert and Goscha, *Falling Out of Touch*, p. 74.

33. *Ibid.*, p. 75.

34. *Ibid.*

35. *Ibid.*, p. 78.

36. Sara Colm, 'Pol Pot: the secret 60s'.

37. *Ibid.*

38. *Ibid.*

39. The Sangkum refers to *Sangkum Reastr Niyum* or Popular Socialist Community, a political movement rather than a political party (although its adherents had to resign from their political parties in order to participate in the Sangkum) which was started by Sihanouk in 1955.

40. Stephen Heder, 'Kampuchea's Armed Struggle: the Origins of an Independent Revolution', *BCAS*, 11, 1 (Jan.–Mar., 1979), p. 5.

41. Milton Osborne, *Politics and Power in Cambodia* (Camberwell: Longman, 1973), p. 89.

42. *Ibid.*, p. 88.

43. *Ibid.*, p. 90.

44. Stephen Heder, "Kampuchea's Armed Struggle," p. 9.

45. Dmitry Mosyakov, "The Khmer Rouge and the Vietnamese Communists," p. 8.

46. Stephen Heder, "Kampuchea's Armed Struggle," p. 20.

47. David Chandler, *A History of Cambodia*, 2nd ed. (Chiang Mai: Silkworm Books, 1993), p. 87.

48. Dmitry Mosyakov, 'The Khmer Rouge and the Vietnamese Communists', p. 8.

49. David Chandler, *A History of Cambodia*, p. 87.

50. *Ibid.*, p. 88.

51. During Hun Sen's first meeting with Sihanouk at Fère-en-Tardenois in 1987, the prime minister told the prince that he had joined the guerrilla movement at the behest of Sihanouk's call following the coup. Serge Thion calls this "a well-intended lie". He dates Hun Sen's commitment to the cause "as a young courier" as probably March 1967. For details, see Serge Thion, *Watching Cambodia* (Bangkok: White Lotus, 1993), p. xxiii. This date is supported by David Chandler, *The Tragedy of Cambodian History: Politics, War and Revolution Since 1945* (Chiang Mai: Silkworm Books, 1991), p. 162. Raoul Jennar suggests the year was 1968.

For biographical details of Hun Sen see Raoul Jennar, *Les clés du Cambodge*, (Maisonneuve et Larose, 1995), p. 206.

52. Serge Thion, *Watching Cambodia*, p. 106.

53. In-flight computer tapes from US aircraft involved show that 43,415 bombing raids were made on Cambodia, dropping more than two million tons of bombs and other ordinance in the period 1970–1975. These records exclude the B-52 raids during the first eight months of 1973. For map and other details, see *Phnom Penh Post*, 14–27 April 2000, p. 13.

54. Acronyms are from the French.

55. Quoted by David Chandler, *The Tragedy of Cambodian History*, p. 201.

56. Timothy Carney, "Communist Party Power in Kampuchea (Cambodia)," p. 7.

57. *Ibid.*

58. Engelbert and Goscha, *Falling Out of Touch*, p. 90.

59. Dmitry Mosyakov quotes Nguyen Co Thach: "Nuon Chea has asked for help and we have liberated five provinces of Cambodia in ten days." Russian State Archive of Modern History (RSAMH), Fund 5, Inventory 75, file 1062. Information on the conversation of the German comrades with the deputy minister of foreign affairs of the SRV Nguyen Co Thach, who stayed on a rest in the GDR from 1 to 6 August 1978. 17 August 1978, p. 70. In "The Khmer Rouge and the Vietnamese Communists," p. 8.

60. Engelbert and Goscha, *Falling Out of Touch*, p. 95.

61. Ben Kiernan, *How Pol Pot . . .*, p. 329. Kiernan suggests that this may have been a resolution passed by the CPK Center, meeting on its own.

62. Engelbert and Goscha quote General Tran Van Tra in *Falling Out of Touch*, p. 100.

63. Cited by Engelbert and Goscha, *Falling Out of Touch*, p. 109, from Manac'h Etienne M., *Memoires d'extrême Asia: Une terre traversée de puissances invisibles, China-Indochina 1972–1973* (Paris: Fayard, 1982), p. 392.

64. David Chandler, *The Tragedy of Cambodian History*, p. 226.

65. "Minutes of Meeting: concerning the matter of children and wives . . . ," *op. cit.* f/n 16.

66. David Chandler, *The Tragedy of Cambodian History*, p. 243. Antonin Kubes claims that thirteen- to fourteen-year old boys formed "a full 70 percent of the Kampuchean army in January 1978." This figure is not corroborated. See *Kampuchea* (Orbis Press Agency: Prague, 1982), p. 109.

CHAPTER 2

1. Francois Ponchaud, *Cambodia: Year Zero* (New York: Holt, Rinehart, Winston, 1977).

2. The figure of 1.7 million is the one most often quoted by journalists. As Michael Vickery correctly notes, however, it is unclear whether this figure refers to deaths over normal or not. PRK figures in 1983 estimated deaths at three million, but methods used to calculate this number were not reliable. This is not intended to deny the scale of premature deaths and killings, only to note that final, accurate figures are still not available.

3. Michael Vickery, *Cambodia: 1975–1982* (Sydney: Allen & Unwin, 1984), Chapter 5.

4. See Timothy Carney, ed., *Communist Party Power in Kampuchea*, p. 56.

5. D. Chandler, B. Kiernan and Boua Chanthou, *Pol Pot Plans the Future: Confidential Leadership Documents from Democratic Kampuchea, 1976–1977* (New Haven, Conn: Yale University, Southeast Asia Studies, 1988), Monograph Series No. 33, p. 218.

6. Quoted by David Chandler, "A Revolution in Full Spate: Communist Party Policy in Democratic Kampuchea, December 1976," *International Journal of Politics*, 16, 3 (1986), p. 131.

7. Ith Sarin, "Life in the Bureaus of the Khmer Rouge (3 June 1972 to 15 January 1973)" in *Sronoh Proloeung Khmer* [Regrets for the Khmer Soul] (Phnom Penh, 28 July 1973), p. 49 and quoted in Carney, *Communist Party Power in Kampuchea*, p. 46.

8. David Ashley, "The End", *Phnom Penh Post*, 7,8 (April 24–May 7, 1998), p. 16.

9. *Ibid.*

10. Stephen Heder, "Democratic Kampuchea: the polls of 1976", *Phnom Penh Post*, 7, 9 (May 8–21, 1998), pp. 16–17.

11. Raoul M. Jennar, *The Cambodian Constitutions* (1953–1993) (Bangkok: White Lotus, 1995), p. 82.

12. Laura Summers, "Defining the Revolutionary State in Cambodia," *Current History*, 71, 422 (1976), p. 215.

13. *Ibid.*

14. Stephen Heder, "Democratic Kampuchea: the poll of 1976."

15. Ith Sarin, *Regrets for the Khmer Soul*, and Carney, *Communist Party Power in Kampuchea*, p. 54. For details of administrative divisions under the DK see Michael Vickery, *Cambodia 1975–1982*, 1999 imprint, Chapter 3, pp. 71–74.

16. George Hildebrand and Gareth Porter, *Cambodia: Starvation and Revolution* (New York: Monthly Review Press, 1976), p. 71.

17. Figures according to Pol Pot quoted by Gavan McCormack,

"The Kampuchean Revolution 1975–78: The Problem of Knowing the Truth", *Journal of Contemporary Asia*, 10, 1–2 (1980), p. 97.

18. Chandler, Kiernan, Chanthou Boua, *Pol Pot Plans the Future*, pp. 13–35.

19. *Ibid.*, pp. 45–49.

20. David Ashley, "The End."

21. Chandler, Kiernan, Chanthou Boua, *Pol Pot Plans the Future*, pp. 168–75.

22. These three famous persons were ultimately executed but, as Michael Vickery points out, there is no reason to associate them with the coup attempt of 1976. Vorn Veth was not arrested until 1978 and his confessions do not indicate an accusation that he opposed Pol Pot in 1976. Hou Yuon's fate is unknown. Vickery suggests that Nate Thayer's Khmer interpreter was mistaken, or that he confused Hou Yuon with Agriculture Minister Non Suon who had been arrested by 1 November 1976 along with more than two hundred others from various ministries, the army and the party apparatus. Personal communication with Michael Vickery, Phnom Penh, September 2000. For details, see Ben Kiernan, *The Pol Pot Regime . . .* , p. 335.

23. Chandler, Kiernan, Chanthou Boua, *Pol Pot Plans the Future*, pp. 177–211.

24. May Ebihara, "Revolution and Reformulation in Kampuchean Village Culture," in D. Ablin and M. Hood, eds, *The Cambodian Agony* (Armonk, NY: M.E. Sharpe, 1987), p. 33.

25. *Ibid.*, p. 35.

26. Figure quoted by Nate Thayer, "Am I a savage person?"

27. *Ibid.*

28. Engelbert and Goscha cite a report sent to Hanoi following the fall of Saigon, showing that 600 Vietnamese personnel had died in armed incidents with Cambodian communists between 1970 and 1975. See *Falling Out of Touch*, p. 121.

29. Dmitry Mosyakov, 'The Khmer Rouge and the Vietnamese Communists', p. 11, citing Fund 5, Inventory 66, file 782. Record of conversation of the Soviet ambassador with the VWP Central Committee Secretary Le Duan, 19 April, 19 April 1973, p. 78.

30. *Ibid.*

31. *Ibid.*, p. 14–15.

32. *Ibid.* In a letter to the *Phnom Penh Post*, 12–15 May, 2000, Stephen Heder corrected his previous estimate of "several thousand" PRC officials present in DK at any one time to 600–700 only. According to internal DK records, he quotes that this number represented "military technicians" who "taught how to fly aircraft, to assemble and employ radar, some things relating to anti-aircraft artillery and to military communications." The remainder were attached to "ministries of civil

administration." He affirms, "There is no clear evidence that any were attached to the Democratic Kampuchea security apparatus."

33. Nayan Chanda, *Brother Enemy: The War After the War, A History of Indochina Since the Fall of Saigon* (New York: Macmillan, 1986), p. 207.

34. Quoted by Nayan Chanda, *Brother Enemy*, p. 208.

35. *Ibid.*, p. 250.

36. Stephen Morris, *Why Vietnam Invaded Cambodia: Political Culture and the Causes of War* (Stanford: Stanford University Press, 1999), p. 109, citing "Report of a conversation with General Secretary of the CPV Central Committee Le Duan," 5 September 1978, TsKhSD, Fond 5, Opis 74, Delo 1061, p. 101.

37. Stephen Heder, "Revolution and Counter-Revolution in Kampuchea," *AMPO*, 12, 3 (1980), p. 28.

38. Nayan Chanda, *Brother Enemy*, p. 255.

CHAPTER 3

1. Quoted by Stephen J. Morris, *Why Vietnam Invaded . . .* , p. 85.

2. Ben Kiernan, 'Conflict in the Kampuchean Communist Movement', *Journal of Contemporary Asia*, vol. 10, nos 1–2, 1980, p. 8.

3. *Ibid.*, p. 23.

4. Antonin Kubes, *Kampuchea*, p. 124.

5. Ben Kiernan, *The Pol Pot Regime: Race, Power and Genocide in Cambodia under the Khmer Rouge, 1975–1979* (New Haven: Yale University Press, 1996), p. 316.

6. *Ibid.*

7. Malcolm Caldwell diary typescript, p. 67, quoted in Ben Kiernan, *The Pol Pot Regime . . .* , p. 316. Malcolm Caldwell was murdered by DK agents the night before he was to have left Cambodia.

8. Ben Kiernan, *The Pol Pot Regime . . .* , pp. 320–323.

9. Details of the rebellion in Region 106 are provided by Ben Kiernan, *Ibid.*, p. 340–345. Ney Pena, later governor of Preah Vihear and briefly minister of the interior for the PRK regime, claimed that the uprising in Siem Reap and also Kompong Thom of February 1976 (sic) was led by comrade Touch, a former GRUNK official. See *Kar Duol Rolum ney Robap Praleypuchsar Pol Pot* [The Downfall of the Genocidal Pol Pot Regime], p. 121–122. For details of the Chikreng uprising and also of the Siem Reap incident see also Michael Vickery, *Cambodia 1975–1982*, pp. 135–138.

10. Antonin Kubes, *Kampuchea*, p. 124.

11. *FEER*, 2 March 1979. Lak On, PRK governor of Ratanakiri, thought that Keo Chenda must have been "confused" because her experience was that Ratanakiri was under tight control until liberation in late December 1978. Interview with author, Phnom Penh, 31 January 2000.

The different perspectives of these two high-ranking PRK officials might bear out the fact that the DK regime varied greatly in its degree of control even within the same local area, or might be due simply to the official position on the regime taken by the government at the time of the interview with Lak On.

12. David Chandler, *The Tragedy of Cambodian History*, p. 288.

13. *Ibid.*, p. 270.

14. *Ibid.*, p. 271.

15. Stephen J. Morris, *Why Vietnam Invaded* . . . , p. 95.

16. *Ibid.*, p. 96.

17. Dmitry Mosyakov, "The Khmer Rouge and the Vietnamese Communists . . . ," p. 19.

18. *Ibid.*, p. 290.

19. Stephen J. Morris, *Why Vietnam Invaded* . . . , p. 94.

20. David Chandler, *The Tragedy of Cambodian History*, p. 271.

21. Elizabeth Becker, *When the War Was Over* (New York: Simon and Schuster, 1986), p. 311.

22. *Ibid.*, pp 311–312.

23. *Ibid.*, p. 318 and Nayan Chanda, *Brother Enemy*, p. 197. Nayan Chanda reported that between 1975 and December 1977 some 300,000 Khmer, Vietnamese and Chinese refugees had fled to Vietnam. For details of Hun Sen's defection see Harish C. Mehta and Julie B. Mehta, *Hun Sen: Strongman of Cambodia* (Singapore: Graham Brash, 1999), Chapter 3.

25. Nayan Chanda, *Brother Enemy*, p. 217.

26. *Ibid.*

27. *Ibid.*

28. Other members were Chea Sim, Ros Samay, Mat Ly, Bun My, Hun Sen, Mean Soman, Meas Samnang, Neou Samon, Ven. Long Sim, Hem Samin, Chey Kanh Nha, Chan Ven, and Prach Sun.

2. References to the Declaration of the FUNSK from *Vietnam Courier*, 1 (1979). See also *Front d'Union Nationale pour le Salut du Kampuchea*, Service d'Information du FUNSK, Janvier 1979.

30. *Ibid.*

31. *Ibid.*

32. *Ibid.*

33. Antonin Kubes, *Kampuchea*, p. 125 and Nayan Chanda, *Brother Enemy*, p. 340. Ney Pena claims that the radio station and the national news agency, SPK, were both established on 3 December 1978. *The Downfall* . . . , p. 153.

34. Timothy Carney, "Heng Samrin's Armed Forces and the Military Balance in Cambodia," *International Journal of Politics*, 16,3 (1986), p. 160.

35. Hun Sen, *Dop Chhnam ney Domnaeur Kampuchea: 1979–1989* [The Ten-Year Journey] (Phnom Penh, December 1988), p. 12.

36. *Ibid.*, p. 21.

37. *Ibid.*

38. Truong Chinh, *A propos du Problème Kampuchéen*, Le Service de Presse de l'ambassade de la République Socialiste du Viet Nam à Paris, 1980, p. 21.

39. Hun Sen, *The Ten-Year Journey*, p. 409.

40. *The Kampuchean People's Revolutionary Party Propaganda Document Concerning the Fifth Party Congress of Representatives throughout the Country*, *op. cit.*, p. 6.

41. *Ibid.* In fact, the name of the party was not resolved until the fourth congress in 1981. "Communist Party of Kampuchea" was regularly used on party documents from 1979 until the fourth congress.

42. Hun Sen, *The Ten-Year Journey*, p. 409.

43. The defection to the Royal Government of Cambodia by Khieu Samphan and Nuon Chea on 25 December 1998, exactly twenty years after the Vietnamese invasion, marked the end of the Khmer Rouge movement.

44. The eight members were Heng Samrin, Pen Sovann, Hun Sen, Chea Sim, Keo Chenda, Chan Ven, Nou Beng, and Mok Sakun.

45. *The Birth of the New Kampuchea* (Phnom Penh: Ministry of Information, Press and Cultural Affairs of the Kampuchean People's Revolutionary Council, 1979), pp 18–23.

46. For a personal account of Hun Sen's escape to Vietnam in June 1977 see Harish C. Mehta and Julie B. Mehta, *Hun Sen: Strongman of Cambodia*, Chapter 3.

47. Mok Sakun died in April 1979, according to Michael Vickery. See Michael Vickery, *Kampuchea: Politics, Economics and Society* (Sydney: Allen & Unwin, 1986*)*, p. 44.

48. Michael Vickery, "Notes on the Political Economy of the PRK," *Journal of Contemporary Asia*, 20, 4 (1990), p. 440.

49. *Ibid.*

50. *Ibid.*, p. 449.

51. *Ibid.*, p. 440.

CHAPTER 4

1. Bui Tin, *From Cadre to Exile: The Memoirs of a North Vietnamese Journalist* (Chiang Mai: Silkworm Books, 1995), p. 117.

2. Personal experiences recounted to author, Phnom Penh, 1990.

3. *FEER*, 9 February 1979, p. 10.

4. *Ibid.*

5. In the 29 June 1979 issue of *FEER*, John McBeth reported Western intelligence sources' "guestimate of about 35,000 KR still under arms"

and that morale was "relatively intact." Figures given for the size of the KR forces were often misleading throughout the next twenty years of their existence because figures for fighting forces, that is, soldiers under arms, were sometimes conflated with the size of the support forces such as porters. Fighting force estimates given by *FEER* varied from 40–50,000 in 1985 to 30–40,000 in 1988 and back to 40–50,000 by the end of 1989.

6. Bui Tin, *From Cadre to Exile*, p. 119.

7. *FEER*, 25 May 1979, p. 24.

8. As stated previously, the name of the party was not resolved until the fourth party congress in 1981, when it officially became the People's Revolutionary Party of Kampuchea. Note that the more literal translation of "politburo" as *kenna kommartikar kariyaley mechem pak* or "committee for the central office of the party" was also used, usually in later documents.

9. "Decision of the center concerning the setting out of duties and the system of organization of the work of the party center, the government and the Front," for Central Committee, First Secretary, 1979 (unsigned, undated).

10. *Ibid.*

11. *Ibid.* Members' names were confirmed by Hun Sen during an interview with the author on 3 August 1999. Seven people were elected to the central committee at the third party congress. At an extraordinary party meeting in February 1979, Say Phouthang, who had been unable to reach the Memot Congress from his rebel base in Koh Kong, was elected to the central committee and replaced Van Sorn in the Administration Commission.

12. "Decision of the center . . . ," *op. cit.*

13. Pen Sovann, interview with author, Phnom Penh, 22 August 1998.

14. "Chan Kiri was not really a man of capacity," according to Pen Sovann, interview 24 March 1998. Perhaps this accounts for one party member's claim that the Party Monitoring Commission to which Say Phouthang was appointed as chairman at the fifth party congress was new. Peter Schier also claimed that it was new. See "Kampuchea in 1985: Between Crocodiles and Tigers," *Southeast Asian Affairs*, 1986, pp. 139–161.

15. "Decision of the center concerning the setting out of duties . . . ," *op. cit.*

16. *Ibid.*

17. *Ibid.*

18. *Ibid.*

19. *FEER*, 13 April 1979, p. 25.

20. "Decision of the People's Revolutionary Council concerning resolving the situation of categories in all ministries and enterprises of the state," No. 29 KBK, for PRC, president, Heng Samrin, undated.

21. *Ibid.*

22. *Ibid.*

23. *Ibid.*

24. Bui Tin, *From Cadre to Exile*, p. 128.

25. "Decision of the center concerning the administration system and working methods between all departments, ministries of the party and the government at all levels, and all ministries with the friend's experts," for Central Committee, First Secretary (unsigned, undated).

26. *Ibid.*

27. *Ibid.*

28. *Ibid*

29. *Ibid.*

30. Ben Kiernan and Chanthou Boua, eds, *Peasants and Politics in Kampuchea, 1942–1981* (London: Zed Books, 1982), p. 382. In the *FEER* of 5 June 1981, Nayan Chanda reported that "the number of Vietnamese civilian advisers—estimated to be about 1,000 in Phnom Penh and several hundred in the provinces—is expected to be reduced shortly," p. 25.

31. "Decision of the politburo: stipulations concerning the duties and system of work administration of the party committee and the people's revolutionary committee of provinces/municipalities," for Central Committee, Politburo (unsigned, undated).

32. *Ibid.*

33. *Ibid.*

34. *Ibid.*

35. Ben Kiernan, "Kampuchea 1979–81," *Southeast Asian Affairs*, 1982, p. 171.

36. "Decision of the politburo . . . ," *op. cit.*

37. *Ibid.*

38. "Decision of the center concerning the state of affairs and duties of the Kampuchean revolution," No. 2SJMCh, for Party Central Committee, 17 July 1979.

39. The Census Department of the Ministry of Planning figures for 1989 give a total of 12,603 villages in 1,545 communes of 153 districts in 21 provinces/municipalities. See "Report of UN Fact-Finding Mission on Present Structures and Practices of Administration in Cambodia, 24 April–9 May 1990," (United Nations, New York, 1990), Annex 36.

40. "Decision of the center . . . ," *op. cit.*

41. *Ibid.*

42. *Ibid.*

43. *Ibid.*

44. Stephen Heder, "Kampuchea: From Pol Pot to Pen Sovann to the Villages" in Khien Theeravit and MacAlister Brown, eds, *Indochina and Problems of Security and Stability in Southeast Asia* (Bangkok: Chulalongkorn University Press, 1983), pp. 16–62. This paper was presented in June 1980.

45. *Ibid.*
46. *Ibid.*
47. *Ibid.*
48. "Decision of the center concerning the setting out of duties . . . ," *op. cit.*
49. Heder, "From Pol Pot to Pen Sovann . . . ," pp. 31–32.
50. *Ibid.*, p. 30.
51. "Report concerning the planned arrangements for restoring cadres in the ministries and provinces," Administration Commission, Central Committee, Communist Party of Kampuchea, 16 August 1979.
52. SPK (*sarpordemien kampuchea*) was the official press agency.
53. "Report concerning . . . ," *op. cit.* In an interview with Chea Soth, Phnom Penh, 12 January 2000, he informed the author that in fact he had gone as first ambassador to Vietnam while Van Sorn went to the USSR.
54. "Report concerning planned arrangements for restoring cadres . . . ," *op. cit.*
55. "Report to the People's Revolutionary Council," No. 6KPR, Ros Samay, Phnom Penh, 11 April, 1980.
56. *Ibid.*
57. "Circular concerning the draft constitution," No. 109/80KB, Vice-President of the PRCK, cde Pen Sovann, signed and stamped, Phnom Penh, 28 May 1980.
58. *FEER*, 16 February 1984, p. 21.
59. "Memo: Concerning Draft Constitution of the PRK," Ministry of Justice, Uk Bun Chhoeun (signed and stamped), Phnom Penh, 8 August 1980.
60. Pen Sovann, interview with author, Phnom Penh, 22 August 1998.
61. *FEER*, 26 September 1980, p. 22.
62. "The plan for disseminating the draft constitution of the PRK" attached to "Various issues raised in discussion concerning the draft outline of the constitution," unsigned, Phnom Penh, 28 February 1981.
63. "Information concerning the announcement and dissemination of the draft constitution of the PRK', No. 02SPrK, for PRCK, chairman, Phnom Penh, 4 March 1981.
64. Raoul Jennar, 'Les Constitutions du Cambodge: Ambitions, Continuités et Ruptures," paper delivered at the International Symposium on Khmerology, University of Phnom Penh, 26–30 August 1996, p. 14.
65. "Motion supporting the Draft Constitution of the PRK," for Central Committee of the Front, Head of Department, Min Khin, Phnom Penh, 16 May 1981.
66. For a thorough analysis of the differences see Michael Vickery, *Kampuchea: Politics, Economics and Society*, pp. 89–105.

67. See the report *Kampuchea: After the Worst*, Lawyers Committee for Human Rights, August 1985.

68. When questioned about this, Hun Sen said, "We had a chairman of the State Council and that was the equivalent to head of state." Interview with author, Takhmau, 3 August 1999.

69. Pen Sovann, interview with author, Phnom Penh, 24 March 1998.

70. "Various issues raised in discussion concerning the draft outline of the constitution," Phnom Penh, 28 February, 1981, attached to 'The plan for disseminating the draft constitution of the PRK', unsigned, undated.

71. "Report of the chairman of the Committee for the Draft Constitution," undated, unsigned.

72. Jerrold W. Huguet, *The population of Cambodia, 1980–1996, and projected to 2020* (Phnom Penh: National Institute of Statistics, Ministry of Planning, 1997), p. 1.

73. Interview with author, Phnom Penh, 26 January 1999.

74. This is the figure quoted by Huguet. However, Desbarats says the reported figure was 6.7 million but "because this count originally excluded the inhabitants of the resistance zones, it was later subject to readjustment". See *Prolific Survivors*, p. 111.

75. Huguet, *The Population of Cambodia*.

76. The sex ratio in 1980 was 86.1 compared with 99.9 in 1962 and an average of 92.06 between 1993 and 1998. See *Provisional Population Totals for the General Population Census of Cambodia 1998* (Phnom Penh: National Institute of Statistics, M.Planning, 1998), p. 25.

77. Roger Kershaw, "Lesser Current: The Election Ritual and Party Consolidation in the PRK," *Contemporary Southeast Asia*, 3,4 (March, 1982), p. 317.

78. "Memo to cde Ung Phan," No. 318KSYT, minister of justice, Permanent Member of the Election Committee, Uk Bun Chhoeun, 30 September 1980.

79. "Draft table: budget for the election for the people's revolutionary committees of *sangkat* and *damban*," unsigned, undated. The use of *damban*, inherited from the DK administration system, is interesting because the word *srok* was already used for the district level. The equivalent level between municipality and *sangkat* was not formally instituted until a 1984 constitutional amendment provided for the *khan* (i.e. a district of the city).

80. "Telegram from Committee for Preparing and Directing the National Election," for National Election Committee, vice chairman, Bou Thong, Phnom Penh, 17 February 1981.

81. "Study document for the election to choose people's revolutionary committees for the commune and *sangkat*," Central Propaganda and Education Commission, unsigned, undated.

82. *Ibid.*

83. *Ibid.*

84. *Ibid.*

85. *Ibid.*

86. *Ibid.*

87. At that same training course, Bou Thong claimed there were 1,373 communes/*sangkat* and that 397 had finished the election.

88. "Report on the opening of a course for training cadres of the committee for preparing the election to choose deputies for the National Assembly throughout the country beginning on 2 April and until 6 April," Dept. PRCK, cadre for compiling reports, Nhiem Son.

89. "Report concerning the activities of Kampuchean women throughout the country in the first quarter of 1981," Women's Association of Kampuchea, unsigned, undated.

90. "Decree-law concerning the elections to choose members for the state assembly of the PRK," No. 03KrCh81, PRCK, President, Heng Samrin, Phnom Penh, 3 March 1981.

91. *Ibid.*

92. The March 1981 "Plan for Preparing and Organizing the Election . . . the Process at the Base" from the Electoral Committee advised that "at each table for helping voters there should be two people, one to help fill out the ballot for the voter and the other to check and observe well that the person helping to fill out the ballot does so properly according to the wishes of the voter." The helper had to check again with the voter.

93. "Pre-Plan for the National Election," unsigned, Phnom Penh, March 1981.

94. *Ibid.*

95. *Ibid.*

96. The Election Council of 19 March 1981,was made up of Say Phouthang, Bou Thong, Uk Bun Chhoeun, Yos Por, Mat Ly, Heng Tiev, Ung Phan, Mean Soman, Nuth Than, Phlek Phirun and Peou Lida (Sisowath Sovethevong Monivong).

97. "Minutes: Final Results of the Election to choose Deputies for the National Assembly of the People's Republic of Kampuchea held on 1 May 1981," Election Council to Choose Deputies for the National Assembly, undated, unsigned.

98. *FEER*, 8 May 1981, p. 15.

99. *Ibid.*

100. "Decision of the Council of Ministers," No. 148 SRJ, for Council of Ministers, Chairman, Pen Sovann, Phnom Penh, 23 November 1981.

101. Details confirmed by Hun Sen, interview with author, Takhmau, 3 August 1999.

102. "Announcement Concerning the Working System of the Permanent Commission of the Council of Ministers," No. 01/BK, minister, Cabinet of the COM, Ung Phan, 31 March 1982.

103. Ung Phan was a member of the small group including Hun Sen, that defected and escaped to Vietnam in 1977. During the SOC he attempted to form a new party and barely survived an assassination attempt. He later joined the royalist party, FUNCINPEC, which he effectively split in 1997 in the dramatic events leading up to the coup of July that year.

104. "Law concerning the organization of the people's revolutionary committee at all levels," Article 1. (Unsigned, undated copy).

105. For biographical details of Pen Sovann, see Raoul M. Jennar, *Les clés du Cambodge*, p. 242. Details about Chan Si from official biography, State Archives, Phnom Penh.

106. *FEER*, 4 April 1980, p. 23.

107. For further details, see Ben Kiernan, *How Pol Pot . . .*, p. 358.

108. It is not clear either in the Chan Si biography or in the Nayan Chanda interview why, when or for how long both men were inside Cambodia during the 1970–1975 civil war period. Nayan Chanda notes the disparity but the question was not pressed.

109. Nayan Chanda, *FEER*, 4 April 1980.

110. Pen Sovann, interview with author, Phnom Penh, 22 August 1998.

111. For an analysis of Pen Sovann's dismissal see Nayan Chanda, "First round to Hanoi," *FEER*, 11 December 1981, pp. 8–9. Chea Soth told the author that by the end of 1981, Pen Sovann would not listen to advice from anyone, neither the Vietnamese nor his fellow Khmers. Interview with Chea Soth, Phnom Penh, 12 January 2000.

112. *FBIS*, 3 December 1981.

113. *Ibid.*

114. Pen Sovann, interview with author, Phnom Penh, 22 August 1998.

115. *Ibid.*

116. Information from unnamed source, Phnom Penh, 25 August 1998.

117. Bui Tin, *From Cadre to Exile*, p. 123.

118. *Ibid.*

119. Eric Pape, "Ex-Top Communist Pen Sovann Explains Political Rebirth," *The Cambodia Daily*, 13 May 1997, p. 13.

120. *Ibid.*

121. Personal communications with author, Phnom Penh.

122. "Memo concerning the report on the progress and difficulties in the method of working," No. 1732KSK, Ministry of Agriculture, minister, Kong Sam Ol, Phnom Penh, 28 March 1983.

123. "Circular concerning resolving the requests of the people," No. 02SR, for Council of Minister, Acting Chairman (signed and stamped), Chea Soth, Phnom Penh, 31 January 1984.

124. *Ibid.*

125. *Ibid.*

CHAPTER 5

1. This figure and the figures that follow for 1968 are taken from "Statistical Year-Book of Cambodia, 1968," Ministry of Planning, Kingdom of Cambodia.

2. Ney Pena, *The Downfall* . . . , p. 58.

3. Hildebrand and Porter, *Cambodia: Starvation and Revolution*, p. 33.

4. *Ibid.*, p. 32.

5. *Ibid.*

6. For details of the KR "guns before rice" policy, see Wilfred Burchett, *The China Cambodia Vietnam Triangle* (Chicago: Vanguard Books, 1981), p. 169. Someth May refers to this in *Cambodian Witness* (London: Faber and Faber, 1986). R.S. and S.T. in personal conversation with the author spoke variously of trucks coming directly into the ricefields to take the harvest (northwest zone) and of harvests being placed in local storehouses (eastern zone).

7. Jacqueline Desbarats, *Prolific Survivors*, p. 60.

8. *Ibid.*

9. Personal recollection by former resident of Kompong Siem District, Kompong Cham Province, in conversation with the author, Phnom Penh, 1998.

10. See, for example, Heng Hung, *Lbech Yuon Neng Krom Ayong* [Vietnamese Tricks and the Puppet Group] (Phnom Penh, 28 November 1996), p. 26.

11. Nayan Chanda reported that "barely 5 percent of the land normally put under the main six-month crop has been planted with rice," *FEER*, 17 August 1979, p. 16.

12. Ea Meng-Try, "Cambodia: A Country Adrift," *Population and Development Review*, 7, 2 (June 1981), p. 219.

13. Jacqueline Desbarats, *Prolific Survivors*, p. 99.

14. Hun Sen, *The Ten-Year Journey*, pp. 232–33.

15. "Request to Provincial People's Revolutionary Committees," People's Revolutionary Council of Kampuchea, President, Heng Samrin (signed and stamped), 7 April 1979.

16. *Ibid.*

17. *Ibid.*

18. "Circular concerning agricultural production in the 1979 wet season," People's Revolutionary Council of Kampuchea, for President of PRCK, Ros Samay (signed and stamped), Phnom Penh, 26 May 1979.

19. *Ibid.*

20. *Ibid.*

21. "Decision of the center concerning the state of affairs and the duties of the Kampuchean revolution," No. 2SJMCh, for Central Commit-

tee, Communist Party of Kampuchea, 17 July 1979. By the middle of 1980, a strictly confidential report ("Report on all work in the first six months and general duties for the second half of 1980," unsigned, undated) said the number of hungry people "may be more than four million." This report commented that the organization and management of emergency aid had improved, but there were still abuses such as taking the famine relief to "hire workers, receive guests and to buy basic government materials"; there was also negligence in the storing of the food for famine relief. Evidence of the government's efforts to organize famine relief is given in a telegram dated 26 June 1980 from Duong Sarom, president of the Committee for Receipt of International Humanitarian Assistance and member of the Famine Steering Committee to comrade president of the People's Revolutionary Committee of Svay Rieng Province (No: 611/6KTJT), with instructions for filling out the form for a census of the needy to be tallied district by district. On 9 June 1980, the PRC made a decision (No. 127.80) to set up a Committee for the Salvation of the Hungry, with Kong Sam Ol as chairman. On 16 January 1981, Kong Sam Ol sent a report to Heng Samrin in the form of a table showing the distribution of food aid to twelve provinces between July and September 1980. According to the table, the neediest province was Kompong Speu (1,056,669 people in need), followed by Kompong Cham (1,036,264) and Takeo (517,620). Svay Rieng had 310,119 people in need, virtually the entire population of the province.

22. "Announcement of the PRC and the Central Committee of the FUNSK concerning the state of affairs for the first six months of 1979 and duties for the future," for PRC and the Central Committee of the FUNSK, president, Heng Samrin, Phnom Penh, July 1979.

23. *Ibid.*

24. "Report on all work in the first six months and general duties for the second half of 1980" marked "Strictly Confidential," unsigned, undated.

25. "Distributing agricultural produce within the solidarity groups for increasing the harvest," unsigned, undated.

26. *Ibid.*

27. *Ibid.*

28. *Ibid.*

29. *Ibid.*

30. *Ibid.*

31. At the third party plenum it was admitted that the people had commandeered draught animals after 7 January and the government did not know how to deal with the situation ("Decisions of the third party plenum," Central Committee of the Communist Party of Kampuchea, Permanent Committee, No. 14 SMRCh). The decision said that some families had sold the animals for meat, which caused friction within the

krom samaki. In 1980, there were only about 700,000 draught animals in the country, or 40 percent of the number that existed before the war; many had died of disease during the Pol Pot era. The shortage of draught animals remained a severe obstacle throughout the PRK regime, and the special arrangements which effectively paid plowmen twice the rate of other agricultural laborers created significant inequalities in the village from the very beginning of the PRK.

32. *Ibid.*

33. Telegram No: 33–80 KB to Ministries of Agriculture, Industry, Central Commerce, Communications & Transport, Propaganda, Information & Culture, People's Revolutionary Committees and Administrative Committees of every province and municipality from People's Revolutionary Council of Kampuchea, president, Heng Samrin, 27 June 1980.

34. Draft Report, "Concerning the purchase of staple food (*spieng*) in the 1980–1981 wet season and selling manufactured goods to the farmers," Phnom Penh, 25 July 1980.

35. *Ibid.*

36. *Ibid.*

37. *Ibid.*

38. *Ibid.*

39. "Plan: Expanding the Family Economy," unsigned, undated.

40. *Ibid.*

41. *Ibid.*

42. *Ibid.*

43. *Ibid.*

44. *Ibid.*

45. *Ibid.*

46. For details, refer to "Summary of opinions expressed by cde Pen Sovann, chairman of the Council of Ministers, at the second session of the Council of Ministers, 28–29 July, 1981," Cabinet of the Council of Ministers, for minister, cde Msaos Luos.

47. Text from Office of the Minister, Ministry of State Commerce. Received by Council of Ministers Cabinet, signed, Ung Phan, 15 November 1980.

48. *Ibid.*

49. *Ibid.*

50. *Ibid.*

51. *Ibid.*

52. *Ibid.*

53. *Ibid.*

54. *Ibid.*

55. "Summing up the results of buying rice in the 1981–1982 season," Council of Ministers, Central Commission for Buying Rice.

56. Chea Soth was the chairman of this commission, the minister of

commerce was his deputy and representatives of Commerce, Finance, the National Bank, Communications and Transport, and the Cabinet of the Council of Ministers were members. There were provincial commissions also with appropriate administrative structures at district and commune level for buying paddy and selling commodities to the farmers.

57. "Summing up the results of buying rice . . . ," *op. cit.*

58. *Ibid.*

59. "Report of ministry of agriculture to Council of Ministers at the meeting of 17 June 1982," for Minister of Agriculture, signed and stamped Mat Ly, Phnom Penh, 16 June 1982.

60. "Circular concerning defeating the ruses of the enemy in the exchange of paddy for some goods from Vietnam," No. 43SR, for Council of Ministers, chairman, Chan Si, Phnom Penh, 13 November 1982.

61. *Ibid.* A commercial agreement was signed by Cambodia and Vietnam in mid-1981. "Report on Commercial Relations and Economic Cooperation Between PRK and SRV," Ministry of Planning, Department of General Planning, unsigned, undated, begins: "On 2 May 1981 a Kampuchean economic delegation led by comrade Taing Sarim signed in Hanoi a Commercial Protocol between Kampuchea and Vietnam for 1981 and a Treaty for Economic Cooperation (of non-refundable assistance) between the two countries for 1981–1982." The value of goods listed in the protocol was 3,124,175 *roubles.*

62. *Ibid.*

63. *Ibid.*

64. "Ideas of comrade vice chairman of the Council of Ministers and Minister of the Ministry of Planning," unsigned, undated.

65. *Ibid.*

66. "Situation and duties to strengthen the *krom samaki* for increasing the harvest," undated, unsigned. Viviane Frings identifies the date and source of this text which was reproduced in "The Work of Strengthening the Production Solidarity Groups," PRK, Ministry of Agriculture, Part I, Phnom Penh, 1985, p. 2. See "The Failure of Agricultural Collectivization in the PRK," p. 16.

67. *Ibid.*

68. *Ibid.*

69. *Ibid.*

70. *Ibid.*

71. *Ibid.*

72. *Ibid.*

73. *Ibid.*

74. *Ibid.*

75. *Ibid.*

76. "Confidential report concerning the situation of implementing the duties of defending and building the country in the first half of 1984 and

directions for duties in the latter half of 1984 of the Council of Ministers," No. 09 RBK, for Council of Ministers, vice chairman, Hun Sen (signed and stamped), Phnom Penh, 20 July 1984.

77. *Ibid.*

78. *Ibid.*

79. Murray Hiebert, "Cambodia and Vietnam: Costs of the Alliance," *Indochina Issues 46*, May 1984, pp. 4–5.

80. *Ibid.*

81. *Ibid.*

82. "Decision of the 9th party plenum concerning the management and use of agricultural land," No. 255SRMCh, for Party Central Committee, secretary general, Heng Samrin (signed and stamped), Phnom Penh, 3 August 1984.

83. *Ibid.*

84. Viviane Frings, "The Failure of Agricultural Collectivization in the People's Republic of Kampuchea (1979–1989)" (Working Paper 80, Center of Southeast Asian Studies, Monash University, 1993), p. 26.

85. Hun Sen, *The Ten-Year Journey*, pp. 311–12.

86. *Ibid.*, p. 313.

87. Viviane Frings, "The Failure of Agricultural Collectivization . . . ," p. 27.

88. *Ibid.*

89. *Ibid.*, p. 28.

90. *Ibid.*, p. 29.

91. Chhoy Kim Sar, Touch Varine, Kham Phalin, Prak Sophea, *Rural Women and the Socio-Economic Transition in the Kingdom of Cambodia* (Phnom Penh: Ministry of Women's Affairs, January 1997), p. 14.

92. Hun Sen, *The Ten-Year Journey*, p. 260.

93. "A number of matters concerning the clarification of the value of money and the price of goods in Kampuchea in the time ahead," unsigned, undated.

94. *Ibid.*

95. Michael Vickery followed the *riel*'s progress at unofficial market rates: in 1981 it was approximately 50 to $1; by early 1986 it was 155–160; early in 1987, 120; by late 1988, 150–55; and in 1989 down to 180–90, "not out of line with the reported economic growth in the same period, and still a far better record than the Vietnamese experience." See Michael Vickery, "Notes on the Political Economy of the PRK," *Journal of Contemporary Asia*, 20, 4 (1990), p. 452.

96. *Ibid.*

97. *Ibid.*

98. *Ibid.*

99. *Ibid.*

100. *Ibid.*

101. "Summary report on changing the currency and pricing," unsigned, undated.

102. *Ibid.*

103. "Circular concerning the matter of determining the system of selling some foodstuffs and utensils at state prices to cadres, workers and staff in 1980," No. 49/80KBK, for PRCK, president, Heng Samrin (signed and stamped), Phnom Penh, 25 March 1980.

104. Each child in the family was provided with 10r per month and 8 kg of rice.

105. "Circular . . . ," *ibid.*

106. *Ibid.*

107. "Revised list of sale prices for goods on sale in Phnom Penh markets," unsigned, undated, 1980.

108. "A number of issues about prices," unsigned, undated, 1980.

109. "Outline of the report on the matter of circulating the paper currency, instituting salary supplements and child support," unsigned, undated, 1980.

110. "Concerning the state budget," unsigned, undated.

111. *Ibid.*

112. *Ibid.*

113. *Ibid.*

114. Hun Sen, *The Ten-Year Journey*, p. 250.

115. "Minutes of working meeting of the PRCK concerning restoring the rubber plantations," Dept. PRCK, director, Ung Phan, Phnom Penh, 15 December 1980.

116. "Summary of opinions expressed by comrade Pen Sovann, chairman of the Council of Ministers, at the second session of the Council of Ministers, 28–29 July 1981."

117. *Ibid.*

118. "Decree-law concerning tax on imports," No. 15KrJ, for Council of State, president, Heng Samrin (signed and stamped), Phnom Penh, 27 November 1982.

119. Report concerning the work of managing the collection of taxes on imports in Kompong Som and Koh Kong since the issuing of the Decree-law No. 15KJ of 27 November 1982', No. 272/83 KHV, minister for the Ministry of Finance, Chan Phin (signed and stamped), Phnom Penh, 15 February 1983.

120. *Ibid.*

121. *Ibid.*

122. *Ibid.*

123. *Ibid.*

124. *Ibid.*

125. *Ibid.*

126. *Ibid.*

127. *Ibid.*

128. "Announcement guiding improvements to the implementation in practice of Decision No. 54SSR of March 22, 1984 of the Council of Ministers concerning the set rate of tax on imported goods," No. 236KHV, minister of the Ministry of Finance, Chan Phin (signed and stamped), Phnom Penh, 22 March 1984.

129. "Report: The financial situation and the proposed state budget for 1984 to the National Assembly, sixth session, first legislature," (confidential), submitted by comrade Chan Phin, minister, Ministry of Finance.

130. *Ibid.*

131. *Ibid.*

132. *Ibid.*

133. "Report: The financial situation and the proposed state budget for 1984 to the National Assembly, sixth session, first legislature," (confidential), submitted by comrade Chan Phin, minister, Ministry of Finance.

134 *Ibid.*

135 *Ibid.*

CHAPTER 6

1. Hun Sen, *The Ten-Year Journey*, p. 416.

2. *Ibid.*

3. *Ibid.*, p. 418.

4. *Ibid.*, p. 424.

5. *Ibid.*, p. 421.

6. Timothy Carney, "Heng Samrin's Armed Forces . . . ," p. 160.

7. Douglas Pike notes, "As of mid-1983 (KPRAF) reportedly stood at about 25,000 men, although its desertion rate was running so high (50 percent a year at that time) that such a figure was meaningless," *PAVN: People's Army of Vietnam* (Novato: Presidio Press, 1986), p. 276.

8. During the author's interview with Hun Sen, Takhmau, 3 August 1999, the prime minister made the point that unlike the armies of the PLA and the PAVN, the KPRAF troops were constantly engaged at the front during those ten years and that such comparisons were invalid. He did not deny the general criticism.

9. "Decision of the center concerning the state of affairs and the duties of the Kampuchean revolution (Draft)," No. 2 SJMCh for Central Committee of the Party, 17 July 1979.

10. "Announcement of the PRCK and the Central Committee of the FUNSK, concerning the state of affairs for the first six months of 1979 and duties for the future," PRCK, July 1979.

11. "Decision of the center concerning the state of affairs . . . ," *op. cit.*

12. *Ibid.*
13. *Ibid.*
14. *Ibid.*
15. *Ibid.*
16. *Ibid.*
17. References to "the debt of blood" are frequent in the early documents. The expression refers to those who were known to have killed during the Pol Pot regime.
18. *Ibid.*
19. *Ibid.*
20. *Ibid.*
21. *Ibid.*
22. *Ibid.*
23. *Ibid.*
24. *Ibid.*
25. *Ibid.*
26. *Ibid.*
27. *Ibid.*
28. *Ibid.*
29. "Circular concerning increasing the work of the propaganda and education movement for our brother intellectuals," No. 11SRMCh, for Central Committee of the CPK, secretary general, Pen Sovann, Phnom Penh, 22 November 1979.
30. "Circular concerning increasing the work of the propaganda and education movement for our brother intellectuals," No. 11SRMCh, for Central Committee of the CPK, secretary general, Pen Sovann, Phnom Penh, 22 November 1979.
31. *Ibid.*
32. "Decision concerning the matter of cadres," Central Committee, First Secretary, 1979.
33. *Ibid.*
34. *Ibid.*
35. *Ibid.*
36. *Ibid.*
37. *Ibid.*
38. *Ibid.*
39. *Ibid.* For graphic descriptions of the people's revenge, see Someth May, *Cambodian Witness*. Summary people's justice in the days and weeks after the arrival of the PAVN/FUNSK troops in late 1978 and early 1979 seems to have been condoned by the Vietnamese and the skeleton Cambodian administration. In the absence of courts or even a legal system during the early months of the regime, justice was *ad hoc* and arbitrary. Later, there were arrests and punishments according to law for involvement in the KR killings. Him Huy, for example, who rose from prison

guard at S-21 (Tuol Sleng) Prison to deputy chief of security there by 1977, was arrested in 1984 and detained without trial "for about 10 months—three months in jail and 7 months in a reeducation camp working in the rice fields." Him Huy's account is given by Bou Saroeun, "Tuol Sleng torturer: 'What I've said is enough,'" *Phnom Penh Post*, 22 January–4 February, 1999, p. 3. The only trial of KR leaders during the PRK period was that of Pol Pot and Ieng Sary, who were tried in absentia during the tribunal held in Phnom Penh on 15 August 1979.

40. *Ibid.*

41. *Ibid.* Sino-Khmers were temporarily excluded from official positions. However, as in virtually every other country in Southeast Asia, the educated skills and commercial dynamism of the ethnic Chinese community were assets far too valuable to forego. In any event, while Hun Sen told a visiting diplomat in October 1989 that there were 62,000 ethnic Chinese living in Phnom Penh at that time (of a total city population of close to one million), in fact, many Phnom Penh citizens, including high government officials, could lay claim to some Chinese ancestry. The status of ethnic Chinese in the PRK was not clarified until the issue of "Circular Concerning the Ethnic Chinese in Kampuchea," No: 40 SR, for Council of Ministers, vice chairman, Chea Soth (signed and stamped), Phnom Penh, 22 October 1982. The circular recognized that there was concern that "the Beijing Chinese expansionists, American imperialists and other imperialist groups, the Thai reactionaries along with their lackeys, Pol Pot, Khieu Samphan, Son Sann, have used some ethnic Chinese to be their lackeys in order to do espionage activities, psychological warfare, economic sabotage, creating panic in the markets, et cetera." The circular considered the matter to be "important, complicated and long-term" but it recommended that "we should implement it taking care not to be impetuous." The policy recommendations came down strongly on the side of encouraging solidarity while exercising vigilance and doing thorough checks.

42. *Ibid.*

43. "Decisions of the third party plenum, 1980," No. 14SRMCh, Central Committee of the CPK, Permanent Committee.

44. *Ibid.*

45. *Ibid.*

46. Michael Vickery notes that the first National Congress of the Kampuchean Youth Association for National Salvation was held 25–27 November, 1983 and was attended by 300 delegates. Vickery, *Kampuchea*, p. 118.

47. "Decisions of the third party plenum . . . ," *op. cit.*

48. *Ibid.*

49. *Ibid.*

50. *Ibid.*

51. *Ibid.*

52. *Ibid.*

53. "Circular concerning completion of the work of building core groups, admitting new party members and recognizing the party status of former party members," No. 196 SRMCh, Central Committee, Communist Party of Kampuchea, 30 July 1980.

54. *Ibid.*

55. "Directive concerning the work of expanding the party," No: 241 JTMCh, Administration Commission, 19 October 1980. The inclusion of Kandal farmers among the 'moneyed classes' indicates that life was indeed returning to normal. Kandal province surrounds the capital city. Its proximity to city markets, the rich alluvial soil and easy access to good supplies of water in many parts of the province give Kandal farmers more opportunities for wealth creation than most Cambodian farmers have.

56. *Ibid.*

57. "Monitoring the work of building the party and the core groups in the first eight months of the year and the outlook for the end of the year," for Party Committee for Ministries and Departments around the Center, unsigned, Phnom Penh, 28 September 1980.

58. "Study Document for the Party Plenary Congress: Building the strength of the Marxist-Leninist party is the key factor in the success of the Cambodian revolution," for Party Central Committee, Pen Sovann, 3 April 1981.

59. *Ibid.*

60. *Ibid.*

61. *Ibid.*

62. *Ibid.*

63. *Ibid.*

64. "Information of the central committee of the PRPK concerning the results of the fourth party congress," Phnom Penh, 8 May [sic], 1981.

65. "Extracts from a speech delivered by comrade Bou Thong on the occasion of the announcement of the results of the fourth party congress," No. 004KChM-NP, Central Propaganda Commission.

66. Note that in this document the "private economy" was defined as "the family economy of the farmers, the craft economy, small-scale industry, everyday transport, small exchanges."

67. "Decisions of the fourth congress of the PRPK," Central Propaganda and Education Commission.

68. *Ibid.*

69. *Ibid.*

70. For names see Michael Vickery, *Kampuchea*, p. 74.

71. "Summary Report," No. 343KhMB, Party Central Committee, Phnom Penh, 18 April 1982.

72. "Ideas of comrade vice chairman of the Council of Ministers and Minister of the Ministry of Planning," unsigned, undated, 1982.

73. Michael Vickery, "The Cambodian People's Party: Where Has It Come From, Where Is It Going?," *Southeast Asian Affairs* (Singapore: ISEAS, 1994), p. 109.

74. Anecdote recounted to author, Phnom Penh, 1996.

75. Anecdote recounted to author, Phnom Penh, 1994.

76. Jacques Bekaert says there were two official biographies. See *Cambodian Diary:* . . . , p. 128. The State Archives also hold two official biographies which are not essentially different.

77. "Decree of the Council of State," No. 33KR, for Council of State, president, Heng Samrin, Phnom Penh, 20 December 1984.

78. "Information concerning the special session of the PRPK Central Politburo on 27 December 1984," No. 04SRMCh, Politburo, secretary general, Heng Samrin (signed and stamped), Phnom Penh, 1 January 1985.

79. This often stated belief is referred to by Thomas Clayton, quoting former and current officials of the ministries of education and finance: "In 1984 Chan Si was sick. The Vietnamese were suspicious of his loyalty and told him, "Please go recuperate in the Soviet Union." In those days, you had to fly through Vietnam to go anywhere . . . He received some injections for the trip from the Vietnamese, and he died of these injections. In fact, he was killed by the Vietnamese so he would not oppose their policies." See Thomas Clayton, *Education and the Politics of Language*, pp. 104–105.

80. "Revelations by Pen Sovann about Hun Sen," Sam Rainsy, Phnom Penh, 26 April 1998, SRP Web-site.

81. "Sam Rainsy Uses Pen Sovann to Attack Hun Sen's Background," *The Cambodia Daily*, 1 May 1998, p. 11.

82. *Ibid.*

83. In his interview with the author, Phnom Penh, 3 August 1998, Pen Sovann was adamant that Chan Si had died in 1987, not 1984.

84. Eyewitness accounts provided by one high-ranking government official and by a Cambodian medic, Phnom Penh, 1998.

85. Timothy Carney, "Heng Samrin's Armed Forces . . . ," p. 150.

86. *Ibid.*

87. *Ibid.*, p. 158. For PAVN troop numbers stationed in Cambodia between January 1979 and April 1985, see Douglas Pike, *PAVN*, p. 70.

88. *Ibid.*, p. 150.

89. Unofficial translation from the Vietnamese text, quoted in *Vietnam Courier*, No. 3, March 1979, pp. 5–6.

90. Anon., "The Military Occupation of Kampuchea', *Indochina Report*, Singapore, 3, July–Sept. 1985. Note that Oddar Meanchey province

was jointly administered with Siem Reap province. During the PRK, this was Siem Reap/Oddar Meanchey province.

91. *Ibid.*, p. 8.

92. *Ibid.*, p. 10.

93. *Ibid.*, p. 18.

94. "Announcement of the PRCK and the Central Committee of the FUNSK concerning the situation for the first six months of 1979 and duties for the future," for the PRCK and the Central Committee of FUNSK, Heng Samrin, July 1979.

95. *Ibid.*

96. *Ibid.*

97. "Decisions of the center concerning the state of affairs and the duties of the Kampuchean Revolution," No. 2SJMCh (Draft), 17 July 1979, Central Committee, Communist Party of Kampuchea, 17 July 1979.

98. *Ibid.*

99. *Ibid.*

100. *Ibid.*

101. Timothy Carney, "Heng Samrin's Armed Forces . . . ," p. 164.

102. "Agreement between the Ministry of Defense of the SRV and the Ministry of Defense of the PRK concerning Vietnam's assistance to Kampuchea for the upgrading of training of commanders, cadres, staff, and technicians" (Draft), Phnom Penh, June 1981.

103. Letter to comrade Chairman of the Council of Ministers of the Socialist Republic of Vietnam, No. 23 LS, (from) chairman of the Council of Ministers of the People's Republic of Kampuchea, Chan Si (signed and stamped), Phnom Penh, 30 June 1982.

104. "Agreement concerning the distribution of troops and military cooperation between the PAVN and the KPRAF (Draft)," Phnom Penh, June 1981.

105. Noted in "Report on construction of the system of defense on the Kampuchea-Thailand Border in the 1987–8 dry season and directions for the 1988 wet season," No. 15RBK, Hun Sen, 21 June, 1988.

106. "Distribution of Vietnamese Military Experts in Kampuchea (Accompanying Document)."

107. For organogram of the KPRAF in 1986–87, see Frank Tatu, "National Security" in Russel R. Ross, ed., *Cambodia—A Country Study* (Library of Congress, Federal Research Division, 1987), p. 282.

108. The Ministry of the Interior Annual Report for 1981 listed twenty parties or fronts supporting either Son Sann or Sihanouk that were involved in anti-PRK activities apart from the KR guerrillas.

109. See "Undeclared War Against the PRK," Ministry of Foreign Affairs Press Department, Phnom Penh, 1985.

110. Details of "the network of saboteurs and political agitators" are

provided in "The Great Anti-Kampuchean Conspiracy," Department of Press, Ministry of Foreign Affairs, PRK, April 1983.

111. "Decisions of the center . . . ," No. 2SJMCh (Draft), *op. cit.*

112. Lawyers Committee for Human Rights, *Kampuchea: After the Worst*, p. iv.

113. Michael Vickery, "A Critique of the Lawyers Committee for International Human Rights, Kampuchea Mission of November 1984," *Journal of Contemporary Asia*, 18 (1988), pp. 108–116.

114. "Report of the UN Fact-Finding Mission . . . ," p. 132.

115. "Advice and instructions concerning the struggle against the traitors of the revolution and caring for the security situation in these new conditions," Party Central Committee, 1979, (unsigned).

116. *Ibid.*

117. *Ibid.*

118. "Decision concerning arrangements for firming and having a system for the Kampuchean People's Security Forces (*nokorbal*)," No. 143SRJ, for Council of Ministers, chairman, Pen Sovann, Phnom Penh, 20 November 1981.

119. *Ibid.*

120. "Sub-decree concerning setting out the duties, rights and organization of the Ministry of the Interior," No. 04ANKr, for Council of Ministers, chairman, Chan Si (signed and stamped), Phnom Penh, 11 January 1983.

121. *Ibid.* (Article 1)

122. References in Memo No. 23LS to cde Chairman of the Council of Ministers of the SRV, for People's Council of Ministers of the PRK, Chan Si, Phnom Penh, 30 June 1982, and "Report evaluating the cooperation and support and the implementation of the agreement of cooperation between the MOI of the PRK and SRV, 1983–84," Ministry of the Interior, unsigned, undated. Note that in the report, the date of the agreement is incorrectly given as 1982.

123. "Report evaluating the cooperation and support . . . ," *op. cit.*

124. *Ibid.*

125. *Ibid.*

126. "Annual Report from 1 January to 20 October 1981," No. 004MHP, minister of the interior, Khang Sarin. Khang Sarin, Khmer Viet Minh and former chief of the Military Committee of Phnom Penh, replaced Chea Sim as minister of the interior when Chea Sim was appointed president of the National Assembly at its first session in 1981.

127. Pol Pot remained chairman of the Supreme Commission and commander-in-chief. It was assumed in diplomatic circles at the time that the change was a cosmetic one. See John McBeth, "Seeking a cleaner official image," *FEER*, 4 January 1980, p. 11.

128. "Annual report . . . ," *op. cit.*

129. *Ibid.*

130. *Ibid.*

131. *Ibid.*

132. *Ibid.*

133. *Ibid.*

134. *Ibid.*

135. *Ibid.*

136. *Ibid.*

137. *Ibid.*

138. *Ibid.*

139. *Ibid.*

140. "Report on step 1 of the joint campaign on the battlefields of Siem Reap/Oddar Meanchey from November 1 to November 20, 1981," Chan Seng, Chief of Command and Le Tanh, Deputy Chief of Command, C80 Combat Force, Command Group, Siem Reap.

141. *Ibid.*

142. *Ibid.*

143. *Ibid.*

144. *Ibid.*

145. *Ibid.*

146. *Ibid.*

147. *Ibid.*

148. *Ibid.*

149. Timothy Carney, "Heng Samrin's Armed Forces . . . ," p. 182.

150. "Nothing much to cheer on Kampuchea's birthday," *Bangkok Post*, 7 January 1984. See Jacques Bekaert, *Kampuchea Diary 1983–1986*.

151. "The Military Occupation of Kampuchea," p. 2.

152. The term "conscription" was used with caution. During the author's interview with Hun Sen, in response to a questions about the start of military conscription (*komnaen toap*) in 1984, he replied, "We call it obligation (*katapekech*)." Article 1 of that decree-law read, "Citizens of the People's Republic of Kampuchea between the ages of 18 and 25 are selected to serve in the army in order to defend the motherland."

153. "Decree-law concerning military service," for Council of State, President, Phnom Penh, 1984.

CHAPTER 7

1. "Announcement of the PRC and the Central Committee of the FUNSK concerning the situation for the first six months of 1979 and duties for the future," Heng Samrin, Phnom Penh, July 1979.

2. "Minutes–Congress of the FUNSK from 27–28 September 1979," signed by note-taker, 4 October 1979.

3. *Ibid.*

4. Helen Ester, *Vietnam, Thailand, Kampuchea: A firsthand account* (Canberra: Australian Council for Overseas Aid, March 1980) p. 5. Note that the figure of three million was the consistent official estimate right throughout the PRK regime and it was more or less confirmed by the findings of research into the crimes of Pol Pot which was conducted over nine months to July 1983. That official research commission put the total number of dead at 2,746,105. Details of this research are given later in this chapter.

5. "*Prakas* of the PRCK and the Central Committee of the FUNSK concerning the state of affairs for the first six months of 1979 and duties for the time ahead," for PRC and the Central Committee of the FUNSK, president, Heng Samrin, Phnom Penh, July 1979.

6. "Report on the third national congress of the Front, 20, 21, 22 December 1981," No. 2219.81 KRS, for the Secretariat of the National Council of the United Front for the Construction and Defence of the Motherland, vice president, Chhun Iem, 22 December 1981.

7. *Ibid.*

8. *Ibid.*

9. 'Report on preparatory congress of the central committee of the Front for Building the Motherland: 17–18 December 1981', No.2218–81 AMR, for the Secretariat of the National Council of the United Front for Construction and Defence of the Motherland of Kampuchea, unsigned, 19 December 1981.

10. "Decree-law concerning the system of general education," No.30KrJ, for Council of State, President, Heng Samrin (signed and stamped), Phnom Penh, 20 November 1986.

11. "Directive for implementing the decree-law concerning the system of general education," No. 04SRNN, for Council of Ministers, chairman, Hun Sen (signed and stamped), Phnom Penh, 22 August 1987.

12. *Ibid.*

13. *Ibid.*

14. *Ibid.*

15. *Ibid.*

16. *Ibid.*

17. Judith Banister and Paige Johnson, "After the Nightmare," p. 99.

18. "PRK Summit on Adult Education—National Day for Raising a Movement to Eradicate Illiteracy, 19 June 1980," Phnom Penh, Ministry of Education.

19. Sub-Decree (No. 04ANKr) was issued by the Council of Ministers on 3 February 1988 to set up the University of Phnom Penh with the role of "cultural and scientific/technical training centre of the nation, com-

bining the work of scientific research with production and social livelihood."

20. Author's experience, Phnom Penh, 1988. In the early years, university entrance was based on its own merit test.

21. "Report summing up the results of the campaign against illiteracy
and for complementary education," National Committee for the Campaign, unsigned, undated.

22. "PRK summit on adult education . . . ," *op.cit.*

23. *Ibid.*

24. *Ibid.*

25. "Report of the national committee for the campaign against
illiteracy and for complementary education concerning the summing up
and evaluation of the results of the literacy movement and complementary education over the past two years, especially in the first half of 1982
and directions and measures for implementation for the last year of the
three year plan," for National Committee, Campaign Against Illiteracy
and for Complementary Education, president, Heng Samrin, Phnom
Penh, 8 August 1982.

26. This number was later adjusted to 1,075,105, of whom 63 percent
were women. See "Report summing up the results of the campaign against
illiteracy and for complementary education," National Committee for the
Campaign, unsigned, undated.

27. "Directive concerning objectives, duties, aims and measures for the
second three-year plan to fight illiteracy and for complementary education: 8.9.83–8.9.86," No: 04 SRNN, for Council of Ministers, acting
chairman, Chea Soth (signed and stamped), 31 January 1984.

28. "Report summing up the results of the campaign against illiteracy
and for complementary education," National Committee for the Campaign, unsigned, undated.

29. *Ibid.*

30. *Ibid.*

31. Rajalakshmi Rama Rao & Binie Zaan, *An Analysis of Female-Headed
Households in Cambodia*, National Institute of Statistics, Ministry of Planning, Phnom Penh, My 1997.

32. *Ibid.*, p. 12.

33. Helen Ester, *Vietnam, Thailand, Kampuchea* . . . , p. 47.

34. "Report on all work in the first six months and general duties for
the second half of 1980," unsigned, undated.

35. Jacqueline Desbarats, *Prolific Survivors*, p. 111.

36. "Report concerning the state of affairs in all areas for the nine
months of 1981 and duties for the final quarter and first quarter of 1982,"
unsigned and undated.

37. "Circular concerning the work of health in the time ahead," No.

55SRMCh, for Party Central Secretariat, Say Phouthang (signed and stamped), Phnom Penh, 13 February 1985.

38. "*Prakas* of the PRCK . . . ," July 1979.

39. Helen Ester, *Vietnam, Thailand, Kampuchea* . . . , p. 45, quoting Ms Mien Som An, president of the Revolutionary Women's Association of Kampuchea.

40. *Ibid.*, p. 40

41. *Ibid.*

42. "Circular concerning the administration of practice according to a number of points in the policy for martyrs and disabled veterans and army families," No. 35SR, for COM, Chairman, Chan Si, Phnom Penh, 1 October 1982.

43. Letter from the chairman of the COM to comrade president of the COS, No. 11LS, for COM, chairman, Hun Sen (signed and stamped), Phnom Penh, 30 January 1985.

44. "Report concerning the situation of the implementation of the duties of defending and building the country in 1984 and objectives for duties in 1985," No. 14RBK, for Council of Ministers, vice chairman, Chea Soth, Phnom Penh, 5 December 1984.

45. "Report concerning the situation of applying the socio-economic plan for the nine months of 1987 and the measures for implementation of duties in the fourth quarter," No. 07RBK, for Council of Ministers, chairman, Hun Sen, Phnom Penh, 27 October 1987.

46. "Minutes of meeting concerning the matter of children and wives of Kampuchean cadres who gave their lives after coming back from northern Vietnam' attached to letter addressed to Ministry of Disabled Veterans and Social Action, No. 864 JTMCh, for Central Administration Commission, vice chairman, Iou Samom, Phnom Penh, 12 September 1986.

47. "Circular concerning the implementation of the policy on religion," No. 453/80KB, for Central Committee of the Front and for PRCK, president, Heng Samrin (signed and stamped), Phnom Penh, 5 December 1980.

48. *Ibid.*

49. *Ibid.*

50. *Ibid.*

51. "Circular concerning the system of entering the Buddhist monkhood," No. 24-82SR, for Front Central Committee, for PRCK, president, Heng Samrin (signed and stamped), Phnom Penh, 5 June 1981 (2524).

52. *Ibid.*

53. *Ibid.*

54. *Ibid.*

55. Vu Can, "Buddhism and Socialism in Kampuchea," *Vietnam Courier*, 9 (1982), p. 31.

56. "Circular concerning becoming a Buddhist novice," No. 03. 89KJRS, for National Council of the United Front for the Construction and Defence of the Motherland Kampuchea, president, Chea Sim (signed and stamped), Phnom Penh, 24 April 1989.

57. "Report, 1980," No. 407 (KH.V.Ph), for Ministry of Propaganda, Culture and Information, assistant to the minister, Phnom Penh, January 1981.

58. *Ibid.*

59. *Ibid.*

60. *Ibid.*

61. *Ibid.*

62. *Ibid.*

63. "Decision concerning the setting up of a committee to report on and care for the Angkorian temples," No. 49SSR, for COM, chairman, Chan Si, Phnom Penh, 16 March 1984.

64. "Report on the financial situation and the proposed state budget for 1984, to the National Assembly, 6th session, first legislature," Council of Ministers, Ministry of Finance. As noted previously, when the *riel* was issued in March 1980, it was worth one-quarter of one US dollar at the official rate; in 1981 its black market value was fifty to the dollar and throughout the rest of the decade it fluctuated between 120 and 160 to the dollar. In 1987, the official rate was adjusted to 100 to the dollar.

65. Helen Ester, *Vietnam, Thailand, Kampuchea . . .*, p. 47.

66. "Circular concerning caring for and protecting the bones of corpses of the people who suffered in the genocidal regime of Pol Pot, Ieng Sary, Khieu Samphan," No. 37SR, for Council of Ministers, vice chairman, Chea Soth (signed), Phnom Penh, 8 September 1981.

67. "Decision," No. 1619–82, for National Council for the KUFCDM, president, Chea Sim (signed and stamped), Phnom Penh, 5 October 1982.

68. *Ibid.*

69. "Minutes: Summing up the crimes of the Beijing Chinese hegemonists and their lackeys Pol Pot, Ieng Sary, Khieu Samphan in the period 1975–78 against the people of Kampuchea," Commission for Researching the Crimes of the Pol Pot Regime, Min Khin, 25 July 1983.

70. *Ibid.*

71. The likelihood of double-counting was virtually inevitable according to this method; nor does it seem to have allowed for natural mortality rates.

72. *Ibid.*

73. *Ibid.*

74. "Minutes concerning the working meeting of the Permanent Committee of the National Council of the KUFCDM," No. 1100-83:KRS, Phnom Penh, 3 August 1983.

75. *Ibid.*

76. *Ibid.*

77. *Ibid.*

78. "Decisions: Third Conference of the National Council of the KUFCDM, 15–17 November [sic] 1983."

79. "Report concerning the situation of the implementation of the duties of defending and building the country in 1984 and objectives for duties in 1985," No. 14RBK, for Council of Ministers, vice chairman, Chea Soth.

80. Hun Sen, *The Ten-Year Journey*, pp. 485–86.

81. Critical assessment of the mass organizations was made by Heng Samrin in 1986. This is discussed in the concluding chapter.

CHAPTER 8

1. Robert Muscat noted, "From 1984 to 1986 the PRK put the rate of growth in national income at 3.5 percent, reflecting the plateauing of growth in economic activity . . . " See *Cambodia: Post-Settlement Reconstruction and Development* (Columbia University, NY: Occasional Papers of the East Asian Institute, 1989), p. 25.

2. In an interview with Nguyen Co Thach, former Foreign Affairs Minister of Vietnam, Raoul Jennar was told that Hun Sen "betrayed us" by accepting conditions for multi-party elections in 1993. Personal communication.

3. Memo No. 12LS to Comrade President of the Council of State, for Council of Ministers, Chairman, Hun Sen, Phnom Penh, 5 February 1985. Reference: Decision of the Politburo, undated.

4. Tim Huxley, "Cambodia in 1986: The PRK's Eighth Year," *Southeast Asian Affairs*, 1987, pp. 161–73.

5. According to figures provided by the Ministry of Education, 1990, "In all, 2,650 Cambodian students completed degree programmes between 1983 and 1989 in the USSR, East Germany, Vietnam, Bulgaria, Czechoslovakia, Hungary, and Cuba." Quoted by Thomas Clayton, *Education and the Politics of Language*, p. 129.

6. Memo No. 11LS, for Council of Ministers, vice chairman, Chea Soth, Phnom Penh, 28 January 1988.

7. *FEER*, 12 January 1989.

8. *Ibid.* In 1987, Kong Sam Ol became the third deputy prime minister and the following year was made minister responsible for the Cabinet of the Council of Ministers.

9. *FEER*, 25 December 1986. Hun Sen also gives this figure in *The Ten-Year Journey*, p. 416.

10. *FBIS*, 15 October 1985 (Phnom Penh Domestic Service)

11. *Ibid.*

12. *Ibid.*

13. Nayan Chanda, "Cambodia in 1986," *Asian Survey*, 27/1, January 1987, pp. 115–23.

14. Hun Sen, *The Ten-Year Journey*, p. 421.

15. *Ibid.*, p. 424.

16. One party member interviewed was admitted in 1989, having been an active core group member since 1979. Following her application for membership, her biography was rigorously checked and when an inconsistency was discovered following interviews conducted by the party monitors with people in her home village, her preparatory period was extended as a form of discipline. Conversation with author, Phnom Penh, January 2000.

17. For a detailed analysis of the fifth party congress, see Peter Schier, "Kampuchea in 1985: Between Crocodiles and Tigers," *Southeast Asian Affairs*, 1986, pp. 139–161.

18. According to one party member, Say Phouthang was consulted on all major issues, most notably conditions for the return of the king in 1991. She believed that old age and ill-health were more likely reasons for Say Phouthang's apparent decline. Conversation with author, Phnom Penh, January 2000.

19. Report of the Council of State concerning the Election to choose Members of the National Assembly's Second Term of Office to the tenth session of the first legislature of the National Assembly, for Council of State, president, Phnom Penh, January 1986.

20. *Ibid.*

21. *Ibid.*

22. "Law concerning the inspection and resolution of accusations, protests and denunciations of citizens," president of the National Assembly, Chea Sim, July 1982.

23. *Ibid.*

24. Memo No. 137/82TPKR to the Council of Ministers, "Law Concerning the Stipulations of Supervisory Regulations for the Protests and Denunciations of Citizens," for the minister, Ministry for Monitoring State Affairs, vice minister, Dauk Dan, 12 July 1982.

25. 'Report concerning Activities of the National Assembly between Sessions 9 and 10', unsigned and undated

26. *Ibid.*

27. "Decree-law concerning the organization and activities of the People's Supreme Court and the attorney general attached to the Supreme Court," No. 34KrCh, for Council of State, President, Heng Samrin (signed and stamped), Phnom Penh, 26 August 1987.

28. "Report of the United Nations Fact-Finding Mission . . . ," p. 109.

29. *Ibid.*

30. *Ibid.*

31. "Rapport sur les activities de l'assemblée nationale accompliés dans l'intervalle dès 14 et 15emes sessions de la 1re legislature," unsigned, undated.

32. *Ibid.*

33. *Ibid.*

34. *Ibid.*

35. "Report concerning the activities of the National Assembly in the interval between the 15th and 16th sessions of the first legislature," unsigned, undated.

36. *Ibid.*

37. *Ibid.*

38. *Ibid.*

39. "Minutes of Meeting of 1–2 February 1989," Chan Ven, secretary general, Council of State.

40. *Ibid.*

41. *Ibid.*

42. *Ibid.*

43. *Ibid.*

44. *Ibid.*

45. *Ibid.*

46. "Circular concerning the campaign for serving agricultural production and ensuring the livelihood of the people in the time ahead," No. 02SR, for Council of Ministers, chairman, Hun Sen, Phnom Penh, 4 February 1985.

47. *Ibid.*

48. "Report concerning the state of affairs of implementing the defence and construction of the country in the nine months of 1985 and objectives and duties in the fourth quarter of 1985," No. 05RBK, for Council of Ministers, chairman, Hun Sen, Phnom Penh, 15 October 1985.

49. *Ibid.*

50. *Ibid.*

51. *Ibid.*

52. Michael Eiland reported that the price of rice and fish, the national staple diet, doubled in just six months during 1985. See "Cambodia in 1985: From Stalemate to Ambiguity," *Asian Survey*, 26/1, pp. 119–25.

53. "Decision concerning increasing regional allowances for cadres, staff and state workers," No. 35SSR, for Council of Ministers, chairman, Hun Sen, Phnom Penh, 8 February 1985.

54. *FBIS*, 15 October 1985, op. cit. Note that "private economy in 1985 meant something quite different from the "private economy" referred to during the fourth party congress in 1981 when it was defined as "the fam-

ily economy of the farmers, the craft economy, small-scale industry, everyday transport, small exchanges." See "Decisions of the fourth congress of the PRPK," *op. cit.*

55. *Ibid.*

56. "Report to the National Assembly concerning the law for changes to Article 12 of the PRK Constitution," No. 01RBK, for Council of Ministers, chairman, Hun Sen, Phnom Penh, 1 February 1986.

57. "Memo to Council of State concerning the request to change the tax policy for industrial commerce," No. 27LS, for Council of Ministers, chairman, Hun Sen, Phnom Penh, 1 April 1985.

58. Tim Huxley, "Cambodia in 1986," p. 164.

59. *FEER*, 15 May 1986, p. 25.

60. "Memo to Council of State concerning request to change the tax policy . . . ," No. 27LS, *op cit.*

61. *Ibid.*

62. *FEER*, 7 May 1987, p. 38.

63. *Ibid.*

64. *Ibid.*

65. "Decision concerning changes in the rate of foreign exchange," No. 116SSR, for Council of Ministers, chairman, Hun Sen, Phnom Penh, 12 September 1987.

66. *Ibid.*

67. "Decision concerning the livelihood of cadres, staff, workers," No. 130SSR, for Council of Ministers, chairman, Hun Sen, Phnom Penh, 30 September 1987.

68. "Decision concerning changes to the salary system of cadres, staff and workers," No. 17SSR, for Council of Ministers, chairman, Hun Sen, Phnom Penh, 9 February 1989.

69. *Ibid.*

70. Hun Sen, *The Ten-Year Journey*, p. 489.

71. *Ibid.*

72. "Decision concerning the right of mastery of production and exploitation of state industrial enterprises," No. 13SR, for Council of Ministers, chairman, Hun Sen, Phnom Penh, 4 October 1988

73. *Ibid.*

74. *Ibid.*

75. "Decree-law concerning foreign investment in the State of Cambodia," No. 58Kr, for Council of State, president, Heng Samrin, Phnom Penh, 26 July 1989.

76. Neither the Vladivostok statement nor later statements concerning normalisation of relations between USSR and China provided the usual reassurance that it would not be at the expense of any third country. See Nayan Chanda, "Not Soft on Cambodia," *FEER*, 1 January 1987, pp. 11–13.

77. John Pedler, "Cambodia: A Report on the International and Internal Situation and the Future Outlook," London, April 1989, p. 15.

78. "Directive concerning building the socio-economic plan for 1987," No. 17SRNN, for Council of Ministers, vice chairman, Chea Soth, 16 August 1986.

79. Tim Huxley, "Cambodia in 1986," p. 163

80. "Decision concerning expanding the socialist commercial network in the time ahead 1986–87," No. 02SRJ, for Council of Ministers, chairman, Hun Sen, Phnom Penh, 2 September 1986.

81. *Ibid.*

82. *FEER*, 7 May 1987, p. 38.

83. "Account of the Commission for the Economy and the Budget," draft, unsigned, undated.

84. *Ibid.*

85. *Ibid.*

86. *Ibid.*

87. *Ibid.*

88. *Ibid.*

89. *Ibid.*

90. *Ibid.*

91. "Memo to comrade Chairman of the Council of Ministers concerning the problem of shortages of drugs and the possibilities of resolving it," No. 1289, Yit Kimseng, Phnom Penh, 15 October 1987

92. *Ibid.*

93. "Report concerning the results of implementing the state budget for nine months of 1987 and the plan for the fourth quarter and estimates for implementation throughout 1987," No. 08RBK, for Council of Ministers, chairman, Hun Sen, Phnom Penh, 27 October 1987.

94. A meeting of key ministers on 15–16 October 1987 which was held to discuss the budget report revealed that the stolen rubber was crossing the Kompong Cham border into Tay Ninh province of Vietnam. See "Information concerning the meeting of the Council of Ministers, 15–16 October 1987," No. 1328SJN, for Minister Responsible for the Council of Ministers Cabinet, vice minister, Cham Prasith, Phnom Penh, 27 October 1987.

95. "Report concerning the situation of applying the socio-economic plan for the nine months of 1987 and the measures for implementation of duties in the fourth quarter," No. 07RBK, for Council of Ministers, chairman, Hun Sen, Phnom Penh, 27 October 1987.

96. *Ibid.*

97. *Ibid.* Both long-term and short-term Vietnamese advisers received salary and provisions from the PRK budget.

98. The 1995 qualitative survey referred to in Chapter 5 claimed, "In 1986, the *krom samaki* definitely ended," but no evidence is offered for

the claim. The researchers found "a few regions" such as in Kompong Chhnang and Svay Rieng where collective work ended in 1988, and even two villages where it did not end until 1991 because "land sharing was not agreed by people: some received more than others. There was no justice, and this leads people to be disappointed and be resentful towards the authorities." *Rural Women and the Socio-Economic Transition . . .*, *op. cit.*, pp. 14–15.

99. "Law concerning changes to Articles 15,16 and 17 of the PRK Constitution," president of the national assembly, Chea Sim, Phnom Penh, 11 February 1989.

100. Serge Thion, *Watching Cambodia*, p. 88.

101. *Ibid.*

102. Peter Schier, "Kampuchea in 1985: Between Crocodiles and Tigers," p. 156.

103. In "Cambodia in 1986 . . . ," Huxley wrote: ". . . huge areas of the country were in reality 'no-man's land.' Cadres sent to north-western districts in 1985 had found that in some places people had never had contact with PRK administrators. In response to this situation, which effectively provided a political and administrative vacuum that might be filled by the resistance, Phnom Penh reportedly rusticated civil servants from various ministries for up to three months at a time, in order to tighten the central government's control of the provinces." This statement is pieced together from information given in a *FEER* article by Nayan Chanda, 15 May 1985, where he ascribed the 'no-man's land' reference to East European sources in Phnom Penh. Huxley's re-shaping of that article actually represents something different from the original article's intention.

104. "Report concerning the study of establishing a new province by cutting off a number of districts of Battambang and Siem Reap/Oddar Meanchey," No. 70LS, for Council of Ministers, chairman, Hun Sen, Phnom Penh, 10 September 1986.

105. Decision No. 02SRJ of the Council of Ministers, 2 September 1986, states, "The district level has just been built." "Decision concerning the duties and the administrative structure of the District People's Revolution Committee," No. 71SSR, was issued on 10 May 1988.

106. "Circular concerning the concrete implementation of the duties of the Commune People's Revolutionary Committees," No. 02SR, for Council of Ministers, chairman, Hun Sen, Phnom Penh, 17 March 1988.

107. "Circular concerning collecting debts from the people," No. 04SR, for Council of Ministers, chairman, Hun Sen, Phnom Penh, 21 March 1988.

108. *Ibid.*

109. *Ibid.*

110. "Minutes of the Ordinary Session of the Council of State, 1–2

February 1989," secretary general of the Council of State, Chan Ven, Phnom Penh, 2 February 1989.

111. *Ibid.*

112. *Ibid.*

113. *Ibid.*

114. Viviane Frings, "The Failure of Agricultural Collectivization . . . ," pp. 51–65. Embedded quotation p. 65.

115. *Ibid.*, p. 55.

116. *Ibid.* Here Frings draws on an interview with Eva Mysliwiec who worked in Cambodia for international humanitarian organizations from 1980 onwards.

117. Francois Grunewald, "The rebirth of agricultural peasants in Cambodia," *Cultural Survival Quarterly*, 14/3, 1990, pp. 74–76.

118. Hun Sen, *The Ten-Year Journey*, p. 314–15.

119. *Ibid.*

120. *Ibid.*

121. Hun Sen, interview with author, Takhmau, 3 August 1999.

122. *Ibid.*

123. Viviane Frings, "Cambodia after decollectivization (1989–1992)," *Journal of Contemporary Asia*, 24/1, 1994, pp. 49–66.

124. *Ibid. Rural Women and the Socio-Economic Transition* . . . states un-equivocally that "official land distribution was done in 1986 according to the number of family members," *op. cit.*, p. 17. The report argues further that "Until 1985, no one could sell nor buy land" despite the fact that in some provinces land distribution was actually carried out in 1984–1985. According to the report, in the 1986 land distribution, a family with six members received 76 *aar* of land, where one *aar* is equal to one hundred square metres.

125. *Ibid.*

126. *Ibid.*

127. Viviane Frings, "The Failure of Agricultural Collectivization . . . ," p. 69.

128. "Minutes of Permanent Meeting of the Council of Ministers concerning the socio-economic plan for the period 1991 to 2005 in the PRK [sic]," No. 69KNH.PS, secretary/note-taker Sim San, Phnom Penh, 13 May 1989. The other six in attendance were vice-chairmen Say Chhum and Tea Banh, Chea Chanto, Kong Korm, Keo Samut and Msaos Luos.

129. *Ibid.*

130. *Ibid.*

131. *Ibid.*

133. "Report concerning implementation of the duties of nine months of the state plan and objectives for the fourth quarter of 1989," No. 14RBK, for Council of Ministers, Chairman, Hun Sen, Phnom Penh, 11 October 1989.

134. Interview with author, *op. cit.*

CHAPTER 9

1. Most of the information in this chapter is reproduced from the author's paper, "The K5 Gamble: National Defense and Nation Building under the People's Republic of Kampuchea," *Journal of Southeast Asian Studies*, 32 (2), June 2001, pp. 195–210.

2. *FBIS:AP*, 4 January 1985, "The VPA and Its Lofty International Duty in Friendly Cambodia," from *Tap Chi Quan Doi Nhan Dan*, December 1984.

3. Peter Schier, "Kampuchea in 1985 . . . ," p. 140.

4. *Ibid.*

5. *Ibid.*

6. "*kor*" is the first letter of the Khmer alphabet. "K5" is the common transliteration.

7. Robert Karniol, "Rebels on the march," *FEER*, 23 October 1986, p. 20.

8. There were, in all, eight of these plans. K6, for example, related to the plan for the defense of the belt around Phnom Penh (*kar karpier kravat Phnom Penh*). This information was corroborated by government officials, including Nhim Vanda, through reliable intermediaries for the author, Phnom Penh, 25 November 2000.

9. In 2000, SRV Deputy Prime Minister Nguyen Tan Dzung signed an agreement with the Cambodian government for a special joint operation to locate and repatriate the remains of Vietnamese soldiers who died in Cambodia during the First, Second and Third Indochina Wars. Their statistics show a total of 10,000 soldiers dead or missing during the decade 1979–1989. An estimated 20,000 Vietnamese soldiers were wounded throughout those years. These figures were reported by Agence France-Presse, "VN Admits Toll of Occupation" in *The Cambodia Daily*, 20 July 2001. Figures given by the Vietnam Defense Ministry at the time of the final withdrawal of Vietnamese troops from Cambodia in September 1986 were that approximately 23,000 Vietnamese soldiers had died and 55,000 had been wounded since 1979.

10. "The Military Occupation of Kampuchea," p. 2.

11. Paul Quinn-Judge, "The sound and fury," *FEER*, 22 August 1985, p. 38.

12. Hun Sen, interview with author, Takhmau, 3 August 1999.

13. Report concerning the state of affairs of implementation of the K5 Plan in the 1984-1985 dry season and directions and duties for the plan in the 1985–1986 dry season, No. 52/85, for Central Leadership Commit-

tee for K5 and vice minister for Ministry of National Defense, Soy Keo, 4 July 1985.

14. Soy Keo is said to have been dismissed for grand corruption involving the illegal sale of timber from the northern border regions, according to remarks made to the author by a former government official, Phnom Penh, November 2000. "Minutes concerning the report on the work of K5," No. 02KNH, Cabinet of the Council of Ministers, note-taker Bun Ny, Phnom Penh, 26 April 1986.

15. Reference to Chea Dara, *ibid.* Khvan Seam reference in "Information concerning session of the Permanent Commission of the Council of Ministers to discuss the report concerning the building of the Kampuchea-Thai border defense system in the year so far and directions for 1987," No. 46SJN.S.R., Prieb Pichey, vice-minister, Cabinet of the Council of Ministers, Phnom Penh, 14 January 1987.

16. "Minutes of the ordinary session of the Council of State 1–2 February 1989." Nhim Vanda was a vice minister of the Ministry of Planning until 1988 when he was transferred to the same level position in the Ministry of Defense in charge of logistics. He was made Lt. Gen. in January 1989. He became "vice president" of the K5 committee in February that year. See Raoul Jennar, *Les cles du Cambodge*, p. 233.

17. "The Military Occupation of Kampuchea," p. 21.

18. *Bangkok Post*, 16 May 1986 in *Kampuchea Diary 1983–1986.*

19. "Report concerning the state of affairs . . . ," *op. cit.*

20. *Ibid.*

21. *Ibid.*

22. "Circular concerning gathering the strength of the people to participate in and contribute to the defense of the nation to serve the campaign and to care for the security of the routes of communication," No. 48SR, for Council of Ministers, Chairman, Pen Sovann, Phnom Penh, 9 November 1981.

23. Martin, *Cambodia: A Shattered Society*, p. 222.

24. "Circular concerning organizing and leading a *bralong branang* movement of loving the nation to defend and build the motherland," No. 343SRMCh, for Central Secretariat of the PRPK, Say Phouthang, Phnom Penh, 2 October 1982.

25. *Ibid.*

26. "Memo," No. 98SJN, for Council of Ministers, Chan Si, Phnom Penh, 20 November 1982.

27. *Ibid.*

28. "Decision concerning manpower levy for the people to serve the defense of the country," No. 28SSR, for Permanent Committee of the Council of Ministers, Chairman, Chan Si, Phnom Penh, 21 February 1983.

29. *Ibid.*

30. Martin, *Cambodia: A Shattered Society*, p. 222.

31. "1983–1984 Dry Season Situation," No. 194/84BY, campaign commander, Men Vanna, 22 May 1984.

32. Rodney Tasker, "Hanoi's headache," *FEER*, 19 January 1984, p. 32.

33. *Ibid.*

34. "1983–84 Dry Season . . . ," *op. cit.*

35. Esmeralda Luciolli, *Le Mur de bambou*, pp. 107–8.

36. "Decision concerning the handing over of the duties for the implementation of the K5 Plan to the provinces/municipalities and the relevant ministries/departments," No. 155SSR, for Council of Ministers, chairman, Chan Si, Phnom Penh, 28 September 1984.

37. "Plan for materials, budget, laborers," attached to "Report concerning the state of affairs of implementation of the K5 Plan in the 1984–85 dry season . . . ," *op. cit.*, 4 July 1985.

38. "Report to the National Assembly concerning the construction of the Kampuchea-Thailand border defense system for the dry season of 1986–1987 and directions for the wet season of 1987," Council of Ministers, unsigned, Phnom Penh, 10 July 1987.

39. "Report concerning the construction of the system of defense on the Kampuchea-Thailand border in the 1987–1988 dry season and directions for the 1988 wet season," Council of Ministers, chairman, Hun Sen, Phnom Penh, 21 June 1988.

40. "Decision concerning announcement of the use of souvenir certificates . . . ," No. 63SSR, for Council of Ministers, Chairman, Hun Sen, Phnom Penh, 16 February 1985.

41. "Accompanying Document No. 1 attached to Decision concerning distribution of duties to ministries and provinces/municipalities in the implementation of the plan to build a defense line along the Kampuchea-Thailand border," No. 48SSR, for Council of Ministers, chairman, Hun Sen, Phnom Penh, 12 February 1985.

42. *Ibid.*

43. During his interview with the author, Hun Sen said that "the funding and provisions for the military were all carried out by the Vietnamese."

44. *Bangkok Post*, 11 April, 1986. See Bekaert, *op. cit.* According to Ministry of Finance officials, Cambodia's debt to the former USSR and its allies is estimated at $1.1 billion and Russia alone is owed an estimated $800 million by Cambodia. These figures were reported by Deutsche-Press-Agentur, "Hun Sen to visit Russia, seek debt reduction" in *The Cambodia Daily*, 8 February 2001.

45. "Report concerning the state of affairs . . . ," *op. cit.*

46. "Decree-law concerning the obligation to defend the motherland,"

No. 26KrJ, for Council of State, President, Phnom Penh, 4 September 1985.

47. "Directive concerning the extension of the decree-law on the obligation to defend the motherland," No. 02SRNN, for Council of Ministers, chairman, Hun Sen, Phnom Penh, 27 January 1986.

48. Luciolli, *Le Mur du bambou*, p. 123.

49. *Ibid.*, p. 120.

50. Personal conversation with the author, Phnom Penh, 1998.

51. "Report concerning the checking on the situation of the implementation of K5 in Battambang Province', for delegation, Chhea Thang, Phnom Penh, 30 December 1985.

52. *Ibid.*

53. *Ibid.*

54. *Ibid.*

55. "Directive concerning the leadership of a *bralong branang* movement to build a system to defend the Kampuchea-Thailand border, K5," for COM, Chairman [sic], Chea Soth, Phnom Penh, 20 December 1986.

56. "Report to the National Assembly concerning the construction of the Kampuchea-Thailand border defense system for the dry season of 1986–1987 . . . ," *op. cit.*, 10 July 1987.

57. "Minutes of meeting concerning the hearing of the report," No. 127KNH.PK, Cabinet of the Council of Ministers, note-taker Bun Ny, Phnom Penh, 29 August 1989.

58. Jacqueline Desbarats, *Prolific Survivors*, p. 99.

59. Personal communication with the author, Phnom Penh, 1999.

60. This corrupt practice is referred to in the "Report to the National Assembly concerning the construction of the Kampuchea-Thailand border defense system for the dry season of 1986–1987 . . . ," *op. cit.* 10 July 1987.

61. "Order concerning protection of security and caring for order along the Kampuchea-Thailand border," No. 14BBJ, for Council of Ministers, Chairman, Chan Si, Phnom Penh, 12 November 1984.

62. "Sub-decree concerning the setting up of a committee for the movement of bringing back the enemy who have lost the way at all levels," No. 23ANKr, for Council of Ministers, vice chairman, Chea Soth, Phnom Penh, 27 November 1984.

63. "Directive concerning the work of the movement for the misled in the wet season of 1985 and the beginning of the dry season in 1985–1986," No. 151SRMCh, for Central Party Secretariat, Say Phouthang, 22 April 1985.

64. *Ibid.*

65. *Ibid.*

66. *Ibid.*

67. *Ibid.*

68. *Ibid.*

69. *Ibid.*

70. *Moulinaka* (Mouvement pour la Libération Nationale du Kampuchea) was established on the border in 1979 by merging several small Khmer Serei groups into a single body. Its original leader, Kong Syleah was reportedly poisoned in the summer of 1981 and succeeded by In Tam, a former leader of the Democratic Party. In Tam, who broke with the royalist faction in 1985, was a member of the committee which drafted the SOC Constitution of 1989.

71. "Report concerning the state of affairs of implementing the defense and construction of the country in the nine months of 1985 and objectives and duties in the fourth quarter of 1985," No. 05RBK, for Council of Ministers, chairman, Hun Sen, Phnom Penh, 15 October 1985.

72. Bruce Roscoe, "Wooing the waverers," *FEER*, 30 May 1985, p. 22.

73. Nayan Chanda, "A qualified recovery," *FEER*, 15 May 1986, p. 28.

74. "Report to the National Assembly concerning the military situation, the work of K5 and the work of the movement for the misled in the first half, 1989," No. 11RBK, Council of Ministers, chairman, Hun Sen, Phnom Penh, 6 July 1989.

75. See "Declaration on the policy of national reconciliation of the People's Republic of Kampuchea," in *Vietnam Courier*, No. 11, 1987, p. 13.

76. Bekaert, *Bangkok Post*, 16 May 1986, *op. cit.*

77. John McBeth, "A Borderline battle," *FEER*, 21 February 1985, p. 16. In mid-1986, the KR reportedly had "as many as two-thirds of their 30–40,000 forces inside Cambodia at any given time" according to Rodney Tasker, 'The reality of coalition', *FEER*, 10 July 1986, p. 12.

78. "Directive concerning the management of Lake Tonle Sap," No. 06SrNN, for Council of Ministers, chairman, Hun Sen (signed and stamped), Phnom Penh, 19 April 1985.

79. "Report concerning the military situation—Report to the Session of the National Assembly," Council of Ministers, unsigned, undated.

80. The three revolutionary movements which had been in force throughout the PRK years were to encourage production, to defend security and strengthen the armed forces, and to build the genuine revolutionary force (i.e. the party).

81. "Report concerning the military situation . . . ," *ibid.*

82. "Circular concerning increasing the management of labor throughout the country," No. 04SR, for Council of Ministers, chairman, Hun Sen, Phnom Penh, 12 April 1989.

83. "Report concerning the military situation for the first six months of 1988 for the 15th Session of the National Assembly," No. 17RBK, for Council of Ministers, chairman, Hun Sen, Phnom Penh, 25 June 1988.

84. "Circular concerning increasing the management of labor . . . ," *op. cit.*

85. "Report summing up the situation of caring for political security and social order for 1988," No. 008RBK, Ministry of the Interior, Minister, Sin Song, Phnom Penh, 30 January 1989.

86. *Ibid.*

87. *Ibid.*

88. Murray Hiebert, "The shadow of war," *FEER*, 7 May 1987, p. 37; Murray Hiebert, "Standing alone," *FEER*, 29 June, 1989, p. 18.

89. Nayan Chander, "A troubled friendship," *FEER*, 9 June 1988, p. 16.

90. According to Hun Sen, ". . . in general, by June 1988, all the Vietnamese advisers were withdrawn from Cambodia." Interview with author, Takhmau, 3 August 1999.

91. "Report concerning the construction of the system of defense on the Kampuchea-Thailand border in the 1987–1988 dry season and directions for the 1988 wet season," No. 15RBK, for Council of Ministers, Chairman, Hun Sen, Phnom Penh, 21 June 1988.

92. *Vietnam Courier*, No. 3, 1989, p. 13.

93. "Joint declaration of the government of the PRK, of the government of LPDR and the government of SRV on the total withdrawal of Vietnamese volunteer forces from Kampuchea," 5 April 1989.

94. Unknown student, conversation with the author, Phnom Penh, 26 September 1989.

95. KPRAF troop figures given by Frank Tatu (*op. cit.*, p. 286) and *FEER*, 7 September 1989, p. 16. The lower figure for the militia is given by that *FEER* article and the higher one by Hun Sen in an interview with the author, 3 August 1999. Murray Hiebert quoted estimates of 45,000 regulars and another 50,000 provincial forces and district and village militia (*FEER*, 29 June 1989). PAVN spokesman, Gen. Nguyen Van Thai told Murray Hiebert that the PRK had "no less than 200,000 troops, including militia" (*FEER*, 12 January 1989).

96. Murray Hiebert, "The war winds down," *FEER*, 12 January 1989, p. 17.

97. Heng Hung, *Vietnamese Tricks and the Puppet Group*, Phnom Penh, 28 November 1996, p. 5.

98. John McBeth, "No news from Hanoi," *FEER*, 14 February 1985, p. 16.

99. Hiebert, "Cambodia: Guerrilla Attacks Curb Development," pp. 1–6

100. Robert Karniol, "Rebels on the march," *FEER*, 23 October 1986, p. 21.

101. *Ibid.*

102. *Ibid.*

103. Rodney Tasker, "Dry-season dominance," *FEER*, 6 November 1986, p. 44.

104. Murray Hiebert, "The shadow of war," *FEER*, 7 May 1987, p. 36.

CHAPTER 10

1. Michael Vickery, *Kampuchea*, 1999 imprint, p. 284.

2. Maurice Godelier, *Pespectives in Marxist Anthropology* (Cambridge: CUP, 1977), p. 45.

3. Theda Skocpol, *States and Social Revolutions*, p. 114.

4. *Chbab Phseng Phseng* [Codes de conduites] (Cedoreck: Centre de Documentation et de Recherche sur la Civilisation Khmere, 1986).

5. David Chandler, "Normative Poems (*Chbap*) and Pre-Colonial Cambodian Society," *Facing the Cambodian Past*, p. 59.

6. L. M. Hanks, "Merit and Power in the Thai Social Order," *American Anthropologist*, 64, 1962, p. 1252.

7. Someth May, *Cambodian Witness*, p. 209.

8. Ieng Sonnary. The author is grateful to Beth Goldring for a copy of the transcript of her interview with Sonnary in Phnom Penh, early 1999, for a project commissioned by the Asian Human Rights Commission.

9. David Chandler, "Normative Poems . . . ," p. 59.

10. David Chandler, "A Revolution in Full Spate," *Facing the Past*, p. 258.

11. Kate Frieson, "The Pol Pot Legacy in Village Life," *Cultural Survival Quarterly*, 14, 3, 1990, p.72.

12. *Ibid.*

13. Serge Thion, *Watching Cambodia*, p. 87.

14. David Chandler, "A Revolution in Full Spate," *Facing the Past*, p. 258.

15. James Scott, "Revolution in the Revolution . . . ," p. 120.

16. Theda Skocpol, *States and Social Revolutions*, pp. 31–32.

17. Noam Chomsky and Edward S. Herman, *After the Cataclysm*, p. 155.

18. Noam Chomsky, *ibid.*, with reference to Kenneth Quinn.

19. Serge Thion, *Watching Cambodia*, p. 10.

20. *Ibid.*, p. 44.

21. Interview with Ministry of Education official, Phnom Penh, in 1992 and 1994, cited by Thomas Clayton, *Education and the Politics of Language*, p. 97. One must beware of comments made about the PRK during this period. The UN-supervised election took place in 1993. It was preceded (and followed) by a barrage of anti-socialist propaganda and the interviewees may have wanted to appear to be on the "right" side.

22. Interviews with Ministry of Education officials, *ibid.*, p. 100.

23. Interviews with Ministry of Education officials, *ibid*.

24. *Ibid.*, p. 101.

25. *Ibid.*, p. 102.

26. *Ibid.*, p. 146.

27. Personal conversation with the author, Kompong Thom province, January 1999.

28. Personal conversation with author, Phnom Penh, 1999.

29. Interview with a higher education administrator, cited by Thomas Clayton, *Education and the Politics of Language*, p. 141.

30. *Ibid.*

31. John Hoffman, "The Coercion/Consent Analysis of the State under Socialism," in Neil Harding, ed. *The State in Socialist Society* (Albany: State University of New York Press, 1984), p. 139.

32. "Decision concerning building the working class of Kampuchea and turning [it] into a genuine vanguard class imbued with the cause of the Kampuchean revolution," for Party Central committee, secretary general, Heng Samrin (signed and stamped), undated.

33. *Ibid.*

34. "Minutes concerning the meeting between cde Hun Sen, chairman of the Council of Ministers, and cde minister of the interior of SRV and cde minister of the interior of Lao PDR," No. 107KNH, Cabinet of the Council of Ministers, note-taker, Hoy Hoen, Phnom Penh, 15 July 1989.

35. Personal conversation with the author, Phnom Penh, 1990.

36. Response to question by the author, Phnom Penh, 1989.

37. Agence France-Presse, "VN Admits Toll of Occupation," *The Cambodia Daily*, 20 July 2001. The article quotes a "military source" which confirms a report given in *Hanoi Moi*, one of Vietnam's main official daily newspapers. This is a very modest figure. At the time of the final withdrawal in 1989, the Vietnamese death toll for the ten years was given as approximately 23,000. See Chronology.

38. Figure quoted by Cambodian Secretary of State for Foreign Affairs, Sieng Lapresse, "Vietnam Works to Repatriate Soldiers' Remains," *The Cambodia Daily*, 20 September 2001.

39. "Report on the international state of affairs and activities in foreign affairs of the PRK: Speech by Hun Sen to the Fifth Session of the National Assembly, First Legislature," August 1983.

APPENDIX

SOURCE

Undeclared War against the People's Republic of Kampuchea, Ministry for Foreign Affairs of the PRK Press Department, Phnom Penh, 1985, pp. 66–67. (Official English translation and transliteration of place names).

"The People's Revolutionary Army of Kampuchea is maturing in the struggle against its enemies. During the 1984–1985 dry season the PRAK servicemen carried out, jointly with Vietnamese volunteers, a series of successful operations against armed units of the reactionary Khmer groupings and routed eighteen Pol Pot, Son Sann and Sihanouk bases on the Kampuchea-Thai border. The counterrevolution now has not a single inch of land left on the territory of People's Kampuchea.

The chart on the following page shows the counterrevolutionaries' bases, the dates when they were wiped out, and the losses suffered by the enemy."

1. North-West Tropienkul, the Fulro Base, January 4–5, 1985. 901 men were put out of action and 4,221 weapons, 400 tons of ammunition and 14 motor vehicles captured.

2. Phnom Kombot, Choem Khsan, March 18–December 22, 1984. 160 men were put out of action and 372 weapons captured.

3. North-East Olongven, February 25–March 8, 1985. 263 men were put out of action and 42 weapons captured.

4. Chong Chaom, February 25–March 11, 1985. 1,200 men were put out of action, including a Sihanouk general killed during the operation, and 1,500 weapons captured.

5. North-East Yingdonkum, December 25, 1984. 31 men were put out of action, 35 weapons captured, and an A–37 plane was shot down.

6. North-West Ampil, March 5, 1985. 150 men were put out of action and 100 weapons captured.

THAILAND

Si Sophon

Siem Reap

Battambang

Pursat

Kompong Thom

PEOPLE'S REPUBLIC
OF KAMPUCHEA

PHNOM PENH

Kompong Thom

Kampot

7. Srodai, Ampil, January 7, 1985. 500 men were put out of action and 1,300 weapons captured.

8. Phnom Chhokro, December 25, 1984. 150 men were put out of action and 50 weapons and 20 tons of provisions captured.

9. North-West Yingdonkum, December 25, 1984. 150 men were put out of action and 269 weapons and 30 tons of provisions captured.

10. Nong Samet, Nong Chan, February 18-26, 1985. 130 men were put out of action and 93 weapons captured.

11. Phnom Malai, January 6–February 13, 1985. 80 men were put out of action and 250 weapons and 15 tons of provisions captured.

12. Luda, January 31–February 13, 1985. 250 men were put out of action and 800 weapons captured.

13. Chamkasrev, January 11, 1985. 274 men were put out of action and 100 weapons captured.

14. Soksan, December 11, 1984. 26 men were put out of action and 100 weapons captured.

15. West Smetdaeng, January 2–7, 1985. 150 men were put out of action and 44 weapons, 10 tons of ammunition and 1.6 tons of provisions captured.

16. Thalbien Headquarters, February 8–11, 1985. 223 men were put out of action and 1,177 weapons, 75 tons of mortar and artillery shells, 13 motor vehicles and 84 tons of provisions captured.

17. West Pursat, October 2–7, 1984. 100 men were put out of action and 50 weapons captured.

18. Hill 322, December 21–22, 1984. 380 men were put out of action and 121 weapons, 150 tons of ammunition and 25 tons of provisions captured.

CHRONOLOGY

The multiple sources for this chronology appear in the bibliography. Few sources are quoted directly.

1930: Indochinese Communist Party (ICP) founded with responsibility over Vietnam, Cambodia and Laos.

1941: Japanese march into Phnom Penh. Thailand takes advantage of French defeats in Europe and regains control over most of Cambodia's northwest. King Monivong dies and Sihanouk (his 19-year-old grandson) is crowned king by the Vichy French.

1942: Son Ngoc Thanh organizes the first anti-French demonstrations in Phnom Penh in support of the Buddhist nationalists. In Bangkok, Cambodians have established Issarak (Freedom) committees against the French.

1945: The Japanese remove the Vichy French in Cambodia in a *coup de force* and grant Cambodia its "independence" under Sihanouk (13 March). The only minister with genuine nationalist credentials is Song Ngoc Thanh, minister of foreign affairs.

In the "Palace Coup" on 9 August, Sihanouk is forced to appoint Thanh prime minister.

World War II ends and the French return to Cambodia. On 15 October, Thanh is forced into exile in Saigon, then France.

In Hanoi, on 2 September, Ho Chi Minh declares Vietnam independent from France.

Ho dissolves the ICP. Separate national parties will emerge in the 1950s.

1946: The First Indochina War begins between Ho Chi Minh's Vietminh army and the French.

A 67-member Cambodian Constituent Assembly is elected 1 September. Democrat Party (moderate nationalist, founded 1946 in Phnom Penh, with leader Prince Sisowath Yuthevong) wins 50 seats.

1947: Sihanouk approves constitution on 15 July (drafted by Yuthevong who died before the National Assembly met, modeled closely on Fourth French Republic). Fresh elections in December; Democrats win.

1948: Khmer "Issarak" Committee formed in western Cambodia (original group formed 1940). Highly factionalized.

1949: Saloth Sar travels to Paris for studies and stays until 1953 when he returns to Cambodia a committed communist.

Sihanouk dissolves the Assembly and postpones elections. He forms a new government, responsible only to himself, of right-wing Democrats led by Yem Sambaur.

1950: Pro-Vietnamese UIF (United Issarak Front) formed 19 April led by ICP member Son Ngoc Minh.

1951: The Khmer People's Revolutionary Party is created out of the Indochinese Communist Party in June (later to be redated 30 September by Democratic Kampuchea).

Lao Dong Party created with Ho as chair and Truong Chinh as general-secretary.

19 June: first unified command when the VVAK (Vietnamese Volunteers Army in Kampuchea), following directive by Le Duc Tho, decide to create the Khmer Issarak armed forces.

New elections in August give large majority to Democrats under Huy Kanthol.

Son Ngoc Thanh returns to Cambodia in late October.

1952: Sihanouk dismisses government, 15 June, forming new government with himself as prime minister; rules by decree, thus putting an end to political pluralism.

1953: Sihanouk finally moves against Democrats, thereby aligning himself with Lon Nol and the right. At end of January, he appoints a new government headed by Penn Nouth. He begins his "Royal Crusade for Cambodian Independence" in France and in western capitals; wins limited independence from France, 9 November.

1954: Ho Chi Minh's army defeats the French at Dien Bien Phu. The Geneva Conference convenes to settle the Korean and Indochinese conflicts; Vietminh forces would withdraw from Cambodia and Laos. Cambodian Communists and Issaraks not allotted regoupment areas. Cambodian communist leader Son Ngoc Minh and roughly half of the Cambodian communist movement go into exile in North Vietnam.

1955: Cambodian elections. Sihanouk abdicates in favor of his father, Suramarit, and with his new movement, the *Sangkum* sweeps the election on 11 September. *Sangkum* wins all 91 Assembly seats and 82 percent of the vote with Democrats gaining 12 percent and *Pracheachon* (Keo Meas, Non Suon) just 4 percent.

Military aid agreement signed with US in May.

1955–60: Cambodian communists concentrate on organizing in Phnom Penh as well as in the countryside.

1958: *Sangkum* wins massive victory in Assembly elections; alone amongst the opposition, *Pracheachon* fielded five candidates, four of whom withdrew at the last minute. Only Keo Meas wins a seat in Phnom Penh. Sihanouk selects all *Sangkum* candidates, including a few young, left-wing intellectuals including Hou Yuon, Hu Nim and Chau Sau, who all were given cabinet posts.

1959: An attempted coup led by Sam Sary and Dap Chhuon.

The in-country leader of the Cambodian communist movement, Sieu Heng, publicly defects to Sihanouk's Royal Government.

1960: Suramarit dies. Sihanouk's neutralist policies are approved by national referendum and the prince is appointed chief-of-state and his mother, Kossamak, appointed to symbolize the throne.

Communists hold secret congress on 30 September in Phnom Penh railway station and found a Cambodian Marxist-Leninist party, the Workers Party of Kampuchea (to be renamed the Communist Party of Kampuchea in 1966). Tou Samouth elected party general secretary, Nuon Chea deputy and Saloth Sar as third-ranking politburo member. Ieng Sary is elected to the central committee.

1962: General elections and all 77 *Sangkum* candidates are returned unopposed. Sihanouk incorporates a number of members of the *Sangkum*'s left-wing faction into his new cabinet, including Khieu Samphan, Hou Yuon and Hu Nim.

20 July: Pol Pot becomes acting CPK general secretary following the disappearance of Tou Samouth.

National Census: of economically active population age 10+, 80 percent engaged in agriculture and forestry; 65,000 professional and technical workers (equal to 2.6 percent of national workforce); artisans and factory workers equal 4.1 percent; small numbers of transport, mining, retail trade workers; government and military employees and religious leaders make up the rest. Of entire population age 10+, 57 percent are illiterate; only 2 percent have graduated from primary school, 0.4 percent have graduated from secondary school. Of those literate or with any education, the vast majority are males. (see Banister)

1963: On 20–21 February, Pol Pot is confirmed as Cambodian Communist Party leader at the third party congress in Phnom Penh. Membership of new politburo and central committee confirms dominant position of Saloth Sar's supporters and the weakening of the position of the old Viet Minh-trained revolutionaries.

Sihanouk publishes a list of leading subversives. Saloth Sar and Ieng Sary flee Phnom Penh to build their movement in the maquis.

19 November: Sihanouk renounces US economic and military aid, alleging that Washington was supporting right-wing rebels operating from Thailand and South Vietnam. Funding replaced by increased aid from USSR and China. New economic measures include nationalization of all banking business and import-export businesses.

1964: Cambodia complains to Security Council about incursions of US-South Vietnamese forces. Cambodian relations with South Vietnam had deteriorated rapidly during 1963 as a result of the incursions and accusations by Saigon that Sihanouk was allowing NLF and NVA troops to establish bases in eastern Cambodia. Diplomatic relations broken off in late August.

1965: The US and Australia send combat troops into Vietnam for the first time.

Late that year and early 1966, Pol Pot spends five months in China.

1966: De Gaulle visits Cambodia in September and condemns US policy in Southeast Asia.

11 September: general elections are held but this time Sihanouk does not designate the candidates and well over 400 candidates stand. Although new assembly is dominated by the *Sangkum* right, led by Lon Nol, Khieu Samphan, Hou Yuon and Hu Nim on the left are elected with large majorities. Lon Nol is appointed prime minister (Sihanouk appoints a left-wing "counter-government").

Sihanouk allows Vietnamese communists use of border areas and a seaport.

1967: Peasant-led insurrection (April–August) against rice tax in Samlaut in the northwest following government policy forcing peasants to sell their rice crop to the state to pre-empt sales to the NLF. Sihanouk accuses the communists (KR) and on 22 April names Khieu Samphan and Hou Yuon as responsible for Samlaut insurrection. They flee Phnom Penh. Student demonstrations in Phnom Penh in protest over their "murder."

30 April: Lon Nol resigns after car crash; Sihanouk forms emergency government headed by Son Sann.

1968: KR launch widespread guerrilla campaign throughout (western) countryside in January, spreading to over half the provinces by the end of the year. Sihanouk steps up repression of the left.

Lon Nol returns as defense minister to halt rapidly deteriorating security situation.

1969: US begins secretly to bomb Cambodia (key NVA positions in the east) in March. Sihanouk announces resumption of diplomatic relations with the US (Emory Swank, ambassador).

NLF forms a provisional revolutionary government which Sihanouk recognizes.

Lon Nol appointed prime minister in August, Sirik Matak as his deputy, of a right-wing cabinet; serious blow to Sihanouk's personal authority and his neutralist policies.

Ho Chi Minh dies.

1970: 18 March, Sihanouk overthrown.

In March, anti-Viet Cong riots in the southeast spreading to Phnom Penh where demonstrators attack the North Vietnamese and PRG embassies. Lon Nol issues ultimatum ordering all Vietnamese troops to withdraw from Cambodian territory. (Banister & Johnson claim 200,000 Vietnamese citizens of Cambodia expelled to Vietnam; reported that 5,000 Khmer communists—the 1954 Khmer Vietminh group—returned to Cambodia after coup).

23 March: Sihanouk announces he has formed an anti-Lon Nol resistance with the KR (National United Front of Kampuchea, FUNK) and on 24 March issues a communiqué calling on his supporters to take up arms against Lon Nol. In the countryside, there is an almost spontaneous outburst of unrest with mass demonstrations in Kompong Cham, Siem Reap and Takeo (brutally suppressed by army with hundreds of peasants killed and thousands arrested). Resistance forces, Khmer Rumdoh, swell from four thousand in March to 30,000 in 1975, trained by Vietnamese.

May: US/ARVN forces invade Cambodia; in response the Vietnamese communist forces' move deeper into southern and eastern Cambodia.

Sihanouk and KR form a government-in-exile in China with Beijing-based GRUNK, headed by Penn Nouth.

9 October: the Khmer Republic is proclaimed and the monarchy officially abolished.

1971: 20 October, state of emergency declared (deteriorating security situation, inflation); on 16 October the National Assembly is deprived of its legislative powers. In December, Lon Nol launches Chenla II with terrible casualties. Relations between Khmer Rouge and Khmer Rumdoh strained by this stage (operating separately by end of 1972).

1972: In June, Presidential Palace in Phnom Penh is bombed by So Pothra (husband of Botum Bopha, favorite daughter of Sihanouk; he then flew off to the KR-controlled zone); forty-seven killed but Lon Nol unhurt; state of emergency declared.

1971–1972, several hundred Cambodian communists sent from Hanoi to aid the revolution (some of them had been in exile in Vietnam since 1954); were suspected of Vietnamese sympathies and in 1972–1973 most of them were secretly purged; by end of 1972 when Vietnamese communist troops withdrew from Cambodia (part of ceasefire agreements reached in Paris by Vietnam with US), the KR leadership was in the hands of those who had remained in Cambodia in the 1950s and 1960s and were antipathetic to Vietnam.

1973: 24–26 January, Kissinger's demand for KR–Lon Nol negotiations is rejected by Pol Pot; Pham Hung warns this will bring heavy punishment from US.

27 January, Paris Agreement on ending the war in Vietnam is signed; Cambodian communists refuse to negotiate despite US pressure on the republican government to broaden its base; the intensive B-52 bombing begins and continues until August (257,465 tons of bombs).

KR take over majority of the fighting in Cambodia while the Vietnamese communists retreat to border areas.

February and March, Sihanouk visits the liberated zones.

11 May: In Tam again appointed to post of prime minister. He resigns on 7 December and is replaced by Long Boret.

15 August: US bombing of Cambodia ends after Congress blocks funding following miscalculated hit on Neak Luong, killing over 130 people, mainly civilians.

The KR order the creation of cooperatives in all their zones.

By year end, reports of armed clashes between KR and Khmer Rumdoh units (see Nayan Chanda, 72).

1974: Lon Nol proposes unconditional peace talks with the KR, bowing to pressure from the US (who were prepared to accept a Laotian-style coalition government) but rejected within hours by Sihanouk (who had lost control of the FUNK). The KR win control over the insurgency movement, purging communists returned from North Vietnam and ethnic Vietnamese.

Population Movements: In period 1971–1974, 34,000 refugees to Thailand and another 120,000 (mostly ethnic Vietnamese) to Vietnam. (see Banister)

1975: KR enter Phnom Penh on 17 April and city is evacuated.

24 April: Ieng Sary returns to Phnom Penh from China where he had asked for direct commodity aid, no longer through Vietnam.

30 April: fall of Saigon.

Early May: Democratic Kampuchea orders its armed forces to land on Phu Quoc island; attack Tho Chu island and encroach on Vietnamese territory in a number of border regions from Ha Tien to Tay Ninh with loss of life; later KR say its lack of topographical knowledge was responsible; 515 Vietnamese residents of Tho Chu were abducted and killed.

12 May: *Mayaguez* captured by KR sailors, leading to US bombing and major incident.

14 June: Vietnam seizes Puolo/Koh Wai (returned to Cambodia on August 10).

June: Pol Pot goes to Hanoi and Beijing for unpublicized meetings. Negotiations begin on arms aid (see Nayan Chanda, 14).

18 August: China pledges generous economic aid ($1 billion over five years including $20m in grant aid) to visiting DK delegation.

By September, more than 150,000 Vietnamese have flooded into Dong Thap, An Giang, Tay Ninh (ethnic Khmer and Chinese forced to returned); KR territorial invasions continue in late 1975 and early 1976.

At year's end, the second evacuation of city people from Southwest to Northwest occurs inside Cambodia.

Population movements: 10,400 Cambodians fled to Laos (returned by 1987 under agreement between Lao PDR and PRK).

1976: 5 January: DK Constitution.

Early February: secret Sino-Cambodian military aid agreement (demonstration of their shared perception of Vietnamese hegemony as the region's principal menace).

12 February: joint Lao-VN communique declaring a "special relationship" and promise to increase solidarity among Laos, Cambodia, Vietnam.

20 March: elections to the People's Representative Assembly.

2 April: Sihanouk resigns as head of state (had returned in September 1975); kept under "palace" arrest.

13, 14 April: DK government is announced with a new cabinet headed by Pol Pot following three-day meeting of Assembly.

4–18 May: preparatory meeting for a proposed June summit between Vietnam and DK to discuss border issue is suspended at request of Kampuchean side and border incidents continue but decrease in number until beginning of 1977.

2 July: official reunification and renaming of the PRG and DRV governments as the Socialist Republic of Vietnam

End of August: Three-day meeting ends with DK decision to totally collectivize agriculture and industry and to introduce nationwide communal kitchens.

9 September: death of Mao Zedong (Zhou Enlai had died 8 January).

27 September: Pol Pot temporarily resigns (nominally for health reasons) and Nuon Chea is acting PM). Pol Pot reemerges in late October and from then into the next year launches war against rival pro-Hanoi zonal armies and their supporters. 250 top party, army, administrative officials in every region and many thousands of CPK members eliminated.

6 October: arrest of the Gang of Four and Cultural Revolution is finished.

1977: First three weeks of January, Kampuchean regular forces attack civilian settlements in six Vietnamese border provinces.

24 February: Beijing announces no new aid to Vietnam; no rapprochement.

15–28 March: almost daily encroachments on Vietnamese territory from Ha Tien to An Giang provinces (about 100km stretch of border).

Late March: KR decision to begin campaign to physically exterminate all ethnic Vietnamese still remaining in Cambodia and to go on the offensive in attacking Viet Nam.

30 April: KR attacks on villages and townships in An Giang, killing civilians and burning houses; timed to coincide with second anniversary of the liberation of Saigon and with preparations for May Day.

April, May: escalation of border incursions (terrible attacks on An Giang, particularly on night of 30 April preceding Vietnamese anniversary celebrations and May Day celebrations, as well as major military buildup with Chinese military assistance, increasing KR army from six divisions in 1975 to eleven by April. Vietnam retaliates with aerial bombing but neither side reports developments along border.

12 May: Hanoi announces that its economic zone extends to 200 miles from its shores.

7 June: Central Committee of VCP sends letter to DK side giving accounts of Kampuchea violations and proposing talks to stop such incidents; no response.

8 June: Pham Van Dong's acrimonious encounter with Li Xiannian adds urgency to Hanoi's search for security (Nayan Chanda, 93).

11 June: Ha Tien shelled and again during raid on 14th; Vietnam proposal for private talks on border rejected. (see Nayan Chanda, 82)

June: Hun Sen flees to Vietnam. (see Nayan Chanda, 197)

17 July: top party cadres of the Eastern Zone gather in a secret location to work out their strategy against VN; resolution urged the combatants to be ready to annihilate the Vietnamese if they invaded Cambodia. (Nayan Chanda, 96)

18 July: Laos and Vietnam sign a 25-year Treaty of Friendship and Cooperation.

24 September: KR attackers kill hundreds of civilians in Tay Ninh Province in a series of raids in which more than 1,000 Vietnamese civilians in a 240 km border stretch are killed by Kampuchean forces between now and November in "acts of barbarism that defy the imagination"; Vietnam counterattacks and three months of armed conflict follow.

27 September: Pol Pot finally emerges as the Communist Party leader in Cambodia.

28 September: Pol Pot begins triumphant tour of China, his first public appearance.

Purge of Northwest Zone begins.

5 October: Chinese military attaché in Phnom Penh signs protocol for delivery of arms, result of agreement for nonrefundable military aid signed in February 1976.

October: Vietnam army launches first important (unpublicized) military operation against Cambodia; moves armored columns up to 15 miles into Svay Rieng and feigns retreat; Hanoi now takes first steps in forming anti-Pol Pot resistance in VN.

3 December: Vice premier (and Politburo member, leader of Dazhai Commune) Chen Yonggui visits Cambodia for 10 days.

17 December: Lao president, Prince Souphanouvong arrives, urges Pol Pot not to disrupt the unity of the three Indochinese countries.

Border war with Vietnam starts (or at least declared public by Kampuchea) 25 December and on 31st Cambodia and Vietnam break off diplomatic relations. Vietnamese infantry and artillery, including elite 9th Division, launch massive attack from half a dozen points and move along Routes 1 and 7; hundreds of Khmer solders killed and wounded. KR retaliate by sending reinforcements to Eastern Zone and win diplomatic coup by denouncing its aggression to the world (see Nayan Chanda, 214). Third Indochina War begins.

Population Movements: 60,000 Khmers go back to Vietnam with the Vietnamese troops; since 1975, some 300,000 Khmer, Vietnamese and Chinese refugees had escaped to Vietnam; now army-assisted exodus was presented to the world and UNHCR asked to assist the displaced. Vietnamese recruit and train men and women to fight Pol Pot.

1978: 6 January: Vietnamese troops withdraw; KR present this as a great historic victory publicly but begin new and ferocious wave of purges.

10 January: China signs annual agreement on supply of goods and payments with Vietnam (not yet ready to openly pressure Vietnam, wary of Vietnam's steadily growing ties with Moscow).

18 January: Madame Deng Yingchao (wife of Zhou Enlai) visits Cambodia to urge moderation; is refused permission to see Sihanouk; suggestions of moderation in relations with Vietnam also rejected.

5 February: Hanoi proposes ceasefire and negotiation with Cambodia (Vietnamese negotiator makes secret trip to Peking).

Mid-February: meeting of Vietnamese Politburo to study plan for setting up a Cambodian resistance organization; then Le Duan and Le Duc Tho (who takes over responsibility of directing Hanoi's Cambodia policy) meet separately with Cambodian party cadres of the 1954 school and those escaped from the purges; Say Phouthang still leading armed resistance within Southwest Zone.

24 March: Vietnamese government moves against markets of Cholon; currency of the South abolished on 3 May (estimated that more than half the money in circulation and most of gold and dollar holdings in the South were in Cholon, a virtual economic counter-power).

April: massive exodus of the Hoa from Vietnam triggers crisis in Sino-Vietnam relations.

22 April: First Khmer rebel brigade formed in Vietnam.

10 May: Radio Phnom Penh broadcasts the call to exterminate the Vietnamese race and "purify" its ranks.

24 May: Pol Pot launches full-scale attack against the Eastern Zone. So Phim dies in action or commits suicide; Heng Samrin, commander of 4th Division, and about 1,000 loyal troops go to the jungle; other zonal leaders like Chea Sim, Mat Ly, Men Chhan, Uk Bun Chhoeun and Sim Kar take to the jungle with some 3,000 armed men and 30,000 civilians and for almost two months after the end of May, Kompong Cham, Prey Veng and Svay Rieng are a battlefield for hit-and-run attacks against Central troops, communal kitchens destroyed, cattle and communal property divided.

China denounces Vietnam for treatment of ethnic Chinese.

June: Vietnam makes crucial decision to use military force against Pol Pot. Hanoi starts Khmer-language broadcasts calling for an uprising. Historic turning point for Vietnamese revolution to affect Vietnam's relations with all major power and with Southeast Asian neighbors as well as organization of the domestic economy.

28 June: Vietnam joins COMECON.

3 July: China halts economic and technical aid to Vietnam following Vietnam's admission to COMECON on June 28; decides to "teach Vietnam a lesson" for its arrogant and ungrateful "behavior ($20 billion given by China as aid during the war) and would show Moscow that China was ready to stand up to its bullying.

End July: Son Sen in Beijing seeking China's military commitment against Vietnam; is urged to bring back Sihanouk to head the government. Airlift of arms and ammunition to Cambodia, along with hundreds of advisers.

July: vengeance killings begin in Eastern Zone (probably more than 100,000 executions) and about one-third of the population were moved to western Cambodia where half of them would die.

Early September: Vietnamese launch another operation inside Cambodia to contact Heng Samrin and his followers and escort them back to Vietnam.

21–22 September: Le Duc Tho meets with KR defectors and survivors of the 1954 school and decides to make a decisive military push against Pol Pot in December; work begins to set up the Kampuchean National United Front for National Salvation.

11 October: President Carter shelves normalization with Hanoi pending the establishment of ties with Beijing.

By 12 October: Vietnamese divisions deployed in Dac Lac, Tay Ninh, An Giang provinces and MiGs on standby at Chu Lai, Bien Hoa and Can Tho air bases in the South; special defence precautions in Ho Chi Minh City. Vietnamese units actually occupy stretches of Cambodian territory along border.

3 November: Vietnam signs 25-year friendship treaty with Moscow. USSR granted facilities for Soviet navy and air force in Vietnam as price for Soviet insurance against China. Vietnam is promised all arms and equipment needed and economic assistance including emergency food aid of 1.5 m tons of grain. Vietnam, brought to disastrous dependence on one large friend.

5 November: another Chinese delegation visits Cambodia (KR had begun campaign to improve its international image by hosting a series of friendly delegations; of concern to Vietnam); Deng Xiaoping tours noncommunist Southeast Asia.

November: Khmer Kampuchea Krom youth recruited into the liberation movement; 500 sent to Ca Mau for military training; would accompany Vietnamese units in drive into Takeo in January 1979. Operation in Kratie mid-month secured area for use as a 'liberated zone', chosen as site to unveil the FUNSK. (For description of event see Nayan Chanda, 339)

3 December: formation of a Cambodian national salvation front, FUNSK, led by Heng Samrin and a 14-member central committee (in the 'liberated zone' of about 600 sq. miles of Krek, Memot and Snoul

districts held by the Vietnamese troops. An eleven-point program is adopted which includes among its aims the overthrow of the "reactionary Pol Pot–Ieng Sary clique" and the introduction of policies 'tending towards genuine socialism'.

15 December: US-China normalization.

25 December: Vietnam and United Front forces advance into Cambodia (100,000 VN troops and air force along with 20,000 Front soldiers). (See Nayan Chanda, 341)

Population Movements: From 1975–1978, 34,039 refugees to Thailand; 150,000 mainly Chinese and Khmer Cambodians to Vietnam.

1979: 2 January: Sihanouk smuggled out to China; CPK formally decides to abandon cities and resume guerrilla war.

5 January: Capture of Takeo; congress in Memot to reorganize the party, Kampuchean People's Revolutionary Party.

7 January: DK leadership departs Phnom Penh by train; Vietnam/FUNSK capture Phnom Penh; newly formed party immediately called on to assign duties among 66 delegates assembled for congress (elected seven-member Standing Committee headed by Pen Sovann).

January 8: announcement of the establishment of the eight-person People's Revolutionary Council to rule Cambodia, headed by Heng Samrin.

11 January: Ieng Sary goes to Beijing to seek aid for DK.

12 January: The PRK is founded, quickly recognized by Vietnam, Laos and the USSR and allies. Many western countries announce cessation of aid to Hanoi.

12 (or 13) January: ASEAN calls for immediate withdrawal of Vietnamese forces from Cambodia (but Sino-Thai agreement providing for use of Thai territory to arm the KR); Vietnam and PRK exchange ambassadors.

14 January: secret Thai-Chinese meeting to support guerrilla war against Vietnamese in Cambodia.

End January: by now, some 17 regular PLA divisions (c.225,000 men) assembled near Vietnamese border.

16 February: Pham Van Dong arrives in Phnom Penh and 25-year friendship treaty with Vietnam is signed during the visit (military clauses provide legal grounds for presence of Vietnamese troops in Cambodia).

17 February: Chinese offensive against northern Vietnamese provinces (One-Month War with human wave tactics but PLA suffer heavy casualties; a war nobody won).

17 March: Hun Sen admits presence of Vietnamese troops in Cambodia for first time (not until July did Vietnamese acknowledge they had played a role in overthrowing Pol Pot).

19 March: Sihanouk breaks relations with KR against Chinese advice.

23 March: Treaty of Friendship in Phnom Penh between PRK and Lao PDR.

21 April: 50,000 refugees cross into Thailand; Thai soldiers drive many back into Cambodia to be executed by the oncoming KR; when fighting subsides in late June, there are at least 250,000 Cambodians along border in camps.

In Cambodia, people organized for agricultural production with partial recollectivization in May (15-family solidarity teams).

8 June: Thai authorities attempt forcible repatriation of more than 42,000 Cambodian illegal immigrants (trucked to Preah Vihear temple, given food for eight days); international outcry.

June: US agrees to send aid, but only to Thai border area.

June and July: DK attacks in cultivated areas mean agricultural production at virtual standstill.

2 July: Cyrus Vance, US Secretary of State, calls for direct famine relief to Cambodia but waits three months before US makes a contributions (in October).

20 July: major conference on Indo-Chinese refugees in Geneva.

15–20 August: People's Revolutionary Tribunal opens in Phnom Penh to try Pol Pot and Ieng Sary *in absentia*.

5 September: Pham Van Dong declares the situation in Cambodia to be "irreversible" at Havana Meeting of the Non-Aligned Nations.

Famine decimates the DK ranks and UNICEF and ICRC begin to supply them with food.

21 September: DK wins Kampuchean seat in the UN by 71 votes to 35 with 34 abstentions.

26 September: Phnom Penh grants approval to UNICEF and ICRC for large-scale relief operations in Cambodia.

29 September: Second Congress of the FUNSK; Heng Samrin re-elected president; Central Committee enlarged from 14 to 35, of whom 15 are of non-communist background.

9 October: Formation of KPNLF led by Son Sann with Chheam Vorm and Dien Del on the border said to have forces of 5,000 men.

19 October: Thai government declares open door policy to all Indochinese people seeking asylum; this leads to major international aid effort and building of Khao I Dang with housing for 200,000 which opens on 21 November (numbers peaked in May, 1980 at 130,000).

Massive aid shipments provided by UNICEF, ICRC and a number of voluntary agencies arrive in Kompong Som and Phnom Penh.

November: Vietnam secures effective military control over most important parts of the country.

5–17 December: KR Congress creates a new government with Khieu Samphan as prime minister in place of Pol Pot, commander-in-chief of armed forces and CPK Secretary.

December: Soviet invasion of Afghanistan.

Population movements: By December 1979, perhaps one million Khmers encamped along border in the flat country north of Aranyaprathet, living on aid and trade spin-offs (see Evans and Rowley).

1980: January: Foreign ministers of Lao, Cambodia and Vietnam meet in Phnom Penh to announce a unified stand on Cambodian problem and other international issues (beginning of regular bi-annual affairs).

20 March: Decision on reintroduction of money to encourage private enterprise and the expansion of agricultural production.

First DK dry season counter-offensive declared: attacks on trains and lorry convoys.

April: currency introduced (4 *riel* =$1, black market rate 16r=$1)

June: trial of Hem Krishna and fifteen other members of the *Sereikar* underground movement (11 of them were officials of PRK).

5–7 June: Hem Krishna and accomplices sentenced; other underground movements crushed, e.g. "Movement of the Khmer Soul" headed by In Sothea.

Vietnam begins withdrawing administrative advisers and by end of year about half have withdrawn.

17 June: Thailand starts repatriating Cambodian refugees (9,000, most from Sa Kaeo camp controlled by KR), prompting Vietnam forces to launch a surprise attack along the boundary and into Thailand on 23rd and seal the border north of Aranyaprathet, halting cross-border relief operations and further repatriations; unanimously denounced by ASEAN.

7 July: India officially recognizes the Heng Samrin regime, the only non-communist Asian country to do so.

September: DK defeats move to have the Kampuchea seat in UN declared vacant;

November: Le Duc Tho (in charge of whole Kampuchea dossier) makes secret visit to Phnom Penh and conducts training course at the Palace for top officials of PRK focusing on the "new state" of the Kampuchean revolution, the current political status of Kampuchea, the organization of the PRK central government and its relations with foreign countries.

Year-end administrative population count shows that midyear population was 6.50m (86 percent male), then adjusted to 6.59m at end of year. Projection from last (1962) census was 9.3m (see Banister & Johnson). From this demographic data, Banister & Johnson conclude there was no nationwide famine 1979–1980 despite severe food shortages in several regions.

1979–1980 Population movements: 100,000 return from Vietnam; 172,380 flee regional food crises and travel to Thailand.

1980: large-scale Vietnamese immigration, including many of those who had migrated to Vietnam 1970–1978. Estimated total of 500,000 by 1991, admitted by Phnom Penh officials to the Economist Intelligence Unit.

By year end, KR fighting force estimated at 40,000.

1981: January: Hanoi, Vientiane and Phnom Penh call for a regional conference of Southeast Asian nations to discuss Kampuchean question.

25 February: Food and Agriculture Organization releases report on food situation in Cambodia—widespread starvation had been overcome but economy remained extremely fragile and without further international assistance, serious malnutrition could quickly return. During 1981 poor weather conditions (flooding in southeast and drought in the west and southwest) meant the food situation deteriorated again, making Cambodia dependent on relief aid during the 1982 wet season.

March: Funcinpec organized with Sihanouk as president and In Tam vice president and commander in chief of the armed forces. The front represents a regrouping of some dozen organizations.

1 May: election of a National Assembly and local elections by people living in government-controlled areas; 117 seats contested by 148 candidates with 99.17 percent of the 3,417,339 electors voting.

26 May: Fourth Congress of the KPRP opens in Phnom Penh. Front is renamed Kampuchean United Front for National Construction and Defence (KUFNCD) as a mass organization assisting the Party.

27 June: PRK Constitution adopted and Council of State and a Council of Ministers to replace the PRC, with party general secretary and defense minister, Pen Sovann, as prime minister, thereby confirming his position as the dominant figure in the regime.

13 July: UN international conference on Cambodia (representatives of 79 countries plus observers from 25 others) opens in New York and adopts resolution calling for the withdrawal of Vietnamese forces (Cambodia represented by KR government; representatives from PRK not invited).

4 September: Under pressure from the West, China and ASEAN, Sihanouk, Son Sann and Khieu Samphan meet in Singapore and "agree to express the desire to form a united front" to combat the PRK and SRV.

4 December: Pen Sovann is ousted as general secretary of the PRPK and is replaced by Heng Samrin.

6 December: DK announces the end of the CPK. By year end, the guerrilla war had increased sharply, rendering large parts of Cambodia insecure.

First withdrawal of Vietnamese forces takes place with 137th division leaving (not witnessed by foreign observers).

Population Movements: few arrivals to Thai camps documented but by 1981, over 300,000 of the refugees had found permanent residence in France, Australia, the US and elsewhere; a similar number remained in the camps (Chandler, in Mabbett, 254)

1982: 27 March: Fifth Congress of the Vietnamese Communist Party.

May: directive of Council of Ministers approves settlement of Vietnamese who had come into Cambodia since 1979 "engaged in occupations which contribute to the rehabilitation and development of the economy" (see Nayan Chanda, 454).

22 June: Coalition Government of Democratic Kampuchea (CGDK) of three rebel factions created in Kuala Lumpur with Sihanouk president, Khieu Samphan vice president and in charge of foreign affairs, and Son Sann prime minister.

July: Vietnam announces planned withdrawal of troops from Cambodia. On July 14, six "volunteer" units return; border talks in Hanoi (no result).

July: new agreement signed on economic and technological aid with USSR valid for one year, covers agriculture, transport and communications; Air Kampuchea commences, manned by Soviet pilots flying Soviet planes; Kampuchea sends rubber, tobacco, wood and handicraft products to USSR.

25 October: UN General Assembly votes ninety to twenty-nine with twenty-six abstentions to reject Lao amendment to accept committee report except without regard to credentials of DK (the empty chair principle); until now Vietnam has tried to have the PRK replace DK.

27 November: Decree law on income taxes, import taxes passed by State Council; implemented early 1983.

Official birthrate of seven percent (up from 1.93 percent in 1978).

Population Movements: few arrivals to Thai camps documented.

1983: February: Vietnam-Laos-Cambodia Joint Economic Committee established (bi-annual meetings).

1 March: China outlines five-part plan for a Cambodian settlement (includes suggestion of UN-sponsored election).

Late March: annual ASEAN meeting in Bangkok. Thais win out over SRV-Malaysian overtures for talks and possibility of SRV-ASEAN talks failed even to make the agenda.

1 April: Vietnamese forces attack rebel position along the Thai border.

May: black market rate 35–40 *riel* =$1; civil servant salary 120–200r/month; rice costs 3r/kg (1r at state shops).

2 May: first partial withdrawal witnessed by foreign journalists (had been two earlier in 1981 and 1982); up to 10,000 according to Vietnamese and Cambodian claims. Cuu Long group of divisions including one infantry division and six brigades and regiments.

May–July: more than 7,450 refugees to KPNLF camp at Ampil from Siem Reap, Battambang and Oddar Meanchey suggest possible insecurity in the region.

23 July: Sihanouk alleges "hundreds of thousands of Vietnamese colonists" have settled in Cambodia. SRV's Paris Embassy claims that while some 500,000 Vietnamese had lived in Cambodia before 1970, only 30,000 currently live there.

September: Since May, more than 10,000 refugees have arrived in Ampil, with others reported in O'Bok and Sokh Sann.

December: Vietnamese officials admit to "very serious mistakes" some months before in Siem Reap.

Military activity increasing: unofficial figures put PAVN casualties for the year at 2,500; Nationalist army (Son Sann) reportedly has 15,000 trained men; DK said to number 25,000 men.

Population Movements: few arrivals to Thai camps documented.

1984: January: Le Duc Tho chairs political course for KPRP Central Committee and the PRK Council of Ministers.

KPRP Central Committee issues special directive requisitioning all Khmers (aged 18–45) to undertake *"polakam karpie mietophum"* (labor for national defense).

27 January: KR attack Vietnam's main military and logistic supply center in Siem Reap; KR also claim attacks in Kompong Thom, Battambang, Pursat and even the outskirts of Phnom Penh.

2 April: Chinese forces launch shelling campaign against Vietnam and tension along Sino-Vietnam border increases significantly.

6 June: Two PAVN infantry brigades (690, 688), Regiment 550 as well as a number of independent battalions leave Kampuchea.

June–July: clashes between NADK and the ANS (National Sihanoukist Army) and even KPNLF (similar to incidents in 1983); Sihanouk offers his resignation on 6 September proposing that Ranariddh take over as head of the CGDK.

July–August: In France, the "defection" of Keat Chhon (and two Thioun brothers); he had been DK roving ambassador.

August: Intelligence sources say NADK could be 40,000-strong and a group of 200 cadres, trained in China, have recently returned to the battlefield.

18 November: Dry-season offensive begins (first offensive against KPNLF bases), the heaviest to date and by April 1985 almost all of the main rebel bases along the border have been overrun; in February as many

as 18,000 Vietnamese troops succeed in forcing KR out of their stronghold in Phnom Malai.

30 November: Hun Sen in Paris as guest of French Communist MP; told newsmen that a meeting between himself and Sihanouk would be impossible as long as Prince was allied to Pol Pot. French officials have tried to arrange a meeting with Sihanouk but the meeting did not take place; China absolutely opposed to any contact.

December: Field sources say NADK is present in almost every province inside Cambodia and that border camps less and less important as staging posts.

31 December: SPK reports that prime minister Chan Si died of heart disease in Moscow.

Population Movements: at year end, 208,995 Cambodians pushed into Thailand from their camps on the Cambodian side of border following the November offensive.

By 1985, more than 175,000 Vietnamese civilians had settled in Cambodia (according to Fraser, "Vietnam Struggles with Exploding Population" in *Indochina Issues*, No. 57, May 1985, 5).

1985: January 14: Hun Sen elected by National Assembly as chairman of the Council of Ministers.

January: PAVN moves two new divisions in front of Phnom Malai bringing Vietnamese military presence in Kampuchea to the same level as before the various withdrawals (according to Western diplomat). By 18 February, the KR bases were completely lost by NADK.

January: PAVN over-run KPNLF camps (Sikh San, Bakseu, Rythisen, Prey Chan/Nong Chan and, finally, Banteay Ampil the main base and HQ; decision to separate the civilians (to Site 2) and the soldiers and to send a large number of troops now at the border to the interior.

March: ANS lose battle for Tatum and make decision similar to that of KPNLF, civilians mainly in Site B.

3 April: fifth withdrawal of Vietnamese troops (group of 52 divisions including brigades 7703, 7706, 9906). Figures say that 40,000 have left since 1982 when the first withdrawal took place. Assuming originally 200,000, now no more than 150,000–160,000.

Heng Samrin not present at withdrawal parade; constant rumors that he is about to be purged.

3 April: Cabinet meeting of CGDK; Khieu Samphan says situation would become more complicated for the Vietnamese now that the border camps have been eliminated, with resistance moving around and more difficult to catch; intelligence sources claim KR are setting up strong parallel administration around the Great Lake which takes over control of the area during the night.

24–25 May: SPK announces appointment of Thong Khon as chairman of the PRC of Phnom Penh (Keo Chenda is stood down).

2 August: ANS sabotage team blows up ammunition depot, and Aug. 10, a building located in a Vietnamese military compound in Siem Reap with 34 Vietnamese casualties and at least 27 wounded. ANS agent claims success because of support of soldiers and civilians from the PRK.

16 August: at two-day conference of the Indochinese ministers in Phnom Penh, Vietnam announces target date of 1990 for complete withdrawal (previously 1995); Hun Sen states main reason is success of 1984–1985 dry season offensive. Sihanouk retaliates by warning that one million Vietnamese would be settled in Cambodia by then.

1 September: Pol Pot "retires" as military leader of KR with Son Sen replacing him as commander in chief with Khieu Samphan as KR president. News welcomed by China and ASEAN claiming it removed a serious obstacle to peace talks.

25 September: Announcement of five-year terms of compulsory military service for men aged 18–30. 12 October: Fifth Congress of the Cambodian Communist Party opens with 250 delegates from the party's twenty-two divisions; Heng Samrin re-elected as party general secretary and central committee doubled to 45 (31 full members and fourteen non-voting alternate members) with five new politburo and three new secretariat members elected. Heng Samrin announces details of the country's first five-year plan (1986–1990) to concentrate on food supplies, rubber, timber and aquatic products; existence of a mixed economy was an "objective reality of history." Private sector formally legalized and endorsed.

17 November: Lon Nol dies in exile.

December: major split in KPNLF, mainly over command of military affairs; dissidents to Son Sann regroup under the Provisional Central Committee for Salvation (PCCS).

Population Movements: early in year, towards end of the offensive, assumed that KR military and associated civilian populations crossed into Thailand; estimates of this "hidden population" vary widely but generally range from 50,000 to 100,000; assume a figure of 70,000 (Banister & Johnson).

1986: Dry Season Offensive: characterized by renewed military activities of the resistance forces and the continuation of the K5 Plan started in 1984 to stop further infiltration of men and supplies into Kampuchea; clashes all over the country with main effort at the villages; PAVN use more and more air support; problems of lack of combativity and complicity of PRKAF with the resistance; many defections.

February: Government fiat prolongs the National Assembly of 1981 by a further five-year term.

17 March: CGDK issue their eight-point proposal, the group's national charter (codified in September) with calls for phased withdrawal of Vietnamese forces supported by UN-monitored ceasefire, followed by negotiations leading to free elections and possible formation of a quadripartite coalition. Proposal quickly rejected by Phnom Penh and Vietnam.

18 March: SPK announces Khang Sarin replaced by Ney Pena as interior minister; Sin Song appointed to new Ministry for the Inspection of State Affairs, and Say Chhum replaces Kong Sam Ol at Ministry of Agriculture.

28 March: major resistance coalition attack on Battambang.

By 20 June: Oddar Meanchey and Siem Reap are part of the same administrative entity following a restructuring of the provincial organization.

June: KPRAF celebrate 35th anniversary; important foreign visitors including high-ranking Soviet delegation.

June: Vietnamese troop withdrawal; usual foreign observer skepticism with many of them claiming it is little more than a troop rotation; Hanoi maintains that so far, about one third of its troops have left since 1981.

June (late) to mid-July: series of meetings involving senior Vietnamese military personnel in Siem Reap and border areas and Soviet advisers at a meeting in Samrong.

August: Sihanouk has meetings in Singapore with Lee Kwan Yew and in Jakarta with Suharto.

November: Pol Pot said to have left border headquarters for China and medical treatment; very sick; also rumors of factional struggles within DK.

December: Sixth Congress of the Vietnam Communist Party.

Population Movements: 1986–1989 great deal of movement from Cambodia to Thai border and back, engaging in trade or the guerrilla struggle or just seeking UN-provided food.

1987: 5 January: serious armed clashes on Sino-Vietnam border.

3 June: Amnesty International releases report detailing human rights abuses carried out by the Phnom Penh government and claiming that thousands of political prisoners had been detained without trial and tortured since 1979.

June: supplementary elections for NA held in six provinces increasing the National Assembly to 123 deputies.

27 August and 8 October: PRK program of political settlement based on national reconciliation as main elements.

2–4 December: meeting between Hun Sen and Sihanouk in France represents first substantive negotiations between opposing factions but resulted in little more than an agreement to hold further talks.

1988: 20–21 January: further talks in France between Hun Sen and Sihanouk; Hun Sen announces they are in broad agreement on the question of the political structure of a post-settlement Cambodia but disagreement over timing; Hun Sen wants elections before formation of government and Sihanouk the reverse.

14 March: Sino-Vietnam dispute worsens over the Spratley Islands.

22 June: Do Muoi elected prime minister of SRV.

25–28 July: first face-to-face talks between all Cambodian factions open in Indonesia (JIM 1).

3 November: UN General Assembly and ASEAN-sponsored resolution calls for 'creation of an interim administration authority' to govern the country in the period between a troop withdrawal and free elections; also a seeming attack by ASEAN on KR, affirming that there could be 'no return to universally condemned policies and practices of a recent past' in Cambodia.

Within Cambodia, state firms granted management autonomy and piece rates are introduced to increase production (industry represents only 5 percent of GDP)

1989: 19 February: JIM 2 opens in Jakarta but makes little progress on key issues.

February: PRK government implements its "land to the tiller" program, recognizing private ownership of land and real estate and the rights of inheritance.

5 April: Vietnam sets firm deadline for full troop withdrawal in joint statement by SRV-Lao-Kampuchea announcing all Vietnamese volunteer troops would be withdrawn from Cambodia by the end of September 1989, regardless of whether or not a political solution had been found.

30 April: State of Cambodia replaces the PRK when the National Assembly adopts numerous amendments to the Constitution which had been proposed by an *ad hoc* commission. Flag changed, Buddhism re-established with its pre-1975 prerogatives, death penalty abolished, private property recognized and free market economy introduced (also beginning of separation of powers although political nature of the party remains unchanged).

15–18 May: Cambodia issue is raised at the Sino-Soviet summit in Beijing (the Gorbachev visit). Soviet troop withdrawals from Afghanistan and Mongolia during early 1989 meant that only the Cambodian problem remained as an obstacle to Sino-Soviet normalization.

30 August: Paris International Conference on Cambodia (32 days) ends in stalemate; delegates deeply divided over the issue of the inclusion of the KR in any future Cambodian government.

26 September: Vietnam completes its troop withdrawal from Cambodia; the SRV Defense Ministry announces that approx 23,000 Vietnamese soldiers had died and 55,000 had been wounded since 1979. The vir-

tual collapse of the Paris conference meant that no international supervision mechanism had been established to verify the Vietnamese troop withdrawal; despite Western military assertions to the contrary, both China and Thailand issued statements after the withdrawal alleging that Vietnamese soldiers remained in Cambodia.

22 October: KR guerrillas score major victory, capturing Pailin less than a month after the withdrawal.

1990: 26 February: JIM 3 opens; primarily concerned with a new Australian peace plan which proposed a large-scale UN involvement in Cambodia; received favorably at the UN Security Council in January and February.

9 August: National Assembly session ends after dismissal of Ung Phan (communications minister) and Chheng Phon (propaganda and culture minister) following power struggle in June and July when Chea Sim reportedly had gained ground against Hun Sen.

28 August: Security Council agrees on a Cambodian peace plan (P-5) demanding establishment of a 12-member Supreme National Council composed of Cambodian leaders from all factions. The SNC would occupy Cambodia's seat at the UN but would turn over most of its powers to the UN until the election of a new government; also called for an initial ceasefire followed by phased disarmament and the halt of military supplies to the warring factions.

4 September: secret two-day Sino-Vietnam summit ends in China; discussions centered on Cambodia, the main issue blocking Sino-Vietnamese normalization. On 16 September China opens its southern border with Vietnam at the "Friendship Pass".

10 September: The factions approve the P-5 peace plan at JIM 4 in its entirety and commit themselves to placing it within a comprehensive political settlement at a future meeting of the Paris International Conference on Cambodia. Agreed on the formation of a twelve-member SNC which would also occupy the UN seat during the transitional period.

1991: 1 May, cease-fire proclaimed by all sides in Cambodia (first independent confirmation of its violation came on 19 May with KR artillery attack in Battambang.)

Early June: Jakarta SNC meeting (KR declare the cease-fire over but other three factions broadly observed the cease-fire from 1 May).

6 June: Sihanouk announces his intention to return to Phnom Penh for the first time since 1979, for a two-month visit beginning November 1991.

23 October: Paris Peace Agreement (Agreements on the Comprehensive Political Settlement of the Cambodia Conflict which contains the so-

called UN Plan) signed by the four Cambodian factions and 18 foreign ministers.

1992: March: UN Transitional Authority in Cambodia (UNTAC) established; Yasushi Akashi, UN Special Representative arrives with John Sanderson, Force Commander.

1993: 23 May: national elections.
24 September: adoption of new constitutional monarchy.

BIBLIOGRAPHY

A Group of Cambodian Jurists. *People's Revolutionary Tribunal Held in Phnom Penh for the Trial of the Genocide Crime of the Pol Pot–Ieng Sary Clique, Documents (August, 1979)*, Phnom Penh: Foreign Languages Publishing House, 1990.

Ablin, David A. and Marlowe Hood, eds. *The Cambodian Agony*. Armonk, N.Y.: M.E. Sharpe, 1987.

Abrams, Floyd and Orentlicher, Diane. *Kampuchea: After the Worst— A Report on Current Violations of Human Rights*. New York & Washington: Lawyers Committee for Human Rights, 1985.

Acharya, A., Lizee, P. and Sorpong Peou. *Cambodia—The Paris Peace Conference (1989): Background Analysis and Documents*. Millwood, New York: Kraus International Publications, 1991.

Adamson, Walter L. *Hegemony and Revolution: A Study of Antonio Gramsci's Political and Cultural Theory*. Berkeley: University of California Press, 1980.

Amnesty International Report, *Kampuchea (Cambodia)* 1979, 1986, 1987, 1988.

Artistic Programme: Presented by a group of artists of the People's Republic of Kampuchea in honor of the distinguished delegations of Socialist Republic of Tchecoslovakia, 15 February 1980.

Artistic Programme to be shown at the first anniversary of the birth-day of the People's Republic of Kampuchea.

Ashley, D.W. *Pol Pot, Peasants and Peace: Continuity and Change in Khmer Rouge Political Thinking 1985–1991*, Indochinese Refugee Information Center, Institute of Asian Studies, Chulalongkorn University, October 1992.

Barnett, Anthony. "Inter-Communist Conflicts and Vietnam." *BCAS*, 11, 4, (Oct.–Dec., 1979).

Bartu, Friedemann. "Kampuchea—The Search for a Political Solution Gathers Momentum." *Southeast Asian Affairs*, 1989.

Becker, Elizabeth. "Kampuchea in 1983: Further from Peace." *Asian Survey*, 24,1, (January 1984).

Becker, Elizabeth. "The Progress of Peace in Cambodia." *Current History*, 88, 537, (April 1989).

———. *When the War Was Over*. New York: Simon & Schuster, 1986.

Bekaert, Jacques. *Kampuchea Diary 1983–1986: Selected Articles*. Bangkok: DK Books, 1987.

———. *Cambodian Diary: Tales of a Divided Nation 1983–1986*. Bangkok: White Lotus, 1997.

Boggett, David. "Democratic Kampuchea and Human Rights: Correcting the Record." *AMPO*, 11, 1, (1979).

Bottomore, T. and Goode, P. *Readings in Marxist Sociology*. New York: OUP, 1983.

Bui Tin. *From Cadre to Exile: The Memoirs of a North Vietnamese Journalist*. Chiang Mai: Silkworm Books, 1995.

Bull, David. *The Poverty of Diplomacy: Kampuchea and the Outside World*. Oxford: Oxfam, 1983.

Burchett, Wilfred. *The China Cambodia Vietnam Triangle*. Chicago: Vanguard Books, 1981.

Carney, T.M., ed. *Communist Party Power in Kampuchea (Cambodia): Documents and Discussion*. Ithaca: Cornell University, Southeast Asia Program (Southeast Asia Program, Data Paper No. 106), 1977.

———. "Heng Samrin's Armed Forces and the Military Balance in Cambodia." *International Journal of Politics*, 16, 3, (1986).

———. "Kampuchea in 1981: Fragile Stalemate." *Asian Survey*, 22, 1, (January 1982).

———. "Kampuchea in 1982: Political and Military Escalation." *Asian Survey*, 23, 1, (January 1983).

Chak Saroeun Sakhonn, Dumas Soula Marie-Lucy, Kyheng Chanmalis, Panh Meng Heang. *Cambodge Actuel: Chronologie 1953–1987*. Saint Maur des Fosses: ADECA Editions, 1987.

Chanda, Nayan. *Brother Enemy: The War After the War, A History of Indochina Since the Fall of Saigon*. New York: Macmillan, 1986.

———. "Cambodia in 1986: Beginning to Tire." *Asian Survey*, 27, 1, (January 1987).

———. "Cambodia in 1987: Sihanouk on Center Stage." *Asian Survey*, 28,1, (January 1988).

———. *Cambodia's Future: The View from Vietnam*. Occasional Paper No. 12, Center for Southeast Asian Studies, Uni. Wisconsin, 1987.

———. "Civil War in Cambodia?" (source unknown/CDRI Library, Phnom Penh)

———. "Vietnam's Economy: 'Bad but not Worse.'" *Indochina Issues*, 41 (October 1983).

Chandler, David. *A History of Cambodia,* 2nd ed. Chiang Mai: Silkworm Books, 1993.

———. "A Revolution in Full Spate: Communist Party Policy in Democratic Kampuchea, December 1976." *International Journal of Politics,* 16, 3, (1986).

———. *Australia, Asean and Cambodia.* Melbourne: Dyason House Papers, 10, 1, (September 1983).

———. *Brother Number One: A Political Biography of Pol Pot.* Chiang Mai: Silkworm Books, 1993.

———. "Cambodia in 1984: Historical Patterns Re-Asserted?" *Southeast Asian Affairs,* 1985.

———. *Facing the Cambodian Past: Selected Essays 1971–1994.* Chiang Mai: Silkworm Books, 1996.

———. "Kampuchea: End Game or Stalemate?" *Current History,* 83 (1984).

———. "Reflections on Cambodian History." *Cultural Survival Quarterly,* 14, 3 (1990).

———. "Revising the Past in Democratic Kampuchea: When was the Birthday of the Party." *Pacific Affairs,* 56, 2 (Summer 1983).

———. "Strategies for Survival in Kampuchea." *Current History,* April 1983.

———. "The Constitution of Democratic Kampuchea (Cambodia): The Semantics of Revolutionary Change." *Pacific Affairs,* 49, 3, (University of British Columbia, Fall 1976).

———. *The Tragedy of Cambodian History: Politics, War and Revolution Since 1945.* Chiang Mai: Silkworm Books, 1991.

Chandler, David and Kiernan, Ben eds. *Revolution and Its Aftermath in Kampuchea: Eight Essays.* New Haven, Conn: Yale University (Southeast Asia Studies, Monograph Series No. 25), 1983.

Chandler, David P., Kiernan, Ben and Boua, Chanthou. *Pol Pot Plans the Future: Confidential Leadership Documents from Democratic Kampuchea, 1976–1977.* New Haven, Conn.: Yale University (Southeast Asia Studies, Monograph Series No. 33), 1988.

Chang, C.Y. "The Sino-Vietnam Rift: Political Impact on China's Relations with Southeast Asia." *Contemporary Southeast Asia,* 4, 4 (March, 1983).

Chang Pao-Min. "Beijing Versus Hanoi: The Diplomacy over Kampuchea." *Asian Survey,* 23, 5 (May 1983).

———. *Kampuchea Between China and Vietnam.* National University of Singapore: Singapore University Press, 1985.

———. "Kampuchean Conflict: The Continuing Stalemate." *Asian Survey,* 27, 7 (1987).

Chhab Phseng Phseng [Codes de conduites]. Paris: Cedoreck, 1986.

Chea Chanto. *Samettephal Seddhkech-Sangkumekech robas Pracheachon*

Kampuchea reye pel dop boun chhnam 1979–1993 [Socioeconomic Achievements of the Kampuchean People for the 14 Years, 1979–1993]. Phnom Penh: Faculty of Economics, November 1996.

Chhor Kim Sar, Touch Varine, Kham Phalin, Prak Sophea. *Report: Rural Women and the Socio-Economic Transition in the Kingdom of Cambodia*. Phnom Penh: Ministry of Women's Affairs, 1997.

Chomsky, Noam and Herman, Edward S. *After the Cataclysm: Postwar Indochina and the Reconstruction of Imperial Ideology. Vol. II of The Political Economy of Human Rights*. Boston: South End Press, 1979.

Chufrin, Gennady I. "Five Years of the People's Revolutionary Power in Kampuchea: Results and Conclusions." *Asian Survey*, 24, 11 (November 1984).

Clayton, Thomas. *Education and the Politics of Language: Hegemony and Pragmatism in Cambodia, 1979–1989*. Hong Kong: CERC, The University of Hong Kong, 2000.

Communiques of the Tenth Conference of the Foreign Ministers of Laos, Campuchia and Vietnam (17th and 18th January, 1985). Press Department, Ministry of Foreign Affairs, People's Republic of Kampuchea. January 1985.

Corfield, Justin. *A History of the Cambodian Non-Communist Resistance, 1975–1983*.

Clayton, Victoria: Monash University Centre of Southeast Asian Studies, 1991.

———. *Khmers Stand Up!: A History of the Cambodian Government 1970–1975*. Monash Papers on Southeast Asia, No. 32, Monash University Centre of Southeast Asian Studies, 1994.

Correze, Francoise *Kampuchea:Espoirs-Réalités*. Hanoi: Fleuve Rouge, 1982.

Crimes des Dirigeants Chinois contra le Kampuchea. Ministère des Affaires Étrangères de la République Populaire du Kampuchea. Phnom Penh, Avril 1984.

Curtis, Grant. *Cambodia: A Country Profile* fiA Report Prepared for the Swedish International Development Authority. Phnom Penh, August 1989.

Davies, James C. "Toward A Theory of Revolution." *American Sociological Review*, 27,1 (Feb. 1962), pp. 5–19.

Declaration of the People's Republic of Kampuchea on the Political Solution to the Kampuchean Problem, October 8 1987. Ministry for Foreign Affairs Press Department, Phnom Penh.

"Democratic Kampuchea's Statement on General Elections." Source: Monitoring Digest, 76, 1981, 2 April 1981. *Journal of Contemporary Asia*, 3, 1 (1981).

Desbarats, Jacqueline. *Prolific Survivors: Population Change in Cambo-*

dia 1975–1993. Program for Southeast Asian Studies, Arizona State University, 1995.

Documents on the Kampuchean Problem, 1979–1985. Department of Political Affairs, Ministry of Foreign Affairs, Bangkok, Thailand.

Duiker, William J. "The Legacy of History in Vietnam." *Current History*, 83 (1984).

Ea Meng-Try. "Cambodia:A Country Adrift." *Population and Development Review*, 7, 2 (June 1981), pp. 209–28.

Ebihara, M. "Return to a Khmer Village." *Cultural Survival Quarterly*, 14, 33 (1990).

Ebihara, May M. Mortland, Carol A., and Ledgerwood, Judy eds. *Cambodian Culture Since 1975*. Ithaca: Cornell University Press, 1994.

Eiland, Michael. "Kampuchea in 1984: Yet Further From Peace." *Asia Survey*, January 1985.

———. "Cambodia in 1985: From Stalemate to Ambiguity." *Asian Survey*, 26, 1 (January 1986).

Elliott, David W. P. ed. *The Third Indochina Conflict*. Boulder, Colorado: Westview Press, 1981.

Emmerson, Donald K. "The Stable War: Cambodia and the Great Powers." *Indochina Issues*, 62 (December 1985).

Engelbert, thomas and Goscha, Christopher E. *Falling Out of Touch: A Study on Vietnamese Communist Policy Towards an Emerging Cambodian Communist Movement, 1930–1975*. Centre of Southeast Asian Studies, Monash Asia Institute, Monash University, Paper Number 35, 1995.

Entwhistle, Harold. *Antonio Gramsci: Conservative Schooling for Radical Politics*. London: Routledge & Kegan Paul, 1979.

Evans, Grant and Rowley, Kelvin. *Red Brotherhood at War*. London: Verso, 1984.

Far Eastern Economic Review (issues 1979–1989)

Femia, Joseph. "Hegemony and Consciousness in the Thought of Antonio Gramsci." *Political Studies*, 23, 1 (1975). pp. 29–48.

Francisco, Ronald A., Laird, Betty A., Laird, Roy D. *The Political Economy of Collectivized Agriculture/A Comparative Study of Communist and Non-Communist Systems*. New York: Pergamon Press, 1979.

Frieson, Kate. "The Political Nature of Democratic Kampuchea." *Pacific Affairs*, 61, 3 (Fall 1988). 1979.

Frieson, Kate. "The Pol Pot Legacy in Village Life." *Cultural Survival Quarterly*, 14, 3 (1990).

Frings, Viviane. "The Failure of Agricultural Collectivization in the People's Republic of Kampuchea (1979–1989)." Working Paper 80. Centre of Southeast Asian Studies, Monash University, 1993.

————. "Cambodia After Decollectivization (1989–1992)." *Journal of Contemporary Asia*, 24,1 (1994).

Front d'Union National pour le Salut du Kampuchea. Service d'Information du FUNSK, Phnom Penh, Janvier 1979.

Front Policy Regarding Overseas Kampucheans. PRK, Phnom Penh, 1985.

Giddens, Anthony. "Four Theses on Ideology." *Canadian Journal of Politics & Social Theory*, 7, 1–2 (1982), pp. 18–21.

Gittings, John. "Kampuchea." *The Asia and Pacific Review*, 1985.

Godelier, Maurice. *Perspectives in Marxist Anthropology.* Cambridge: Cambridge University Press, 1977.

Goldfrank, Walter L. "Theories of Revolution and Revolution Without Theory: The Case of Mexico." *Theory & Society*, 7 (1979), pp. 135–165.

Goldstone, Jack A. "Theories of Revolution: The Third Generation." *World Politics*, 32 (1979–80), pp. 425–53.

Grant, Jonathon S., Moss, Laurence A.G. and Unger, Jonathan. *Cambodia: The Widening War in Indochina.* New York: Washington Square Press, 1971.

Grunewald, Francois. "The Rebirth of Agricultural Peasants in Cambodia." *Cultural Survival Quarterly*, 14, 3 (1990).

Hanks, L. M., Jr. "Merit and Power in the Thai Social Order." *American Anthropologist*, 64 (1962), pp. 1247–1261.

Harding, Neil ed. *The State in Socialist Society.* Albany: State University of New York Press, 1984.

Heder, Stephen R. "From Pol Pot to Pen Sovann to the Villages" in Khien Theeravit and MacAlister Brown, eds. *Indochina and Problems of Security and Stability in Southeast Asia.* Bangkok: Chulalongkorn University Press, 1983.

Heder, Stephen R. *Kampuchean Occupation and Resistance.* Asian Studies Monographs No. 027. Institute of Asian Studies, Chulalongkorn University, January 1980.

————. "Kampuchea's Armed Struggle: The Origins of an Independent Revolution." *BCAS*, 11, 1 (Jan.–March 1979).

————. "Racism, Marxism, labelling, and genocide in Ben Kiernan's "The Pol Pot Regime." *South East Asia Research*, 5, 2 (July 1997).

————. "Revolution and Counter-Revolution in Kampuchea." *AMPO*, 12, 3 (1980).

Heng Hung. *Lbech Yuon neng Krom Aayong, sangkhep "Anakut Kampuchea?"* [Vietnamese Tricks and the Puppet Group, in short, "Cambodia Future?"]. Phnom Penh, undated.

Heng Samrin. *La révolution du Kampuchea est Irreversible* Département de Presse, Ministère des Affaires Étrangères de la République Populaire du Kampuchea, 1984.

354

Hiebert, Murray. "Cambodia: Guerrilla Attacks Curb Development." *Indochina Issues*, 69 (September 1986).

———., ed. "Cambodia: Perspectives on the Impasse." *Indochina Issues*, 64 (Feb.–March 1986).

———. "Cambodia and Vietnam: Costs of the Alliance." *Indochina Issues* 46 (May 1984).

Hildebrand, George C. and Porter, Gareth. *Cambodia: Starvation & Revolution*. New York: Monthly Review Press, 1976.

Hun Sen. *Dop Chhnam ney Domnaeur Kampuchea: 1979–1989* [The Ten-Year Journey of Cambodia]. Phnom Penh, December 1988.

———. *La Solidarité Kampuchea-Vietnam*. Commission de Propagande et d'Education, Phnom Penh, 1982.

Huxley, Tim. "Cambodia in 1986: The PRK's Eighth Year." *Southeast Asian Affairs*, 1987.

Indochina: Vietnam, Laos, Cambodia Country Profile 1989–1990 Annual Survey. The Economist Intelligence Unit.

Ith Sarin. *Sronoh Proloeung Khmer* [Regrets for the Khmer Soul]. Phnom Penh, 28 July 1973.

Jennar, Raoul M. *Les clés du Cambodge: Faits et chiffres, repères historiques, profils cambodgiens, cartes*. Paris: Maisonneuve & Larose, 1995.

———. *Les Constitutions du Cambodge: Ambitions, Continuites et Ruptures*. Paper delivered at the International Symposium on Khmerology, 26–30 August, 1996.

———., ed. *The Cambodian Constitutions (1953–1993)*. Bangkok: White Lotus, 1995.

Jumsai, Brig. Gen. M.L. Manich. *History of Thailand and Cambodia*. Bangkok: Chalermnit Press, 1987.

Kampuchean Humanitarian Assistance Programmes: The International Community's Response. New York: UN. 1986.

Kattenburg, Paul M. "'So Many Enemies': The View From Hanoi." *Indochina Issues* 38, (June 1983).

Kellner, Douglas. "Ideology, Marxism, and Advanced Capitalism." *Socialist Review*, 42 (1978), pp. 37–66.

Kershaw, Roger. "Lesser Current: The Election Ritual and Party Consolidation in the People's Republic of Kampuchea." *Contemporary Southeast Asia*, 3, 4 (March 1982).

Kershaw, Roger. "Multipolarity and Cambodia's Crisis of Survival: A Preliminary Perspective on 1979." *Southeast Asian Affairs*, 1980.

Keyes, Charles. "Buddhism and Revolution in Cambodia." *Cultural Survival Quarterly*, 14, 3 (1990).

Khien Theeravit and MacAlister Brown, eds. *Indochina and Problems of Security and Stability in Southeast Asia*. Bangkok: Chulalongkorn University Press, 1983.

Kiernan, Ben. *How Pol Pot Came to Power: A History of Communism in Kampuchea, 1930–1975.* London: Verso, 1985.

———. "Kampuchea 1979–1981, National Rehabilitation in the Eye of an International Storm." *Southeast Asian Affairs,* 1982.

———. "Conflict in the Kampuchean Communist Movement." *Journal of Contemporary Asia,* 10, 1–2 (1980).

———. "Origins of Khmer Communism." *Southeast Asian Affairs,* 1981.

———. "Roots of Genocide: New Evidence on the US Bombardment of Cambodia." *Cultural Survival Quarterly,* 14, 3 (1990).

———. *The New Political Structure in Kampuchea.* Melbourne: Dyason House Papers 8, No. 2, December 1982.

———. *The Pol Pot Regime: Race, Power, and Genocide in Cambodia under the Khmer Rouge, 1975–1979.* New Haven: Yale University Press, 1996.

———. "Vietnam and the Governments and People of Kampuchea." *BCAS,* 11, 4 (Oct.–Dec., 1979).

———., ed. *Genocide and Democracy in Cambodia: The Khmer Rouge, the United Nations and the International Community.* New Haven, Conn.: Yale University (Southeast Asia Studies, Monograph Series 41), 1993.

Kiernan, B. and Chantou Boua, eds. *Peasants and Politics in Kampuchea, 1942–1981.* London: Zed Books, 1982.

Kiljunen, Kimmo. *Kampuchea: Decade of the Genocide.* London: Zed Books, 1984.

Klintworth, Gary. *The Vietnamese Achievement in Kampuchea.* Working Paper No. 181, ANU Strategic & Defence Studies Centre, Canberra, May 1989.

———. *Vietnam's Intervention in Cambodia in International Law.* Canberra: AGPS, 1989.

Kobelev, Yevgeni and Solntsev, Nikolai. *Kampuchea: Rising from the Ashes.* Moscow: Planeta Publishers, 1988.

Kono Yasushi. *Cultural Aspect of Cambodia' Reconstruction* (Summary of Reports published by Institute of Asian Cultures of Sophia University, Tokyo, on visits to the PRK in March 1988 and March 1989). Phnom Penh (undated).

Kubes, Antonin. *Kampuchea.* Prague: Orbis Press Agency, 1982.

La Grande Conspiration Anti-Kampuchéenne. Département de Presse, Ministère des Affaires Étrangères, République Populaire du Kampuchea. Avril, 1983.

L'Education en République Populaire du Kampuchea. Ministère de l'Education, Phnom Penh, 1987.

Leifer, Michael. "Obstacles to a Political Settlement in Indochina." *Pacific Affairs,* 58, 4 (Winter 1985–86).

———. "Kampuchea 1979: From Dry Season to Dry Season." *Asian Survey*, 20,1 (1980), pp. 33–41.

———. "Kampuchea in 1980: The Politics of Attrition." *Asian Survey*, 21, 1 (1981), pp. 93–101.

Liste du Corps Diplomatique. Ministère des Affaires Étrangères, Département de Protocole, PRK, 1983.

Long, Simon. "China and Kampuchea: Political Football on the Killing Fields." *The Pacific Review*, 2, 2 (1989).

Luciolli, Esmeralda. *Le Mur de bambou: Le Cambodge après Pol Pot.* Paris: Régine Deforges, 1988.

Lutz, William and Brent, Harry. *On Revolution.* Cambridge, Mass.: Winthrop, 1971.

Mabbett, Ian and Chandler, David. *The Khmers.* Chiang Mai: Silkworm Books, 1995.

Mack, Andrew. "America's Role in the Destruction of Kampuchea." *Politics* 16,1 (May 1981).

Mackerras, Colin and Knight, Nick. *Marxism in Asia.* London: Croom Helm, 1985.

Marks, Tom. *Making Revolution: The Insurgency of the Communist Party of Thailand in Structural Perspective.* Bangkok: White Lotus, 1994.

Martin, Marie Alexandrine. "Vietnamised Cambodia, A Silent Ethnocide." *Indochina Report*, 7 (July–Sept., 1986).

———. "Social Rules and Political Power in Cambodia." *Indochina Report*, 22 (January–March, 1990).

———. *Cambodia: A Shattered Society.* Berkeley: University of California Press, 1994.

May Someth. *Cambodian Witness.* London: Faber and Faber, 1986.

Mazlish, B., Kaledin, A. D., Ralston, D.B. *Revolution: A Reader.* New York: Macmillan, 1971.

McAuliff, J. and McDonnell M. Byrne. "The Diplomatic Dance: Cambodia on the International Stage." *Cultural Survival Quarterly*, 14, 3 (1990).

McCormack, Gavan. "The Kampuchean Revolution 1975–1978: The Problem of Knowing the Truth." *Journal of Contemporary Asia*, 10, 1/2 (1980).

McMillen, D. H. ed. *Conflict Resolution in Kampuchea.* Working Papers of the Second International Conference on Indochina, Centre for the Study of Australian-Asian Relations, Division of Asian and International Studies, August 1988. Griffith University, 1988.

Miller, D. B. ed. *Peasants and Politics: Grass Roots Reaction to Change in Asia.* Edward Arnold: Melbourne, 1978.

Moise, Edwin E. "Land Reform and Land Reform Errors in North Vietnam." *Pacific Affairs*, 49, 1 (Spring, 1976).

Montagu, John. "Kampuchea." *The Asia and Pacific Review*, 1985.

Morris, Stephen J. *Why Vietnam Invaded Cambodia: Political Culture and the Causes of War*. Stanford: Stanford University Press, 1999.

Mosyakov, Dmitry. "The Khmer Rouge and the Vietnamese Communists: A history of their relations as told in the Soviet archives." [Translation from paper in Russian journal *Vostok* (Orient), No. 3, August 2000.] Documentation Centre of Cambodia (DC-Cam) website.

Muscat, Rober J. "Cambodia: Post-Settlement Reconstruction and Development." Occasional Papers of the East Asian Institute, Columbia University, NY, 17 August, 1989.

Mysliwiec, Eva. *Punishing the Poor: The International Isolation of Kampuchea*. Oxford: Oxfam, 1988.

Newman, R. S. "Brahmin and Mandarin. A Comparison of the Cambodian and Vietnamese Revolutions." Working Paper No.15, Centre of Southeast Asian Studies, Monash University, 1978.

Ney Pena. *Kar Duol Rolum ney Robap Praleypuchsar Pol Pot* [The Downfall of the Genocidal Pol Pot Regime]. Printery of Pracheachon Newspaper, Phnom Penh, 1991.

Nguyen Khac Vien et Francoise Correze. *Kampuchea 1981: Témoignages*. Paris: Doanket, 1981.

Nichols, John. *Cambodia: And Still They Hope*. ACFOA Development Dossier No. 25, Canberra, July 1990.

Novib. *Report of a Mission to Kampuchea by Netherlands' Members of Parliament/Politicians March 13 to 24, 1989*. The Hague, April 1989.

Ogura, Sadao. "Hanoi's Southeast Asia Policy and Cambodia." *Pacific Community*, 14 (Fall 1981).

Osborne, Milton. *Politics and Power in Cambodia*. Longman: Australia, 1973.

————. "Kampuchea and Vietnam: A Historical Perspective." *Pacific Community*, 19, 3 (April 1978).

————. "Peasant Politics in Cambodia: The 1916 Affair." *Modern Asian Studies* 12, 2 (1978).

Panaritis, Andrea. "Cambodia: The Rough Road to Recovery." *Indochina Issues* 56 (April 1985).

Pedler, John. *Cambodia: A Report on the International and Internal Situation and the Future Outlook*. London, April 1989.

People's Revolutionary Tribunal held in Phnom Penh for the Trial of the Crime of Genocide Committed by the Pol Pot-Ieng Sary clique (Summary). Ministry of Information, Press and Cultural Affairs of the

People's Republic of Kampuchea, August 1979. Phnom Penh: Foreign Languages Publishing House, 1990.

Phnom Penh Post (various issues, 1997–1998)

Pike, Douglas. *PAVN: People's Army of Vietnam*. Novato: Presidio Press, 1986.

Pilch, Imogen. *Prospects for the Neutralisation of Kampuchea*. Australia-Asia Papers No. 43, Centre for the Study of Australian-Asian Relations, Griffith University, December 1988.

Pilger, J. and Barnett, A. *Aftermath: The Struggle of Cambodia and Vietnam*. London: New Statesman, 1982.

Policy of the People's Republic of Kampuchea with Regard to Vietnamese Resident. Press Department, Ministry of Foreign Affairs, People's Republic of Kampuchea. September 1983.

"Pol Pot's Interview with Yugoslav Journalists," 17 March 1978. *Journal of Contemporary Asia*, 8 (1978).

Ponchaud, Francois. *Cambodia: Year Zero*. London: Allen Lane, 1978.

Porter, Gareth. "Towards a Kampuchean Peace Settlement: History & Dynamics of Sihanouk's Negotiations." *Southeast Asian Affairs*, 1988.

———. "ASEAN and Kampuchea: Shadow and Substance." *Indochina Issues* 14, (February 1981).

———. "Vietnam-ASEAN Relations: A Decade of Evolution." *Indochina Report*, 2 (April–June, 1985).

Pouvatchy, Joseph R. "Cambodian-Vietnamese Relations." *Asian Survey*, 26, 4 (April 1986).

———. *The Vietnamisation of Cambodia*. ISIS Seminar Paper, ISIS Malaysia, 1986.

"President Heng Samrin Presents the Draft Constitution to the National Assembly." Source: Monitoring Digest, No. 147,1981, (27 June 1981). *Contemporary Southeast Asia*, 3, 2 (1981).

Quinn-Judge, Paul. "The Khmer Resistance: State of the Union." *Indochina Issues* 40 (September 1983).

Quinn-Judge, Sophia. 'Kampuchea in 1982, Ploughing Towards Recovery'. *Southeast Asian Affairs*, 1983.

Rajalakshmi Rama Rao and Binie Zaan. *An Analysis of Female-Headed Households in Cambodia*. National Institute of Statistics, Ministry of Planning, Phnom Penh, Cambodia, May 1997.

Randle, Robert F. *Geneva 1954: The Settlement of the Indochinese War*. Princeton, New Jersey: Princeton University Press, 1969.

Réalisations dans le Domaine de l'Education: Exposition à l'occasion de 1er Anniversaire de la Grande Victoire 7.1.79. Ministère de l'Education, Phnom Penh, 7.1.80.

Report of the United Nations Fact-Finding Mission on Present Structures and Practices of Administration in Cambodia. New York: United Nations, 24 April–9 May 1990.

Retboll, Torben. "Kampuchea and the Reader's Digest." *BCAS*, 11, 3 (July–Sept.1979).

Reynell, Josephine. *Political Pawns: Refugees on the Thai-Kampuchean Border.* Oxford: Refugee Studies Programme, 1989.

Ross, Russell R. ed. *Cambodia—A Country Study, 3rd ed.*, first printing 1990. Library of Congress, Federal Research Division (research completed in 1987).

Rot-thoamenunh (sekkedei prieng), 1980 [Constitution (Draft)] by the Advisory Group of the Draft Constitution from 7 January–17 April, 1980 at No. 90 Tousamuth Blvd (formerly Norodom Blvd), Phnom Penh.

Sagar, D. J. *Major Political Events in Indochina, 1945–1990.* New York: Facts on File Inc., 1991.

Schier, Peter. "Kampuchea in 1985: Between Crocodiles and Tigers." *Southeast Asian Affairs*, 1986.

Scott, James C. "Revolution in the Revolution: Peasants and Commissars." *Theory & Society*, 7 (1979), pp. 97–130.

Sekkedei Prakas Ompi Koalka Samkhansamkhan robas Kenapak Pracheachon Kampuchea [Announcement Concerning Important Principles of the Cambodian People's Party]. Phnom Penh (undated).

Sewell, William H. "Ideologies and Social Revolutions: Reflections on the French Case." *Journal of Modern History*, 57 (1985).

Shapiro, Toni. *Dance and the Spirit of Cambodia.* PhD Diss. Cornell University, 1994.

Shawcross, William. *Cambodia's New Deal.* Contemporary Issues Paper No. 1, Washington: Carnegie Endowment for International Peace, 1994.

———. *Sideshow: Kissinger, Nixon and the Destruction of Cambodia.* London: Hogarth Press, 1991.

———. *The Quality of Mercy: Cambodia, Holocaust and Modern Conscience.* London: Andre Deutsch, 1984.

Skocpol, Theda. *States and Social Revolutions: A Comparative Analysis of France, Russia, and China.* Cambridge: Cambridge University Press, 1979.

———. "Cultural Idioms and Political Ideologies in the Revolutionary Reconstruction of State Power: A Rejoinder to Sewell." *Journal of Modern History*, 57 (1985).

Smith, Frank. *Interpretive Accounts of the Khmer Rouge Years: Personal Experience in Cambodian Peasant World View.* Occasional Paper No. 18, Center for Southeast Asian Studies, University of Wisconsin-Madison, 1989.

Sodhy, Pamela. "A Survey of U.S. Post-Vietnam Policy and the

Kampuchean Dilemma, 1975–1989: A Southeast Asian View." *Contemporary Southeast Asia*, 11, 3 (Dec., 1989).

Solarz, Stephen J. 'Cambodia and the International Community'. *Foreign Affairs*, Spring, 1990.

Spragens, John Jr. 'Hunger in Cambodia, Getting Beyond Relief'. *Indochina Issues* 43, (February 1984).

"Statement of the Government of SRV on Vietnamese-Kampuchean Border Issue, Hanoi, 31 December, 1977. Statement by the Government of Democratic Kampuchea." *Journal of Contemporary Asia*, 8 1(978).

Statistical Year-Book of Cambodia, 1968. National Institute of Statistics and Economic Research, Ministry of Planning, Kingdom of Cambodia.

Stromseth, Jonathan. *Time on Whose Side in Cambodia?* ISIS Paper 2, Chulalongkorn University: ISIS Thailand, 1988.

Stuart-Fox, Martin *Vietnam in Laos: Hanoi's Model for Kampuchea*. Essays on Strategy and Diplomacy, No. 8. The Keck Center for International Strategic Studies, 1987.

Sukhumbhand Paribatra. *Kampuchea Without Delusion*. ISIS Malaysia: ISIS ASEAN Series, 1986.

Summers, Laura. "In Matters of War and Socialism, Anthony Barnett Would Shame and Honor Kampuchea Too Much." *BCAS*, ll, 4 (Oct.–Dec., 1979).

———. "Defining the Revolutionary State in Cambodia." *Current History*, 71,422 (December, 1976).

———. "Consolidating the Cambodian Revolution." *Current History*, 69,411 December, 1975).

Szelenyi, Ivan, ed. *Privatizing the Land*. London: Routledge, 1998

Tan Ten Lang. *Economic Debates in Vietnam: Issues and Problems in Reconstruction and Development (1975–1984)*. Research Notes & Discussions Paper No. 55, ISEAS: Singapore 1985.

Tarr, Chou Meng. "A Talk with Prime Minister Hun Sen." *Cultural Survival Quarterly*, 14, 3 (1990).

Thai Policy vis-à-vis Kampuchea. Ministry of Foreign Affairs, People's Republic of Kampuchea, September 1983.

Thayer, Carlyle A. "The Vietnam People's Army Today." *Indochina Issues* 72 (January 1987).

The Birth of the New Kampuchea. Ministry of Information, Press and Cultural Affairs of the Kampuchean People's Revolutionary Council, Phnom Penh 1979.

"The Causes of the Suffering of the Cambodian People: A Possible Solution"—Remarks of His Excellency Mr Son Sann, Prime Minister of the Coalition Government of Democratic Kampuchea, and President of the Khmer People's National Liberation Front, at the Council on Foreign Relations, New York, on 29 September 1982. Source: Information Office of the KPNLF, Bangkok. *Contemporary Southeast Asia*, 4, 4 (1983).

The First Women's Congress Throughout the Country 28th to 30th October, 1983. Revolutionary Women's Association of Kampuchea, The People's Republic of Kampuchea.

The Great Anti-Kampuchean Conspiracy. Department of Press, Ministry of Foreign Affairs, People's Republic of Kampuchea. April 1983.

"The Military Occupation of Kampuchea." *Indochina Report*, 3 (July–Sept. 1985).

"The Vietnamisation of Kampuchea: A New Model for Colonialism." *Indochina Report*, Pre-publication Issue, October 1984.

Theeravit, Khien and Brown, Macalister, eds. *Indochina and Problems of Security and Stability in Southeast Asia: Papers and Discussion of the Conference held at Chulalongkorn University, Bangkok, 18–21 June, 1980.* Bangkok: Chulalongkorn University Press, 1983.

Thion, Serge. *Watching Cambodia.* Bangkok: White Lotus, 1993.

Thion, Serge and Vickery, Michael. *Cambodia Background and Issues: A Research Paper prepared for the Church World Service Kampuchean Program.* Phnom Penh, September 1981.

Tilly, Charles. *From Mobilization to Revolution.* New York: Random House, 1978.

Truong Buu Lam. *New Lamps for Old: The Transformation of the Vietnamese Administrative Elite.* ISEAS Occasional Paper No. 66, Maruzen Asia, 1982.

Truong Chinh. *A Propos du Problème Kampuchéen.* Le Service de presse de l'Ambassade de la République Socialiste du Viet Nam à Paris, 1980.

Truong Nhu Tang. *Journal of a Vietcong.* London: Jonathan Cape, 1986.

Tukdei Angkor Pachebon [The Land of Angkor Today]. Phnom Penh: Ministry of Information and Culture, 1984.

Um Khatharya. "Cambodia in 1988: The Curved Road to Settlement." *Asian Survey*, 29, 1 (January 1989).

Undeclared War Against the People's Republic of Kampuchea. Press Department of the Ministry for Foreign Affairs of the PRK. Phnom Penh, November 1985.

Une Solidarité Indéfectible. Department de Presse, Ministère des Affaires Étrangères de la R.P.K. Phnom Penh, 1984.

Van der Kroef, Justus. "Cambodia: From 'DK' to 'People's Republic.'" *Asian Survey*, 19, 8 (1979).

———. "Kampuchea: Protracted Conflict, Suspended Promise." *Asian Survey* 24, 3 (1984), pp. 314–34.

Vietnam Courier (1979–1989)

Vickery, M. "A Critique of the Lawyers Committee for International Human Rights, Kampuchea Mission of Nov., 1984." *Journal of Contemporary Asia*, 18, 1 (1988).

———. *Cambodia 1975–1982*. Sydney: Allen & Unwin, 1984.

———. *Cambodia 1975–1982, 2nd ed.* Chiang Mai: Silkworm Books, 1999.

———. "Cambodia (Kampuchea): History, Tragedy & Uncertain Future." *BCAS* 21, 2–4 (1989).

———. "Cambodian Political Economy 1975–1990." *Cultural Survival Quarterly*, 14, 3 (1990).

———. "Cambodia's Tenuous Progress." *Indochina Issues* 63 (January 1986).

———. *Kampuchea: Politics, Economics and Society.* Sydney: Allen & Unwin, 1986.

———. "Notes on the Political Economy of the PRK." *Journal of Contemporary Asia*, 20, 4 (1990).

———. "The Cambodian People's Party: Where Has It Come From, Where Is It Going?" *Southeast Asian Affairs* 1994, ISEAS: Singapore, 1994.

———. "The Rule of Law in Cambodia." *Cultural Survival Quarterly*, 14, 3 (1990).

Vo Nguyen Giap. *People's War People's Army.* New York: Frederick A. Praeger, 1962.

Watts K., Draper C., Elder D., Harrison J., Yoichi Higaki, Salle J–C. *UNDP Report of the Kampuchea Needs Assessment Study.* August 1989.

Willmott, W. E. "Analytical Errors of the Kampuchean Communist Party." *Pacific Affairs*, 54, 2 (Summer 1981).

INDEX

CPSIA information can be obtained
at www.ICGtesting.com
Printed in the USA
BVHW072323161021
618821BV00004B/8